The Life of the Copper Eskimos

Diamond Jenness

The Life of the
Copper Eskimos

Diamond Jenness

OXFORD
UNIVERSITY PRESS

OXFORD
UNIVERSITY PRESS

Oxford University Press is a department of the University of Oxford.
It furthers the University's objective of excellence in research, scholarship,
and education by publishing worldwide. Oxford is a registered trade mark of
Oxford University Press in the UK and in certain other countries.

Published in Canada by
Oxford University Press
8 Sampson Mews, Suite 204,
Don Mills, Ontario M3C 0H5 Canada

www.oupcanada.com

Library and Archives Canada Cataloguing in Publication
Jenness, Diamond, 1886-1969, author
The life of the Copper Eskimos / Diamond Jenness.

(The Wynford Project)
Includes index.
ISBN 978-0-19-901786-7 (pbk.)

1. Inuit. I. Title. II. Series: Wynford Project

E99.E7J4783 2015   971.9004'9712   C2015-900524-8

Cover image: Diamond Jenness with Copper Inuit at Bernard Harbour, Nunavut.
1914. Fritz Johansen, Canadian Museum of History, Gatineau, 42232.

Oxford University Press is committed to our environment.
This book is printed on Forest Stewardship Council® certified paper
and comes from responsible sources.

MIX
Paper from
responsible sources
FSC® C004071

Printed and bound in Canada

1 2 3 4 — 18 17 16 15

The Life of the Copper Eskimos
Preface to the Wynford Edition

"Each man delights in the work that suits him best."
—Homer

One hundred years ago, on August 28, 1914, Diamond Jenness, a New Zealand–born anthropologist with the Canadian Arctic Expedition, arrived at Bernard Harbour, a sheltered inlet along the mainland shore of Dolphin and Union Strait, and for the time being, headquarters of the expedition's six-man scientific section, the Southern Party. Coronation Gulf lay to the east, and to the north, Victoria Island. This was, and remains today, the homeland of Copper Inuit or Inuinnait—"the people," in their Inuinnaqtun dialect. Vilhjalmur Stefansson, the expedition's leader, made preliminary observations of the little-known group he called Copper Eskimos—a cluster of a dozen or so local bands—while travelling through the region's western precincts in 1910–11. Despite following in another anthropologist's footsteps, Jenness nonetheless met with an opportunity both fleeting and rare: the chance to study at first-hand a population barely touched by contacts with the Western world, contacts that had already brought an array of changes, big and small, elsewhere in the Arctic. Writing at a moment when reconstructing the traditional—that is, pre-contact—lifeways of the continent's indigenous peoples engaged anthropologists first and foremost, Clark Wissler mused that Jenness might well be "the last to come in contact with this original, but now passing, type of Eskimo culture."[1]

In the wake of his renowned researches in the Trobriands during the First World War, Bronislaw Malinowski famously pronounced that the "proper conditions" for getting "the hang of tribal life" rested with learning the local language and living "right among the natives. . . ."[2] For the better part of two years, this is precisely what Jenness did, criss-crossing the country and immersing himself in the day-to-day routines of camp and trail in the different seasons, and at one point spending six uninterrupted months (May to November) travelling with the Puivlirmuit across the band's inland summer range in southwestern Victoria Island. The highlight of their itinerary, it bears mention, was a much-anticipated late-spring rendezvous with a few Kanghirjuarmuit families, denizens of Prince Albert Sound. Stefansson, a tireless self-promoter, reported discovering "Blond Eskimos" at the Sound during his previous expedition, proclaiming them long-lost descendants of Inuit–Greenlandic Norse parentage. "They show no signs of 'blondness' that do not appear in the more southern Eskimos" was Jenness's initial impression, one he subsequently substantiated in a formal refutation of the explorer's controversial claims published in the *American Anthropologist*.[3]

The tangible product of his Coronation Gulf fieldwork was considerable, amounting to some 2,500 artefacts of traditional manufacture, 90 wax cylinder recordings, and over 200 photographs, all on deposit in Ottawa's Victoria Memorial Museum, forerunner of the National Museums of Canada. Added to this were extensive collections of oral traditions, cat's cradles, song texts, lexical and anthropometric data, and with them, notebooks containing detailed descriptions of everything from house construction and hunting techniques to shamanic performances and observance of taboos. Finally, Jenness kept a diary, as all expedition members were required to do. Although he later felt ashamed of its contents, thinking them "childish and egotistical," in fact, its pages brim over with illuminating, day-by-day reflections on the research, the researcher, and the researched, and are peppered with ruminations on what the future might hold for a people spared, at least so far, the ruinous "kiss of the white man."[4]

In the years to come, much of this material made its way into print, including the diary, published posthumously.[5] *The People of the Twilight*, a memoir explicitly written for a popular audience, is the most widely read of his long list of titles. Yet *The Life of the Copper Eskimos*, the first of Jenness's five contributions to the official series of Southern Party reports, is surely the most noteworthy, and influential, in scholarly circles. Long regarded as a classic of arctic ethnography—"the best description of a single Eskimo tribe," in the estimation of some—it rivals, and arguably surpasses, Franz Boas's foundational 1888 monograph, *The Central Eskimo*, by virtue of the scope and depth of its treatment, the latter a reflection of Jenness's hard-won capacity to work without an interpreter constantly at his side, as his Victoria Island sojourn amply demonstrates.[6] For its time, moreover, it constitutes an exemplary piece of ethnographic method and writing, one with few parallels in its near-total reliance on participant-observation, then something of a novelty, not the de rigueur field method it would soon become; its use of vignettes, many exposing the anthropologist's various involvements in the social scene; and its explication, à la Boas (and later, Malinowski), of native perceptions of their own culture—the insider's point of view, as more recent generations of students have come to know it.[7] Last but hardly least, portions of the work constitute an empirical test of French ethnologist Marcel Mauss's hypothesis, proposed in 1904, that Inuit social, moral, and religious life alternate in form and intensity with the seasonal shift from winter to summer. Careful not to dismiss the proposition outright, Jenness concluded instead that the key argument, an early experiment in the analytical strategy now known as cultural ecology, appeared not to stand up in the light of two years' worth of observation around the Coronation Gulf region. "Changes in their environment, it is true, produce marked changes in their economic life," he explained; "But their social organization and religious life continue unchanged. . . ." Rather, the evidence suggested an alternative interpretation of causation, one made obvious in both the outer (e.g., community size) and inner (e.g., taboos) dimensions of life: the land–sea dichotomy.[8] Some years after those words were written, Jenness revisited the entire matter in a letter to Mauss himself, apologizing, on the one hand, for thinking the theory a tad "overdrawn," while on the other, crediting its principal assumptions with having "opened my eyes to many things that I would otherwise have overlooked."[9]

While it is true that the Arctic's natives and explorers have long held a grip on the popular imagination, it is no less true that for nearly all of us, this fondness "is just our voyeur's fascination with hard times being had by other people."[10] What better backdrop could there be for recounting the other side of Diamond Jenness's story, the so-called back-story—how it is the New Zealander came to do the work he did at Coronation Gulf in the first place. Pure chance is probably as good an explanation as any for the way events unfolded. Yet for a life-long devotee of the Classics, as was Jenness, a more satisfying take is to imagine his northern odyssey playing out in the hands of the Fates, especially the hands of Klotho, the mythical spinner of the thread of mortal life. Either way, the evidence makes for a compelling case.

...

Until the telegraphed invitation from Canada reached him at home on the outskirts of Wellington in late February 1913, the very idea of going to the Arctic likely never crossed Jenness's mind, not even as a youngster, dreaming, as boys do, of high adventure. Freshly returned from year-long fieldwork in New Guinea, an informal apprenticeship after diploma studies at Oxford, he envisioned a future in the South Pacific, continuing research and, banking on his being the first New Zealander to earn formal credentials in anthropology, landing a university faculty position, preferably at Victoria College, his alma mater. Yet timing, as the saying goes, is everything, and at that point, it was definitely not working in his favour. For one thing, there was then only a single, gainfully (if precariously) employed anthropologist in the entire country, curator Elsden Best, at the Dominion Museum. For another, the field was not yet recognized as an academic discipline on any campus, a situation that dragged on for six years before the University of Otago took the plunge in 1919, hiring a different native son (and Jenness's boyhood schoolmate), Cambridge grad Henry Skinner.[11] Barring an instant outbreak of anthro-mania nationwide, the odds of his aspirations being realized any time soon looked long, even prohibitive. So, with nothing more promising on the near-horizon than becoming a school teacher, and with cautious optimism that one thing might lead to another in Canada after the expedition, the 27-year-old bachelor made the decision that a great many others make at least once in life—*why not?* Besides, the pay on offer, $500 per year plus expenses, made for a more respectable alternative than depending on his parents' generosity any longer than strictly necessary. Six weeks later, affairs in order, he bid family and friends adieu and embarked on the 7,000 mile sea voyage from Auckland to Victoria, British Columbia. Odd to say, some while was yet to pass before he learned why he had been invited to "join Stefansson. . . and study Eskimos for three years" at all. That turned out to be the doing of Canadian anthropologist, and fellow Oxonian, Marius Barbeau, glad to help a friend in a day when paying jobs of any description were scarce everywhere, not just in New Zealand.[12]

Practically everything Jenness then knew about the Inuit came from hurriedly reading through a handful of published reports after arriving in Canada on the last day of April, weeks ahead of the expedition's mid-June departure. Understandably, he was delighted to find that Stefansson had recruited a second anthropologist to the voyage, by coincidence, also on Barbeau's recommendation. Better still, it happened that his new colleague, a 34-year-old Parisian named Henri Beuchat, was a veritable font of information on the subject immediately to hand, no less an accomplished scholar in the wider field of New World cultures, past and present. Beuchat's special interest in the American Arctic traced back a decade when, as a student at the Sorbonne, he assisted Marcel Mauss in putting together the selfsame analysis of seasonal variations in social morphology that factored so prominently in Jenness's investigations. As luck would have it, the sizeable descriptive literature that professor and pupil combed through for the project, a hodgepodge of mainly nineteenth-century works treating groups from Greenland to Alaska, contained next to nothing on the very population whose territory the Southern Party was preparing to visit. This proved incentive enough for Beuchat to take leave from his job minding France's prehistoric monuments for the Ministry of Fine Arts in order to fill this glaring hole in the global ethnological map. And just as Mauss's ideas, which he naturally intended to re-examine, had broken new theoretical ground, so, too, would his going to the field, something few French anthropologists did at the time. Not to be overlooked, the expedition also offered escape, if only temporary, from the hum-drum of workaday life, and, or so he fervently hoped, reprieve from the episodic depressive moods to which he was prone.[13]

The Canadian Arctic Expedition was Stefansson's brainchild. Managerial and financial responsibility for it, however, belonged solely to the dominion government. Organized into two parties, the Northern and the Southern, each had its own mission—respectively, geographic exploration in the Beaufort Sea, and multi-disciplinary scientific research at Coronation Gulf—and operated under the authority of different departments and branches of the federal bureaucracy. Supervision of Jenness and Beuchat's fieldwork fell to Edward Sapir, chief of the Geological Survey's anthropological section, established only three years before. If local conditions allowed, as their formal instructions stated, they were expected to conduct ethnological and archaeological investigations in separate regions— Beuchat in the stretch of country from Coppermine River to the Gulf's eastern limits, his junior associate on Victoria Island. Otherwise, they were free to settle on a division of labour for working together as a team, a division best arranged in accord with their individual areas of expertise. Familiarity with the relevant literature and a knack for languages and phonetic transcription made Beuchat the logical choice to delve into linguistics, as well as social and intellectual life. This last task involved collecting ethnographic details in the form of texts—narrative accounts and stories taken down in the original—a method then in high vogue among ethnologists trained at Columbia under Franz Boas, Sapir prominent in their ranks. For his part, Jenness would concentrate on subsistence practices, material culture, and anthropometry.[14] Though crucial to disciplinary practice at the time, applying callipers and tapes had a way of becoming disagreeable for measured and measurer alike, a lesson he learned through hard experience in the tropics. (To his relief, the Inuit were unfazed by the poking and prodding, finding the proceedings both amusing and profitable—matches and steel needles for the women, fish hooks for the men—and were ever-ready "to tender assistance and advice.")[15] But of the many lessons that first taste of fieldwork taught him, surely the most important was that relying on interpreters was a poor substitute for working with informants in their own language. Managing little better than a rudimentary grasp of the Bwaidogan dialect spoken on Goodenough Island, his field site out in the Solomon Sea (and next-door to the Trobriands), he fretted afterwards about everything he had missed—above all else, coming to terms with how natives themselves understand their own world. Determined to do things differently this time, he enlisted Beuchat to tutor him in linguistics, and for homework, pored over William Thalbitzer's study of north Greenlandic speech, one of the useful titles to be found in the expedition's well-stocked library.[16]

On June 17, 1913, with a crowd of dignitaries, journalists, and well-wishers gathered at dockside, the expedition's flagship, *Karluk*, every inch of shipboard space jammed with passengers and freight, set sail from Esquimalt. Twenty-one days at sea brought them to Nome, on Alaska's Bering Strait coast. Almost as soon as their feet touched dry land, Stefansson whisked his fellow anthropologists off to a nearby camp where they laid eyes on Inuit—actually, north Alaskan Iñupiat, from nearby King Island—for the very first time in their lives. Keen to learn what they could, a Franco-Canadian priest stationed in town, Père La Fortune, agreed to interpret for them the next day, but a last-minute change of plans cut short their time ashore. A second vessel, *Alaska*, was supposed to ferry the Southern Party's eight scientists from Nome to Coronation Gulf by way of a rendezvous with *Karluk* at Herschel Island, a winter haven for whaling ships situated just inside Canadian waters. Without warning, the expedition's mercurial commander ordered Beuchat and Jenness (and magnetician William McKinley) back aboard *Karluk* for an earlier than expected exit. Switching vessels, as Stefansson explained it, was intended to get them to Herschel Island ahead of their mates aboard the smaller and slower *Alaska*, time enough to get a head start on research with the Inuit who frequented the place—people from the Mackenzie Delta, now called the Inuvialuit.[17]

Had either man been clairvoyant, neither would have re-boarded. Indeed, no one would have climbed the gangway onto the aging (and recently retired) whaler. What their northward journey held in store were unusually heavy floes, heavy enough to impede *Karluk*'s eastward progress after it rounded Point Barrow, then halt it altogether before winds, sometimes gale-force, drove the ship, now imprisoned in ice, on a northwesterly course into the storm-plagued Chukchi Sea, and soon enough, into the teeth of polar winter. Twenty-five people were on board, all of them probably wishing they were anywhere else than where they were just then. The new year was ten days old when the captain sounded the call to abandon ship, *Karluk*'s sparsely reinforced hull no longer able to withstand the relentless heaving and pounding of the ice-choked sea. Jenness was not among those forced to shelter at Shipwreck Camp, a motley collection of tents pitched atop the ice at 73° north latitude, near where the vessel came undone. Klotho had surely been hovering nearby when, back on September 20, the Alaskan shoreline still in sight, Jenness and four others accompanied Stefansson landward in hopes of replenishing the ship's larders with fresh meat. In their absence, *Karluk*, Beuchat still aboard, drifted away, marooning the hunters near the mouth of the Colville River, well to the east of Barrow, northernmost Alaska's largest settlement, and its most reliable point of supply. Remarkably, that day of redemption was actually Jenness's second shot at eluding the miserable fortune that awaited those who remained aboard; weeks earlier, the immortal spinner apparently busy elsewhere, he and Beuchat were forced to turn back when treacherous ice conditions blocked their way to shore.[18] Only later, much later, did Jenness learn that the ordeal had ended tragically for his friend. Physically and emotionally unprepared to cope, the Frenchman succumbed to hypothermia alone, among the ridges of frozen sea, in an ill-advised attempt to reach safe haven on Wrangel Island, 60 miles distant to the east. In all, the aftermath of *Karluk*'s destruction claimed eleven lives. Thanks to the heroics of the ship's master, veteran navigator Robert Bartlett, a dozen survivors, McKinley, of the Southern Party, among them, were eventually rescued from their remote Wrangel Island refuge, an outlier of the Russian Empire, in September 1914.[19]

Considering that he had left behind a trusted colleague and nearly all of his own gear—warm clothes, camera, callipers and tapes, books, even his diary—and, into the bargain, was weakened by recurrent bouts of malarial fever, souvenirs of New Guinea, it is hardly surprising that Jenness fantasized about waiting out his first arctic winter in a modicum of comfort at Barrow.[20] Instead, he put his unscheduled stopover in Alaska to the best possible use: preparing for what lay ahead in Copper Inuit country, in the event he actually made it there. Undergoing a crash course—boot camp captures the experience more accurately—over the ensuing months, he grew accustomed to the rigours of arctic travel and the niceties of living on, and from, the land. Boarding in a native household at Harrison Bay in the depths of winter taught him a few critical lessons, perhaps none as important as the virtue in maintaining an even temper, especially when passing the darkest months with eleven other souls in 180 square feet of living space, and on short rations. His roommates, particularly the children, none older than eight, naturally turned out to be much better language teachers than Beuchat, introducing him in easy stages to the basics of Iñupiaq speech, happily, a near-relative of Inuinnaqtun, and affording ample opportunities to practise what he'd learned. Even so, having his colleague, a veritable "genius for language," with him, or even Thalbitzer's text, would doubtless have made this most crucial of the field anthropologist's tasks just a wee bit easier to handle.[21] Jenness finally caught up with his Southern Party mates in March 1914; they had passed the winter at Collinson Point, east of Harrison Bay, *Alaska*'s farthest advance before ice forced them to find safe harbour. Soon after arriving in camp, he accidentally, if providentially, stumbled across copies of Mauss's treatise and a practicable substitute for Thalbitzer's sorely missed grammar, stray volumes stowed away in some of Beuchat's misplaced luggage.[22] In a eulogy of sorts, Stefansson said of Beuchat that participating in the expedition was his liberation from "libraries, museums, and the exacting trivialities of his Parisian environment." Maybe so. But that didn't stop him from taking along upwards of 100 books from his personal library, including the two that contributed mightily to Jenness's liberation from the pitfalls that dogged his Goodenough researches.[23]

In the waning days of July 1914, inshore waters again navigable, all hands sailed eastward from Collinson Point, reaching Bernard Harbour, via Herschel Island, in late August, one year overdue. And with that, the story of Jenness's time at Coronation Gulf comes full circle, leaving only the lingering hypothetical of how his work there might have differed, how *The Life of the Copper Eskimos* might have differed, had the Fates been more attentive on that late summer day when he and Beuchat failed to reach the Alaskan shore. Of one thing Jenness himself was quite certain, confessing to Mauss that had his colleague lived, ". . . [I] would not have made the mistakes I made, and would have seen more deeply into Eskimo culture."[24] Respectful words expressed in all modesty.

...

One thing did lead to another in Canada after the expedition, as Jenness had hoped, though not right away. First, there was a military hitch that put him in the trenches with an artillery unit for the Great War's final battles, followed by a marital one to Eilleen Bleakney, whom he met and courted in Ottawa before shipping out for Europe. Finally, what started as temporary employment with the Geological Survey's anthropological section before his enlistment became permanent in 1920, thanks in no small part to Edward Sapir's assiduous politicking. Jenness stayed put for two-plus decades, taking up new ethnographic researches with seven different first nations—speakers of languages belonging to the Algonkian, Athapaskan, and Coast Salish language families—and on Sapir's departure for academia midway through 1925, becoming the section's chief cook and bottle-washer, including a frustrating five-year stint as his boss's successor. There was also a return engagement in the Arctic, a part of the world he once vowed never to visit again despite his affection, and lasting concern, for the people of Coronation Gulf.[25]

Serendipity had taken him north the first time out, and it did so again in the mid-twenties, the result of a remarkably perceptive analysis of 2,000 artefacts—some excavated near Cape Dorset, on Baffin Island's southern coast, the rest purchased on Coates Island, at the mouth of Hudson Bay—sent to the Victoria Memorial Museum by government employee L.T. Burwash. In announcing his findings, Jenness concluded—correctly, as things turned out—that the mixed collections contained certain implements whose form and style differed from known Inuit types, and whose darkish patination, an indication of age, suggested they might be the handiwork of a people—he christened them Dorset Eskimos—whose occupation of the eastern Arctic long predated that of its current inhabitants.[26] Coinciding with Danish archaeologist Therkel Mathiassen's rival claim for the antiquity of another early culture, Thule Eskimo, discovered near the modern-day village of Repulse Bay, the stage was set for wide-ranging investigations aimed at piecing together the puzzle of Inuit origins and cultural development across the far north. As his opening contribution, Jenness spent the summer of 1926 at Bering Strait, digging sites at Wales, and then on Little Diomede Island. To his delight, a midden on the fog and storm-bound island produced remnants of yet another early culture, dubbed Old Bering Sea. The next year took him to Newfoundland where he insisted the Dorset-like artefacts that cropped up in a Northern Peninsula potato patch were in fact of Beothuk manufacture, an argument quickly recanted once colleague William Wintemberg unearthed ample evidence in the region of a "pure" Dorset presence.[27] From that point on, Jenness gladly ceded fieldwork to younger, more energetic archaeologists, preferring to serve the cause as recruiter, advisor, and enthusiastic cheerleader.

Retirement in the late 1940s brought a second career of study and reflection, this one free of the fiscal and political constraints of government service, not least, the strictly imposed limits on what could and couldn't be researched and communicated. Atop the list of verboten subjects that were now fair game was Ottawa's management of Aboriginal affairs. Having lived and worked on reserves across the country, Jenness was all too familiar with the deplorable state of material, psychological, and social well-being their residents endured. In a sharply worded essay, he likened their situation to apartheid and its American cousin, Jim Crow, and called for sweeping reforms of a sclerotic system of policies and practices that promised much but, since its inception, had delivered very little.[28] Fittingly, he kept his harshest and most far-reaching criticisms for an examination of past and current conditions in the Canadian Arctic, part of an ambitious, multi-volume history of Inuit administration in four countries. If he had an inkling of what was coming, R.G. Robertson, deputy minister of Northern Affairs and Natural Resources, the study's sponsor, would never have signed off on the project, one meant to evaluate the extent to which different populations had been integrated "into the economy and society of western civilization." Suffice it to say that before the (very lightly emended) manuscript on Canada finally reached the Arctic Institute for publication, a cabal of department bureaucrats, including Robertson, did what they could to bully its author, then in his seventies and in less than robust health, into toning the thing down, or better still, withdrawing it altogether. Resolute to the last, Jenness admitted that while "my claim to Olympic impartiality" might be undone by wider public scrutiny of his views, whatever risk existed "I took with open eyes."[29]

Spanning seven years and resulting in a series of five volumes, Jenness thought of this project as his personal and professional swan song, one final crusade, as he put it, in the name of social and economic justice for the country's first peoples. He died soon thereafter, in November 1969, three months shy of his 84th birthday.

...

When it appeared in 1922, *The Life of the Copper Eskimos* was received as a major contribution to ethnological knowledge, the first systematic investigation of an Inuit population west of Hudson Bay. Since the 1960s and the exponential growth of state power right across the North, it has become something more: a work of historical and political value to the pan-Inuit community as a whole. Throughout the contemporary indigenous world, the cross-generational reproduction of tradition has served to catalyze resistance to totalizing forces in their array of guises. Recent developments in Canada's Arctic bear this out. There, Inuit successes in reasserting inherent rights to self-determination within their ancient lands rest, in good part, on a foundation of shared contemporary identity rooted in a distinctive, customary way of being. Although she made it with reference to photographs he took in New Guinea, Elizabeth Edwards's observation is equally applicable to the artefacts and recordings Jenness collected, the images he captured on film, and even the words he used to convey what the Copper Inuit had taught him—they have acquired new meaning for a new time, helping a people re-engage with their past as part of the ongoing movement to repatriate their future.[30]

Barnett Richling
June 2014

Notes

1   C. Wissler, "Ethnology of the Copper Eskimo," *Geographic Review* 12, no. 3 (1922), 507.

2   B. Malinowski, *Argonauts of the Western Pacific* (London: George Routledge, 1922), 5.

3   D. Jenness, *Arctic Odyssey: The Diary of Diamond Jenness, 1913–1916*, edited by S.E. Jenness. (Gati-

neau: Canadian Museum of Civilization, 1991), 449; D. Jenness, "The 'Blond' Eskimos," *American Anthropologist* 23, no. 3 (1921), 257–67.

4   D. Jenness to A.L. Washburn, [1939]. Canadian Museum of History, Diamond Jenness Correspondence. D. Jenness, *The People of the Twilight*

(Chicago: University of Chicago Press, 1959 [orig. 1928]), 248.

5   Jenness, *Arctic Odyssey.*

6   H.B. Collins, "History of Research Before 1945." In *Handbook of American Indians*, Vol. 5, *Arctic*, edited by D. Damas (Washington: Smithsonian Institution, 1984), 11; D. Riches, "The Force of Tradition in Eskimology." In *Localizing Strategies: Regional Traditions in Ethnographic Writing*, edited by R. Fardon (Washington: Smithsonian Institution Press, 1990), 79–81.

7   J. Berman, "The Culture as It Appears to the Indian Himself: Boas, George Hunt, and the Methods of Ethnography." In *Volkgeist as Method and Ethic: Essays on Boasian Ethnography and the German Anthropological Tradition*, edited by G.W. Stocking, Jr. (Madison: University of Wisconsin Press, 1996), 217–19.

8   M. Mauss, with H. Beuchat, "Essai sur les variations saisonnières des sociétés eskimos: Études morphologie sociale," (Paris: *L'Anée sociologique*, 1904–05), 124; D. Jenness, "The Life of the Copper Eskimos," *Reports of the Canadian Arctic Expedition, 1913–18*, Vol. 11, pt. A (Ottawa: King's Printer, 1922), 143.

9   D. Jenness to M. Mauss, July 7, 1925, cited in B. Saladin d'Anglure, "Mauss et l'anthropologie des Inuit," *Sociologie et Sociétés* 36, no. 2 (2004), 95.

10 Adam Gopnik, *Winter: Five Windows on the Season* (Toronto: Anansi Press, 2011), 67.

11 B. Richling, *In Twilight and in Dawn: A Biography of Diamond Jenness* (Montreal: McGill University Press, 2012), 12, 39.

12 D. Jenness, *Dawn in Arctic Alaska* (Chicago: University of Chicago Press, 1957), 3.

13 Barnett Richling, "Henri Beuchat (1878–1914)," *Arctic* 66, no. 1 (2013), 117.

14 R.J. Diubaldo, *Stefansson and the Canadian Arctic* (Montreal: McGill Queen's University Press, 1978), 63; E. Sapir to H. Beuchat, June 8, 1913; Sapir to D. Jenness, June 19, 1913. Canadian Museum of History, Edward Sapir Correspondence.

15 D. Jenness, "Physical Characteristics of the Copper Eskimos," *Reports of the Canadian Arctic Expedition, 1913–18*, Vol. 11, pt. B (Ottawa: King's Printer, 1923), 5.

16 D. Jenness to R.R. Marett, August 2, 1914. University of Oxford Archives, R.R. Marett Correspondence; W. Thalbitzer, "A Phonetical Study of the Eskimo Language Based on Observations Made on a Journey in North Greenland, 1900–01," *Meddelesler om Grønland* 31 (1904), 1–405.

17 H. Beuchat to C.M. Barbeau, July 15, 1913. Canadian Museum of History, C. Marius Barbeau Correspondence; D. Jenness to G. von Zedlitz, June 29, 1914. Library and Archives Canada, George von Zedlitz Correspondence.

18 D. Jenness to G. von Zedlitz, October 16, 1913.

Library and Archives Canada, George von Zedlitz Correspondence.

19 Eyewitness accounts of the wreck and ensuing ordeal are found in R.A. Bartlett and R.T. Hale, *The Last Voyage of the Karluk: Flagship of Vilhjamur Stefansson's Canadian Arctic Expedition 1913–16* (Toronto: McClelland, Goodchild, and Stewart, 1916); and W.L. McKinlay, *Karluk: The Great Untold Story of Arctic Exploration* (London: Weidenfeld and Nicolson, 1976). On Beuchat's death, see also J. Niven, *The Ice Master: The Doomed 1913 Voyage of the Karluk* (New York: Hyperion, 2000), 164–65.

20 Jenness, *Arctic Odyssey*, 17; D. Jenness to G. von Zedlitz, October 16, 1913. Library and Archives Canada, George von Zedlitz Correspondence.

21 D. Jenness to E. Sapir, December 2, 1913. Canadian Museum of History, Edward Sapir Correspondence; Richling, *In Twilight and in Dawn*, 74–76.

22 Jenness, *Arctic Odyssey*, 168; S. Kleinschmidt, *Grammatik der grönländischen Sprache* (Berlin: G. Reimer, 1851).

23 Stefansson cited in C.M. Barbeau, "Henri Beuchat," *American Anthropologist* 18 (1916), 109; Mme. E. Beuchat to C.M. Barbeau, June 10, 1913. Canadian Museum of History, C. Marius Barbeau Correspondence.

24 D. Jenness to M. Mauss, July 7, 1925, cited in Saladin d'Anglure, "Mauss et l'anthropologie," 95.

25 D. Jenness to G. von Zedlitz, January 11, 1916. Library and Archives Canada, George von Zedlitz Correspondence.

26 D. Jenness, "A New Eskimo Culture in Hudson Bay," *Geographical Review* 15, no. 3 (1925), 28–37; Richling, *In Twilight and in Dawn*, 199–201.

27 D. Jenness, "Archaeological Investigations in Bering Strait, 1926," *National Museum of Canada, Annual Report for 1926* (Ottawa: King's Printer, 1928), 5–13; "The Problem of the Eskimo." In *The American Aborigines: Their Origin and Antiquity*, edited by D. Jenness (Toronto: University of Toronto Press, 1933), 373–96.

28 D. Jenness, "Canada's Indians Yesterday. What of Today?" *Canadian Journal of Economics and Political Science* 20, no. 1 (1954), 342–50.

29 D. Jenness, *Eskimo Administration II. Canada.* (Montreal: Arctic Institute of North America, 1964); R.G. Robertson to Treasury Board, April 28, 1960; D. Jenness to R.G. Robertson, November 4, 1962. Library and Archives Canada, Northern Coordination and Research Centre Correspondence.

30 E. Edwards, "Visualizing History: Diamond Jenness's Photographs of D'Entrecasteaux Islands, Massim, 1911–12—A Case in Re-engagement," *Canberra Anthropology* 17, no. 2 (1994), 14.

Publisher's Note

The Life of the Copper Eskimos was first published in 1922. This facsimile edition faithfully reproduces the original text of the first edition. In the century since, society's attitudes toward Canada's First Nations peoples and indeed the very terms used to denote those societies have changed greatly. So have historical views of first contact between Europeans and the First Nations, relations between French and English Canada, and social attitudes toward gender and ethnicity in general. *The Life of the Copper Eskimos* is an artifact of its time, and it is only fair to say that the twenty-first-century reader may stumble across the occasional expression no longer in common use.

The Life of the Copper Eskimos

Diamond Jenness

Ikpakhuak and his wife Higilak in full dancing costume

REPORT

OF THE

CANADIAN ARCTIC EXPEDITION 1913-18

VOLUME XII:

THE COPPER ESKIMOS

SOUTHERN PARTY—1913-16

OTTAWA
F. A. ACLAND
PRINTER TO THE KING'S MOST EXCELLENT MAJESTY
1923

PREFACE

The series of reports of which this is Volume XII and the first complete volume to be issued, will give the narrative and scientific results of the Canadian Arctic Expedition, 1913–18. The expedition, under the command of Mr. Vilhjalmur Stefansson, was originally planned to remain in the field from 1913 to 1916 and many earlier publications refer to it as the Canadian Arctic Expedition, 1913–16. Although many members of the scientific staff were officers of the Geological Survey of the Department of Mines, the general direction of the expedition for administrative purposes was placed in the hands of the Department of the Naval Service.

As the expedition was planned to work in two comparatively distinct fields at some distance from each other, it was divided into two parties. The Northern Party, whose field was primarily the Beaufort sea and the Arctic archipelago, remained in the field from 1913 to 1918 under the immediate supervision of Mr. V. Stefansson. The work of the Southern Party was confined more particularly to the Arctic mainland and the adjacent islands, under the direction of Dr. R. M. Anderson, and returned in the autumn of 1916. General accounts of the work of the two main parties and subsidiary parties, rosters of the scientific staffs and a portion of their contributions to the results of the expedition have been given in summary reports to the Government and in popular narrative and will be summed up in the forthcoming Volume I of this series.

In order to have the scientific results of the expedition properly worked up, the specimens distributed to specialists, and the reports adequately published, an Arctic Biological Committee was appointed jointly by the Department of the Naval Service and the Department of Mines in January, 1917. This committee consisted of Chairman, Professor E. E. Prince, F.R.S.C., D.Sc., Dominion Commissioner of Fisheries; Secretary, James M. Macoun, C.M.G., F.L.S., Botanist and Chief of the Biological Division of the Geological Survey; Professor A. B. Macallum, F.R.S., M.D., D.Sc., Ph.D., LL.D., Chairman of the Commission for Scientific and Industrial Research (later professor of biochemistry at McGill University); C. Gordon Hewitt, D.Sc., Dominion Entomologist and Consulting Zoologist of the Department of Agriculture; and R. M. Anderson, Ph.D., Zoologist of the Geological Survey, representing the expedition and the Victoria Memorial Museum, the final depository of the specimens collected by the expedition. Various members of the committee took up the editing of different sections, and Dr. R. M. Anderson was appointed general editor of the reports.

The Committee has been at work for nearly five years and reports have been prepared or are in preparation by seventy-three specialists. Dr. Hewitt had fortunately practically completed his work on Volume III (Insects) before his untimely death on February 29, 1920, but Mr. Macoun had not finished his work on the botanical volumes at the time of his death on January 6, 1920. The scope of the committee was later enlarged to include the geographical, topographical, and anthropological work of the expedition and three new members were added in 1920, namely A. G. Huntsman, Ph.D., of the Biological Board of Canada; Edward Sapir, Ph.D., Chief of the Division of Anthropology, Victoria Memorial Museum; and M.O. Malte, Ph.D., Dominion Agrostologist and Honorary Curator (later Chief Botanist) of the National Herbarium.

For convenience in publication and distribution it was arranged that the Department of the Naval Service should issue Volumes I (Narrative of the Expedition), VI, VII, VIII, IX, and X (Marine Biology and Hydrography), and XII (The Life of the Copper Eskimos), while the Department of Mines should issue Volumes II (Birds and Mammals), III (Insects), IV and V (Botany) XI (Geology and Geography), XIII, XIV, and XV (Ethnology), and XVI (Archæology.) Where several different reports are included under one volume, dated separates are issued for distribution to specialists interested in the particular branch covered, and copies are preserved to be bound in the complete series of volumes.

The author of the present memoir, Mr. D. Jenness, M.A. (Oxon.), F.R.A.I., Associate Ethnologist, Victoria Memorial Museum, after graduating from the University of New Zealand in 1908, was a student of anthropology in Balliol College, Oxford University. From 1911 to December, 1912, he was sent by Oxford University as a Research Student to New Guinea, and part of his work there has appeared in a volume entitled "The Northern D'Entrecasteaux," by D. Jenness and A. Ballantyne, Oxford University Press, 1920. After returning from the Arctic Mr. Jenness was on overseas service, with the Canadian Field Artillery from 1917 to 1919, which fact accounts in some degree for the delay in publication of this report.

ARCTIC PUBLICATIONS COMMITTEE.

CONTENTS.

TABLE OF ILLUSTRATIONS

PLATES

TEXT FIGURES

MAPS.

THE LIFE OF THE COPPER ESKIMOS

By D. Jenness

Victoria Memorial Museum, Ottawa, Canada.

INTRODUCTION

When the Canadian Arctic Expedition left Esquimalt, British Columbia, on June 17, 1913, there were two anthropologists on its staff, M. Henri Beuchat, the famous French savant, and myself. Our instructions called for three years research work in the vicinity of Coronation gulf, M. Beuchat devoting his attention more specifically to the language, manners, customs and religious beliefs of the Eskimos of that region—the Copper Eskimos—while I was to study their physical anthropology, technology, and archæology. The first year was a year of disaster. Our largest vessel, the *Karluk*, was crushed in the ice, and several members of our staff, including M. Beuchat, perished either on the ice or on Wrangell island. At the same time the remainder of the expedition found itself doomed to spend its first winter on the north coast of Alaska. From November, 1913, to February, 1914, I lived with the Eskimos near Barrow, gathering folk-lore and compiling a grammar and vocabulary of the language. In March I travelled eastward, and joined the southern party of the expedition at Collinson point, about 100 miles west of the Alaska-Canada boundary. There I continued my linguistic studies for a short time, then at the end of May moved down to Barter island, and spent the next few weeks in excavating some of the ancient ruins on this old trading-site of the Alaskan and Mackenzie river Eskimos. The large collection of archæological specimens now stored in the Victoria Memorial Museum at Ottawa represents but a portion of the ethnological results that were obtained during our first year in the Arctic, when we were still over a thousand miles from our original objective. Indeed it was not until August, 1914, that the southern party of the expedition was able to establish a base at Bernard harbour, on the south side of Dolphin and Union strait, within the territory of the Copper Eskimos. There, with less than two years at my disposal, I had to carry out M. Beuchat's work as well as my own, and attempt as far as possible to cover the whole wide field of anthropological research.

The autumn of 1914 was spent in routine duties around our station at Bernard harbour. We had to unload the vessels, build a house and store-room, set up the meteorological instruments, and collect the driftwood scattered along the coast for fuel during the coming winter. Our only assistant at this period was a young Mackenzie river native named Palaiyak, most of whose time was taken up in hunting. Twice we were visited by small bands of local natives who lingered in our vicinity for two or three days, then disappeared again inland. At the beginning of November, as soon as it was possible to travel along the coast by sled, one of the topographers, Mr. J. R. Cox, accompanied me on a short trip west to Cape Bexley in order to discover whether any of the Eskimos had come down to the coast in that direction. Our journey was fruitless, however, for we found no traces of the natives anywhere.

On November 19, two families of the natives suddenly appeared at our station, and a few days later I joined them at their camp three or four miles east. One of them guided me at the end of the month to the Eskimos on the opposite side of the strait, with whom several days were spent. I visited the latter Eskimos again early in December, and lived with them for about three weeks. The greater part of January was spent in their winter settlement at the Liston and Sutton islands, and time was found to pay a brief visit to another group of Eskimos who were living on the south coast of Victoria island some fifty miles to the northwest. In February I accompanied Dr. R. M. Anderson, the leader of our party, up the Coppermine river, and on the return journey visited the Eskimos of western Coronation gulf. Many of these gulf people accompanied us to Bernard harbour, and settled down beside us, so that it was possible to carry on researches at our own station. Towards the end of the month I accompanied Mr. Cox on a short survey trip along the coast to Locker point, and had an opportunity of paying another visit to the Eskimos in that region.

In April, 1915, the Eskimos, who had been living in large communities on the sea ice all through the winter, began to break up into small bands and slowly travel towards the land at various points along the coast. As they would be hunting and fishing inland throughout the summer, and would probably seldom come near our station, I decided to attach myself to one of their parties during that period and to share their migratory life. An old couple adopted me into their family, and from May to November we wandered about in the southwest of Victoria island. By that time the strait was frozen solidly again and I was able to rejoin the expedition at Bernard harbour.

A large band of natives settled beside our station in the middle of November, and for a month researches were carried on among them without going further afield. They crossed over to the Liston and Sutton islands early in December, and I followed them and spent the greater part of that month and of the following January in their settlement. In February, 1916, accompanied by the Rev. H. Girling, an Anglican missionary who had entered the country the previous summer, I travelled east to the Jamieson islands in order to visit the Bathurst inlet natives. Very bad weather was encountered on both the outward and the homeward journeys, so that we did not reach Bernard harbour again until March 18. A large train of natives from all parts of Coronation gulf followed us to our station and settled down beside us for a month, a very welcome proceeding, as it saved me from the necessity of living in their settlements. On April 20, Mr. Girling and myself set out for his station some 120 miles to the west, at Point Clifton, the topographers of the expedition having reported near this point some ancient houses built of wood and sod after the manner of the western Eskimos. I returned on May 15, and continued my ethnological work among some Eskimo families who had camped beside our house. June was a very busy month, as all our specimens had to be packed and the ship loaded in preparation for our departure as soon as the ice conditions should render navigation possible. Nevertheless, towards the end of the month, I journeyed overland to Cape Krusenstern to examine an old stone house in that vicinity, and to visit the various bands of Eskimos who were trapping salmon in different creeks along the coast. Finally, on July 13, 1916, after spending rather less than two years in the region of Coronation gulf, the expedition sailed out of Bernard harbour on its return journey to civilization, and our field-work came to an end.

I was greatly handicapped during our first year in this Copper Eskimo country by the lack of an interpreter. We had been able to secure the services of only one western native when we entered the region, the Mackenzie river youth Palaiyak. This boy had but the merest smattering of English, and moreover much of his time was inevitably taken up with miscellaneous duties around the station, such as hunting. During the seven months spent with the Copper Eskimos on Victoria island I had no interpreter at all. Conditions were much more favourable in the second year, for Dr. Anderson was able to engage a half-breed Eskimo boy named Patsy Klengenberg to help me in my work. Patsy could neither read nor write at first, but he had a fair conversational knowledge of English and had spoken Eskimo from his earliest years. Although barely sixteen years of age he was strong and hardy, an excellent traveller and a skilful and fearless hunter. Probably no better interpreter could have been found anywhere along the Arctic coast.

Most of my researches were carried out in the settlements of the Eskimos, for it was neither possible nor expedient to keep the natives around our station. Our party of six white men had to live in one small room, and whenever the Eskimos were introduced the house was so crowded that the staff had to retire to their bunks. That there was never the slightest friction, in spite of the inconveniences and discomforts to which they were subjected, was due entirely to their staunch comradeship and friendly co-operation. They often put themselves to considerable trouble in order to obtain information for me, and, without their assistance, the present volume would have been far more imperfect and incomplete. Their help was not confined to the field, for since our return they have generously placed their photographs at my disposal for the illustration of my reports. I take this opportunity of thanking Dr. Anderson and my colleagues for all their assistance.

I am indebted also to the Rev. H. Girling for many friendly criticisms, and for additional information that he has acquired since we left the Arctic. Mr. Girling has spent four years among the Copper Eskimos, from 1915-19, and during that period he has accomplished a great deal of valuable linguistic work. His long residence in the country, and his special gift for acquiring languages, have made him the foremost authority on many matters pertaining to the Copper Eskimos.[1]

The maps and illustrations for the present volume, apart from the photographs, were prepared by O. E. Prud'homme, artist of the Geological Survey.

In this, the first of the ethnological reports, and the only one that is likely to interest the general public, the simplest spelling possible has been adopted for all Eskimo words, in order to make the book more readable. Most, if not all, of these words will be found in one of the later volumes that it is hoped to publish, where a more accurate phonetic system will be employed. These later volumes will deal with the more technical phases of Copper Eskimo ethnology, the physical appearance of the natives, their clothing and implements, their language, mythology and songs. The expedition brought back a large collection of phonographic records, photographs, and ethnological specimens, many of which will be utilized in illustrating the different memoirs.

The main sources of information for all that relates to the ethnology of the Copper Eskimos are the works of Mr. V. Stefansson, the commander of the Canadian Arctic Expedition. Mr. Stefansson obtained an astonishing amount of very valuable information in a comparatively short space of time, and while it was inevitable that a certain number of errors should have crept into his accounts, yet his works will always stand as the basis on which future investigators will have to build. His publications, together with the other works that have been consulted, are given in the bibliography; most of these works are quoted in abbreviated form in the course of the report.

---

[1]The Rev. H. Girling died of pneumonia at Ottawa on Feb. 21, 1920, while he was south on furlough. He was a man of considerable culture and attainments, with large views and larger sympathies. In all practical matters he was exceedingly capable and energetic, while his strong winning personality gained him a great influence over all the natives among whom he worked. He was planning to carry out some ethnological work for the Geological Survey on his return to the Arctic, but his sudden death when only 30 years of age put an untimely end to his career.

CHAPTER I

THE COUNTRY OF THE COPPER ESKIMOS[1]

Although the region inhabited by the Copper Eskimos attains to no very extreme latitudes—hardly more than a few degrees, indeed, beyond the Arctic circle—yet its continental character renders the climate more severe than might otherwise be expected. The Eskimos themselves divide the year into five seasons: winter, *okiuk*, from the middle of November till the end of February, when the sun barely rises above the horizon at noon and for several weeks is missing altogether; early spring, *opinraksak*, from the beginning of March till the latter half of April, when the snow begins to melt; spring proper, *opinrak*, from the end of April till the land is bare of snow; summer, *auyak*, when the days are warm, the snow has left the ground, and for a few short weeks all but the largest lakes are free from ice; and finally autumn, *okiuksak*, when the weather once again grows cold, the lakes freeze over, and the land begins to resume its winter garb. The lengths of the different seasons naturally vary somewhat from year to year, but autumn will roughly include the period from about the middle of September till the middle of November, while summer comprises the months of July and August and the early part of September.

Tbe coldest period is from the middle of January till towards the end of February. In the winter of 1914-15 the average temperatures of the four coldest months were: November −9° F., December −4° F., January −24° F., and February −22°F., while the first fifteen days of March averaged −24° F. For the corresponding months in the winter of 1915-16 the temperatures were, November −12° F., December −19° F., January −17° F., February −25° F., and March up to the 15th, −22° F. The lowest temperatures recorded were −49° F. in the former winter, on January 20, 1915, and −44° F. in the latter, on February 19, 1916. These readings were obtained at Bernard harbour; lower figures were registered at times in other places, but probably the thermometer seldom or never falls as low at any place along the coast as on the plateau to the south.[2]

Winds of extreme velocity are of very rare occurrence. The maximum recorded in winter by the expedition's anemometer at Bernard harbour was 46 miles an hour, on December 7, 1915, whereas at Collinson point, in north Alaska, 80 miles an hour was registered in the winter of 1913–14. It is the long-continued cold with a certain dampness in the atmosphere, and the combination of a strong wind with a low temperature, that renders the climate very severe. In one of the worst blizzards in the winter of 1914-15 the thermometer stood at −30° F. while the wind had an average velocity of 30 miles an hour. In the following winter there were several blizzards when the temperature was below −20° F., and the wind above 20 miles an hour. In March, 1916, almost every man in a settlement of Kilusiktok natives at the Jamieson islands had the marks of severe frost-bites on his face, though there are grounds for believing that the average Eskimo freezes less easily than the average European. Travelling under these conditions is rendered more difficult by the lack of all road-houses; the Eskimo at the end of each day's journey in winter has to build a new snow-hut for himself

---

[1]This chapter deals with the country in its economic aspects only, in so far as they affect the Eskimo inhabitants. For descriptions of its topography, geology and biology the reader is referred to the special reports on those subjects that are being published by other members of the expedition. Cf. also Stefansson, *My Life with the Eskimos* (especially the appendix by Dr. R. M. Anderson), and Anthrop. Papers, A.M. N.H., vol. XIV, pt. I, Introduction.

[2]The Rev. H. Girling informs me that in the winter of 1916–17 his thermometer at Bernard harbour registered −57° F. for three days, and in the following winter it dropped on one occasion as low as −62° F.

and his family. The days too, from November to February, are short—a fine day in mid-December offers only about five hours in which there is light enough for travelling, and in foggy or cloudy weather even this period is greatly reduced.

The break between winter and spring seems to come about the middle of April. Already the days are growing long, and the nights correspondingly short. May sees the triumph of the light with the appearance of the midnight sun. The snow is then rapidly melting from the land, and the creeks and rivers are on the point of breaking out; but the nights are still chilly and strong winds not at all infrequent. June and July are delightful months in an average season, except for occasional fogs which may last two or three days. North and south winds often occur, whereas at all other times of the year the prevalent winds are east and west. The first half of July is perhaps the most pleasant period in the year. Rivers and streams are rushing in full flood and the smaller lakes have lost their covering of ice. All the birds have come back and are joyfully building their nests. The sun circles round in the sky without setting, the air is warm, and in a good season a tent is hardly needed. A few insects, flies and butterflies and bees, have made their appearance, but the weather is not yet hot enough to bring those hosts of mosquitoes that in the height of summer plague animals and men alike. The warmest month is August, when the thermometer sometimes reaches 70° F. on the coast. September marks a decline again, shorter days, colder weather and the departure of all the birds save a very few species. In October winter is already drawing in. The sea is frozen solid in November, and it is possible to travel almost anywhere by sled. December brings back both the cold and the dark.

Generally speaking the coast is low, sloping back in undulating ridges to an interior plateau. The ridges run usually east and west at no great distance from each other, and are connected by numerous short transverse ridges that enclose a network of lakes and ponds of every size and shape. At various points along the shore there are upstanding cliffs of dolomite or diabase. The coast becomes more rocky east of the Coppermine river, and granite makes its first appearance. Nearly all the islands with which Coronation gulf is littered have high upstanding cliffs facing the east and south. Only three rivers carry any great volume of water, the Coppermine (*Kogluktok*), the Tree (*Kogluktualuk*) and the Hood (*Kattimannik*); but there are numerous smaller rivers, the Rae (*Pallik*), the greater and lesser rivers *Kugaryuak*, the *Anialik*, the Wentzel (*Kogluktuaryuk*), the *Utkusikkalluk*, and, on Victoria island, the *Kimiryuak* flowing into Forsyth bay, and the *Kugaluk* which enters the sea behind Bell sland.|

Reindeer moss[1] is abundant in the valleys of most of these rivers, which are therefore favorite haunts for the migratory caribou. Practically the whole of the country lies beyond the northern limit of trees; there are only two places, in fact, where timber is found, viz. in the valleys of the Tree and of the Coppermine rivers, for which reason these two possess a peculiar economic importance.[2] Occasional beds of willow that grow to a height of five or six feet appear as veritable forests among the prevailing heather and moss and grass and tiny flowering plants a few inches high with which the greater part of the country is covered. The driftwood that is found here and there on the sea-shore would be far more valuable to the natives than this scanty vegetation, did not the heather supply them with fuel during the summer months; and the caribou and musk-oxen find sustenance in the moss and grass where man finds none.

---

[1] Reindeer "moss" is the name popularly applied to various s.ecies of lichen, *Cladonia*, and other allied ge era.

[2] A small river, the *Napaktauktuak*, a few miles east of the Coppermine, is said to reach back to timber. The Dease river, though it flows into Great Bear lake, may be considered for our purposes to lie in the basin of the Coppermine, since it is only accessible to the Eskimos by way of the latter.

It is fortunate for the Copper Eskimos that their land lies in the track of a great caribou migration. In the first days of spring the deer that are scattered all over the barren lands west of Hudson bay begin to move northward, seeking their summer pastures on the shores of the Arctic sea and in the great archipelago beyond. The first herds reach the coast as early as the end of April, and the migration continues well into June, when the ice of the straits usually is too unstable to admit any longer of their passage. In July, August and September the deer scatter out, but they muster again on the south shores of Victoria island in October, and cross the straits on their journey south between the end of that month and early December. By Christmas they have disappeared altogether in most places, though a few herds remain all the winter in certain favoured valleys, notably in the basin of the Coppermine river. But when the caribou have gone the sea is frozen solid again, and the natives can track out the breathing-holes of the seals that abound in these waters.

Seals and caribou are the most abundant game animals. Musk-oxen are found east of the Coppermine river, and in the north of Victoria island. Ground squirrels are numerous in certain areas on the mainland, and foxes are fairly common everywhere: wolverines and wolves, on the other hand, are comparatively rare outside of the Coppermine valley, and only an occasional brown bear is encountered even in the places where its natural foods, berries and roots, are most abundant.

Many migratory game-birds, such as ducks, loons and ptarmigan, have their breeding grounds in this region, but not in such numbers as to influence the economic situation to any marked extent. Fish are much more important. Nearly every lake teems with salmon and lake trout, and innumerable schools of salmon[1] migrate up the rivers and streams each year to spawn. These, with the tom-cod that abound in certain bays, furnish about a third of the total food supply of the natives.

The Eskimos have names not only for different divisions of the country, but also for certain subdivisions of them, and most of the creeks and many of the more important lakes, headlands, and islands have also their distinctive appellations. The most westerly district that is still inhabited is the country known generally as *Akulliakattak*, which extends along the coast from about Stapylton bay to Cockburn point and for an indefinite distance behind. The more correct designation for this area is *Akunnik*, for *Akulliakattak* is really only the name for Hope point and for a fair-sized lake behind it, ten miles long perhaps and four miles wide, which is the rendezvous of the Eskimos who have hunted and fished in the interior during the spring and summer. At this lake they sew their new deerskin clothes in the autumn, and make their preparations for going out on the ice of the strait and beginning the winter's sealing. Leaving Lake *Akulliakattak*, they migrate down the stream *Siorak* into South bay. Often they stop a day or two at Cape Bexley to make their final preparations before crossing the strait, whence this cape has received the name of *Ineksarvik*, the "Place where everything is finished." One derivation for the word *Akulliakattak* gives it the meaning of " Short portage", which would refer to an overland route from Stapylton or South bay to the head of the Rae river, a route the Eskimos often take in preference to the long journey round the coast.[2] Mr. J. R. Cox, one of our topographers, made this portage in the course of his surveys, and the brief description he has given of the country will be found a little farther on. The Eskimos say that it abounds in fish, and that caribou are fairly numer-

---

[1] There is no true salmon along the Arctic coast, the fish that is called salmon throughout this memoir being a salmon trout, belonging to the genus *Salvelinus*.

[2] Erdmann (Eskimoiches Wörterbuch), gives the mearing in Labrador as "ein Mittelland," *i.e.*, the and between two bays or gulfs.

ous in spring and summer, though not to the same extent as farther east. In many places near the coast we found the remains of Eskimo caches, and stones set up for deer-drives. Cockburn point is called *Aiyeyak*, and the two small islands off it *Piyumaleksiakuk*.

East of *Akulliakattak* or *Akunnik* is *Noahognik*, a district which includes all that broad triangular peninsula that has its apex at Locker point. Here the country is more irregular, with the ridges higher and the lakes more numerous. Fish are very abundant, and many caribou pass through on their annual migration to and from Victoria island. Bernard harbour is an excellent wintering place for small schooners, but the Eskimos have no name for it, though the small bay next to it, on its eastern side, is called *Ugyuksiorvik*. Off the entrance to the harbour lies Chantry island, *Kikiktaryuak*, the "Big island," so named because it is much larger than the tiny islets and reefs that fringe the coast. In 1914 some of the local Eskimos passed the interval between the summer's hunting and the

FIGURE 1.—Eskimo camp beside a fishing lake behind Bernard harbour

winter's sealing on its northern extremity, for food was scarce, and the men could hunt for seals in the broken ice off the point while the women stayed at home and sewed their winter garments. Other natives gathered at the mouth of a small creek, *Nulahugyuk*, four miles east of Bernard harbour, which issues out of a large lake named *Hingittok* or *Hingiktok*, a few miles inland. In spring large numbers of salmon migrate up this stream to the lake, and at the same time, or usually perhaps a little later, there is a seaward migration of the young salmon out of the lake itself. In 1916 the migration up-stream began in May. Towards the end of June it ceased, and nearly all the Eskimos who had gathered there to fish went inland. But a few days later the young fish, probably two seasons old, began to come down, and at the same time there was a renewal of the upstream migration of the larger salmon. Only one family of Eskimos had remained behind, and they reaped all the benefit. Generally three or four schools, each numbering from six to thirty-six fish, would enter the stream within the twenty-four hours.

About eight miles east of *Nulahugyuk* creek there is another named *Kogluktuaryuk*. Here too the salmon migrate in large numbers, and bearded seals haunt the adjacent waters. North of Cape Lambert, whose dolomite cliffs rise to a height of eighty feet, are the Lambert islands, a favourite sealing-ground of some of the local Eskimos in early spring. Lakes and ponds are very numerous in the country behind this cape. One of the largest is Lake *Kogluktuaryuk*, the source of the creek of the same name; its diameter is about a mile and a half, and it lies a few miles south-west of Cape Lambert. The Eskimos often come here to fish; in the spring of 1916 we saw the remains of a camp on the shore of the lake and three of their caches on the coast just north of it. Willow is scarce here, but heather abundant, so that the natives had no lack of fuel; besides heather they seemed to have used also a few sticks of driftwood which they had carried in from the coast.

In the same spring a band of natives was fishing on another fair-sized creek that flows into Paisley cove. It is called *Noahognik*, and, like the others, issues from one of the many lakes two or three miles inland. Cape Krusenstern is *Nuvuk*, the "Point", and Mount Barrow, in the peninsula behind it, *Uvaiyu*. The low narrow isthmus just north of Mount Barrow is a favourite portage of the Eskimos, as it enables them to avoid the longer route and the rough ice that always gathers round Cape Krusenstern. Another longer portage is often made here, especially by natives coming from the south; they begin from the bay just west of Locker point (*Tikirak*), on the left side of the high bluff *Kikigarnak*, which lies directly behind the point; then, crossing a chain of small lakes and skirting a low hill named *Imneligaryuk*, they issue into the deep bay between Cape Krusenstern and Paisley cove. The small bay at the east end of the shorter portage is a well-known place for tom-cod, and the coast in the vicinity is an excellent hunting-ground for both the rough seal (*Phoca hispida*) and the bearded seal (*Erignathus barbatus*), which are the mainstay of the Eskimos during the winter.

One of the regular routes which the caribou take in their spring migration to Victoria island is across the neck of the Krusenstern peninsula. Eskimo encampments have therefore left their remains on all the highest points in the neighbourhood. On the summit of the hill *Kikigarnak*, behind Locker point, there is a peculiar stone hut which may have been an observation post over the surrounding country. The country to the south and east of here has been described for me by our two topographers, Messrs J. R. Cox and K. G. Chipman, who made a survey of the coast and a part of the hinterland. Mr. Cox begins his account thus:—

"Travelling south from the abrupt limestone cliffs of Cape Krusenstern, one reaches in three or four miles a country for the most part grass-covered and far more pleasant to the eye than the desolate coast of Dolphin and Union strait. From the high land back of Cape Lockyer [Locker point] one may look inland for many miles over a vast grass-land broken only by a ridge of low cliffs that extends from the first bay to the north of Basil Hall bay to Cape Lambert. The same type of country continues to Basil Hall bay, a narrow inlet with shores from fifty to two hundred feet high, which extends in a north-westerly direction for about ten miles from the coast. The low grassy hills at the foot of the inlet are said by the Eskimo to be one of the best places to get deer in the summertime. The south shore of Basil Hall bay runs out to form the low shingly promontory of Cape Hearne. About three miles back from the point there is a fine set of cliffs rising to a height of 205 feet.[1]

---

[1]No name was obtained for Cape Hearne itself, but the cliffs behind it had apparently two names, *Imik* and *Ulugvik*. The bight between Basil Hall bay and Cape Kendall is called *Ituksiorvik*.

"The country to the south and west is again low and grassy till near the foot of the next bay. From this bay to Cape Kendall (*Imnalugyuat*) the foreshore is low and tundra-like, though a few miles inland it rises to a height of two or three hundred feet, in uneven and somewhat rocky terraces.

"At Cape Kendall the dolomite country gives way to the more severe and rough diabase country. From Cape Kendall to some twenty miles up the Rae river (*Pallik*),[1] on the north side, there is an almost continuous series of diabase bluffs which average about 180 feet in height. At the mouth of the Rae river there is a low grass flat several miles wide where there are always deer to be found in the spring-time. The Rae river carries only a small volume of water, and from what one can see of it in the winter-time, has a large number of rapids. About 18 miles from the coast there is a cascade of about ten feet, where, in the summer-time, the Eskimo frequently gather to spear fish. From 20 to 50 miles up the Rae river, the country is for the most part open, grassy and rolling, with occasional isolated diabase buttes. About 32 miles up, the river expands into a lake a third to half a mile wide and eighteen miles long, lying in a trough at the southern edge of the grass country, which extends as far as one can see to the north. A couple of miles to the south the country drops off several hundred feet into what appears to be very rough and rugged rocky country. At the west end of the lake the river passes through a series of low rocky diabase hills for several miles. Here a considerable number of stone caches and shooting shelters were noticed. To the west of these hills the river again expands into a long narrow lake through open grassy country, and after about ten miles breaks up into four small branches. This is practically the head of the river, and here the willows are plentiful and large—growing up to fifteen or twenty feet high. Elsewhere on the river willows are scarce and small, with the exception of a couple of small willow-covered islands in the first lake.

"Striking overland in a northeasterly direction from the head of the Rae river one travels for thirty-five miles through a gently rising grass country with only one low dolomite ridge. Thence to the coast on the south side of Stapylton bay, the country, though still for the most part grassy, is rather more uneven, and one passes three sets of low hills formed of mud and gravel, and holding one or two very small lakes. No large lakes were seen from the head of Rae river to the coast. Eskimo shooting shelters and tent rings were observed amongst the mud hills."

Mr. Chipman then continues the account for the Coppermine river region:—
"The Richardson river [2] comes from the south and southwest and empties into the same inlet as the Rae river. What is apparently a large flat to the south of the Rae is really a triangular flat of which two sides are the Rae and the Richardson. This flat is a feeding ground in the fall and spring for large herds of caribou, and just across the Rae are numerous stones and turfs for drives. The mouths of the rivers are said to be good fishing places, but some distance from the sealing grounds.

"From the Rae to the Coppermine (*Kogluktok*) the country is made up of gentle grassy slopes and valleys broken by diabase hills with the characteristic steep slopes to the south and more even slopes to the north. The former afford good hunting grounds for caribou.

"The Coppermine reaches the coast through two mouths enclosing a large low island, grass covered except for two diabase hills on the northern end.

---

[1] The name *Pallik* has been extended to embrace the whole of the Rae river region.

[2] Mr. Chipman gives two names for this river, *Niakongiak* and *Kugnahik;* the latter means simply "River." I myself obtained (from description only) the name *Walliak*, which was extended to apply to the whole region between the Rae and the Coppermine rivers. From this word comes the name *Walliarmiut*, by which all these western Coronation gulf Eskimos often designate themselves.

This island is a well-known fall gathering place for those Eskimos who have spent the summer up the Coppermine, those who have been in the country of the Rae and Richardson rivers, and for some people from the east. It is a good fishing ground, and when we were there in the spring, herds of caribou were continuously visible.

"Inland from the mouth of the Coppermine, the country is generally tundra, rising evenly and with scattered lakes in the small valleys. Not far above the mouth the river contracts to about half a mile in width and has steeply sloping alluvial cut banks.

"Eskimos travelling inland in the Coppermine river country have as their principal object the securing of wood. Secondary objects are the trade with Indians or white men at or near Great Bear lake, the securing of copper, and the hunting of caribou for the fall clothing skins. Hunting and fishing to supply daily wants are at all times of first importance.

"The generally accepted route of travel on the Coppermine is to go up the west side of the river for some indefinite distance, usually twenty to forty miles, then strike southwest for Dismal lake (*Tasirpik*), and then south to Lake Rouvier (*Imernek*), and west to Great Bear lake (*Imaryuak*). Some of those who this year (i.e. 1916) went to Great Bear lake told me they would return to near the northwest corner of Dismal lake, swing north and even west from there and come back to the Coppermine near its mouth. In all about eighty Eskimos left the mouth of the river this year for inland and of these about half left the main party at various times after ten miles up the river and went west. These said they were going to the places where they found copper. The two latter parties would probably meet at some time before fall.

"A party of three or four families from the Tree river also went inland. They said they would follow up the west branch of the Tree river to where it headed near the Coppermine and then go overland to the Coppermine where they expected to meet and trade with the Indians. These are presumably Dog Rib Indians from Fort Rae. They expected to be gone until the snow was on the ground and to bring wood in addition to the lead and powder they would get from the Indians.

"The party from the Tree river left the coast just a few days before the snow left. The party from the mouth of the Coppermine did not leave the coast until the snow was nearly all gone. Both parties were packing with their dogs.

"The route up the west side of the Coppermine is one of easy travel. Long, gentle, grassy tundra slopes to low rolling country offer no difficulties to either packing with dogs or travel with toboggan. The usual travel is some distance back from the river, and before they strike for Dismal lake, no creeks with steep gullies are met. Travelling toward Dismal lake, the country is level with a good deal of swampy tundra until one commences to climb the long slopes of the so-called Copper mountains. These mountains, which attain an elevation of probably not more than 1,500 feet, are in reality a long series of basalt terraces. Since they occupy a belt of about fifteen miles wide and the terraces are numerous and low, the general effect is of a long gentle slope on the north with a somewhat steeper and more irregular slope to the south. Dismal lake lies just south of this ridge.[1]

" From Dismal lake to Lake Rouvier, the country is more rugged, but there are at least two recognized routes to Lake Rouvier, both of them following the gently sloping valleys of creeks which have numerous lakes. These valleys offer good feeding and hunting grounds for caribou, and the lakes probably contain fish.

---

[1]The Rev. H. Girling writes that "The Eskimos go up the Coppermine to where a line of cliffs running inland comes to an end in a round hill with a definite cutting on the east side. This hill is known as *Koluk-huk*, and from its summit the Dismal lakes are clearly visible. The natives follow the hills to a gully, which leads them to the lakes.'

" Lake Rouvier is the source of what may be considered as the east branch of the Dease river. The route crosses the lake, then cuts east over a low and gently sloping ridge of tundra hills to the south side of the valley of the main Dease river. It follows this to the "Garche" hills, crossing the southeast branch of the Dease at "Big Stick island", and from the "Garche" hills, which are some fifteen miles east of Great Bear lake, the route goes through the timber to the lake.

" With straight travel the above route would occupy about ten or twelve days. The Eskimos of course have to sustain themselves during the trip, and it takes them longer. It would seem that they usually leave the coast with enough dried meat for three or four days. The whole Coppermine valley to its mouth seems to be good caribou country, but within two or three days of the coast the people do not seem to rely on finding them. We ourselves, except for three on the opposite side of the river which we could not get at, saw none until we had left the Coppermine; but from then on we always had plenty and without going out of our way to get them. Caribou offered an abundant supply of food and we had no need to consider fish or other sources of supply. In both Dismal lake and Lake Rouvier, however, fish are known to be plentiful and the Eskimos say that the many small lakes which are abundant throughout the gently rolling tundra country are full of fish. Ducks, loons, bear, etc., are not numerous, but are sometimes used by the people as a source of food.

" Wood for various purposes seems to be obtained most largely from the vicinity of "Big Stick island."[1] This place, about thirty-five miles east of Great Bear lake on the southeast branch of the Dease river, is an area of several hundred acres of excellent timber. It is surrounded by the Barren lands, and is recognized as a good hunting ground both by the Eskimos and by the Indians of Great Bear lake. It is here, when the Indians are hunting, after their return from the summer trips to the trading posts, that the meeting between the two peoples takes place.

" On the Coppermine itself timber comes to about twenty miles from the mouth, but the trees there are small and stunted and consequently neither in size nor in easiness of being worked are they adaptable for use by the Eskimos. From that point on up the river, trees are frequently met with and in places they attain considerable size. In the valley of the Kendall river, which connects Dismal lake with the Coppermine, there is abundant timber, and at the east and west ends of Dismal lake there is a small amount. The balance of the shore of Dismal lake is said to be destitute of trees except for a small clump in a cirque-like basin near the "Narrows." Lake Rouvier has abundant timber on its north side. It was here that Fathers Le Roux and Rouvier had their house. The main valley of the Dease is well timbered, especially as Great Bear lake is approached. In all of this country the timber is confined to the immediate vicinity of the river or lake valley; the surrounding hills and plains are a part of the "Barren lands."

" Mr. D'Arcy Arden, a well-known traveller in the north, who has made his headquarters at the east end of Great Bear lake since 1914, tells me that in 1914 the Eskimos were wandering all through the country south of the east end of the lake as far as Cape McDonnel (which is locally known as Caribou point). From there directly east to the Coppermine, old tent rings and other signs of their camps were numerous.

" It would seem that " Big Stick island " and the country immediately east of Great Bear lake are the main objective points of the Coppermine river Eskimos in their inland excursions in the summer. There it is that they get the wood for various purposes and there it is that they meet and trade with the Indians. If any person were to look for the Eskimos at " Big Stick island "

[1]Cf. Stefansson, Anthrop. Papers, A.M.N.H., Vol. XIV, pt. I, pp. 82-3; My Life with the Eskimo, p. 222.

or elsewhere, it must be remembered that the camps will not be found immediately on the Dease or in the valley, but somewhere on or among the surrounding hills. Old camp sites are very numerous on the north side of Dismal lake, particularly at the " Narrows ", and it is there where both fish and caribou are numerous that they get the supply of fall skins for clothing. They here get caribou both by hunting on land and by spearing from kayaks as the caribou are swimming. Aside from these two main or more permanent gathering places, the country and the camp sites indicate that the Eskimos are wandering around in small parties.

" Except that they go west and south from ten to twenty miles up the Coppermine, nothing is known of the country where those Eskimos who go after copper get their supply and where they spend the summer. The others, however, spend the summer mostly in the country bounded by Dismal lake, the Coppermine, and the east end of Great Bear lake. Throughout this area, timber, caribou and fish are abundant, and the country itself is one of easy travel."

Mr. Cox now takes up the account of the country to the eastward:—

" About ten miles to the east of the Coppermine there is a small river (the *Napaktauktuak*), which runs back into timber and is said to have plenty of fish. Eight miles farther east is the western *Kugaryuak*, which reaches the coast through a wide grass flat. The country from here to the eastern Kugaryuak[1] (28 miles) is broken and rough—typical of the diabase country. The eastern *Kugaryuak* is a fair sized stream and has plenty of willows about the mouth. About ten miles farther east there is a wide steep grassy valley coming down out of the diabase opposite a group of four large islands with striking bluffs. This place is known as *Sallik*, and is said to be a very good place to hunt deer in the spring-time. Immediately to the east of here granite takes the place of the diabase on the coast and continues to about ten miles west of Port Epworth. This is a rough and barren stretch of coast, though doubtless well supplied with lakes. From a grassy bay about twelve miles west of Port Epworth, there is a portage (about one-half to three miles) into a large lake which runs back of the coast to within a third of a mile of the southwest corner of Port Epworth. This route is sometimes used, and the lake holds plenty of fish.

" From the point northwest of the bay mentioned to the large bay just south-west of *Agiak*[2] the coast is bleak and barren diabase, almost entirely devoid of soil and vegetation.[3] A few miles south of the coast, however, lies the granite country, which is relatively much more fertile, though extremely rough and swarming with lakes of all sizes. The Tree river (*Kogluktualuk*) running into the southeast corner of Port Epworth has granite on the east and dolomite on the west. About six miles up from the mouth are fine falls sixteen feet high, below which, and through the rapids which run for about two miles below the falls, the Eskimos do a good deal of fishing. In the summer of 1915, at least a dozen people made their living here—chiefly on fish. There are plenty of willows up to three inches in diameter for fuel. Some ten miles above the mouth, the river forks into two branches of about equal size. Not much is known of the east branch, though it is said to have its source in a large lake, which is also the source of the Hood river or of a branch of it, according to Maffa.[4]

"Both branches of the Tree river run up into the timber about five sleeps up (i.e., 50 to 60 miles). The western branch for about 25 miles up runs through a rather narrow grassy valley with steep ridges on either side. The surrounding

[1]The valleys of both *Kugaryuak* rivers abound in caribou. All this region is known as *Asiak*.

[2]The Eskimos here obtain whetstones for their knives, hence the name *Agiak*, i.e. "Whetstone."

[3]The inland district between Tree river and Bathurst inlet is called *Pingangnaktok*.

[4]Maffa was a Tree river Eskimo who served the expedition as a hunter and guide. It is very improbable however, that the same lake should be the source of two distinct rivers flowing in different directions.

country is full of lakes, most of which have fish. This west branch is said to come very close to the Coppermine river some distance above the big bend in that river, and the Eskimos sometimes make the portage across.

"From the foot of Gray's bay the coast runs in a northeasterly direction to Cape Barrow (*Hanninik*), and is of granite throughout. Three rivers of nearly equal size come out to the coast in this stretch: the *Anialik* at the southwest corner of Gray's bay; the *Kogluktuaryuk* opposite the south end, and the *Utkusikalluk* opposite the north end of Hepburn island (*Igluhugyuk*). In the country lying between the *Kogluktuaryuk* and the *Utkusikalluk* musk-oxen are still to be found in small numbers, and a group of natives was hunting them near the mouth of the *Kogluktuaryuk* as we passed there in the spring of 1916. About the *Kogluktuaryuk*, the coast and the country for a mile or two inland are low and grassy, but elsewhere the granite comes to the beach and the country is excessively rough.[1] Nevertheless, in the numerous tiny valleys there is considerable grass and feed, and caribou are fairly plentiful from March onwards.

"From the foot of the north arm of Inman harbour (*Amaroalligit*) there is a very short portage over into Bathurst inlet a short distance north of Galena point. This is the route generally taken by the Eskimos.

"From Cape Barrow to Detention harbour (*Akeahugyuk*) the country is granitic. From Detention harbour to Kater point (*Naukhiakavik*) the country is much broken and indented with deep bays, and there are many wide grassy valleys and flats—as for instance at the foot of Moore bay, where we saw some tents near the mouth of the river (i.e., in the summer of 1915).

"Practically all of the south and west sides of Arctic sound are open and rather low country. The Hood river (*Kattimannik*) comes in at the southwest side between fairly high mud banks, its mouth spreading out over several square miles of sand flats. At the southeast corner of Arctic sound, there is a small river known as the *Kilusiktok*.[1]

"Banks peninsula is fairly high and rocky (amygdaloid), but has several fair-sized fishing lakes and some grassy valleys. On the east side of Banks peninsula a long sound runs down into "Brown's channel," which is in reality a bay with low grassy country at the foot. A fine set of diabase-capped dolomite bluffs from 800 to 1,000 feet runs along the west side of this low land. A small river (*Hanningaksiorvik*), running out of a lake a short distance inland, drains the valley.

"East of this bay as far as we have gone the mainland consists of a red quartzite which makes a rather rough country. On the peninsula forming the west side of "Brown's channel" is a large tidal lake in a stretch of low land. Here, and in small lakes close to it, is a favourite fishing place of the Eskimos. It is also a good place for caribou.

"With the exception of three, the islands in Bathurst inlet that we visited are so barren and rocky that they are not very much visited by caribou. The three islands that have a fair proportion of grass-land are the two *Kannuyak* islands and *Algak* (the island to the south of *Igloryuallik*), and caribou are plentiful on these islands in the spring-time. *Algak, Ekkalulialuk*, and the northern *Kannuyak* island have good fishing lakes.

"Throughout Bathurst inlet there is good tom-cod fishing anywhere close to the land, especially in bays, channels and near big cliffs. The people we met there were living largely on tom-cod helped out by an occasional caribou, a few lake trout and a considerable number of squirrels. They catch few, if any, seal in Bathurst inlet in the spring-time."

---

[1]This country is called by the natives *Nennitak*.

[2]The whole of the neighbouring district bears the same name.

Banks peninsula was near the most easterly point of the mainland reached by any of the members of our expedition; the country beyond is known only from the journeys of the earlier explorers and of the Royal Northwest Mounted Police patrol in 1917, and from the descriptions of the Coronation gulf Eskimos. The eastern side of Bathurst inlet is known as *Umingmaktok*, while Kent peninsula to the north is *Kiglinguyak*. Farther east is *Asiak*, the country of the Asiagmiut people, while opposite them on the southeast corner of Victoria island is *Ekaluktok*, the home of the Ekaluktomiut. Hanbury says of *Asiak* that it is a very barren country, though caribou, musk-oxen and fish abound, while in winter polar bears are killed on the ice. This was borne out by the statements of an *Asiak* native whom I met near Bathurst inlet, but he added that there were no brown bears, although they are occasionally encountered west of Kent peninsula.

Turning to Victoria island there is the district of *Hanerak*, opposite Stapylton bay, on the other side of Dolphin and Union strait. This was the country of the Haneragmiut before they ceased to exist as a separate unit; it extends from about Cape Baring (*Ikpigyuak*) to the point marked "Cliffs about 80 feet" on Rae's map, nearly northeast of Cape Bexley. Following the coastline around from Cape Baring, the first slight point, which also is marked by Rae "Cliffs about 80 feet," is called *Nauyat*, from the numbers of seagulls ((*nauyat*) which make it their haunt. Between *Nauyat* and Point Pullen (*Sinieluk*), a rocky promontory connected with the mainland behind by a narrow isthmus of sandy clay, is Bell island (*Kikiktaryuk*). A long low sandpit runs out from the west side of Point Pullen towards Bell island, and a small sandy islet lies almost awash half way between the two, but Bell island itself is high and rocky. On it are the ruins of an old wood and sod hut, according to Captain Jos. Bernard, who wintered in a little nook behind Point Pullen in 1913-14. Mount Arrowsmith, directly behind, is called by the Eskimos *Annorillit*, and a peak just to the west of it is *Kingmiktorvik*. The Colville hills are here not more than a mile or two from the sea, and two creeks of considerable size have their outlets in Penny bay. One, the *Attautsikkiak*, rises beside Mount *Kingmiktorvik*, and rushes down in a narrow bed between high steep banks of clay superimposed on dolomite until it reaches the mud flats on the coast. In autumn the stream is diminished to a mere brook, though it evidently pours down a great volume of water in spring. The other creek, the *Kugaluk*, is larger and longer, flowing more from the east and receiving considerable accessions from a number of small lakes. Its banks are wider apart and generally not so high as those of the *Attautsikkiak*, though in one place, about five miles from the sea, where it cuts through a bed of dolomite running northwest by southeast, it forms a beautiful gorge some 300 yards long and from 50 to 100 yards wide, while the cliffs are about 40 feet high. Here the Eskimos often fish in summer, jigging with long lines from a ledge half way down the face of the cliff into a deep pool beneath. Just below the gorge, nodules of pyrites are found in the creek bed, and from time immemorial the Eskimos have come here to gather them, using them to strike fire. The *Kugaluk* also pours its waters into Penny bay, about a mile southeast of the *Attautsikkiak*.

The dolomite cliffs of Cape Hamilton (*Misumeok*) are the most conspicuous feature along this coast.[1] The next small cape a few miles farther east is *Niahognaryuk*, and the coast for a few miles east of that again is called *Kinaruk*. About 25 miles east of Cape Hamilton are the dolomite cliffs of *Tulukak*, the home of "ravens," which have another home in a smaller dolomite cliff just to the west known as *Tulukakak*. To the traveller sledding along the coast, *Tulukakak* seems to be about 50 feet high, with its cliffs running north and south, *Tulukak* itself being a little higher and running approximately east and west. Then follows a shallow bay about 12 miles broad, bounded on the east by the cliffs of *Ingnerin* ("fire-stone," because, it is said, pyrites exists here also). *Ingnerin* is sometimes

---

[1] Rae gives them an altitude of 170 feet.

included in the country of the Akulliakattangmiut, for when that group crossed over from South bay in the autumn, it used to unite with the Haneragmiut at this place and spend the first part of the winter sealing in the vicinity. Although the Haneragmiut are now extinct as a separate group, the Akulliakattangmiut still cross over to *Ingnerin* and do not unite with their eastern neighbours as a rule until after the sun returns, i.e., about February.

Bordering on *Hanerak* is the district of *Puivlik*. Beginning from *Ingnerin*, it seems to reach to about Point Dickens, in the narrow strait just before it broadens out to make Coronation gulf. The general trend of the coast from *Nauyat* to Simpson bay is southeast, with a broad deep bight at Simpson bay. The Colville hills do not dip quite so far south, so that although at Richardson bay they come within a mile or two of the coast, farther east, to the north of Read island, the two are separated by an undulating plain from 10 to 15 miles wide. This plain, like the Colville hills to the north, is full of lakes and ponds, some of which, especially those close to and draining directly into the sea, teem with fish, the sea salmon. North of Read island is the low peak *Kingautak*, a very familiar landmark to the Eskimos. The Colville hills, which are of brown-ish clay formation without signs of any rock exposure, sweep round to the northeast with no apparent break, forming the " Museum range " remarked by Mr. Stefansson. Here there is one very prominent peak, visible even from

Fig. 2.   View of Mount Wivyaurun from Lake Angmaloktok, Colville hills, S.W. Victoria island

Simpson bay in clear weather; Mr. Stefansson called it Mount Bumpus, while the Eskimo name is *Wivyaurun*. Some ten miles NNW. of *Wivyaurun*, in about lat. 69° 45′ N and long. 113° W., is a large lake apparently about ten miles in diameter, though it is difficult in the spring to distinguish islands from shore line even with the binoculars. This is Lake *Tahiryuak*, beyond the Colville divide, a well-known rendezvous where the Puivlik natives of the south meet the Kanghiryuak natives of the north in the later days of spring. From Mount *Wivyaurun*, Museum range (or the Colville hills), for the two here seem identical, appears to continue down to the southward, probably with a trend east.

The Colville hills enclose an enormous number of lakes and ponds, ranging from tiny lagoons a few yards wide to lakes several miles in diameter. All except those that freeze to the bottom in winter abound in lake trout and lake salmon, and the Eskimo inhabitants spend four or five months each year in wandering about from one fishing-ground to another. The ridges themselves are almost devoid of vegetation, but there are pleasant meadows here and there round the margins of the lakes. Most of the deer that remain in this part of Victoria island during the summer, however, find better pasture on the plains nearer the sea.

Several large creeks, almost rivers, flow out of the hills into Simpson bay. One issues out into the sea beside a high knoll named *Tipfiktok*, near where Linklater island is marked on the chart. Still another, known as *Epiullik*, has its exit northeast of Read island[1]. The Eskimos sometimes gather at *Epiullik* in the autumn. More often they assemble at the mouth of the *Okauyarvik* creek a little farther east, in a well-sheltered harbour where Rae marks " 15 May." Bearded seals abound both at this place and at *Epiullik* in the autumn, lying on top of the young ice. *Okauyarvik* is an excellent place from which to start the overland journey to Prince Albert sound in the spring, though the Colville hills can be crossed almost anywhere by sled. The *Okauyarvik* creek has its source in Lake *Kigiaktallik*, one of the larger lakes in the Colville hills, and

Fig. 3.   Frozen falls on Okauyarvik creek, S.W. Victoria island

winds about in a roughly SSW. direction for some 40 miles before it finally reaches the sea. A few miles east of it the *Kimiryuak*, probably the largest creek in this region, falls into Forsyth bay, and a little south of that again, in a rather deep bight just below Clouston bay, falls the *Kogluktok* river. Where the coast approaches nearest to the Liston and Sutton islands there is a point called *Nuvuk;* but beyond this the Eskimo names for the salient topographical features have not been recorded. The whole coast from *Ingnerin* to Lady Franklin point consists of a low gravel ridge, for the dolomite which protrudes in high cliffs farther to the west continues inland when the coast turns south, and the different streams from the interior have to cut deep channels through it on their way to the sea.

---

[1]Between these two streams apparently is the district called *Iglulik;* Read island (or Beads island, for the charts have both names; the natives call it *Kigiktanneuk*) lies about three miles off the shore, and consists of low gravel terraces of dolomite, with here and there boulders of diabase and granite.

In the strait between *Puivlik* and *Noahognik* lie the Liston and Sutton islands. Really there are three islands, called by the Eskimos *Ahungahungak* (Liston island), *Putulik* (Sutton island), and *Illuvillik;* all three are included in the general name *Ukallit.* The two former islands have high dolomite cliffs on their northern and southern faces, and much broken ice gathers around them in winter. Seals, both rough and bearded, are very numerous, so that the Eskimos from both sides of the strait have made this place their winter resort. The Puivlik natives generally make their way along the coast first to *Nuvuk*, for from there they can cross over in a single day; otherwise it would be necessary to camp one night on the ice, and a gale at this time of the year (December) might cause a great crack to open up and engulf them.

The only member of the southern party of the expedition who travelled along the south coast of Victoria island east of Lady Franklin point was Mr. Frits Johansen, one of our biologists, who was there in March, 1916. "The Miles islands," he writes, " consist of diabase with the typical formations of this region, steep and high cliffs on the south and east, low and flat on the north and west. Except in pockets and on gravelly slopes the vegetation was very poor. Few animals occur here, but we noticed tracks of foxes, wolverines, lemmings, hares, ptarmigan and ravens, as well as caribou tracks, it being the time of their spring migration. Only the middle islands contained any driftwood to speak of, and they only on the north and west sides; it was there also that the usual signs of temporary Eskimo encampments were seen, tent-rings, wood-gatherings, and the like, showing that the Eskimos, like myself, used the islands as a pathway from the mainland to Wollaston land. The ice was often very rough and screwed up around the islands, especially where the coast was steep and rocky, but it seemed to have been safe for passage from November on.

" Richardson island, further east, consists solely of diabase. Facing Coronation gulf, there are perpendicular cliffs several hundred feet high, impossible to scale and dropping clear to the water; but facing the sound are gentle slopes of smooth rock clear to the beach, covered more or less with gravel and vegetation. Also the higher land in the interior of the island has good vegetation right to its top and is rather easily scaled from the north side, especially where creeks come down. Numerous caribou were seen here in larger or smaller herds climbing or grazing on the slopes on both sides of the sound. In the sound itself between Richardson island and the coast of Wollaston land are a number of islands. Two, at its mouth, mark the gateway coming from the west, and another half-way up the sound marks the narrowest place and divides it into a northern and a southern arm. The northern route is much the shorter, and along it were found tent-rings of the Eskimos and their meat-caches.

" Murray point is a rocky peninsula of diabase overlying limestone or dolomite, which itself lies on a bed of sandstone. It is connected with Wollaston land by a series of lagoons, sandbars and tundra swamps, over which the Eskimos portage. It was here that I met three families of natives who were living in snow huts in Wellbank bay, where they had been sealing since the autumn of 1915. Some of them had visited the natives of Bathurst inlet that winter, and all had fairly civilized implements, hardly anything being made of copper; there were even guns and ammunition. A few days journey to the eastward, they told me, lay a river named Hagavaktok, which is open till late in the fall and is the only considerable stream along the whole coast to Simpson bay. This Hagavaktok apparently flows into the sea in the neighbourhood of Byron bay.

" The coast of Wollaston land opposite Richardson island consists of steep, high cliffs of diabase, which change a little further west to sandstone ridges that slope gently down to the beach, but rise more quickly inland to a height of about 100 feet. This extends as far as Lady Franklin point. The land along here is more or less covered with gravel, boulders and vegetation, and shows the usual signs of Eskimo settlements, of which the most remarkable were large sandstone slabs laid on edge to form rude rectangular shelters for the hunters. Tracks of caribou were numerous in this place. The 'Mackenzie river' is really a series of creeks that issue from a system of swamps, ponds, and lakes a little way inland. Except on a small basalt island at the mouth of this 'river,' where I found meat caches made from boulders, there were no signs of Eskimo encampments either at the mouth or up inland along the 'river.' A short-cut portage across the base of Ross point is known to the local Eskimos, and I also used it to great advantage. From Lady Franklin point to Wellbank bay, the coast is almost entirely void of driftwood."

Such then is the character of the Copper Eskimo country in so far as we were acquainted with it. Those portions of the mainland and of Victoria island which we did not visit will probably be found to differ in no important respect from the regions already described.

CHAPTER II

THE EXPLORATION OF THE COUNTRY

The first of the early explorers to reach the country of the Copper Eskimos was Samuel Hearne, who travelled overland with a party of Chipewyan Indians to the mouth of the Coppermine river in 1771. Just below Bloody fall they fell in with a band of Eskimos living in five tents on the west side of the river, all of whom they massacred. Another party living in seven tents on the eastern bank managed to make its escape, with the exception of one old man who was so intent on collecting his things that the Indians fell upon him before he could reach his canoe. Only two small pieces of iron were found in the spoils of the twelve tents. Hearne's party, afraid to linger any longer in this region, hastily returned to the south again, and for another half a century the Copper Eskimos were left undisturbed.

In 1819, Captain Franklin, afterwards Sir John Franklin, was placed in command of an expedition sent out to explore the north coast of America eastward from the mouth of the Coppermine river. In 1821 he reached the lower waters of the Coppermine, and found a party of Eskimos at the same place at which Hearne had encountered them, just below Bloody fall. Most of the natives fled, but Franklin was able to communicate with one family, from which he learned that the tribe called themselves Naggeooktormœoot, or Deer-Horn Esquimaux, that they usually frequented the Bloody fall during June and the following months for the purpose of salting [?] salmon, then retired to a river which flows into the sea a little farther west (Richardson river) and passed the winter in snow-houses.

Leaving these Eskimos, Franklin proceeded by boat along the coast to the eastward as far as Point Turnagain. At various places he came on fresh traces of Eskimo settlements, but nowhere did he see the Eskimos themselves. On the return journey he ascended the Hood river for some distance, then struck overland to Fort Providence, on Great Slave lake. No white man since Franklin has ever made this journey, but the Eskimos of the present day follow almost the same route, though some of them ascend the Tree river instead of the Hood.

Richardson and Kendall, in the course of Franklin's second expedition in 1826, travelled eastward from the Mackenzie river in two boats, the *Dolphin* and the *Union*. They encountered first the Eskimos of Kittigaryuit village, in the Mackenzie delta, the inhabitants of which "had heard of the Esquimaux at the mouth of the Coppermine river, and knew them by their name of 'Naggoe-ook-tor-moe-oot' (or Deer-horns), but said they were very far off, and that they had no intercourse with them, adding that all the inhabitants of the coast to the eastward were bad people."

Farther east, these explorers saw recent footsteps of a small party of Eskimos on the beach in the neighbourhood of De Witt Clinton point. Again, "five miles beyond the Harding river, on the extremity of a rocky cape, the Esquimaux had constructed several storehouses of drift timber, which were filled with dried deer's meat and seal-blubber; along with which, cooking kettles, and lamps made of potstone, copper-headed spears, and various other articles, were carefully laid up. The ashes of the recently extinguished fires showed that the natives had quitted this place only a few days."

It is reasonable to suppose that both the foot-prints and the storehouses were due to the same Eskimos, who were probably western natives, since the storehouses were built of wood. They bear out the present-day tradition amongst the Copper Eskimos that the two peoples had intercourse up to two generations ago, i.e., until nearly the middle of the nineteenth century. No Copper Eskimos have ever been seen farther west than Stapylton bay, though traces of them exist as far as Wise point, where they seem to have met their western neighbours. Richardson noticed that they had marked most of the prominent points around Mount Barrow, at Cape Krusenstern, by erecting piles of stones similar to the cairns that the shepherds in Scotland build for landmarks, and adds that these erections were occasionally noticed after doubling Cape Parry, though they were not so numerous. This is precisely what one might expect in a region where two peoples overlapped. At Young point there were several caches of this nature, and near them were some typical implements of Copper Eskimo culture. In 1915, Dr. Anderson noticed about a dozen stone caches and three or four stone tent rings some two hundred yards inland from the sea, eight miles east of De Witt Clinton point. Even as far west as Langton bay these stone caches are found, though there some of them are probably graves, since the western natives often covered their dead to protect them from wild animals and birds of prey. In the vicinity of the Burrow islands, Darnley bay, in 1911, Dr. Anderson discovered a stone cooking-pot broken and mended with copper splices, and a blubber pounder of musk-ox horn, objects that were undoubtedly made by Copper Eskimos.

Richardson and Kendall met none of the Copper Eskimos on this journey, though they found that a party had just quitted Bloody fall, probably frightened by the presence of white men. Back, however, encountered them when he descended the Back or Great Fish river in 1833. All down its course he had noticed their traces, and at Lake Franklin he finally came on a small party fishing. He remained with them only one day, but in that time succeeded in establishing cordial relations. Five years later, in 1838 and 1839, Dease and Simpson explored the coast from the mouth of the Coppermine to beyond Back river. In 1838 they saw two or three Eskimo families below Bloody fall, but the natives were alarmed at their presence and fled over the ice towards some distant islands. Eskimo caches were noticed at various points along the coast east of the Coppermine, placed upon lofty rocks out of reach of beasts of prey; but they saw none of their owners, who had all gone inland to hunt caribou after their winter seal-hunt among the islands. Close to Cape Turnagain was a place where three Eskimo tents had been pitched in the preceding year, with a little stone fire-place on one side, and near Cape Franklin they passed the remains of a larger camp where there were several human skeletons; but they nowhere found recent traces of the people.

In the following year they were more successful. Some thirty Eskimos were encamped at Richardson river, and one family, whose tent was placed on an island in mid-stream, was left behind when the others fled precipitately to the hills. With this family the explorers were able to communicate, and while the information they gathered was of little value, they yet left a favourable impression on the natives which proved of much service to Richardson ten years later. East of Cape Alexander, Dease and Simpson saw vestiges of Eskimos wherever they landed, for the most part very old; but they never fell in with the natives again during their journey.

In 1848 Richardson again made the journey from the mouth of the Mackenzie to the Coppermine river, ascending the latter to Great Bear Lake. On this occasion he was accompanied by Rae, and the party was ferried across the mouth of the Rae river by the Eskimos. Rae returned in the two following years, and explored the coast of the mainland from Cape Lambert to Cape Alexander, and the south coast of Victoria island from Cape Back to Cape Alfred. Besides meeting his old acquaintances on the Rae river, he had an interview with three Eskimos near Cape Flinders, and saw others on a neighbouring island. He says of the Cape Flinders natives, "These people appeared to have been poorly fed as they were much leaner than Esquimaux generally are; they had never been in communication with white people before, and were at first much alarmed, but we very soon gained their complete confidence." The only other place at which he met with natives was along the southwest coast of Victoria island. There were thirteen Eskimo lodges a few miles to seaward of Cape Hamilton, with the inhabitants of which he established relations. None of the women showed themselves, but all the men were well and cleanly dressed in deerskin. They were all very fat, having evidently abundance of seal's flesh and fat, large quantities of which were carefully deposited in seal-skin bags under the snow. It was difficult, he says, to make them understand that no return was expected for some presents he made them.

But though he met with no more natives, Rae found traces of them in several places. Cambridge bay seemed to be one of their favourite resorts, judging by the numerous stone-marks and several caches of provisions, clothing, etc., deposited on the banks of the river there. He observed that it was doubtless an excellent fishing-station immediately after the breaking up of the ice, since he saw many salmon sporting in the transparent waters in the vicinity. Between Cambridge bay and Pelly point there was nothing to indicate that the Eskimos had recently visited the points at which his party touched. One other observation that he made is worth noticing. The Eskimos, he says, have a great respect for caches of any kind. Some that he had made himself on the southwest coast of Victoria island were left untouched, notwithstanding that one, or perhaps all of them had been seen by the natives.

McClure was the next navigator to fall in with the Eskimos. During the spring of 1851 one of his sledge parties came on five families near Berkeley point, at the southern entrance of Prince of Wales strait between Victoria island and Banks island. They seemed very simple and honest, and when presented with anything, they appeared incapable of supposing that anyone would give them an article without expecting an equivalent. His fellow-explorer, Collinson, spent the following winter, 1851-2, in Walker bay, and about fifty of these natives built their snow huts near him. A sledge party under Lieutenant Jago met about a hundred others in Prince Albert sound. None were seen north of 72° 10′ N. in Prince of Wales strait.

Collinson sailed east through Coronation gulf in the following summer, and wintered in Cambridge bay. Rae had seen only caches here, but Collinson met the natives themselves. He says: " The number seen by us in this vicinity I estimated at between two and three hundred, of which between fifty and a hundred returned in the spring; the inner harbour, the large lake west of Mount Pelly, and the peninsula about Cape Colborne, forming their hunting and fishing ground from May until October; at which period they follow the deer to the mainland, where, having first collected together in the neighbourhood of the Finlayson islands, they winter; but the precise spot we did not discover; it could not, however, have been very far from us, as we were visited continually during the winter. I fully expected to have found them on the Finlayson Islands in the spring, as it was usual for them to come from that direction; but on my visit in April, there were no signs of winter huts, although numerous caches showed them to be a place of great resort."[1]

For fifty more years this region remained unvisited, then David T. Hanbury in 1902 made a journey from Chesterfield inlet to Ogden bay, and along the coast to the Coppermine river, which he ascended, as the earlier explorers had done, to Great Bear lake and the Mackenzie river. He first met with the Copper Eskimos, about forty-five people altogether, a few miles inland from Ogden bay; the natives, following their usual custom, gave a dance in his honour. From this point to as far west as Gray's bay small parties of natives were met with in several places; but from there onward no more were seen till he reached the Dismal lakes, where he found four tents, but only three people living in them at the time. Hanbury's journey was one of the most successful that

[1]Collinson, p. 284.

has ever been made in these northern regions, and he has left a very interesting and valuable account of the country he passed through and of the people he encountered.

A Danish trapper and trader, Captain C. Klengenberg, with a small schooner, the *Olga*, spent the winter of 1905-6 in the vicinity of Cape Kendall, on southwest Victoria island. He met a party of the Prince Albert sound natives in the early spring, and they camped near his ship for three days, then disappeared north again. Two years later an American whaler, Captain Wm. Mogg, in the same vessel, wintered in Minto inlet, and met some of the Eskimos there.[1] In 1910, Mr. V. Stefansson, travelling by sled along the coast, visited the Eskimos of Dolphin and Union strait and west Coronation gulf, then continued up the Coppermine to Great Bear lake. In the following year he returned, accompanied by Dr. R. M. Anderson, and visited also the natives of Prince Albert sound. Captain Jos. F. Bernard with his schooner, the *Teddy Bear*, remained in the country for three years; he spent his first winter, from 1910-11, in a bay a few miles east of the Coppermine river, his second, 1912-13, in Bernard harbour, and the last, 1913-14, in a little bight behind Cape Kendall on Victoria island.

A few other travellers, working down to the mouth of the Coppermine from Great Bear lake, have met the Eskimos within the last few years. In the summer of 1912, two brothers, G. M. and L. D. Douglas, accompanied by the geologist, Dr. August Sandberg, descended to the mouth of the Coppermine in the course of their investigations into the copper deposits of this region. They fell in with a considerable number of Eskimos of whom they have published some interesting photographs. Messrs. J. Hornby and C. D. Melville lived from 1908 to 1911 on Great Bear lake; they met some of the Eskimos in their first year[2] and many more later. Mr. Melville returned south in 1911, but Mr. Hornby remained for three years longer.[3] Another traveller, Mr. D'Arcy Arden, was at Great Bear lake from 1914 to 1916. He visited the mouth of the Coppermine with a police patrol in the spring of 1916, and returned to Bear lake again in the following summer with Mr. K. G. Chipman, one of the topographers of the Canadian Arctic Expedition. In 1911, Father Rouvier, of the Order of Mary Immaculate, established a mission on a lake at the head of the Dease river, where Father Le Roux joined him in the following year. At this period the Eskimos were visiting Great Bear lake each summer to trade with the white men and Indians, and in the fall of 1913 the two priests followed some of them north to the mouth of the Coppermine river, and were murdered close to Bloody fall. Two other white men, Messrs. H. V. Radford and T. G. Street, who started from Hudson bay and travelled overland to Bathurst inlet in the summer of 1912, were also killed by the natives. In 1914 the Canadian Arctic Expedition established itself in Dolphin and Union strait and spent two years in exploring the surrounding country. The Anglican mission sent in a party during the summer of 1915; their schooner was blown ashore close to the Croker river, but their leader, the Rev. H. Girling, travelled east in the winter and gained a firm foothold amongst the natives, both in Dolphin and Union strait and in Coronation gulf. Finally, in the summer of 1916, the Hudson's Bay Company established a post in Bernard harbour, which the Canadian Arctic Expedition had just vacated, and other white traders and western Eskimos prepared to follow in their train. The barriers which have separated this country from the outside world for so many centuries have been swept away, and this last outpost of the Eskimo race is now thrown open to the invader.[4]

---

[1]Apparently it was Capt. Mogg who collected the specimens of implements and clothing acquired by the American Museum of Natural History from Capt. Cottle in 1907. See Anthrop. Papers, A.M.N.H., Vol. II, pt. III, p. 314, *et seq.*

[2]See Stefansson, Anthrop. Papers, A.M.N.H., Vol. XIV, pt. I, p. 259.

[3]These two travellers presented some Copper Eskimo specimens to the Victoria Memorial Museum at Ottawa, where they are now on exhibition.

[4]See Stefansson, Anthrop. Papers, A.M.N.H., Vol. XIV, pt. I, pp. 287, *et seq.*

CHAPTER III

THE DISTRIBUTION OF THE POPULATION[1]

Earlier writers have distinguished a number of " tribes " among the Copper Eskimos; but the term "tribe," if we use it at all, should be given a very broad interpretation, for the groups into which these natives divide themselves have none of the permanence and stability that we are accustomed to associate with tribes in other parts of the world. It is true that each group has its local name, a name derived from the district it habitually frequents in summer; but the individual members are constantly changing from one group to another, not merely temporarily for some special purpose, such as the acquisition of stone lamps and pots or the obtaining of wood for sleds and tables, but permanently also, whenever the new district offers greater advantages, especially in the matter of game. At the east end of Coronation gulf, when a native was asked what district he belonged to, he would sometimes answer " Oh, I have many homes. Asiak, Pingangnaktok, Nennitak, Kilusiktok, I have lived in them all, both when I was young and since I reached manhood." Another would say "It makes no difference which you call my home, Puivlik, Kogloktok, Nennitak, Kiglinik or Kilusiktok, for I have lived in all those places." A native who is living in Bathurst inlet one year, may be hunting in the Coppermine region the next, while still later you may find him in south-west Victoria island. In a settlement of Eskimos at the Duke of York archipelago in February, 1915, there were representatives of the following districts: Kilusiktok, Nagyuktok, Asiak, Kogloktok, Pallik, Walliak, Puivlik, Noahognik, Hanerak, Akulliakattak and Kanghiryuak. By representatives in this case is meant that the natives had lived most of their lives in one or other of these districts, although they were all amalgamated at that particular time into one settlement at the west end of Coronation gulf. A year later, in a settlement off the mouth of the Tree river, only four out of thirteen adults called themselves Tree river natives proper (Pingangnaktok); one came from Kilusiktok, one from Asiak near the Coppermine river, one from the Coppermine itself, four from Walliak, one from Noahognik and one from Akulliakattak.

Districts that are poor in game naturally become wholly or partly deserted in time, while others continue to support a considerable population. Generally speaking the tendency of the natives is to keep to the districts in which they were brought up, where every lake and hill, every favourite haunt of fish and caribou, is familiar to them. If an Eskimo migrates to another district he invariably tries to associate himself at first with one of its older inhabitants who can guide him about the country. When our expedition was leaving this region in the summer of 1916, arrangements were made with a trustworthy native named Ikpakhuak to take charge of our station in Bernard harbour till other white men should arrive a month or two later. Ikpakhuak at first was rather unwilling, for his real home was across the strait and the new district was unfamiliar to him; he was not acquainted, he said, with the places in which to find fish and game, and he feared that he might have difficulty in providing food for his family.

The Eskimos, like ourselves, have that indefinable feeling of home in the country they have known since childhood. Some of the natives who wandered in the summer of 1915 over southwest Victoria island had been absent for two or three years in Coronation gulf. Travelling with them I was greatly touched

---

[1]For this whole chapter cf. especially Stefansson, Anthrop. Papers, A.M.N.H., Vol. XIV, pt. I, pp. 25-40 and G.S.C. Museum Bulletin, No. 6, pp. 14-15.

by the joy with which they would recognize each prominent lake and hill, and call up memories of earlier days with which these landmarks were associated. One of their kinsmen had died in that region; they wept as they passed near his grave, and some of them, after the day's fishing was over, went back to visit it, and spent the night there in mourning.

However shifting and changing then the groups may be, a man will be bound to one more closely than to any of the rest, and will usually call himself a member of that group, though he may be living at the time in another far remote. But the longer he remains in his new home the weaker grow the ties that bind him to the old, till finally he merges in the group with which he is living and calls himself by its name. Thus a woman who had spent all her earlier life in the country behind Stapylton bay migrated with her parents to Nennitak, at the east end of Coronation gulf. There after some years she married, and though later she wandered all over the mainland between that place and Stapylton bay, she called herself a Nennitak woman, because most of her kinsfolk lived in that direction and the associations of her first home had become less dear to her. Her husband again was brought up in Walliak, but he spent his youth and early manhood in Kilusiktok, where he became one of the most famous shamans in the country. He was living during the three summers from 1914 to 1916 in the basin of the Coppermine river close to his boyhood home, but he called himself a native of Kilusiktok, and was regarded as such by the rest of his people. It is certainly not true to say of the Copper Eskimos, what Boas remarks of the Eskimos of Hudson bay, that "almost without exception the old man returns to the country of his youth, and consequently by far the greater part of the old people live in their native districts." [1] Yet it may have been true in earlier times, since there is reason to believe that the floating character of the Copper Eskimo groups has been greatly accentuated in recent years.

It is necessary to bear all this in mind, therefore, when attempting to classify the different groups that are actually found in the country at the present day. Mr. Stefansson has given a fairly accurate list of them, and a map showing their relative locations. The most westerly group on the mainland is the one round Stapylton bay, known as the Akulliakattangmiut. They gather in the fall at Lake Akulliakatttak, which is not, as Mr. Stefansson believed, the source of the Rae river, but a large lake, comparatively speaking, some three miles south of South bay. There they sew their new clothing before the sun disappears for the winter night, which in this latitude, allowing for refraction, occurs about November 25; as soon as the ice is firm enough, they migrate out past Cape Bexley. It was at Cape Bexley that one of our sledging parties, on December 23, 1914, found a village they had just deserted. It consisted of eight snow houses, or rather of two double houses and four single ones. Dr. Anderson recorded in his diary, "The natives had evidently come from the south along the coast (of South bay), camped here one night, and gone on this morning, passing just round the point, thence straight out on the ice in the direction of Victoria island. The houses were scarcely iced inside, so the Eskimos must have been short of blubber for fuel, and had probably just come from inland. One double house was about fifty yards north of the others, one double and three single houses were in a close bunch, and a single house was about one hundred and fifty yards south away from the rest." These natives had crossed over to Ingnerin on Victoria island, where they were joined by three families who had spent the summer on Victoria island. Early in January this community was still at Ingnerin, living in eleven snow huts; by March they had moved south into the middle of the strait, and were there joined by some of their eastern neighbours. Two families came with our party to Victoria island in the summer of 1915, others went east, and only about six families returned to the region of Stapylton bay.

[1] Boas, Central Eskimo, p. 466.

Mr. Stefansson found thirteen families encamped on the ice north of Cape Bexley in the spring of 1910, though a settlement of over forty houses but a short time before had been deserted near Hope point. He states that Cape Bexley is a trading rendezvous where people from the east come to visit the Akulliakattangmiut, even from the east coast of Victoria island. This did not happen during the time that the expedition remained in the neighbourhood,[1] though natives from the east end of Coronation gulf visited the Dolphin and Union strait Eskimos when they were camped in the neighbourhood of the Liston and Sutton islands, both in 1915 and 1916. Normally this intercourse took place just before spring, about the beginning of March, when the days were long and travelling much less difficult. In the fall of 1915, however, a large band of Eskimos from the Coppermine river region, attracted by the prospects of trade with the expedition, came west into Dolphin and Union strait, and camped first at Bernard harbour, then with the local natives at one of the Liston and Sutton islands.

Opposite the Akulliakattangmiut, on the other side of the strait, once lived the Haneragmiut, the "people on the side of the land." Mr. Stefansson estimated their number at about forty, and states that "a few of them each year hunt on the mainland with the Akulliakattangmiut or farther east, but the larger number go north into the Colville mountains to a fishing lake called Tahiryuak, where they also get numerous caribou, and where . . . . they some years meet a few representatives of the Kangianermiut." These latter people, he says in another place, are the inhabitants of the mouth of the Rae river. There was a settlement of about seventeen Haneragmiut people near Tulukak which he visited in the spring of 1910.

In the summer of 1915 the region of Hanerak was entirely uninhabited, save for my own party, which extended its wanderings into this portion of the country as well as over Puivlik to the eastward. The Eskimos said that the Haneragmiut were extinct as a separate group; several had died one summer near a small lake named Pisiksitorvik in the Colville hills, and the rest soon became dispersed among the surrounding groups, so that now the district is often uninhabited. In 1916 only one family intended to hunt there; they were encamped on the shore near Point Williams in the month of June, fishing in the lakes and hunting in the hills immediately behind the point. One of our western natives shot a bearded seal on the ice and offered them most of the meat, but they had so much meat and blubber of their own that they refused even to drag the animal to shore and cache it. There are at least two lakes named Tahiryuak in this region, and still another northeast of Prince Albert sound, but the best known of them all is the lake where my party of strait natives met the Prince Albert sound Eskimos in the summer of 1915. This is probably the one that Mr. Stefansson heard of, though the natives who normally meet there are the Kanghiryuarmiut from the north and the Eskimos, particularly the Puivlirmiut, from Dolphin and Union strait.[2]

The Noahognirmiut are the next group to the east on the mainland. In the summer of 1914 there were nineteen people inhabiting this district, all of whom called themselves Noahognirmiut, though two of them when cross questioned named other places as their original homes. During most of the summer they wandered about in two separate bands, but two of the natives kept changing about from one band to the other. In the autumn the two bands came down to the coast at different times. The first to arrive, on November 12th, consisted of two families only, six people in all who made their camp at the mouth of a creek four miles east of Bernard harbour where they had left their caches in the spring. Here they stayed for about three weeks, then, early in December, they crossed the strait and joined the Puivlik Eskimos at the mouth of the Kimiryuak river. The other band, thirteen in

---

[1] Nor has it happened since then, the Rev. Mr. Girling informs me.

[2] Mr. Stefansson has since explained to me that the word *Kangianermiut* in the passage quoted above is obviously an error for *Kanghiryuarmiut*.

number, did not reach the coast till the end of November, when they camped on the north end of Chantry island. On December 5th they migrated across to the Liston and Sutton islands and commenced their winter sealing, though one of the men had already done a little sealing from the mainland. The Puivlik Eskimos from Victoria island joined them just before the new year, and the two groups remained united until the spring.

In the following summer, 1915, about forty Eskimos from various groups wandered about in Noahognik, while most of the nineteen who were there in the previous year went away to other districts. In the spring of 1916 about ninety Eskimos were hunting and fishing in Noahognik, several of whom had come from as far east as Bathurst inlet; many of them, however, probably went down to the Rae river valley about July or August. The increase in the number of inhabitants during these two summers was due to the presence of the expedition and the opportunities for trade that it offered, In earlier times there were probably not more than twenty inhabitants, for the region is noticeably lacking in caribou, especially in mid-summer, when their skins are of the greatest value to the Eskimos.

Opposite the Noahognirmiut, on Victoria island, are the people called Puivlirmiut, who wander in summer over all the country between the Colville

Fig. 4. A group of Copper Eskimo men and boys who spent the summer of 1914 in Noahognik

hills and the shores of Simpson bay as far south as Point Dickens. When I first met them at the end of November, 1914, they were encamped some two or three miles up the estuary of the Kimiryuak river in nine double houses, houses, that is to say, that comprised two rooms each, with a single passage way leading to both. There were then 56 people, but the number was increased to 62 a few days later by the addition of two families from Noahognik. In the following summer eighteen natives, all closely connected by kinship or by marriage, were hunting and fishing in the districts of Puivlik and Hanerak; in the autumn they all gathered together at the mouth of the Okauyarvik creek. Three other families (thirteen people), who were wandering at the same time a little to the southeast, came down in the autumn to Clouston bay. In 1916, late in the spring, more than thirty people were encamped at the south end of Clouston bay, and one family had gone to the northwest; all of them intended to spend the summer in Puivlik.

In the month of December, when the sealing on the ice commences, the Puivlik and Noahognik Eskimos regularly unite at the Liston and Sutton islands, the particular island each winter being determined by the condition of the ice in the vicinity and the positions of the best sealing grounds.   The Akulliakattak Eskimos used to join the Haneragmiut at the same time a little to the west, either on the south coast of Victoria island near Ingnerin, or else in the middle of the strait between that place and Cape Bexley.   At Christmas, 1914, the number of natives at the Liston and Sutton islands was 75, whereas at Ingnerin there were about 40.   In the following year about the same period there were no natives at all at the latter place, but 139 at the former, since all the Eskimos in the strait, and even some from Coronation gulf, had assembled at Bernard harbour a short time before in order to trade with the expedition. In February, after the sun returns, the island groups usually move west a few miles to new and unexhausted sealing-grounds.   It was during this month, in 1915, that the two bands in the strait amalgamated, and I was assured that this was their usual custom, though the meeting is frequently postponed until March.[1] Some time in March, too, they are regularly visited by the Eskimos of Coronation gulf, and all the groups undergo reshuffling, some of the visitors remaining in the west to spend the summer in the districts bordering on Dolphin and Union strait, while some of the local natives go east to Coronation gulf.

Mr. Stefansson mentions several tribal divisions at the west end of Coronation gulf.   He states that the Kangianermiut or Uallirgmiut, to the number of about 30, occupy the headwaters of the Rae river; the Pallirmiut, who number perhaps 40, occupy the basin of the same river; the Kogluktogmiut, numbering about 30, inhabit the valley of the Coppermine river, and the Kugaryuarmiut, numbering 25, the basin of the Kugaryuak river, eighteen miles east of the Coppermine.   On the opposite side of the gulf, on Victoria island, Mr. Stefansson mentions the Nagyuktogmiut and the Killinermiut, two names, he considers, for a single tribe that numbers about fifty.

Some of these groups are no longer in existence.   Neither myself, nor the Rev. Mr. Girling later, ever heard of a people called Kangianermiut, while as regards the alternative name Mr. Stefansson gives for them, Uallirgmiut (or, as it sounded to me Uwalliarmiut), this was the usual designation of all the Eskimos who gathered for the winter's sealing at the west end of Coronation gulf.   Uwalliak or Walliak (for the "U" is always faint and often imperceptible), as nearly as I could discover, is or was a name for Richardson river, which empties into the same estuary as the Rae.   More rarely these natives were called Pallirmiut, or Rae river Eskimos.   In reality, any division into groups that may have existed formerly has now been obliterated, and even the natives themselves have ceased to make any distinctions.   Some men when pressed would say that they were originally Pallirmiut, but often they would add that the Pallirmiut were extinct now; and whenever they gave themselves a name of their own accord it was generally either Uwalliarmiut or Kogluktomiut. Another group name that was sometimes heard was Asiagmiut, from Asiak, a district that lies apparently between the Coppermine and the Kugaryuak rivers; I never heard any natives call themselves Kugaryuarmiut, though the term would be quite a natural one.   Nagyuktok, according to most of the Eskimos, includes all the islands off the south shore of Victoria island between about 113° W. and 111° W., north and northwest of the Jamieson islands.   Hence they said it was uninhabited in summer, since the natives are unable to exist on small islands at that season, but must go either to the mainland or to Victoria island to the north.   On the other hand one or two natives, when questioned as to where they intended to spend the summer of 1916, said they were going to Nagyuktok, meaning the south portion of Victoria island between perhaps Lady Franklin point and the Richardson islands.   Thus there would seem to

---

[1] The Rev. Mr. Girling informs me that in 1918 they did not amalgamate at all. The Puivlirmiut and Noahognirmiut were camped near Cape Lambert in March, while the Akulliakattangmiut were at the Liston and Sutton islands.

be two uses of the word, one restricting its meaning to the islands just mentioned, the other including with them the country to the northward, which really lies between Puivlik and Kiglinik. Possibly this latter meaning was the older of the two, since the Nagyuktomiut were perhaps the most widely known of all the groups in this region, their fame reaching even to the Eskimos of the Mackenzie delta. The name Nagyuktok, according to some natives, was given to this region because of the abundance of caribou there (*nagyuk*, horn); they seemed not to know of the legend recorded from the Baillie islanders by Mr. Stefansson, that the people were called Nagyuktomiut because they fought for their wives with caribou antlers.[1]

Native tradition, joined to the present confusion of group names, seems to indicate a considerable decrease in the population of Coronation gulf within recent times. The most northerly island in the Duke of York archipelago is named Inyuernerit, "the uninhabited place," because a great number of Eskimos died there long ago.[2] The island is now generally avoided for that reason. In the summer of 1912 or 1913 (my informants were a little indefinite about the exact date) there were fifteen deaths among the West Coronation gulf Eskimos, whereas in the summer of 1914 there was only one.[3] Whatever the reason may be, at the present day at least no definite groups can be distinguished at the west end of Coronation gulf. Natives gather there from all the surrounding regions; some are on their way to the soapstone deposits farther to the eastward; others are seeking for copper or wood between the Coppermine and the Dismal lakes; while others again merely come to hunt in a region where caribou are known to be plentiful. Within the last few years, too, there has been the additional motive of trade with Indians and white men at Great Bear lake. In the autumn these natives assemble at various points according to their hunting grounds in the summer. Some of them gather together on the south shore of Victoria island, others at the mouth of the Rae river; but the majority assemble on one of the small islands a few miles east of the mouth of the Coppermine river, where they have left their caches in the spring safe from the depredations of wolverines and foxes. In winter they all unite into a single settlement close to the Berens islands, and when the sun returns at the beginning of the year they gradually work their way northwards towards Cape Krusenstern, whence visits can easily be made to the natives farther west. A few go east at this season, while natives from east and west join up with this central group till its character is totally changed. Then in the spring, about May, the natives fall back to the coast again, different bands separate according to the localities in which they intend to pass the summer, and the cycle begins over again.

In February, 1915, we found all the natives of this region gathered into one settlement in the Duke of York archipelago. There were twenty-three huts, and the number of inhabitants was somewhere between seventy and eighty. Most of them followed us west in the following month, and spent two or three days at Bernard harbour, and two or three more with the natives in the strait. Three or four families stayed there, the rest moved slowly east again, and dispersed to the land at various places between Cape Krusenstern and the Coppermine river. In the autumn of the same year many of these natives, as soon as the ice enabled them to travel by sled, came again to Bernard harbour—an innovation in their ordinary movements occasioned by the presence of the expedition. Others again came from as far east as Tree river, till by November 29 no less than one hundred and twenty-seven natives were living alongside of us, some in tents, but the majority in snow huts. A few, about fifteen altogether,

---

[1] Stefansson, My Life with the Eskimo, p. 159.

[2] Mr. Stefansson, Anthrop. Papers, A.M.N.H. Vol. XIV, pt. I, p. 131) says that about 40 (?) natives died there some 15 years before, i.e. about 1895.

[3] Possibly there was an epidemic of influenza contracted from the white men or Indians at Great Bear lake. But cf. Amundsen, Vol. II, p. 329.

had not yet crossed over from Victoria island, and a band of perhaps fifty had remained behind somewhere near the mouth of the Coppermine river. These Coppermine people moved northwards at the end of January, and by the middle of February had camped off Locker point in a settlement of fifteen snow huts. Roughly speaking, therefore, at the date of the expedition's arrival, there were

Fig. 5. Eskimo camp off the mouth of the Coppermine river
(Photo by J. J. O'Neill)

about 180 people in Dolphin and Union strait and at the west end of Coronation gulf. Now that other white men and western natives are finding their way into the country, Eskimos from all the surrounding regions will probably gravitate to these parts, and the different groups will amalgamate even more than they have done up to the present.

Farther east there was a small group located around the Tree river, though it extended east as far as Grays bay. Its members called themselves Ping-angnaktomiut, Pingangnaktok being the name of the district south and east of Tree river. Some of the older natives had not moved out of this locality for a great many years. In the summer of 1915 there were nineteen natives (fourteen adults and six children) fishing on the Tree river itself, and ten others (seven adults and three children) fishing on the Anialik river which flows into Grays bay.[1] In February, 1916, seventeen adults and eight children were living in snow huts about seven miles north of Tree river, and six others (four adults and two children) were travelling between this settlement and Bernard harbour. The majority of these natives moved in to the mouth of the Tree river at the beginning of May, and probably spent the summer in that vicinity.

About seven miles northwest of the most western of the Jamieson islands we found another settlement early in the same year. Here the natives called themselves vaguely Kilusiktomiut, but different groups had their representatives amongst them. A few days before our arrival (on March 2, 1916) they had moved from a still larger settlement some ten miles northeast, where we found the twenty-nine snow-huts they had just abandoned. Thirty-five of their number had gone west to Bernard harbour, and about half the remainder went northeast. About a dozen of the latter were seen by the biologist, Mr. F. Johansen, in Wilbank bay on Victoria island on March 26, and a month later a sledging party met them in Bathurst inlet. At the beginning of May about thirty of these Kilusiktok natives were encamped on Hepburn island, whence they moved across into Grays bay a week or two later. At that time thirteen other natives were fishing about three miles east of Cape Barrow, and seven

---

[1] Hanbury found natives fishing at Grays bay in the late spring of 1903.

more were at Banks peninsula. The remainder of the inhabitants of Bathurst inlet were lost to view inland, but more than fifty deserted snow-houses were seen on one of the Barry islands, Igloryuallik; the natives had evidently erected them in the previous autumn before they went out on the ice to seal, for a similar settlement was noticed a few miles farther north. After spending the summer in the country round Bathurst inlet the Eskimos regularly return at its close to this island of Igloryuallik to sew their winter clothing, while the natives round Grays bay repair at the same time to the north end of Hepburn island.

A few Eskimos fish and hunt each summer on the opposite shore of Victoria island. The only name that I could obtain for this district was Kiglinik, and for the people Kiglinirmiut. Kiglinik means literally "the back country," and so might easily be applied to any district that lay north of any other. The Rev. Mr. Girling tells me that the Bathurst inlet natives often use the term Kiglinirmiut for any Victoria island Eskimos, even the Puivlirmiut to the westward. Nevertheless the word seemed to have a more restricted meaning as well, and to designate that portion of Victoria island that lies directly opposite Bathurst inlet. The natives here are never very numerous. They gather in the autumn somewhere on the coast till their winter clothing is completed, then move out on the ice and combine with the natives from the opposite shore. The total population at this end of Coronation gulf is apparently somewhere around two hundred.

Hanbury says [1] that the natives between Cape Bathurst and the Copper-mine river are called Kuyakiyuarmiut, but the name seemed unknown to the Eskimos I met. Probably what he heard was Kugaryuarmiut, the people of the Kugaryuak river. There is a small river flowing into the bottom of Arctic sound, which, with the country surrounding it, is known by the name of Kil-usiktok. Strictly speaking therefore, the Kilusiktomiut should be only those people who make this their summer home.[2] Actually, however, the name is used, both in Coronation gulf and farther west, for all the natives who spend the winter on the ice off Bathurst inlet. The western natives sometimes call these people Umingmaktomiut, from Umingmak, the high land on the east side of Bathurst inlet not far from the Barry islands. Mr. Stefansson heard of a rumour of a permanent village in this place, but rightly suspected its truth; probably it merely referred to the great autumn gathering at Igloryuallik. He mentions, too, the Kogluktualugmiut, or Tree river people (Kogluktualuk is the local name for the Tree river), who call themselves also the Utkusiksaligmiut,[3] and the Kogluktuaryumiut or people of the Kogluktuaryuk river which flows into Grays bay. None of these names seem to be used at the present day, though a few natives call themselves Nennitagmiut, or inhabitants of the district of Nennitak, which seems to be the country behind Cape Bathurst. As a matter of fact, any locality can potentially give its name to the people who habitually frequent it, so that it is possible at any time for a new group to arise and for an old one to drop out of existence.[4]

The natives say that the region about Bathurst inlet was very densely populated up to some three generations ago. Many of the people were then stricken with sickness and died; their bones are said to be visible still on a small island near Igloryuallik.[5] The country was thus left almost uninhabited, but it

---

[1]Hanbury, p. 177.

[2]Mr. Stefansson was mistaken in supposing the Kilusiktomiut to be a Victoria island people.

[3]I think Mr. Stefansson may have been misled here by the meaning of the word *Ukkusiksalik*—"The place that possesses material for making pots," and the fact of soapstone existing in this region. The Ukku-siksaligmiut, according to the testimony of the Coronation gulf natives themselves, dwell much farther east. They are usually located by other writers, e.g. Boas, at the mouth of Backs river, or between Backs river and Wager inlet.

[4]The Rev. Mr. Girling informs me that two new group names were adopted about 1917. The people who hunt in Southern Victoria island in what has been called Nagyuktok now call themselves Tuktuk-tomiut (i.e. the Caribou-hunters), while some natives who spent the summer round the Napaktoktok river a little west of Tree river call themselves Napaktoktomiut.

[5]Dease and Simpson found several human skeletons near Cape Franklin in 1838 (J.R.G.S. Vol. 9, p. 325).

was gradually peopled again by natives from the surrounding districts. This would account for the present distribution of the population, the great numbers that dwell in Bathurst inlet, and the comparatively few that are scattered along the south coast of Victoria island and between Bathurst inlet and the Coppermine river on the mainland. The tradition is borne out also by the statements of individual natives as to their birthplaces. Relatively few of the men who were sealing off Bathurst inlet in the winter of 1916 had been born in that region; they had gone there from Umingmaktok, or from the Coppermine river area, or else from the opposite shore of Victoria island. Others again had been born there, but their parents or grand-parents were immigrants. One old man stated that his grandfather had come there by sled from Asiak, beyond Kent peninsula, accompanied by five other families.[1] Four of the families returned to Asiak, but the other two, including his grandfather, stayed on in Bathurst inlet, where their descendants are living still.

Two natives from Asiak, beyond Kent peninsula, were living off Bathurst inlet in the winter of 1916. One had come in the autumn, and was passing his first winter in the country. He had married a Kilusiktok woman, but intended to return in the spring to his native home and take his wife back with him. The Asiagmiut, he said, were more numerous than the Kilusiktok natives with whom he was living, more numerous too than the Ekaluktomiut on the opposite side of Dease strait. Mr. Stefansson understood from the Prince Albert sound natives that the Asiagmiut might number between fifty and a hundred, and this would correspond to my own information. Kent peninsula probably forms part of their country, though it is called by a name of its own, Kiglinguyak; nothing is known as to its inhabitants, if there be any at all at the present time. The Asiagmiut who visit the Bathurst inlet natives seem to travel by the same route as Hanbury, between Kent peninsula and the mainland. Rae met three natives near Cape Flinders, and Hanbury found others all the way from the east side of Kent peninsula to Ogden bay. Near Ogden bay there were six families in one settlement, and forty-five natives in another, but Hanbury does not mention to what group they belonged; possibly they were Asiagmiut also. Probably there are many local groups in this region just as elsewhere, though their names are not known to the western natives, who usually call all the people east of them Kivalirmiut (i.e., Easterners). Beyond the Asiagmiut, Coronation gulf natives know of the Netsilingmiut and one or two other groups, but they could give us no estimate concerning their numbers.

We did not meet with any natives from Ekaluktok, though some of them visited and traded with the Bathurst inlet people in the spring of 1915, returning to their own country again before the ice broke up in the strait. The population of this group, according to the reports of other natives, was somewhere about fifty. The Rev. Mr. Girling has written to me stating that one of his mission parties, led by the Rev. E. Hester, visited the Ekaluktomiut in the winter of 1918, when they were encamped midway between Victoria island and Kent peninsula. At that time they numbered only a few families. Mr. Stefansson deduced a much higher estimate for the group, about two hundred, judging by the accounts he received from the Prince Albert sound natives; but either his estimate is exaggerated or only a small portion of the tribe frequents Dease strait. It was possibly these people whom Collinson met in the neighbourhood of Cambridge bay, though they then numbered between two and three hundred. More probably, however, they were Kiglinirmiut, since that group appears to have been far more important formerly than now.[2] Rae found no recent indications of people between Cambridge bay and Pelly point, but Lieutenant Hansen came upon thirty or forty natives in the neighbourhood of Taylor island. He under-

---

[1]His grandfather's name was Kingaulik; the other men in the party were Arnauyuk, Aumeyok, and Aitauk, and two others whose names he could not remember.

[2]Collinson, p. 284. The Bathurst inlet patrol found many of the Bathurst inlet natives calling themselves 'Killin-e-miut.'

stood from them that they were Kilnermiun, i.e., Kiglinirmiut, but Mr. Stefansson asserts that they were Ekaluktomiut.[1] I am rather inclined to believe, however, that Hansen was right, or at least that some of them may have been Kiglinirmiut. It is worth noting that on his return journey Hansen saw two of their sled trails running south to De Haven point, indicating that two families at least intended to pass the summer somewhere on the southeast coast, not inland from Albert Edward bay; the season was too late for them to be crossing the strait. The two groups are certainly contiguous, and Schwatka expressly states that the Netsilingmiut and the Ugyulingmiut used to meet the "Qidneliq" of Coronation gulf, which indicates that the latter people were accustomed to travel eastward.[2] Mr. C. Leden tells me that the Eskimos on the west shore of Hudson bay apply the term Kiglinirmiut to the inhabitants of Bathurst inlet. But until these eastern natives have been actually visited and studied, it is better to leave their exact numbers and group divisions undefined.[3]

One region has not been mentioned, the west coast of Victoria island, where two groups are now living, the Kanghiryuarmiut of Prince Albert sound and the Kanghiryuatjagmiut of Minto inlet. Lieutenant Jago, who was with Collinson in 1852, met about a hundred natives in Prince Albert sound who probably belonged to the former of these two groups. About fifty other natives were wintering at the same time near Walker bay, in which region McClure had met five families. Our chief knowledge of these groups, however, comes from Mr. Stefansson, who visited the Prince Albert sound people in the spring of 1911, when he estimated their number at two hundred or a little over. The northern party of the Canadian Arctic expedition had a base at Cape Kellett from 1914 to 1916, and in 1915 another was established near Armstrong Point, in Prince of Wales strait. From both of these places our people had many dealings with the northern natives, and Mr. G. H. Wilkins, the photographer of the expedition, made the same estimate of their number as Mr. Stefansson. Mr. Wilkins further informs me that in the winter of 1914-15 the Kanghiryuarmiut were encamped near the entrance of Prince Albert sound, while the Kanghiryuatjagmiut, who comprised only about half a dozen families (Mr. Stefansson estimated their number at twenty) were living outside of Minto inlet, close to the shore of Banks island. In the following winter fully half of the Kanghiryuarmiut joined their northern neighbours, so that the two settlements were about evenly divided. Two families of Prince Albert sound natives whom I met in the summer of 1915 just north of the Puivlik district, said that the main body of their people had gone to a lake called Tahiryuak close to some copper deposits a day's journey northeast of the sound. They had not met the Kanghiryuatjagmiut that winter, nor did they know of the presence of white men at Cape Kellett. Members of the two groups then would seem to have met in the late spring or summer of that year, either on the ice or somewhere inland. In the winter of 1917-18 again, the Rev. Mr. Girling informs me, some two hundred Kanghiryuak natives were camped a little south of Holman island at the northwest corner of Prince Albert sound. Where the Kanghiryuatjagmiut were at that time he could not say.

The Eskimos of Dolphin and Union strait assert that the Kanghiryuarmiut were much more numerous in former times than they are now. About 1875 (Higilak, a woman of about 45 years of age, was said to be a baby at the time) a great storm broke up the ice in Prince Albert sound early in the spring, and many of the natives were drowned. Others again perished through famine. The ice never left the shore one summer, and was consequently very heavy and broken the following winter. The natives could find very few seal-holes in the piled-up ridges, and many of them starved to death. Quite recently

[1]Amundsen, Vol. II, p. 329; Stefansson, My Life with the Eskimo, p. 283 *et seq.*
[2]Science, Vol. IV, 1884, p. 543, quoted by Boas, Central Eskimo, p. 465.
[3]Further information on this region that has come to hand later will be found in the appendix.

again they were overtaken by another famine, so severe that they were reduced to eating the frozen corpses of their dead, and in one instance at least a boy was actually killed and eaten.

Mr. Stefansson states that a large group called Ugyulingmiut perished from famine to the north of Minto inlet. The name Ugyulingmiut was vaguely familiar to the natives of Dolphin and Union strait, but they seemed to think that the tribe dwelt somewhere to the eastward. Early explorers located a group with this name in the neighbourhood of King William island.[1]

All the groups or tribes that have now been described, from Dolphin and Union strait in the west to Ogden bay in the east, including Victoria island and Banks island, form a fairly homogeneous unit. The most noticeable variation that could be observed throughout this region was in the intonation of the voice. The natives of Prince Albert sound have a much higher range of inflection than the natives south of them. They speak in high-pitched tones, "in their heads" as it were, but usually drop to a lower and more normal key at the end of the word or clause. This peculiarity, however, is not confined to Prince Albert sound; it is adopted by some of the Eskimos in Bathurst inlet and farther east, and is said to be characteristic also of the Ekaluktomiut, so that at the present day at least it is not confined to any single area. Apart from this there is nothing, either in the physical appearance of the natives[2] or in their culture, that would distinguish one group or area from another, while the differences in dialect are infinitesimal. The uniformity of culture throughout the region, and its marked difference from the culture of the Eskimos in all other places, justifies Mr. Stefansson in giving these natives a separate appellation, and his term "Copper Eskimos" (i.e., Eskimos who use copper instead of stone in their implements) very aptly seizes upon their most striking characteristic.

The total population of the country would seem to be between 700 and 800. At the close of 1914, 115 of these were living in Dolphin and Union strait, about 75 at the west end of Coronation gulf, 200 at the east end, and about 215 in Prince Albert sound and Minto inlet. From Kent peninsula to Ogden bay the population is probably not more than 150. Mr. Stefansson's estimate is somewhat higher; if we add together the numbers that he assigns to each tribe his total would come to about 1,100, but then he apparently overestimated the population a little everywhere except in Prince Albert sound and Minto inlet.

The Copper Eskimos, like the Eskimos of Greenland[3], show a preponderance of males over females. Of the 127 natives who gathered at Bernard harbour in November, 1915, 67 were males and only 60 females. The disparity was apparent both in the adults and the children, 46 men as compared with 42 women, and 21 boys as against 18 girls. At the settlement off the mouth of the Tree river in February, 1916, there were only 11 males to 14 females, but this was an exceptional case, and the inequality was in the children, 6 girls to 2 boys, not in the adults. Probably as many females are born as males, but the mortality among them is higher; for the Eskimos, like many tribes that live by the chase, much prefer boys to girls, and in times of hardship or distress it is always the latter who suffer first.

No statistics were obtained as to the mortality in this region. Amongst adults death was nearly always due to natural causes, either old age or the perils that are inseparable from life in the Arctic; an occasional murder added to the number. The natives were remarkably healthy: measles, influenza, tuberculosis, and venereal diseases, all common amongst Eskimos elsewhere, were unknown here. Occasionally they were assailed with diarrhoea or with indigestion, and colds were frequent at the beginning of winter, but the only malady that ever proved fatal was an insidious stomach trouble that may have

[1] Cp. Boas, Central Eskimo, p. 456 *et seq.*
[2] The physical characteristics of the Copper Eskimos will be dealt with in a separate memoir.
[2] Except those of Smith sound. See Kroeber, Bulletin A.M.N.H., Vol. XII, 1899, p. 268.

been a form of ptomaine poisoning. Parry mentions this disease at Iglulik in Baffin island.[1] He says; "The complaints of those that died at their huts, therefore, did not come under observation. It appears, however, to have been acute inflammation of some of the abdominal viscera, very rapid in its career. In the generality, the disease assumed a more insidious and sub-acute form, under which the patient lingered for awhile, and was then either carried off by a diarrhoea, or slowly recovered by the powers of nature." In one case that I observed the man was attacked very suddenly and died within a few days, while in another the patient lingered for many months. In the first case the victim fell ill early in the winter, when the natives were still eating caribou meat and fat that had been secured during the previous summer and fall; in the latter the man had been quite well during part of the summer at least, but was ill when I saw him in December and hardly able to walk. The exact origin and nature of the disease, however, is uncertain, nor had we any means of ascertaining its frequency. With the influx of traders and missionaries into the country the conditions of life are fast changing. Famine looms less in the foreground, but in its place European diseases are threatening the health of the communities and bid fair to rival all other causes in their effect on the death-rate.

[1]Parry, Vol. 4, p. 75.

CHAPTER IV

TRADE AND INTERCOURSE[1]

All the groups of the Copper Eskimos maintain a constant intercourse with one another, but naturally the extent of their relations varies inversely with the distance between them. Mr. Stefansson believes that prior to 1830 there was a continuous chain of habitations along the coast from Langton bay to Coronation gulf. It is true that ruins of wood and sod houses have been found at various places between Cape Lyon and Cape Krusenstern, all dating back probably at least a hundred years, but the fewness and rude character of these remains seem to indicate the presence of occasional travelling parties of western natives or temporary settlements that lasted but one or two winters, rather than any permanent habitations.[2] Moreover, while seals are plentiful along the coast, caribou seem to be rather scarce, so that there would be little inducement for natives acquainted with the more bountiful districts east and west of them to fix their homes in this region. It is worth pointing out in this connection that Richardson and Kendall saw no dwellings in 1826, but only a few store-houses built of drift-wood at Young point, where the Eskimos had cached their things for the summer while they themselves wandered inland.

The Copper Eskimos have no traditions that would point to their having lived farther west than now. They know, however, that their ancestors up to two generations ago used to meet the western natives in the vicinity of Wise point. These western natives, who came from the country of Avvak (Cape Bathurst), traded mainly for stone lamps and implements of copper, giving in exchange iron knives; it was only rarely that they purchased stone pots, since they had pots of clay that they themselves made. How far back these relations date is uncertain. Higilak, an Akulliakattak woman of about 45 years of age, said that long ago a party of Copper Eskimos travelling west came upon a large settlement of Eskimos on a point near the mouth of a great river that had high cliffs along one bank; before that time they had not known there were people to the west of them. The Copper Eskimos married some of the strangers' women and afterwards frequently went west again to meet them. Once they found them living with Indians, but this was in a different place.

Awallook, an Eskimo who was living on the Richardson river, told Simpson that he had heard there were Eskimos far west who wore labrets, but that he had never seen any himself[3]. We met an old woman of the same name at the west end of Coronation gulf in the winter of 1914-15. When she was a little girl, she said, strange people came from the westward to Dolphin and Union strait, but they never reached Coronation gulf; they were not white men, but Eskimos like themselves. She had heard that her own people had come to the Rae river district long ago from the west. Another elderly man named Anerak, who belonged to the same group, said that the Copper Eskimos used to meet and trade with the western natives near some high cliffs on the sea-shore (one of the promontories near Wise point). Occasionally some of the western natives would return with them, while a few of the Copper Eskimos would sometimes go west. He himself many years ago made a journey to this place, hoping to meet these people, but became frightened when he found the place deserted and turned back home.

---

[1]For this chapter see especially Stefansson, Anthrop. Papers, A.M.N.H., Vol. XIV, pt. I, pp. 17-19, 25, 133 *et seq.*, and G.S.C., Museum Bulletin No. 6.
[2]But see Appendix, where the opinion expressed here is modified in the light of more recent information.
[3]Simpson, Discoveries, p. 347.

Two western Eskimos, a man and a woman, once stayed with the Copper Eskimos, according to a native from Bathurst inlet. The man soon died, but the woman lived for a great many years among them. A year or two afterwards another western native named Uksokak joined the Copper Eskimos. These three natives had come by sled along the coast in spring, not by boat in summer. Panigyuk, a very old woman who died at Cape Bathurst about 1913, and who had seen the boats of Richardson's party in 1848, was said to be a native of Nagyuktok and to speak the Copper Eskimo dialect. Higilak's grandfather had married a woman named Allikammik who had come east from Avvak; she was one of three western women who had married Copper Eskimos. It was in this generation, Higilak said, that the intercourse between the two groups came to an end.

Mr. Stefansson attaches much importance to the trade connections between the Cape Bathurst Eskimos and those of Victoria and Banks islands by way of Cape Parry and Nelson head. It was always the western Eskimos, he says, who crossed the strait, and then it was only by sled, late in March or early in April. The Cape Bathurst natives still remembered this trade route, but knew nothing of the one along the coast to Dolphin and Union strait. The Copper Eskimos, on the other hand, had clear recollections of the latter route, but not of the former. From the large number of ruined houses round Franklin bay and Cape Parry it is quite certain that many years ago (just how many we cannot really estimate, but probably not much more than a century) there must have been a considerable population in this region. In spite of this, however, it is hard to believe that they could have had any regular communication with Banks island by sled, for there is a very strong current off Cape Parry, and the sea is sometimes open throughout the entire winter. The Cape Bathurst natives are well aware of this, and moreover they have always been chary of going far out on the ice at any time. While it is not improbable therefore that small parties did cross over to Nelson head on two or three occasions, it is highly unlikely that this could ever have been a regular trade-route. Moreover no traces were found at Nelson head that would indicate visits from western natives, no remains, for example, like the stone graves or houses of wood and sod that were discovered in Dolphin and Union strait. The northern party of our expedition had a base at Cape Kellett, and Mr. G. H. Wilkins, the photographer, made one or two journeys along the southern coast of Banks island, of which he furnishes the following account:—

"The first sign of there having been human inhabitants of Banks island was found on the side of the valley near the southwest coast and about thirty miles from Cape Kellett. Here we found a tent ring which had been formed many years ago, for it was almost completely overgrown with moss. Nearby were several small sticks of driftwood which had been hacked by some blunt instrument. Although the camp site looked so old. the chips of wood were still in a good state of preservation.

"As we continued along the coast toward Cape Kellett, we found a number of these camp sites. Some were situated on the side but near the breast of a hill, while others were directly on top. It was generally noticed that those on the side of the hill had some musk oxen horns or bones lying about nearby, and usually in the vicinity one would find semicircular 'blinds built' of sods for the most part, but later on in the northern part of the island we found these 'blinds' built of stone. (The stones were not available on the southwestern part of the island.) They rarely were higher than nine inches high and I never saw one higher than eighteen inches at the highest part. These were used to hide behind to shoot the musk oxen.

"About twenty miles from Cape Kellett and about a mile from the beach I found a skull very much weather worn and so fragile that it was difficult to handle without it crumpled. It is among the collection of specimens at Banks island together with another which I found seven miles from Cape Kellett.

This one was much larger and stronger. Near, too, was found an old whittling knife and a short-bladed knife much rusted. There was a grassy mound of earth nearby, but we could find no further trace of instruments having been left there. At the head of the sand spit which forms Cape Kellett, is a large deserted village of thirty or more houses. They seem to have been built of sod around a frame work of whale bones. Some of the houses are now crumbling away owing to the inroad of the sea, but the majority of them are still intact, but very much overgrown with moss and tundra. The earth nearby is very much stained with whale or seal oil, and in the heat of summer there is still an odor of decaying animal matter to be noticed in the vicinity. In winter this attracts a number of foxes that dig in the snow and throw up yellow stained turf, but one cannot see that they get anything to eat for their pains. Because of having to do other work connected with the boats of the Expedition, I was unable to do any digging around here; but there is no doubt that the site is a rich field for anthropologists.

"During the course of the expedition I travelled almost the complete circumference of Banks island, crossed overland over the southern section

(Photo by G. H. Wilkins)

Fig. 6. View of the south coast of Banks island, near Cape Lambton

and hunted over the country for many miles inland from nearly all parts of the coast. The ruined village at Cape Kellett was the only one seen, but one could scarcely go twenty-five miles in any direction without seeing a tent ring or some chips of drift wood, showing that at some time or other it had been a hunting ground of some human race."

In reading this account we are at once struck by the fact that it was at Cape Kellett that the western natives established a settlement, not at Nelson head; further that there was this one settlement only, for no other ruins were found anywhere else along the coast. The tent rings and the semicircular "blinds" for hunting seem rather to indicate Copper Eskimos, for we find similar remains in every part of Victoria island and on the mainland around Coronation gulf. Another point to notice is that the inhabitants were essentially whale and seal hunters, and this presupposes the possession of the large skin boats called umiaks. Here we have a basis for a reasonable theory. Whales are very common between the mainland and Banks island, and they have always been hunted by the Cape Bathurst natives. In their large skin boats these Eskimos must often have travelled far out to sea, and known of the great land north of them; so in the days when their communities were still flourishing a colony hived off one summer and established itself at Cape Kellett. No doubt it still kept up a connection with its home country, mainly by boat, perhaps, since to cross the ice by sled directly is probably almost as difficult as from Cape Parry to Nelson head, unless, of course, the season is an exceptional one. It is not unlikely that even by boat the natives usually crossed between Cape Parry and Nelson head, for not only is the distance much shorter, but both these points are high and conspicuous, whereas Capes Bathurst and Kellett are low and sandy.

How long the settlement lasted and when it died out we have no knowledge, but from the overgrown condition of the ruins it could hardly have been less than a century ago and may have been much longer. The isolation of the place, and the absence, so far as we know, of any similar ruins along the coast, seem to indicate that the rest of Banks island was uninhabited at the time, or at least that the two peoples had no contact with each other.[1] This would explain why the Victoria island natives who now seal round Nelson head have no knowledge of any trade-relations with their neighbours across the strait, although a Kanghiryuak native told Mr. Wilkins that he had followed a bear so far out on the ice that he had seen the land on the other side.

The Copper Eskimos had no intercourse with the Indians of Great Bear lake until Mr. Stefansson brought them together in 1910; since then they have regularly visited the lake each summer and traded their dogs for guns and ammunition. Up to 1910 they were afraid of the Indians, and apparently never reached quite as far as Bear lake, its north end at least.[2] They have a tradition that long ago some Indians came up from the south and massacred many of the Walliak natives, after which they went away west, carrying with them the Eskimos' pots. Possibly there is some reference in this to the massacre at Bloody fall. Higilak told me that the Eskimos never fought with the Indians, though the latter would steal their copper and pots. Once when the Indians were close to a party of Eskimos the latter kindled a great fire and threw the ashes into the eyes of their enemies. Natives from Bathurst inlet at the present day often travel overland in summer to the country between the Coppermine river and McTavish bay. Much of their journey to the Coppermine can be made in kayaks, since there are numerous lakes everywhere, as Franklin found on his first journey. Caribou too are abundant, and every summer scores of them are herded into the lakes and speared from kayaks. I was unable to learn whether the Eskimos often came into contact with Indians along this route; probably not, for we found little or no evidence in their culture and traditions that would indicate any established relations. Mr. Chipman met some Tree river Eskimos in the spring of 1916 who were heading for the upper reaches of the Coppermine in order to trade with Dog Rib Indians from Fort Rae; but presumably this was a new departure in their movements, and dated back no more than three or four years. The amicable relations established between the two races in 1916 were still further improved in the following year, when a band of 17 Indians from Fort Rae and Great Bear lake descended to the mouth of the Coppermine river to visit a white trader named Klengenberg.[3] Thus European influence, after extending slowly north for several centuries, is at last making itself felt in this region, and for the first time since Hearne's day the Indians have ventured to approach the Arctic coast.

---

[1]Various considerations, too lengthy to deal with in this volume, incline me to believe that the Copper Eskimos are comparatively recent immigrants into the country that they now occupy.

[2]Cf. Simpson, Discoveries, p. 347; Stefansson, My Life with the Eskimo, p. 216.

[3]Report of the Bathurst Inlet Patrol, p. 38.

One route, the main one perhaps, to the Akilinnik [Thelon] river and the Eskimos of the interior, has its starting point in Bathurst inlet. Mr. Stefansson, influenced perhaps by Hanbury's account, has stated that the Copper Eskimos begin their overland route from Ogden bay. Hanbury certainly found Eskimos in that neighbourhood who were on their way to the Akilinnik, and others whom he had actually met on that river in 1899. No doubt the more eastern people do take this route, the Asiagmiut for example, and perhaps some of the Kanghiryuarmiut and Ekaluktomiut as well; but the natives of the east end of Coronation gulf usually start from Bathurst inlet. Sometimes they leave in winter and make the journey by sled, carrying seal-blubber for fuel and living on caribou and musk-oxen; sometimes in summer, packing their goods and provisions on their backs. One old man, the shaman Ilatsiak, had visited the Akilinnik no less than three times, crossing in early winter and returning the following spring. He lived on caribou, he said, and instead of seal-blubber used caribou fat for fuel and light. Their supplies, however, frequently ran out, and then they would sit crouched up on their skins, shivering with the cold. The inland natives, he said, frequently endure the same hardships.

Victoria island natives sometimes follow the same route, for a Kilusiktok Eskimo informed me that many Ekaluktomiut had come to his country on their way to the Akilinnik. A more easterly route, used perhaps by the Asiak natives, follows the course of the Ellice river.[1] No Indians are ever encountered between the coast and the Akilinnik, and usually no Eskimos either, though sometimes the northern people meet the Backs river natives, since the Backs or Saningaiyok river is only six days' journey from the sea at Bathurst inlet. Ilatsiak said that it has five tributaries, and that finally it enters the country of Ukkusiksalik, somewhere east of Kilusiktok, but more distant probably than Netsilik.

The Copper Eskimos secured guns and ammunition and knives from the Akilinnik people in exchange for the skins of caribou, musk-oxen and foxes. Ilatsiak had bought from them a saw, an axe, powder for his rifle, two big snow-knives and a few things of lesser importance. At the same time the Copper natives obtain wood from which to make their sleds and weapons. Sometimes they stayed with the Akilinnik people for a year or two, and went down to Chesterfield inlet with them to meet and trade with white men; occasionally too, an Akilinnik native would return with them to Bathurst inlet. These inland natives, however, being ignorant of the method of seal-hunting on the ice in winter, could never remain for any long period with their northern neighbours, but were compelled to hasten south again in quest of caribou and musk-oxen.

An Akilinnik native visited the expedition at Bernard harbour about Christmas, 1915. He told us that his people have a regular formula to describe the natives of Bathurst inlet; translated it ran: "They are good people to meet, they are pleasant companions. They always have plenty of seal-meat. They are a friendly people. Whenever they go sealing they always secure plenty of seals."

South of the Akilinnik the Coronation gulf natives know of a people called Aligattalingmiun, who live on a large river close to the country of the white men. In the land of these Eskimos they say there is one very large river with five smaller rivers leading to it (tributaries?), and the white men live on the one farthest away. Ilatsiak had seen some of these Aligattalingmiun, who were living on a tributary of the Akilinnik at a place called Kanralasiorvik, where many caribou crossed the river in the fall during their annual migration south-

---

[1]Cf. the Report of the Bathurst Inlet Patrol.

wards. The strangers were living in very large tents and possessed a numbe of kayaks, which they would lash together when ferrying big loads across th rivers and lakes.

Only within quite recent times did the Coronation gulf Eskimos meet with any of the Pallik Eskimos from the southwest hinterland of Hudson bay.[1] A Kilusiktok hunter named Sikoaluk, who died a few years ago, came upon a few of these natives while hunting to the south of Bathurst inlet, probably in the vicinity of Backs river. Kaksavik, a Pallik Eskimo who visited our station at Bernard harbour in December, 1915, left his native district in 1912 and migrated to the country of Saningaiyok or Backs river,[2] because of the abundance of caribou and musk-oxen in that region. In the summer of 1914 he met some Bathurst inlet natives who told him that white men were living to the westward, so as soon as the fall set in he left two of his wives and their children inland, and with his third wife, and a young couple from the Akilinnik, travelled north and west till he came to Bernard harbour. He stayed with us for three days, then crossed to the Liston and Sutton islands to visit the local Eskimos. They immediately held a dance in his honour, which he returned on the following day; on the third he left again for Backs river.

Ilatsiak, the Kilusiktok shaman whom I have mentioned, gave an account of how two Akilinnik natives named Kitiraiyak and Innitak met two Back river natives named Pattuyak and Pakunnuak. In friendly rivalry they strove to knock each other down. One succeeded in throwing his adversary, but the latter quickly rose and knocked him down in turn, tearing his clothes; his companion, too, was equally successful. After the wrestling was over they lived together for a few days and traded for various goods. On another occasion a party of Eskimos was living on a grassy flat beside a large lake named Tahiryuak not far from Backs river; another band was living on the opposite side of the lake, behind a long spit that projected into the water. One day four men from the flat lashed two of their kayaks together and crossed over to visit their neighbours; two sat in the kayak holes and paddled, while one lay across the bows and the other across the sterns. As they drew near the spit five natives went forward to meet them, and one of the paddlers, Pitiganna, cried out, "We have come from the place where the long grass grows beside the lake. We have come in two kayaks lashed side by side, to visit you dwellers on the spit." As soon as the kayaks grounded the man in the bow jumped ashore holding a knife in his hand, and the other three followed quickly after. The five strangers approached them, one grasping a spear. First they had a wrestling contest to find out which side was the stronger, then the visitors went up to the tents and they all ate together and traded.

Natives from Dolphin and Union strait and from the west side of Coronation gulf seldom travel beyond Bathurst inlet. My Eskimo Ikpakhuak, whose home was in Puivlik, had never been farther east than Cape Barrow, though he knew of the Netsilingmuit, a ferocious people who stabbed strangers in the arms and head and killed them. He had even heard of the Aivilingmiut, who dwell somewhere beyond the Netsilingmiut, but more than this he did not know. The natives at the east end of Coronation gulf, on the other hand, have met some of the Netsilingmiut at an inland named Putulik, which was said to be one of a cluster of five small islands a short distance beyond Kent peninsula; the others were named Tigaktok, Anaktok, Kingmiktok and Nallok, the last two perhaps being different names for the same island. Not far from them is a much larger island named Nugluktarvik, which may possibly be Melbourne island. These places apparently are all in Asiak, and the natives from either side travel there to meet one another.

---

[1]Cf. Stefansson, My Life with the Eskimo, p. 251.
[2]The Backs river natives are called Saningaiyomiut. Kaernermiut, an alternative name Mr. Stefansson gives them, means "the people of the flat land."

Ilatsiak, who had thrice visited the Akilinnik region, had also been three times to Netsilik, or at least had visited those people three times. Many white men, he said, men without chins on their faces,[1] go to that country in ships, and the Netsilingmiut barter with them for knives. Somewhere in that direction also, he believed, were a people with long claws on their hands with which they tear strangers to pieces.

The father of Kingollik, a Bathurst inlet native still living, once made a trip to the country of Netsilik, and his sister married a Netsilik man. Other Bathurst inlet natives had also visited that country, and have met natives there from other groups, Aivilingmiut (Repulse bay natives?), Mallorektomiut who live behind them (*tungani*, i.e. north?), and Ukkusiksalingmiut (Wager bay inland to the mouth of Backs river). One man who is still living, the father of a young Tree river native, married a woman of Asiak and made a journey to the country of the Aivilingmiut. The Netsilingmiut, these Coronation gulf natives say, have a very peculiar manner of welcoming strangers; they give them a buffet on the head or shoulder with their fists. Their mittens deaden the force of the blow to some extent; nevertheless it is no mere tap, for in one case at least a visitor was "killed for a time" (i.e., stunned) by a buffet behind the ear.[2] The country of Netsilik is almost devoid of driftwood, consequently its people are eager for sleds and other objects of wood which the western natives possess, though the Netsilingmiut also purchase stone lamps and pots. In exchange they give the Copper natives articles of iron, such as knives and harpoon heads. A few of the Netsilingmiut had guns from white men, but not knowing how to use them, they broke them up, the western natives say, for the sake of the iron.[3] One Eskimo in Coronation gulf had heard of white men who visited the shores of Netsilik and Ukkusiksalik one summer in two ships, but left again before the sea froze over; one of the ships had four masts, the other only two. He had heard too that a Bathurst inlet native who had migrated to Netsilik after the death of his parents had finally boarded a ship of the white men and sailed away with them. Evidently this is a reference to the Eskimo named "Manni," whom Amundsen took west with him when he left the Netsilik country.[4]

Returning to the northwestern natives—those inhabiting the regions of Prince Albert sound and Minto inlet—there were three routes at least by which they communicated with their southern and eastern neighbours. Some of them used to follow round the coast past Cape Baring and meet the Eskimos of Dolphin and Union strait in the neighbourhood of Cape Hamilton early in the spring, about April. Captain Klengenberg fell in with them near this place in the winter of 1905-6, and in the spring of 1915, when I travelled along the coast to Cape Kendall, some Prince Albert sound natives were camped only a few miles farther north, as we learned a few months later. The Hanerak natives, when that group still existed, and the natives from Akulliakattak across the strait, regularly fell back in this direction in the spring of the year after they had associated with the Puivlik and Noahognik Eskimos east of them and come into contact there with visitors from Coronation gulf; and although the Hanerak group is now dispersed, the Akulliakattak natives still often return to the neighbourhood of Point Williams before crossing the strait to their own country. Nor was it only their kinsmen of Dolphin and Union strait that the Kanghiryuak natives encountered here, but apparently western Eskimos as well. On Bell island, close to Cape Kendall, Captain Jos. Bernard found some stone cairns used as graves, and the ruins of three old sod houses

---

[1]See Stefansson, Anthrop. Papers, A.M.N.H., Vol. XIV, pt. I, p. 302; *My Life with the Eskimos*, p.179.

[2]Cf. Boas, *Central Eskimo*, p. 609.

[3]A Puivlik native informed me that the Kanghiryuarmiut obtained some guns from McClure's ship, the *Investigator*, but as they did not know how to use them they broke them up. They had not seen any of the white men who abandoned this ship in Mercy bay.

[4]Amundsen, Vol. II, p. 114.

that formerly had wooden frames. In two similar ruins that he found at the bottom of Lady Richardson bay, some 800 yards from the beach beside a stream, the posts were still partially preserved; they were made of driftwood logs split into halves, the original diameters of the logs being about two feet. Cape Hamilton is visible from Wise point on a clear day, and we know from the traditions of the Copper Eskimos that they frequently met the western natives at Wise point. It seems very probable therefore that some of the western natives crossed over to Victoria island to meet the northern people, and spent the winter there, building from logs of driftwood houses of wood and sod like those they used in their own country; for we can hardly attribute these remains to the Copper Eskimos, who are, or were until recently, entirely unfamiliar with dwellings of this character.

The second route which the northern Eskimos follow is inland to Lake Tahiryuak, which is roughly about ten miles in diameter and studded with islands of every shape and size. It lies approximately in lat. 69° 50′ N. and long 112° W. Several families of the northern natives usually come here each summer to meet the Puivlik Eskimos from the south, though sometimes they meet about thirty miles to the southwest at the small lake of Numikhoin in the Colville hills.[1] In the summer of 1915 we waited several days at this latter place hoping that they would join us; when they failed to appear we went on to Lake Tahiryuak, where we met two families that had just arrived from Prince Albert sound. When the first family appeared on the first day of June all the Puivlik natives lined up on top of the bank overlooking the lake to give

Fig. 7. Puivlik Eskimos welcoming visitors from Prince Albert sound at Lake Tahiryuak
S.W. Victoria island

them a welcome. The leading man of the visitors called out as he drew near us, *ilanaitut?* "Are the people friendly?" and the Puivlik natives all joyfully shouted, "Yes, they are friendly." One of our party, Kesullik, then rushed down the slope, and wrestled with one of the visitors, pretending to push him away, and exclaiming *nunaga, nunaga*, "It's my land," while the visitor answered *tikittunga*, "I have reached it, I have come." Every one was greatly excited,

---

[1]In December, 1914, a Puivlik Eskimo promised to guide me to the Kanghiryuarmiut the following spring. It was too cold to cross the hills in winter, he said, while the route round the coast (via Cape Baring) was too long.

and gathered, laughing, around the wrestlers. Some of us were strangers and had to introduce ourselves, so the leader of the Kanghiryuarmiut came and stood before each one of us in turn and asked us our names. As soon as the introductions were over we helped the newcomers to drag up their sled and unload it, then watched them set up their tent, after which we all filed inside and ate of their food. Two of the Puivlik men in the afternoon erected a dance-house of snow, roofing it over with skins and with the sheet that covered my sled, since the temperature at this time of the year would not permit of the usual dome of snow. The ceremonial dance of welcome took place in the evening, though everyone was eagerly watching for the second family of the northern natives to arrive. This did not happen till midnight, when a little girl ran out to meet them and assure them that they were welcome, while the rest of us remained on the bank. Again we filed into their tent and ate some of their food, but the dance that was to be given in their honour was postponed till the following day.

A little trading was carried on between the two groups late in the evening of the first day, but most of it took place the following morning before breakfast. It was done individually, sometimes out of doors, sometimes in one or other of the tents. The northern natives brought polar bear skins, copper-headed ice-chisels, musk-ox skins and a few miscellaneous articles like polar bear mittens, which they exchanged for iron knives, tins, deerskin clothes, tent poles, etc.; the regular price for an ice-chisel was an iron snow-knife. One of the Puivlik women exchanged a small knife for a stone pot, the northern woman being given an old pemmican can to serve her for cooking instead.[1]

Economically these northern Eskimos are of little importance to their southern neighbours, at least at the present day. Most of the things that are lacking to the natives of Dolphin and Union strait are more easily procurable from the Coronation gulf Eskimos during the winter, when they can be packed on sleds, than from the Kanghiryuak during the summer, when many of their possessions are cached on the coast and only what is absolutely necessary is ever carried inland. Musk-ox skins and ladles of musk-ox horn can be obtained, through the Coppermine natives, from the people of Bathurst inlet, while, as regards copper, the Coppermine natives themselves can easily supply all that is needed. In fact it would seem that the Coppermine valley, rather than either Victoria island or Bathurst inlet, was always the main source of the supply of this metal, the amygdaloidal nodules scattered over the surface being perhaps more numerous and more accessible here than elsewhere. At all events most of the Dolphin and Union strait natives possessed one or more nodules from this region, which they had either gathered themselves or obtained by barter. From one Puivlik native we obtained a solid block weighing nearly forty pounds which had come from the Coppermine; originally it had been twice as large. It must be remembered, however, that iron has largely superseded copper during the last ten or fifteen years; and that while the softer metal alone was procurable the deposits at the head of Prince Albert sound must have been far more important economically than they are now.

The most valuable commodity that the Kanghiryuak natives furnish at the present day is the skin of the polar bear, small strips of which are in use everywhere for icing the runners of sleds, and in many cases also for footpads when sealing. Even polar bear skins however can be obtained by the southern Eskimos in other ways. Occasionally a stray animal wanders down into Dolphin and Union strait in the early part of the winter and is killed; or one will linger on the land near Cape Baring during the summer, where the Puivlik natives in 1915 killed a mother and its cub. The animals rarely, if ever, penetrate into Coronation gulf, but the Eskimos of that region can obtain their skins by bar-

---

[1] Cf. Stefansson, My Life with the Eskimo, p. 273.

tering with the natives beyond Kent peninsula, where polar bears are said to be numerous. Altogether, therefore, the Eskimos of Prince Albert sound are at a disadvantage now in regard to their southern neighbours, on whom they are largely dependent for stone lamps, pots and wood.

The third route that these northern natives follow in the maintenance of trade relations is eastward. According to Mr. Stefansson they ascend a river named Kagloryuak at the head of Prince Albert sound, cross a divide and descend the Ekaluktok river to Albert Edward bay. Somewhere in this region they meet the Ekaluktomiut, and a few of them sometimes journey south to Ogden bay on the mainland and make their way to the Akilinnik river. Some of them, no doubt, do follow this route at times, but since both the Ekaluktok and the Kanghiryuak natives visit the Bathurst inlet people by way of Dease strait, it would seem reasonable to suppose that there is a shorter route overland, probably from the deep inlet on the south side of Albert Edward bay to Cambridge bay or perhaps even Anderson bay, whence they could either turn west into Dease strait or south to the Ellice river.[1] Somewhere on the divide between the Kagloryuak and the Ekaluktok rivers there must be a regular meeting place between the two groups, for the son of a Prince Albert sound woman whom we met at Lake Tahiryuak visited the Ekaluktomiut somewhere inland one summer, and was drowned a few weeks later on his way back.

There is always much trade, of course, between neighbouring groups, and even between members of the same group. In the spring of 1915 a woman in Dolphin and Union strait went round the whole settlement trying to buy a tent-pole. Brisk barter took place when the west Coronation gulf Eskimos visited this settlement in March. One woman bought musk-ox skins with some cartridges she had received from the expedition, another sold a large wooden table. Dolphin and Union strait natives purchase stone lamps and pots, musk-ox ladles, blubber pounders, sled-toggles, and skins both of deer and of musk-oxen from the Eskimos of Coronation gulf, besides of course copper and implements made of it. As their own region, however, furnishes them with few commodities for bartering, many, perhaps the majority, of these strait natives at some time in their lives make special journeys eastward, in order to collect their own copper and wood in the valleys of the Coppermine and Dease rivers, and to hew out their own lamps and pots near Tree river.

Mr. Stefansson has greatly magnified the difficulty of making stone pots and lamps, naturally enough, for he never saw their manufacture. He says, "To make a large pot (inside measure say 9 by 40 inches and 7 inches deep) is said to take all a man's spare time for a year, and some take two years to the making of a pot. Lamps are more quickly made. Certain individuals are considered expert pot-makers, and many others attain old age without ever having made a large pot, though all have owned one or more. We have here the beginning of division of labour, the germ of a 'trade.' These pot and lamp makers furnish the best example known to me both of specialization of industries by tribes and of the division of labour among individuals."[2]

Two members of the staff of our expedition, Mr. J. R. Cox and Mr. J. J. O'Neill, watched the manufacture of a lamp about 3 feet long at Port Epworth in July, 1915. The workman, who was only a young man of about twenty-five years, hewed his block out of the solid rock in a single day. Two days later his lamp was finished, though he worked only at odd intervals. At the same time the children were amusing themselves by making small lamps and pots from two to eight inches long. Working steadily, even an unskilled native could make the largest lamp in use in three days, and a pot would take him very little longer. A Dolphin and Union strait woman wandered east with her

---

[1]But see the appendix, where this subject is discussed in the light of more recent information.
[2]Geol. Survey Canada, Museum Bulletin, No. 6, 1914, p. 28.

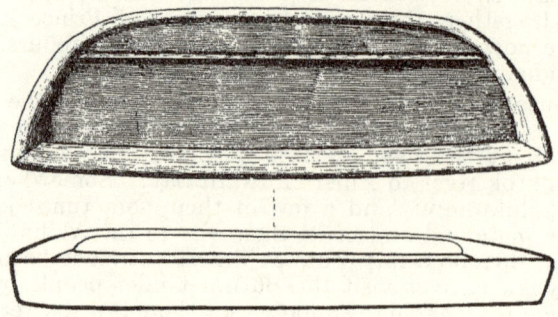

Fig. 8. A typical Copper Eskimo lamp, carved out of soapstone

husband one spring, spent the summer around Tree river, and returned to her own land the following winter with a large lamp and a pot that they had made. This was in fact the object of their journey, although neither of them had ever seen a lamp or a pot manufactured before. The majority of the natives of Coronation gulf do the same thing at some time or other in their lives, for fresh soapstone (talc chlorite schist) such as is found at Tree river requires no great skill in handling, and can be adzed quite easily even with so soft a metal as copper. It is only natural that the local natives should often make extra pots and lamps for trading purposes, but they by no means specialize in this industry, nor rank in any way as professional stone-cutters.

Fig. 9. Maffa, a Tree river native, making a stone lamp   (Photo by J. R. Cox)

Little need be added to Mr. Stefansson's descriptions of the manner in which strangers are welcomed.[1] The shouting of *taima* as a sign of peaceable intentions seems to be a Hudson bay usage not employed by the Copper Eskimos among themselves, although they are doubtless fully aware of its meaning.[2] The ordinary method of signifying peace is to hold up the arms so that the strangers may see you are carrying no weapons. A party of Noahognik Eskimos, coming down to the coast in the early fall of 1914, found us established at Bernard harbour. They approached our tents to within about 200 yards, and, standing in line on the crest of the ridge, alternately raised their open hands above their heads, and, stooping, lowered them again towards the ground, thus signifying that they had lain their weapons on the ground and held nothing in their hands. We laid our rifles on the ground (we had been hunting seals), returning their gestures, and twice again they repeated their signs as we approached.

In November of the same year I engaged a Noahognik native named Aksiatak to guide me to the Puivlik settlement across the strait. Skirting along the coast of Victoria island we fell in with four Eskimos, all coming from different directions. Aksiatak ran ahead at top speed, flinging up his arms to indicate peace; the four Eskimos likewise started to run, converging towards their settlement. Soon my companion was hidden from view behind a ridge, and when I came up with him about a mile farther on he and the strangers were together. The four natives gave the peace signal as I approached and arranged themselves in line, the tallest man on the right. He told me his name, I told him mine, and the process was repeated all along the line. Then we started out again towards their settlement. As we drew near, Aksiatak ran ahead with a local native on each side of him, shouting "White man, white man," while the other two ranged themselves on either side of me and told me to run also. Men and women and children immediately began to pour out of the huts and rush to meet us. All the men and some of the women introduced themselves one after another, pressing round me in an excited throng; then an elderly native led me into his hut.

The presence of women in the party is a sure sign that no hostility need be apprehended. The custom of carrying a knife when going to meet strangers has often been noticed.[3] It is done even when the visitor knows there is nothing to fear. As a Coronation gulf native expressed it, "We carry knives in our hands when we go out to welcome strangers, just as the Netsilingmiut greet them with a buffet in the face. They have one custom, we have another." The visitor is always expected to confirm the good relations by presenting his hosts with some of the food he has brought, and they in turn send him dainty portions of whatever they happen to have on hand. A dance is given to welcome him during which he is especially marked out for honour by some leading man in the community. The compliment is returned on the following day when the visitor and his people give a dance in return. Trading may occur at any time after the visitors have settled down in the camp and eaten some food.

---

[1] My Life with the Eskimo, p. 172, 190 *et seq.*; Anthrop. Papers, A.M.N.H., Vol. XIV, pt. [I, pp. 235, 301. Cf. Parry, Vol. II, pp. 165-6.
[2] See Hearne, p. 379; Douglas, p. 204.
[3] See Back, p. 381; and Stefansson, Anthrop. Papers, A.M.N.H., Vol. XIV, pt. I., p. 264.

CHAPTER V

DWELLINGS

Materials from which to construct a dwelling are very limited among the Copper Eskimos. There is no standing timber anywhere along the coast, and the shores are almost bare of drift-wood. To obtain the wood they need for sleds and household furniture the natives must travel south for many days far into the interior. It is true that a little spruce still grows within thirty and even twenty miles of the coast in the valley of the Coppermine river, but it is all too small and stunted to be of any great value. The natives at the western end of Coronation gulf obtain their timber from the neighbourhood of Great Bear lake, while the eastern people often travel down to the Akilinnik river for the same purpose, though the journey takes them half the year.

One would hardly expect then to find in the Copper Eskimo country huts of wood and sod such as dot the coastline everywhere from Alaska to Baillie island. Traces of these, however, are not altogether lacking, for ruins of old wooden houses have been noticed at various places from Cape Lyon to Coronation gulf. There are six or seven on the small islands off Cape Lyon, and six, very old and covered with grass, about fifty yards from the shore between Deas Thompson and De Witt Clinton points, a little east of the Roscoe river. Fourteen similar ruins near the mouth of the Inman river were examined by the Rev. H. Girling, and the implements he recovered from them conclusively prove that the inhabitants of that site were western natives.

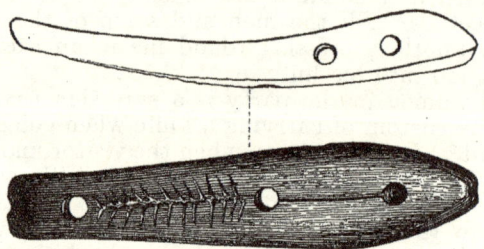

Fig. 10. A fish-hook of caribou antler, from a ruined house beside the Inman river

These places are outside the limits of the Copper Eskimo country, but there are other ruins of the same type that lie within them. Four or five were found on Chantry island in the spring of 1918, and about the same time seven others were noticed at Cape Krusenstern, and one on an island off Locker point. Mr. W. G. Phillips, the Hudson Bay Company's factor at Fort Bacon (Bernard harbour), tells me that the houses of Cape Krusenstern were built of wood, rock, and a good quantity of whalebone, and that the specimens gathered from them were strange to the Copper Eskimos. In one of the houses there seemed to have been an open fireplace, for the gravel was burnt in one spot and massed together with oil; in each of them there was a well or hole in the middle lined with flat stones. Captain Bernard's discovery of wood and sod houses on south-west Victoria island has been mentioned in the previous chapter. Almost certainly these dwellings were erected by western natives several generations ago, for the Copper Eskimos build their houses of snow blocks only, and never on any occasion employ wood in their construction.

The early explorers found stone huts on the islands of the Parry archipelago similar to those that are still used by the natives of Smith sound.[1] Mr. Stefansson discovered one of these huts near the mouth of the Kimiryuak river, but his Copper Eskimo companion was afraid to let him enter it—why I do not know, since other natives have frequently been inside.[2] Captain Bernard found another on Bell island not far from the ruins of the wood and sod houses of the western natives; he excavated the floor to the depth of about a foot, but found nothing but stones and a few seal-bones. Larger than either of these, according to the natives, is a stone hut at Tutukok, near Lady Franklin point. I was not able to examine any of these huts, but visited one on the top of Kikigarnak hill behind Locker point. In shape it resembled a truncated cone, built of flat slabs of dolomite laid roughly one on top of another. Its height was about 6 feet, while the inside diameter diminished gradually from 4 feet 6 inches at the bottom to 2 feet 6 inches at the top. There was a small door facing WSW., 2 feet 6 inches high and 1 foot 6 inches wide, the bottom being raised 1 foot 4 inches above the level of the floor. From an architectural point of view the most interesting feature was the use of the cantilever principle in closing the roof.[3] The space to be covered was roughly circular, with a diameter of a

Fig. 11. Old stone hut near Locker point

little more than two feet. Apparently no s'ngle slab to hand was large enough, so the builders used several smaller slabs instead. Two sufficed to cover about half the space on the south side; another was laid over the northern segment, resting on the wall, and the interspace was filled in with two overlapping slabs. Both the roof and the sides had many chinks and openings through which the wind and rain could enter. A rude flooring had been laid with slabs of dolomite, and near the doorway, close to the outer walls, were two stone rings where some Eskimos had evidently set up their tents in shelter from the east wind. About fifteen yards to the northwest was a pillar of seven or eight dolomite slabs laid one on top of another, though with what object it is hard to imagine. Elsewhere,

[1]See C. R. Markham, p. 169 *et seq.*
[2]My Life with the Eskimo, p. 274 *et seq..*, 288; Anthrop. Papers, A.M.N.H., Vol. XIV, pt. I, p. 297
[3]Cf. Peary. The Secrets of Polar Travel, 1917, pp. 136-7.

on the summit of the same hill, was another tent-ring, with its hearth-stones close beside it, and a low wind-break of stones from behind which the country north and east could be scanned for several miles.

Birds and animals had evidently been the latest occupants of the hut for we found their bones scattered both above and below the floorstones. The ground was frozen hard, and I had no time to stay and excavate. It is hardly possible that the structure could ever have been a dwelling, since there was barely room for a man even to squat inside. The natives gave varying accounts of its origin. Some said it was made by white men long ago, possibly Rae's party when it tried in vain to cross the strait to Victoria island.[1] Certainly if it was intended for an observation post looking out on the gulf to the east and south, no better site could have been chosen anywhere. Another version assigned it to the *tornrin*, the dwarf people who were driven underground by the Copper Eskimos long ago.[2] They were responsible, too, for a curious structure that we found on the plain behind Cape Lambert. It was made of large flat slabs of dolomite set on edge in the shape of a rectangle, about 8 feet long by 4 feet wide, and from 1 foot to 1 foot 6 inches high. It was unlike the remains of a Copper Eskimo camping-site, and may have been due to the western natives. Whether the stone houses should be assigned to the same origin (stone being used because of the lack of driftwood), or whether they belong rather to that earlier people who have left similar remains round Hudson bay and in the Parry archipelago, must be left uncertain until the Copper Eskimo country and the adjacent regions have been more fully explored and we have more information concerning the distribution of these houses.[3]

The only types of dwellings known to the Copper Eskimos are the snow-hut and the tent. Sometimes a traveller finds them with neither, but camping instead under the open sky; only rarely, however, for it is seldom that a man can sleep with comfort out of doors in this region. Occasionally of course night overtakes a hunter without a tent, and without any means of building a snow hut. He will then wander round for a time, searching for his camp, and when weariness overcomes him, squat down on the ground or snow for a while and fall asleep, with his chin resting on his chest, his legs outstretched, and his arms withdrawn inside his coat and folded against his body. In time the cold awakens him and he rises and resumes his journey. In June and July, sometimes too in August, a party will often leave its tents and journey off to hunt or fish for a few days in some adjoining district, carrying only sleeping-bags and a few skins. Such open-air bivouacs are very pleasant as long as the weather remains fine; the warm hours of the morning are generally given over to sleep, and the party does not stir till nearly noon. Should rain come on or a fog arise they can soon construct a rude shelter by converting their ice-chisels, fish-spears and walking-sticks into tent-poles and stretching their skins around and over them. At the end of May, 1915, we made a trip of some 50 miles to meet the Eskimos of Prince Albert sound. Two families in our party left their tents behind. At first they merely set up a wind-break, driving a row of sticks into the ground at an inclined angle and spreading their skins over them; later, when we had to wait for several days at the rendezvous, they ranged their poles in an oval and made a regular tent. Then a blizzard struck them, and the howling

---

[1] See Richardson, p. 178.

[2] Cf. Boas, Central Eskimo, p. 635; Meddelelser om Grønland, Vol. XXXIX, p. 688 *et seq.*

[3] The stone huts on Southampton island which were used for meat caches had no doorway, but were opened at the top (Boas, Bulletin IV, A.M.N.H., Vol. XV, p. 475). Captain Bernard tells me, however, that the natives of Adelaide peninsula build huts like those among the Copper Eskimos for trapping foxes. A bait of meat or fish or blubber is laid on the floor, the door cl sed, and the roof either opened, or closed with a lightly balanced stone that will cave in when the fox steps on it. Once the animal has entered the trap it is unable to escape. I cannot help thinking, however, that this is a secondary use, the structures being originally intended, perhaps, for meat-caches. The doorway would be convenient, but not absolutely essential.

wind drove eddies of snow inside their tent under its flapping edges, so they built a low circular wall of snow-blocks and raised their tent on that. A few weeks later in similar circumstances they made a wall with turf instead of snow. It was only about a foot high, but it anchored down the edges of their tent and kept the rain from flooding it. In August of the same year, during a gale of driving sleet and snow, two men without a tent stretched some deerskins over a gap between two crags and weathered it out in comparative comfort. Mc-Clintock mentions the case of an old woman near Pond's bay (Pond's inlet) who had neither hut nor tent, but a sort of lair constructed of a few stones and a seal-skin spread over them, so that she could crawl underneath.[1] These, however, are exceptional cases. Normally the Copper Eskimo lives in a snow-hut through the winter months, and moves into a deer-skin tent as soon as the warmth of spring renders his house untenable.

The first step[2] in constructing a snow-hut is to find a suitable site. Not only must the snow be deep enough but it must also possess a certain firmness. It must not be crumbly, as it is when granular, or soft as when freshly fallen, otherwise the blocks will fall to pieces at the slightest touch; as for its depth, that should be at least a foot. There are two ways of cutting snow-blocks, horizontally and vertically, and it depends on the depth of snow which one the native will employ. In the former method a rectangle is cut to the size required and the block is undercut for as far as the knife will reach. A kick below will now release it, and slightly raise one side so that it can be lifted in the hands. Sometimes careful pressure with the foot on top will break it off where a kick beneath would crack it. The depth at which the undercut is made decides the thickness of the block. This is the only method possible when the snow is shallow. Vertical cutting requires deep snow, for here it is the width of the block that is regulated by the depth. A few rapid cuts with the knife, a few vigorous kicks to scatter the loose snow, and a space is cleared from which the first block can be cut away. A cut on each side gives it its length, and the knife is run backwards and forwards underneath to give the width of the block One face and the sides are now clear, and all that remains to be done is to determine its thickness and separate the remaining face. This is the only delicate part of the operation. The first cut must not be deep, otherwise the block will be sure to crack on one side before the knife has reached the other. Usually the man runs his knife along the back face twice, cutting free about half its surface; then he stabs it down about the middle, when the block breaks off as a rule and falls towards him. If this should not release it he stabs it again on the side that he thinks is holding, and sometimes on the other side as well. Once the first block has been extracted the others proceed more easily, since there is more open space in which to work and their shape is already half outlined. Vertical cutting is quicker and easier than cutting horizontally, besides which there is more snow in the same surface area. Then too the deeper down you cut in making your house the less high you have to build. It makes no difference if you come to ice, for a floor of ice is quite as good as one of snow. A deep snow-drift gives you half your wall already built. With a small house almost all the blocks required can be taken from the floor, but should more be needed they can soon be obtained outside and pushed in through an opening cut in the bottom of the wall.

One or sometimes two men therefore build up the house from the inside, while the housewife and the children make an outer rampart all around it about six inches or a foot away, and fill the interspace with soft snow. The arrangement of the first tier of blocks naturally determines the size and shape of the subsequent house. A Mackenzie native who was building us a hut in

---

[1]McClintock, p. 133.
[2]Cf. Stefansson's account in Anthrop. Papers, A.M.N.H., Vol. XIV, pt. I, p. 6 *et seq.*, and Amundsen, Vol. II, ch. VIII.

which to shelter the dogs made the diameter of his first tier far too great, so that instead of his walls approaching in a perfect Byzantine dome, they mounted skywards almost to a cone. A more skilful workman might have made a symmetrical dome despite the diameter, but the art of building snow-huts is fast dying out amongst the western natives.

The critical stage in the building of a snow hut comes with the second tier, for then the spiral form commences and judgment and experience are required to know at what place to begin. The younger men often seek the advice of their elders; and I have seen even an old woman correct a youth and show him where to begin his coil. Often the spiral form is barely noticeable when the hut is finished, and one has the impression that the blocks are set up anyhow. The neatest workmen make their blocks rectangular, and lay them so that the joints will come in steps, no block falling exactly over the one below. As each is laid in place the knife is run along the joints and the block punched sharply on the top to fit it tightly against its neighbours. Thus the builder follows round his spiral, curving gradually inwards till only a small opening remains above. The final stage is the most critical of all, for the roof will collapse if made too flat, and part of the structure may cave in from an accidental knock, or the unskilful jointing of a block. The joints are therefore bevelled, but even so it is sometimes necessary to hold one block up with the hand till it is wedged securely by the next. The keystone requires skilful handling. It is roughly trimmed to shape, then pushed up through the opening in the roof and gently lowered from above. The left hand poises it above the hole, while with the right the builder trims its edges and those of the blocks against which it sets.

The structure is now complete, but many chinks and gaps remain where the blocks fit imperfectly together. These must be closed from without, if the housewife has not already done this after making her rampart. Small blocks of hard snow are jammed into the larger gaps, and all the joints are filled with soft snow, which acts like mortar and cements the blocks together. It matters little if a few chinks still remain on top, for the warmth inside the hut sets a current of air flowing upwards and outside; but unless the lower wall is tight the house will be very draughty and uncomfortable. This cannot happen as long as an outer rampart is built all round, but the temporary hut for one night's occupation only has usually no such rampart; instead, soft snow is packed tightly round the base of the lower tier, and into all the joints.

Not every hut is built so carefully. Sometimes the shape is oval, the length much greater than the breadth. Then the side walls are gradually brought together till a row of longer blocks laid across like beams will close the roof. But this is a very slovenly way of building. More often the hut is dome-shaped, but the blocks are entirely unsymmetrical, being set up in any manner so long as they hold together. The spiral form is then quite absent, although the same care is still required in beginning the second tier. Even the rule that no joint should come directly above the one below is not adhered to, and the joints come anywhere. This in fact is the usual form of hut, and the perfect dome built with symmetrical blocks arranged in a continuous spiral which earlier writers have so consistently depicted is of very rare occurrence. In fact not every native has the necessary skill to make it, besides which it requires more time and labour. But every man can build a snow-hut of some kind or another, and must indeed at the end of each day's journey that he makes in winter. He may have travelled many miles, dragging a heavy sled, and darkness is almost upon him before he begins his hut; naturally, then, he is much too tired to care about its shape so long as it provides his family and himself with a comfortable shelter for the night.

The hut that we were describing was complete indeed, but it had neither furniture nor door. If snow-blocks from without were used in building it there will be a hole in one of the bottom blocks through which to pass them in; if no such hole exists one is quickly cut out with the knife. Now the woman goes inside, carrying her snowshovel with her, levels the floor in the front half and raises a bank behind it to form the sleeping-platform. Often in building the hut the man will cut his blocks from the front part only, leaving the snow behind at its natural level, which is now one tier above the floor; this gives a platform already made, and he has merely to pass in the furniture for his wife to arrange in order.

While the wife is thus busy within, the man must construct a passage for his hut. This is a simple operation, merely the building of two straight walls about three feet apart and from four to five feet high roofed over at the top with horizontal blocks. Before he begins it he closes the hole through which the furniture was passed and does not cut the doorway until after the passage is finished. The hut is thus hermetically sealed, and time is given the woman to light her lamp and warm the room before her husband enters. In making the door he pokes his knife through the wall at the end of the passage, cuts out an arch about two feet high, and calls to his wife within to give it a kick; the block falls outwards into the passage and is quickly dragged away. The man's work is now finished, save that he must pile all bags and pokes and lashings, that are not wanted in the house, on top of the rampart outside, and dispose his sled in safety for the night.

Meanwhile his wife is arranging the house within. Usually a gap is made in the middle of the sleeping-platform where clothes and other articles can be conveniently stowed away. Then she arranges the platform itself, covering it over with mats of willow twigs tied together with rawhide thongs, and bridging the gap with three or four planks. Musk-ox skins are laid on top of the matting, and on these again the deerskins, in two layers, the lower ones having the fur side downwards while the upper skins have the fur on top. In the upper skin— each is called a *kak*—not only should the fur be upwards, but the hair should lie towards the door; for, like a carpet, they must be swept from time to time and naturally the sweeping is done outwards on to the floor along the set of the hair. The sleeping-bags, the men's tool-bags, the women's sewing-kits and various other articles are strewn indiscriminately on top of the skins till bedtime, when the room is tidied up.

In front of the platform the lamp and table with their appurtenances occupy half the floor space, while the door comes in the middle of the arc at the very bottom of the wall. Usually, but by no means invariably, the lamp is to the left of the door, as seen from the inside. The natives have a curious device for supporting the lamp and table, and every family adopts the same method. One piece of the furniture consists of a long board shaped like the letter **L,** but widest at the elbow. This is used to form a strut, the long end, the top of the **L,** being driven into the wall of the house, while the short end rests directly upon the floor or on top of a small block of snow. The table is a long flat board resting at one end on the elbow of the strut; the other, like the strut, to which it is at right angles, is driven deep into the wall. It thus lies parallel to the front of the sleeping platform, from which it is separated by a narrow space along which the wife can move freely in and out. Both table and platform stand some two feet above the floor.

Two poles run parallel to the table and just behind it; on one side their ends are resting on the strut, while on the other they are driven into the snow wall of the hut. On top of these is placed the lamp, a shallow trough of stone with a partition usually along the back; sometimes, instead of a single lamp of large dimensions two smaller ones are used, placed end to end. Care must be taken to set the lamp horizontally, or with a slight tilt forward so that the oil will run towards the wick. Some contrivance is then required for suspending the cooking-pot above it, so a short stick, notched at its upper end, is planted vertically on the edge of the main strut near its elbow; another stick is now laid across it at right angles, parallel to the strut below, with one end resting in the notch, and the other driven into the wall; this gives a second strut on top of the first. Two poles are laid across this new strut, parallel with those supporting the lamp, and the drying rack, an oval hoop of wood with rawhide webbing, is set on top of them. From the foremost pole, the one that lies nearest the sleeping platform, the pot is suspended by two cords in such a way that it hangs about half an inch above the flame of the lamp, while from the pole behind shoes and other small articles that require drying are suspended. If two families share a dwelling, or the man has a second wife, another lamp and its outfit is set up in similar fashion on the opposite side of the hut. Often the space is vacant, and a little girl will play at housekeeping in this corner, erecting a lamp there for herself, either a small one made of soapstone in the usual manner, or merely a hollow pebble from the beach.

Fig. 12. Interior of a snow hut

Houses intended for more than one night's occupation nearly always have windows made of ice. These are chipped out with ice chisels from fresh-water lakes or streams in the fall of the year, and are roughly squared so that each side will be from 2 feet to 2 feet 6 inches long. The window is let into the wall behind the lamp, or sometimes just above the door, either as soon as the hut is built or more usually on the following morning; it thus lights up the fore part only, but the snow itself is semi-translucent, so that as long as the sun is shining a window is hardly needed at all. In the twilight hours of midwinter, however, even the front of the hut beneath the window is only dimly lit up, while the back and sides are in deep obscurity. One house we saw had a window in its passage, but this was very unusual; apparently the family has an extra 'pane' which they determined to put to use. Very large houses, especially dance-houses, often have two "panes" let in side by side, with but one block of snow between them. The frost which settles on these windows is scraped away with a woman's knife, just as the natives farther west scrape their gut windows; these latter, by the way, are totally unknown in Coronation gulf.[1]

Some houses have a small recess built in a corner near the door; this is for storing meat, or for housing a litter of pups. Sometimes the passage is broadened in one place for the same purpose. Often two houses are joined together, or several unite round a common forecourt which forms the village dance-house. The Eskimo is very skilful in modifying the shape of his hut to suit his needs. One snow-hut in which I lived was dripping badly, besides which it had an awkward shape, so its owner knocked out the roof and part of one side and built it up afresh. The warmth of the hut had transformed the inner face of each snow-block into ice to the depth of about an inch, so that he had to chop it away with a small hatchet. This transformation of the snow to ice explains the solidity of a snow-hut, which is so great indeed that a full-grown man can stand on the very top of the roof without its collapsing. The same native who had thus re-shaped his dwelling once made a chimney of snow-blocks in a small snow hut when we were trying to cook inside with chips of driftwood. He derived the notion no doubt from the stove pipes at our station, but it showed at least his versatility and his skill in handling snow.

A snow-hut is a very comfortable dwelling even in mid-winter, unless the temperature falls unusually low and a blizzard is raging out of doors. Even then, in a well-built hut with a long semi-subterranean[2] passage, the natives are not uncomfortable, provided that the lamp can be kept burning to its full extent.

If the temperature of the hut rises above the freezing-point, the ceiling immediately begins to drip. This often happens when the meals are being cooked, or when the house is filled with people. Slight dripping can usually be stopped by chipping away the ice at the place from which the drops are falling, or by holding against it a lump of snow, which will freeze against the wall and lower the temperature at that spot. Neither method, however, will permanently stop it, unless the temperature of the hut is lowered as well. Often when the ceiling of a hut is thus plastered with lumps of snow, they themselves become soaked like sponges and fall on the inmates' heads; I have seen this happen to a native lying in his sleeping bag, with a rather amusing result. The only sure remedy is to knock a small hole in the roof, so that the cold air streaming in will freeze the walls again. Old huts are pitted with many holes where the roof and walls have dripped and melted away. By day the natives take no notice unless the weather is stormy, but at night, before going to bed, someone will often go outside and close all the chinks with snow. It is not always pleasant, though, to stumble about in the darkness and clamber up on to the roof, so frequently they merely block the largest holes from inside with scraps of skin or mittens, or with handwipers of ptarmigan skins, and let the others remain. The door is closed with a block of snow, dragged inside and set in place from within, with loose snow cementing the edges. It is not wise to close up the hut too tightly, however, or the air becomes foul and suffocating. In the fall of 1914, I was travelling with a Copper Eskimo across Dolphin and Union Strait, and carefully closed up every chink and cranny in our first snow-hut, in order to increase its warmth. Early next morning our lamp refused to burn, and it was only then that we realized how impure the air was and quickly broke open the door.[3]

---

[1] The owner takes his window out to pack on his sled at every migration, and his wife hands him the bedding through the hole it leaves in the wall. Mr. Stefansson saw a number of deserted huts with such holes in them, and his first interpretation of them as windows was as correct as his second. The window is naturally set above or nearly above the lamp, and as this may be on either side of the door, the window may be also, not, as Mr. Stefansson thought, on one side only. Anthrop. Papers, A.M.N.H., Vol. XIV, pt. I, p. 247.

[2] *i.e.*, partly under the surface of the snowdrift.

[3] Cf. Stefansson, My Life with the Eskimo, p. 245 *et seq.*

In the fall, before the sea is frozen solidly over, the Eskimos often build their huts on the very edge of the land.[1] The rise and fall of the tide then frequently splits the ice, and cracks the hut above it. The roof threatened to cave in on this account in one house, but its owner propped it up with a pole, one end of which rested on the floor while the other was jammed beneath a board laid flat against the roof. In 1915 our first snow-hut in the fall was built above a tide-crack, and during the night we were awakened several times by loud reports like gun-shots; next morning we found our hut was split from one side to the other. On another occasion the house-wife was dressing and stepped from the sleeping platform to the floor, when suddenly she sank up to her knees in a pool of slush ice where the tide had oozed up through a crack. Even when badly cracked, soft snow jammed in the seams will hold a house together, unless the cracks are opened further by the next high tide. The walls show wonderful stability, and even half a hut will stand alone and un-supported.

The size of the hut depends on the number of occupants, but the length of the passage is determined by other considerations, mainly by that of warmth. A hut that is built for one night only has hardly any passage at all, while those intended for longer occupation have passages ranging in length from 15 to 40 feet. They are often made quite short at first, and extended when a gale arises. Sometimes the entrance is slightly curved away from the wind, or given a **T**-shape so that one mouth or the other can be closed according to the weather. One man built a dome-shaped roof over his entrance, forming a kind of store-house; but this was very unusual, most natives merely broadening the passage in one place to answer the same purpose. Generally the house is built to face the south so that the window will catch the light of the sun; the passage will then also run towards the south. But the rule is not invariable, since the builder has to modify his plans in accordance with the depth of snow.

A small hut was built for me when I paid my first visit to these Eskimos. It was oval in plan, 10 feet long, 6 feet 9 inches wide, and 4 feet 6 inches high. The blocks were of different sizes, the bottom ones, as usual, much larger than those above. They varied greatly in shape, too, leaving many ill-fitting open corners which were blocked with snow. Soft drift-snow was piled round the bottom of the outside to keep out the draught. The door was a small arch cut in two bottom blocks 2 feet high and 1 foot 10 inches wide. There was no window, but the snow was semi-translucent and gave sufficient light for most purposes during the day. The passage was very short and slightly curved. It was unroofed save for one block over the door, but the next day when a strong wind arose and the snow began to drift my native donned his working clothes and in about five minutes covered it over and slightly extended the mouth so that it pointed away from the wind. The door itself was a snow-block shaped to fit the doorway. It was therefore longer than it was broad and so could be pushed inside; for at night before going to bed the door is always closed from the inside. There was a groove cut in the middle of its inner face so that it could be lifted more readily. Often when the weather is mild the natives merely cover the doorway with a skin or bag, or throw their coats down in the entrance, provided that the dogs are not so starved that they will tear the skins to pieces during the night.

[1]Mr. Stefansson (Anthrop. Papers, A.M.N.H., Vol. XIV, pt. I, p. 50) says that the Kanghiryuarmiut are the only Copper Eskimos, except perhaps the Ekaluktomiut, who ever build winter houses on land or even near land. This is exactly where every tribe does build them in the fall, and again in the late spring.

CHAPTER VI

DWELLINGS (Continued)

Hitherto only the simplest form of house has been described; but there are many varieties, from the single isolated hut to the group of three or four that open on a common dance-house. No rule governs the Eskimos in these matters; they build their huts together or separate as fancy dictates. In view, however, of certain theories that have been put forward on the subject, notably by M. Mauss[1], it may be well to examine the different types of houses that we observed among the Copper Eskimos, without attempting in this place to compare them with the dwellings of Eskimos elsewhere.

Fig. 13 is the plan of a house built by an Eskimo of Dolphin and Union strait at the Liston and Sutton islands in the fall of 1914. It was 10 feet 10 inches long and 9 feet 6 inches wide, with a maximum height of 6 feet 3 inches. The platform was raised 2 feet above the level of the floor and had a maximum length of 6 feet from front to back. The door was 1 foot 11 inches high by 1 foot 9 inches wide, while the window, which was 2 feet 3 inches above it, was 2 feet 3 inches high by 2 feet 1 inch broad. The passage was straight, 13 feet 3 inches long,

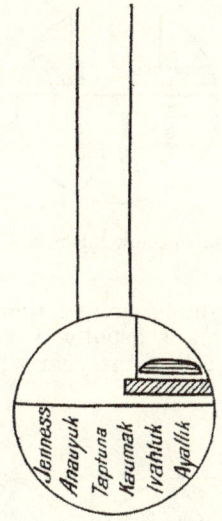

Fig. 13. A typical single-roomed snow hut

with a slight variation in width at different places but averaging about 2 feet 6 inches. The inmates of the hut were Ayallik, a man of about fifty years, his wife Kaumak, a motherly old dame of nearly the same age, their son Ivahluk, a boy about eight years old, another son Taptuna, of about thirteen years, and Anauyuk, a widower, Ayallik's nephew, himself probably forty-five years old. Their sleeping places on the platform, as well as my own during the few days I lived with this family, are given in the figure, and the outlines of the lamp

---

[1]*L'Année Sociologique*, 1906: Essai sur les variations saisonnières des sociétés eskimos. 9me Année, 1906.

and table, showing their positions, are marked in front of the platform.[1]   The hut was a single-roomed dwelling of the ordinary type, built at the end of a day's journey across the strait at the opening of the sealing season.

A development from this type of house is one which has a dance-house in front, built just over the doorway.   Fig. 14 illustrates a dwelling of this kind which was seen at an Eskimo settlement in the Duke of York archipelago, Coronation gulf, in February, 1915.   The hut belonged to a famous shaman named Uloksak, who at this time possessed two wives; each wife kept to her own side of the hut, where she had her own cooking and drying outfit.

Fɪɢ. 14. A single snow hut with a dance-house in front

Sometimes two huts are almost joined together, but their passages open out in opposite directions.   This is usually due to the condition of the snow, and so is more frequent in the fall of the year when its depth is not very great.

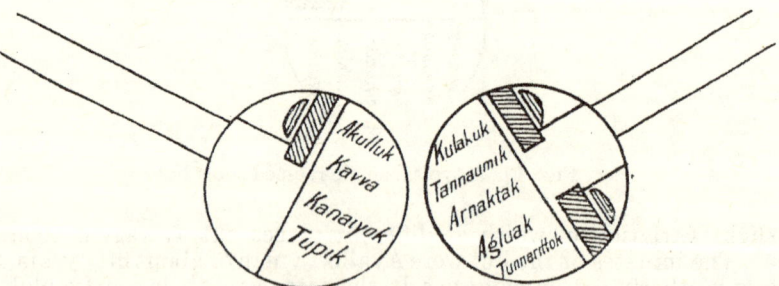

Fɪɢ. 15. Two houses erected side by side, but opening in different directions

Fig. 15 gives the plan of two such huts, erected on the southwest coast of Victoria island in December, 1914, by two men, Kanaiyok and Arnaktak, for their families. Their proximity in this case was due to the limited number of places behind the

---

[1]Eskimos sleep with their heads towards the door, though occasionally when the hut is crowded one or more of them will lie in the opposite direction, as the feet naturally take up less room than the shoulders. Cf. Hall, p. 258.

sandspit where the snow was deep enough to build a house, and the passages were made separate to keep the dogs of the two families from fighting with one another. Kanaiyok's family consisted, besides himself, of his wife Akulluk, their baby daughter Kavva, and his father Tupik. With Arnaktak were his wife Kulahuk and her little son Tannaumik, and two single men, brothers, not closely connected with the family, named Tunnerittok and Agluak; in the previous settlement which the Eskimos had just abandoned these two men had lived in a hut of their own (see Fig. 21).

Sometimes, as in Fig. 16, two houses comparatively far apart have their passages joined near the entrance. This is convenient in stormy weather, when the snow drifts into the passageways and requires constant shovelling. One of these huts was inhabited by a man named Haviuyak, his wife Pikhugyuk, and their unmarried son Avalittok; in the other dwelt Kuniluk, his wife Kormiak and their three boys, Niptanatsiak, Taipanna and Kulitana, the last a baby about twelve months old.

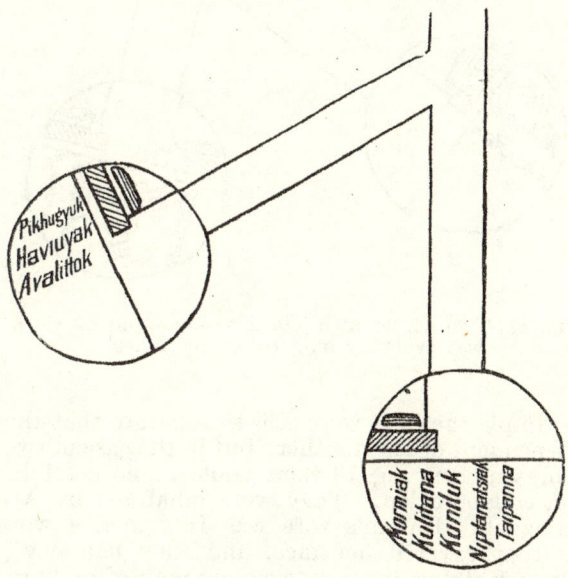

Fig. 16. Two houses erected some distance apart, but joined at their entrances

When I joined the settlement of Puivlik Eskimos on the coast of southwest Victoria island in November, 1914, I went to live in a double hut similar to that represented in Fig. 19, one side of which was inhabited by a man named Haviuyak and his wife Itokanna, the other by Haviuyak's father Haviron and his two younger brothers, Utuallu, a youth of about sixteen years and Haugak, a boy of perhaps eight (see Fig. 22). About a week later an Eskimo named Aksiatak brought his family across the straits and joined the settlement, partly for the sake of company, but mainly because he was short of food and the Puivlirmuit had an abundance of caribou meat and fish. He then built a separate hut on the outskirts of their settlement; but three weeks later, when the whole band migrated some four miles along the coast, he arranged with Haviuyak that they should build their huts together side by side, each with a short passage of its own where the dogs of the two households could sleep apart. This was done in the manner shown in Fig. 17: Haviuyak, with the help of his brother Utuallu, built a large single-roomed hut, while Aksiatak set up a smaller one beside it. Nakitok, the person who is marked as sleeping between Aksiatak and his wife Nik, was their only son, at this time about six years old.

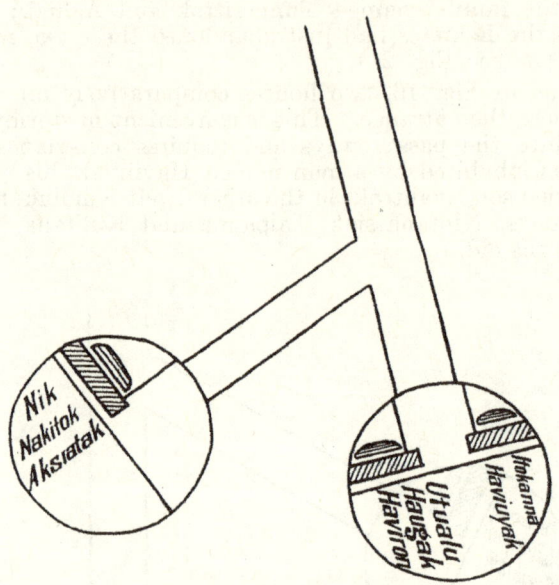

Fig. 17. Two houses with joined passages, one of which
was evidently built before the other

In this last example the huts were still so separate that they might almost be regarded as independent of one another; but in the case of two that lay along-side of the hut represented in Fig. 13 there could be no possible doubt but that they were built in collaboration. They were inhabited by Ayallik's kinsmen, Kallun and Kaminggok. Kallun's wife was Imilguna, a woman remarkable from the freckles that covered her face, and they had one young daughter, Kungaiyuna. Algik, Kallun's brother, a young man of perhaps eighteen years, lived with them as one of the family. Kaminggok was a shaman whose wife Kalyutarun had given him two children, a little girl named Akana, and a baby boy Okomik. The latter had some disease which kept it from growing, so in the winter of 1915-16, when the Eskimos were very short of food, the mother killed it. It was then about three years old, but could neither talk nor walk, having been bewitched, its mother believed, by some evil spirit. Akana, the other child, was about seven years old, and eager to play at house-keeping, so she set up a hollow pebble on one side of the hut to serve as a lamp. Her mother used to give her the wick and blubber, and the child tended the lamp herself. These two houses were so close together that a conversation carried on in normal tones in one could be plainly heard by the people in the other (Fig. 18).

A further stage in complexity is reached when the houses actually combine, forming a single two-roomed dwelling Such was the house of Aksiatak and his kinsman Hitkok at Nulahugyuk creek four miles east of Bernard harbour, in November, 1914, before they crossed the strait to join the Puivlirmiut on the other side. Hitkok's household consisted of himself, his widowed sister Iguak and his nephew Hogaluk, a boy of about fourteen years. The rooms were built as contiguous circles, a small arc of each being left uncovered to form a common forecourt and afterwards roofed over with a dome as in Byzantine architecture. The dance-house, which is usually built over a two-roomed house, is made in exactly the same way, only the dome is much larger, and the roof in consequence higher, so that the builders have to stand on bags to finish it. In Aksiatak's double house an ice window was let into the side of the dome so that it lit up both the forecourt and Aksiatak's room; a similar window was set in the front of Hitkok's room. At the bottom of the forecourt wall, immediately below the window, was the low arched doorway, cut in one of the snow-blocks with a single sweep of the knife. One entered on hands and knees; so narrow in fact was the doorway that a person rather bigger than the average had some difficulty in squeezing through. Half-way along its length the passage broadened, and here was kept the snowshovel, as well as one or two other things

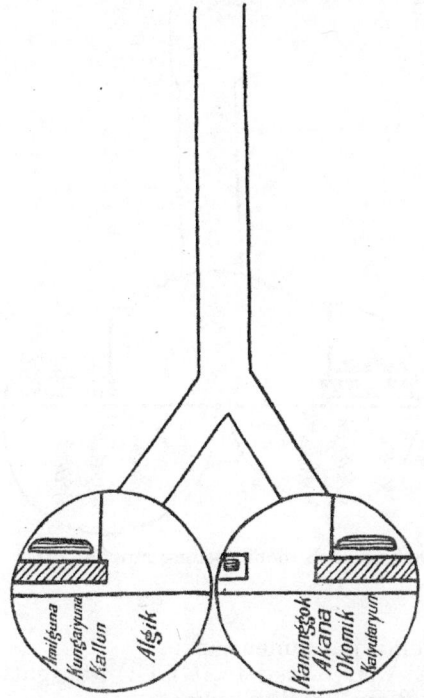

Fig. 18. Two houses built in collaboration, with a single passage for both

which could not conveniently be brought into the house, and would not be damaged by the dogs. The passage then made a sharp curve before issuing out into the open air, so that its mouth, being directed northward, would drift up less easily under the prevailing east and west winds. One day, however, a north wind arose, and Aksiatak had to extend his passage so that it opened towards another point of the compass, a task he performed in a very few minutes. Various sticks, harpoons, etc., were planted upright in the walls around the outside of the house, and bales of clothing were laid on top of the outer rampart.

The dimensions of the two rooms were as follows:—

	Aksiatak's room.	Hitkok's room.
Length (max.)	10′ 5″	11′
Breadth (max.)	6′ 9″	8′ 11″
Height (max.)	5′ 11″	6′ 8″
Height of platform	1′ 3″	1′ 4″
Length of platform	6′	6′ 2″

The door, which was common to the two rooms, was 2 feet 1 inch high by 1 foot 8 inches wide. The window in the forecourt was 2 feet 2 inches high by 1 foot 9 inches wide, and the one in Hitkok's house had approximately the same dimensions. The front wall of the forecourt was about 2 feet in advance of those of the two rooms, but the height was the same as in Hitkok's room.

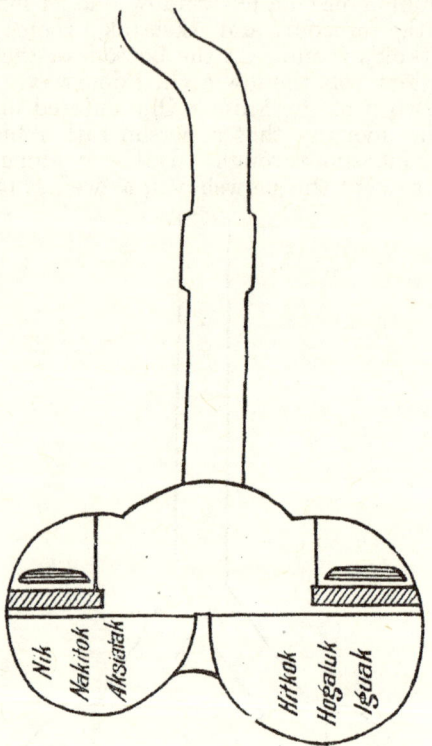

Fɪɢ. 19. A two-roomed dwelling, each room opening into the other, with a door-way common to both

The passage had the following dimensions:—

  Length 17′ (2′ were added to it later, at right angles to the mouth, to keep out the drifting snow)
  Breadth (average) 2′ 6″
  Breadth (maximum) 5′ 8″
  Height (average) 3′
  Height (maximum) 4′ 11″
  The outside entrance was 3′ 4″ high and 2′ 1″ wide.

On November 22, when the temperature outdoors was −2° F. and the lamp in Hitkok's room was burning along only half its length, i.e. about 15″, the temperature inside that room was 35° F. at a distance of three feet from the lamp and 30° F. against the back wall.

In the two-roomed hut just described the rooms were parallel with one another. This, however, is not always the case. Fig. 20 gives the plan of a hut in which they are arranged at right angles. It was built in the beginning of January, 1915, to shelter the families of Ikpakhuak and his nephew Huputaun. It would have been exactly the same as the hut represented in Fig. 19, but for the angle at which the two rooms lay with regard to one another. A few days after its construction the front walls of the two rooms were torn down and a large cupola erected over them to form a dance-house for the community. Where the wall of the dance-house joined his room Ikpakhuak made a bed of willow-matting covered with an old sealskin for one of his dogs that had a litter of pups. His family consisted of his wife Higilak, his nephew and adopted son Haugak, (the son of Haviron in Fig. 17), Higilak's daughter (by a former husband) Kanneyuk, who was about twelve years of age, and myself, since this was the family into which I was formally adopted. The other household comprised Huputaun, his wife Uvillok, their baby boy Kotsik, and a little girl Holoak, of about ten years. Apart from the hut itself the passage was interesting because it had a **T**-shaped entrance, roofed over so that one side or the other could be closed according to the direction of the wind.

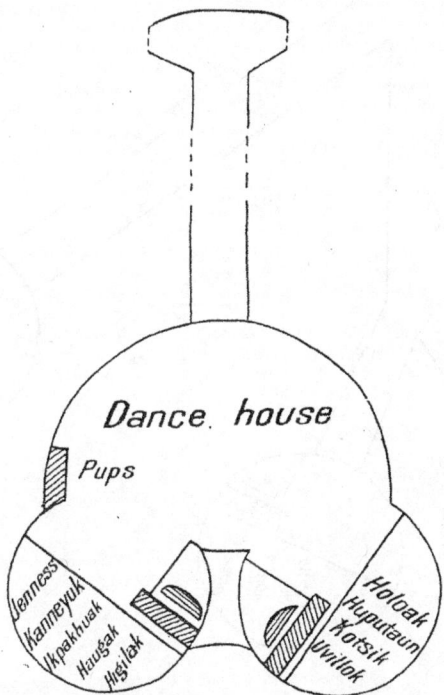

Fig. 20. A two-roomed dwelling opening on a dance-house

So far we have seen two huts coalescing into a single two-roomed dwelling with a dance-house over the forecourt, but nothing in the snow itself prevents three or four huts from coalescing in the same way. The only difficulty lies in the fact that the more numerous the huts that have to be joined together the larger must be the forecourt or dance-house that connects them, and the more difficult it is to construct when the only material that can be employed is snow. Consequently, while the usual custom is to build the dance-house over a two-roomed hut, one built over three rooms is not at all rare, but one over four is very unusual. Still, all these types are found, since the Eskimos are not bound by any rules in the matter and suit their own convenience. Fig. 21 represents a group of three huts where the passages all unite to make a common entrance. They were built in March, 1915, about fifteen miles west of the Liston and Sutton islands, whither the Eskimos had migrated for the sealing in the longer days of spring. Each hut was inhabited by a separate family. In the first was Ikpakhuak's, which was the same as in Fig. 10, save that a young girl, Arnauyuk or Kila, about fourteen years old, had joined it for a short time before her marriage; in the next hut lived Atigihyuk and his wife Kaiyoranna with their little girl Uvillok; and in the third Hitkok and his kinsfolk. The passage of this third hut had a small recess on one side half way along its length, for the same purpose as the widening in the passage represented in Fig. 19.

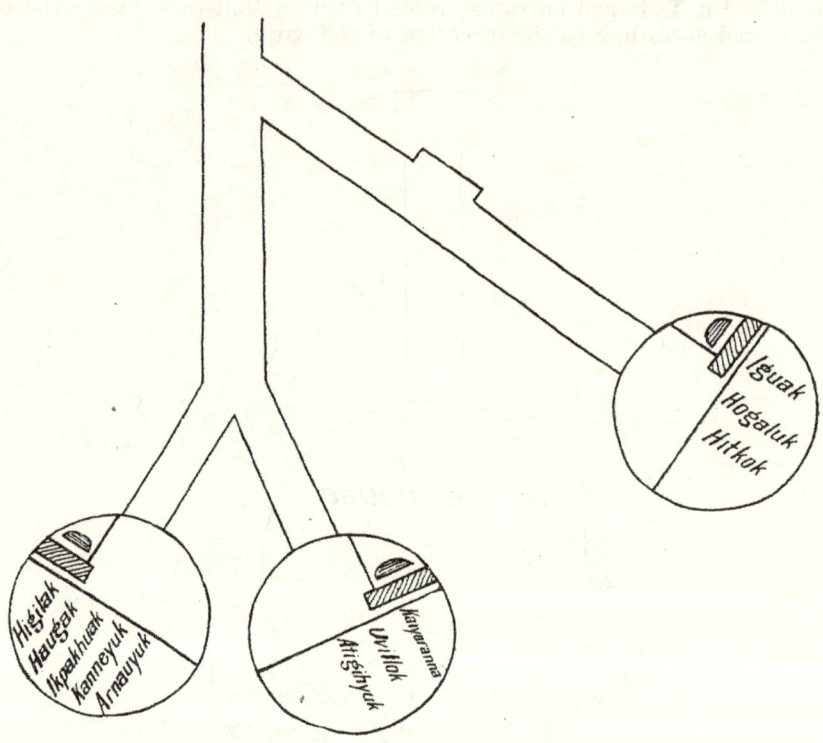

Fig. 21. Three single-roomed dwellings with joined passages

Sometimes two of the three houses coalesce into a single two-roomed dwelling, while the third remains separate, though its passage joins up with the other. This type I observed at the last settlement of the Puivlik Eskimos before they migrated to the coast in December, 1914. The two-roomed hut was the dwelling of Haviuyak and his family (see Fig. 17), while the single hut linked up with it was the home of the two brothers Tunnerittok and Agluak who later went to live with Arnaktak's family (see Fig. 15).

In November, 1915, a three-roomed dwelling was built at Bernard harbour with a dance-house over the common fore-court. Two of the rooms contained two families each, while the third had only one. Each family had its separate lamp, and the different members slept in the usual places; thus the wife slept in the corner where she could superintend the lamp and the cooking, and between her and her husband was their little child, whenever there was one. The family that lived by itself left the settlement before the rest, so the others closed up the front of the empty room with snow-blocks to make their house smaller and warmer (Fig. 23).

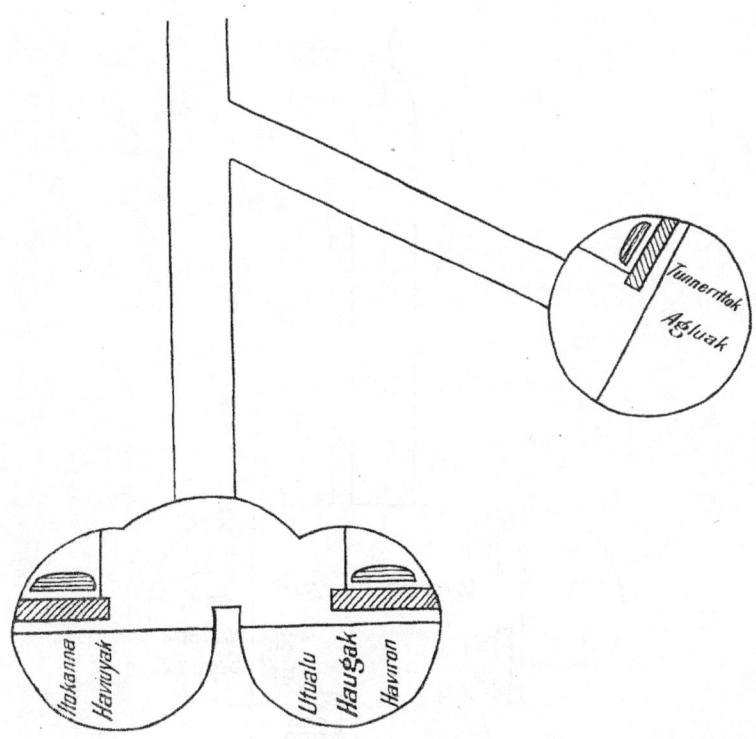

Fig. 22. A two-roomed dwelling joined to a single-roomed hut through the passage

A curious four-roomed dwelling and dance-house was seen at the Liston and Sutton islands in December, 1915. I was not present when it was made and therefore cannot say whether the different rooms were erected at the same time or not. Architecturally two of the rooms must be regarded as excrescences, their only connection with the rest being that their doorways led into the dance-house instead of into a corridor. The dance-house formed the forecourt of the other two rooms, one of which was inhabited by two families not very closely related. Each family, as usual, had its own lamp and furniture, and the places in which the various inmates slept followed the usual custom. The winter that year was very stormy, and both food and blubber were scarce, so that the lamps had to be extinguished in many houses. The two rooms at the back of the dance-house were soon abandoned, as they were cold and uncomfortable unless the lamps were burning full. The other two families were better off as they could bar their doors and make their rooms almost airtight; they therefore remained where they were till February, when the whole settlement migrated some ten miles farther west (Fig. 24).

All the snow-huts among the Copper Eskimos were of one or other of thes e types. The particular form adopted by any family depended on various considerations, the two most important being the amount of snow available and the size of the family. Less space was naturally required where there were no children and a medium-sized hut could conveniently serve two families; besides, with two lamps it could be kept more comfortable, especially when fuel was scarce. Again two families that had not seen each other for some

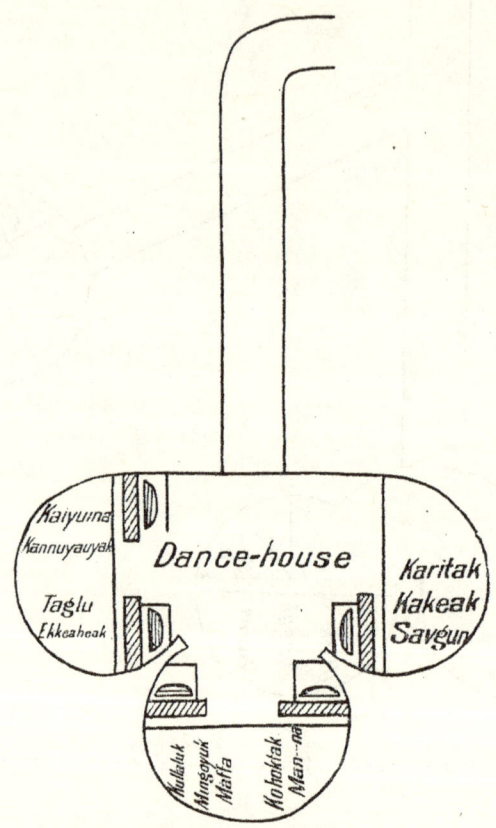

Fig. 23. A three-roomed dwelling with a dance-house

time naturally liked to be together, so they would make their rooms · contiguous or join their passages.[1] The arrangements in one settlement were seldom followed in the next. As each family reached the camping-place the man would choose his site, and those who came up later would have to search round for themselves. Sometimes two would decide to build together before they started out, sometimes not until they chose their sites. It was rare for two families that lived together in one settlement to stay together in the next, apparently because they had tired of each other's company and were anxious for a change. Where two families shared a single room, each as a rule kept to its own side of the hut, though there was never anything to mark a division between them.

---

[1]Mr. Stefansson (Anthrop. Papers, A.M.N.H., Vol. XIV, pt. I, p. 293) says, "I was told that usually, but not always, double houses are built by those who are in the habit of exchanging wives." It is true that they do sometimes build double or two-roomed houses in such cases, but just as often they live in separate huts, and a two-roomed house in itself raises no presumption of wife-exchange.

In February, 1916, I was travelling in Coronation gulf, and in my party were an Eskimo and his wife. They built a snow-hut for themselves each night while the rest of us slept in a tent. One night while we were camped on the ice a blizzard sprang up and raged all the next day. The dogs refused to face it in the morning, so we had to stay where we were until it abated. There was no wood of course on the ice, and we had very little kerosene for our primus lamp, so our tent was cold and uncomfortable. Two of the Eskimos therefore turned out and built an extension to the snow-hut, then broke down the inter-

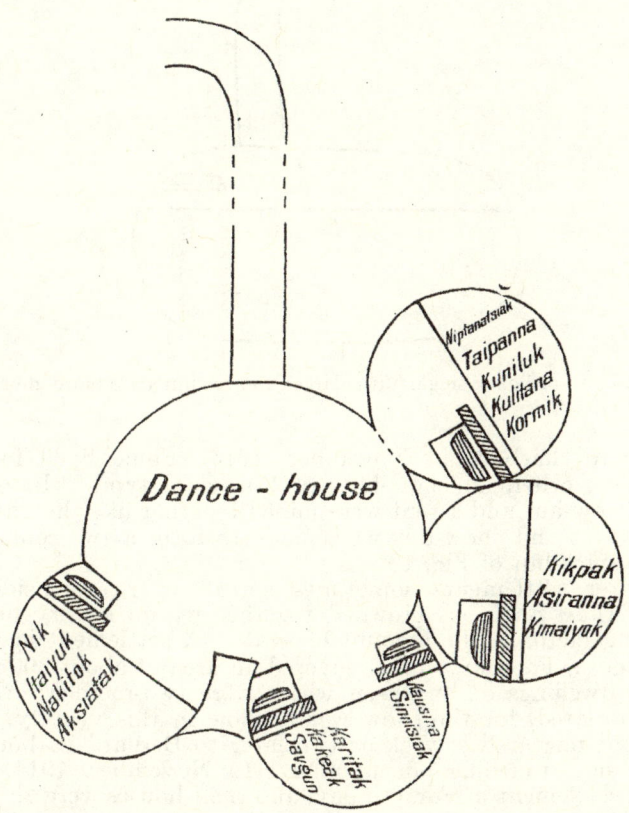

FIG. 24. A four-roomed dwelling with a dance-house

vening wall. This gave an oblong structure, rounded at the ends, with a long platform for the bed and a very narrow space for the floor in front. The woman kept a small blubber lamp burning in one corner, resting on a block of snow. Her place was right beside it, while the rest of us occupied the remainder of the platform. The original passage was left in place, but was slightly extended and its mouth curved away from the wind. The shape of this hut was therefore very unusual, but it was only a make-shift to shelter us while the blizzard lasted. The Eskimos often enlarge a deserted hut in this way to provide a travelling party with accommodation for the night (Fig. 25).

In the fall of the year, when the natives return from inland to resume their winter life, the snow is not everywhere suitable for building a hut. Consequently they have recourse to their heavy spring tents, and only abandon them when they reach some convenient place in which to cache them until the spring. This occasionally leads to curious combinations. A large band of Eskimos

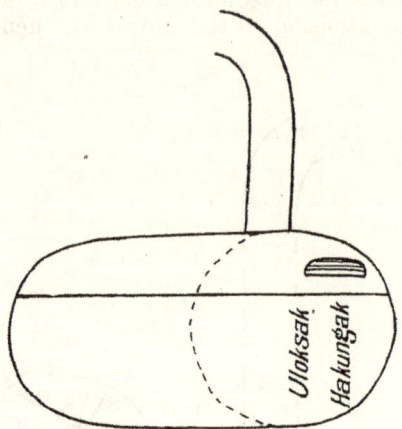

FIG. 25. An ordinary single hut enlarged to accommodate more inmates

settled in Bernard harbour in November, 1915. Some lived in tents with passages of snow, others in snow-huts of the usual types. In one case the passages of a snow-hut and a tent were joined together like the huts in Fig. 17, in another the tent and snow-hut were made to form a two-roomed dwelling, like the double snow-hut of Fig. 19.

These winter settlements sometimes spread over a considerable area, while at other times they are crowded together within a very narrow space. The determining factor is the amount of snow. A settlement in the Duke of York archipelago in February, 1915, covered an area of about 300 x 125 yards. There were 21 dwellings, only five of which were two-roomed; the rest were all single and isolated, for the snow was shallow in this vicinity. When half of the settlement migrated a week or two later to Bernard harbour they built their houses almost touching one another. In November, 1914, the Puivlik Eskimos had a settlement in Forsyth bay, and their houses were all two-roomed, or in pairs with common passages, arranged in a single line along the face of a low ridge. Their next settlement was made behind a sandspit about four miles along the coast. Here most of the houses again were two-roomed, or in pairs, but the line was very irregular and there was a single house standing about 100 yards away from the rest. Their third settlement was at Putulik, one of the Liston and Sutton islands. In this their houses followed roughly the line of the shore, and the single huts were in the minority. At the end of February they migrated to the westward, and were joined by other natives; but now they were living far out on the ice and had no shore to guide their planning, so their huts were scattered in all directions. Fully half of them were detached and single, while the rest were two-roomed or in pairs with common passages. In the middle of March they moved west again, at least all who had not before that time gone eastward and joined the Eskimos of Coronation gulf. One man now set up a large skin tent, the rest building ordinary huts of snow; but since there was only one long drift which offered a sufficient depth of snow they built their houses side by side, some single, others in pairs with the passages linked together; in one case three families joined their passages. Three late-comers had to build some distance away, though still along the same bank of snow; their huts were single, two of them facing south like all the rest, but the third opening northwards, because only in that direction could snow be found to build the passage.

It is clear therefore that M. Mauss' description of the typical snow hut is not applicable to this region. He says, "Il est, d'ordinaire, multiple, composite; c'est-à-dire que deux ou trois iglous s'agglomèrent ensemble et viennent débou-cher sur un même couloir; il est toujours excavé en terre; il est toujours muni d'un couloir dont le débouché est à demi souterrain; enfin, il contient, au mini-mum, deux bancs de neige avec deux places de lampes." In the first place single houses are as common as two-roomed huts, or huts joined in their pas-sages. The entrance is by no means always half-underground; often indeed it is on exactly the same level as the surrounding field of snow, though since the blocks of which it is built are generally cut out of its floor, it usually lies about a foot below that level.[1] Finally it is not true of these Eskimos that the hut contains at least two platforms and two lamps, though this may be the usual type in Hudson bay.[2]

The dance-house is not always built over the huts of the same family or families. At the end of a day's migration the men are usually tired, and gladly retire to rest as soon as their huts are finished and the women have prepared a hasty meal. The dance-house is never built till the following day, or even later. Someone, usually a man of influence, will take the initiative, and a friend or relative will co-operate with him, nearly always, of course, the man over whose house he proposes to build. A dance-house can never stand alone, at least not in winter, because there would be no lamp to keep it warm; and it is preferable to build it in front of a two-roomed house rather than of a single hut because then there will be at least two lamps to heat it.

There are two courses open to the Eskimo in March, when the sun begins to climb higher in the sky and its warmth makes the snow-hut drip intolerably: he may either move at once into his spring tent, or he may build a snow-hut as before, but roof it over with skins instead of with a dome of snow. The latter is the simpler method, but makes an uncomfortable dwelling because the roof is apt to be low. Moreover at this season of the year the Eskimos are already preparing to leave the ice and take to the land for the spring and summer, when a tent is indispensable. Consequently most of them use their tents, though sometimes when these have been cached some distance away the other method must be resorted to for a few days. Hanbury mentions spring snow-huts roofed with skins in the neighborhood of Baker lake.[3] Occasionally they are constructed in the autumn also, when the snow is still too soft to cohere into a dome. We built a hut of this type in Victoria island on October 14, 1915, when travelling inland to pick up our summer caches. The walls settled some-what in the night, and the roof sagged heavily through the weight of the falling snow, so that by morning there was hardly a foot of space between the sleeping platform and the skins above. The hut was comfortable enough as long as we stayed in our sleeping bags, but when we tried to sit up and dress, the roof refused to budge a single inch, and our plight was really a most amusing one.

Each family chooses its own time for removing from a snow hut into a tent. The change nearly always occurs at the end of a day's migration, for at this season of the year no settlement lasts longer than two or three weeks. In

[1]The warmth of the house is materially increased by making the entrance of the outer passageway slightly higher. The Eskimos are fully aware of this; a native told me that his hut was cold because it was built on a sloping bank and the entrance to the passage was lower than the level of the house. It was early in the fall, and he could not remedy the defect, because nowhere else was the snow deep enough to build.

[2]Cf. Boas, Bulletin A.M.N.H., Vol. XV, pt. I, p. 9 *et seq*. and Fig. 140.

[3]Hanbury, p. 75.

1915 one man set up his tent at the end of February; but this was exceptionally early, and no one followed his example till the latter half of March. In the following year the winter was very severe and spring began rather late; no one dreamed of moving out of a snow-hut till the beginning of April. During the first week of that month there were three settlements within twenty miles of Bernard harbour. One, twelve miles east, consisted of five snow-huts and one tent. The second, between the two eastern islands of the Liston and Sutton group, had nine tents and only one snow-hut; the latter belonged to two little girls, who had induced some boys to build it for them that they might play at housekeeping. The third settlement was twenty miles west of the Liston and Sutton islands and consisted of snow-huts only, sixteen in number.

The spring tent of a prosperous Eskimo is very heavy, both on account of its size and from the weight of the deerskins of which it is composed. Skins and poles together weigh upwards of seventy pounds, and occupy a good deal of space on the sled. The tent is as large as, often larger than, a good-sized snow-hut, that is to say it will measure perhaps 15 feet from front to back, with a maximum breadth of 11 feet and a height of about 7 feet. Ten or twelve poles support the ridge-pole, and short sticks, snow-beaters, walking-sticks, etc., poked in behind the poles keep the tent stretched taut. The four or five poles at the far end, which are lashed together at the end of the ridge-pole, give it a semi-circular back. While the man is fastening these together, his wife will lash two others to the front end of the ridge-pole, leaving a triangular opening. The other poles are then ranged along the sides, leaning against the ridge-pole without being lashed, and the tent is drawn all round the frame, encircling it on the back and sides and half closing up the front.

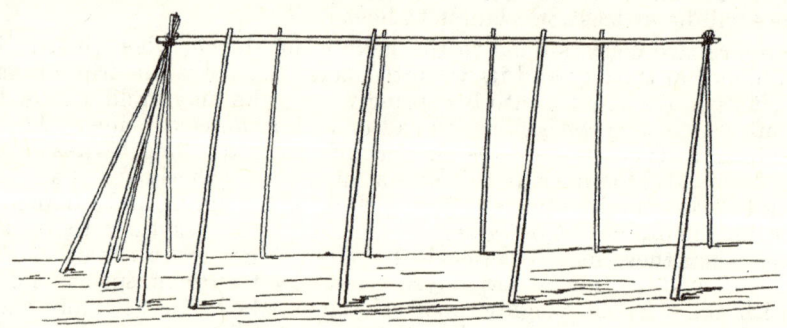

Fig. 26. The frame of a spring tent

The woman now laces the tent along the ridge-pole and halfway down the front, while the husband anchors it securely around the bottom with stones or blocks of snow. If the weather is still cold, and the snow is suitable, a low snow wall is first erected and the tent poles planted on top. Then a foot or so outside it another low wall is made all round and the interspace filled with soft loose snow. Into this low wall the edges of the tent are pegged, and more loose snow is stamped over it to keep out any draught. Finally, on top, are placed the bags of clothing and other articles that are not required inside the tent.

The front of the tent is now broad and gaping, but the sleeping platform must be arranged before it is closed up, the table and lamp and drying rack set up on snow-blocks, and the bedding and household utensils passed inside. After this is done a short passage of snow-blocks is built as in the case of an ordinary hut. Sometimes the passage is made before the goods are passed inside, for there is still a gap between the end of the passage roof and the apex of the front wall of the tent. When everything is entered this gap is closed with a skin, which is tied or jammed in some way at the top and covered with snow at the bottom.

Such a tent is rectangular, but with rounded ends to give it more space. Sometimes, however, the front is finished off square, if the family is small and has little property to keep inside. The ridge-pole is often inclined so that the back of the tent is higher than the front. The gaping seam along the ridge can be stuffed with scraps of skin, odd mittens, hand-wipers of ptarmigan skins and anything else that lies to hand. The tent itself is generally made of caribou skins obtained in spring, the hair of which is long and loose and consequently unfit for clothing; about fifteen are required for a single tent. It is generally erected with the hair side out, as Mr. Stefansson says, but the rule is not invariable. Usually it takes about three days to sew a tent after the skins are scraped, but if the woman is very industrious, she may finish it in two. In the spring of 1915 a woman finished a tent in two days, while her mother-in-law was nearly a week in making one but a little larger; the second woman, however, was sewing other things at the same time, besides doing most of the cooking for our party. Her tent was not as strong as she had hoped, for the spring skins soon rotted and began to tear in several places; so in the fall, when our hunting was very successful and we had plenty of serviceable skins, she put fifteen of them aside to make a new tent.

An hour is easily consumed in setting up one of these tents, with its outer wall and passage of snow. They are very comfortable, however, and rather more spacious than the ordinary snow-hut. The doorway is the same as in a snow-hut, an oval gap in the snow, on a level with the bottom tier of blocks or sometimes a little lower, the snow-blocks for the passage walls being taken out of the floor. In stormy weather a wind-break of snow is often built along one side of the tent. As a rule there is no need of a window, for the days are long in spring and the obscurity inside the tent is rather a relief from the dazzling glare outside; occasionally, however, the passage is slightly enlarged at the side of the door and a window of ice inserted in the side. On April 15th, 1915, a tent in which the flame of the lamp extended about 18 inches gave a temperature of 43° F. at the front of the sleeping-platform, though the thermometer outside stood at zero. In the late spring, and also in the fall, when the snow is shallow or melting, a patch of bare ground is chosen for the camping-site and the edges of the tent are held down with large stones; a passage is impossible in such cases.

The interior arrangements of the spring tent are the same as in the snow-hut. When erected over a floor of snow it has a sleeping-platform, table and lamp exactly like the hut. On bare ground a platform is impracticable, but the bedding is arranged in the same way, though on a level with the floor. If the family still have a lamp and blubber they set it on the ground in the usual place, and arrange the cooking pot above it on two stones, one on each corner of the lamp. In most places, however, by the time the snow has melted there is plenty of other fuel available, willow or heather or the *Dryas octopetala*, and the stone lamp is cached away until the fall. In fine weather cooking takes place out of doors, but whenever it is cold or windy a hearth is made just inside the doorway. The smoke soon fills the tent and slowly drifts out of the entrance; if it becomes unendurable the flap in the rear of the tent is raised a little, and the current of air that pours in drives the smoke through the doorway.

Another kind of tent is occasionally seen, a conical tent like the Indian tipi. Unlike the tipi, however, the skin covering reaches to the very top of the cone, for the blubber lamp, if properly trimmed, gives out hardly any smoke and a venthole is unnecessary. This tent, like the rectangular one, can be raised on snow-blocks and furnished with a passage; one that I saw in Coronation gulf was about 18 feet high, while its diameter at the bottom was about 20 feet. Possibly this was the kind of tent that Hearne saw at the mouth of the Coppermine river, though his description is far from clear. It is much less common than the rectangular tent, yet the Copper Eskimos have used it for as long as they can remember. The conical tent described by Murdoch from Barrow, Alaska, and by Mr. Stefansson from the Mackenzie delta, differed from the Copper Eskimo type in that only four or five of the poles reached the apex of the cone, the remainder leaning against a hoop that passed over the principal poles some 6 feet from the ground.[1]

(Photo by R. M. Anderson).

FIG. 27. A spring tent with an outer wall and passage of snow-blocks

The inland Eskimos of northern Alaska, and some of the Mackenzie natives, often use bee-hive tents of an altogether different shape; originally they were made of deerskin, but this has now been superseded by cloth. The frame is of pliant willow sticks, which are bent over in pairs and lashed together to form a series of arches.[2] The Copper Eskimos, however, are unacquainted with this style of tent, which is more akin to one used by the Indians.

The summer tent of the Copper Eskimos has the same shape as their rectangular spring tent, only it is much smaller and made of lighter skins. Often indeed, they use not deerskins but sealskins, from which the hair has been

---

[1]Murdoch, p. 86; Stefansson, Anthrop. Papers, A.M.N.H., Vol. XIV, rt. I, p. 26 *et seq.*
[2]See the excellent photographs in E. de K. Leffingwell, The Canning River Region, Northern Alaska, Interior Department, U.S.G.S., Professional Paper 109, Plate VII., Washington 1919.

removed, or sometimes both deerskins and sealskins combined; a family from Prince Albert sound had a tent even of musk-ox skins. Walking-sticks, ice-pick handles, and fish-spears serve for poles, with the addition of one or two light sticks that are generally carried along for this specific purpose. The doorway is more open than in the spring tent, since the ends are rarely long enough to meet in front without making the interior too restricted; even with the end partly open the occupants barely have room to stretch themselves out at night. Such a tent is comfortable and airy enough in fine weather, but it affords very poor shelter in a storm. The rain drips through the seam along the ridge, and the wind beats in through the open door while the poor Eskimo crouches shivering within. He can raise it up on walls of turf, or in the fall on snow-blocks, and block his door with a spare skin, but these are sorry makeshifts; so, before the rigour of the autumn overtakes him, he generally retraces his foot-steps and recovers the heavy tent he used in spring.

(Photo by R. M. Anderson)

Fig. 28. A summer tent at the fishing lake behind Bernard harbour

The interior arrangement of the summer tent differs in no way from the spring tent as above described. Often both in spring and summer two tents are joined together so as to have a common entrance, like the common passage of a two-roomed hut. They then lie, not in a straight line, but at an obtuse angle with one another so that the walls meet together on the side facing the common door. Just as in the snow-hut, more than one family sometimes sleep in a single tent; but, as every household has a tent of its own, this seldom occurs except when one is visiting another, or when a party wanders off on a hunting or fishing excursion for a few days, and leaves most of its property behind.

All over the country the Eskimos have left traces of their camping sites in the shape of rings of stones that have once held down their tents, with the hearth-stones lying a few feet to one side. Early explorers have often noticed these in other regions.[1]   There are remains of caches too, heaps of stones that have covered meat or blubber or clothing to protect them from the wolverines and foxes.   Near Bernard harbour there were many remains of all these kinds. Some of the rings were very small and may simply have been weights to hold

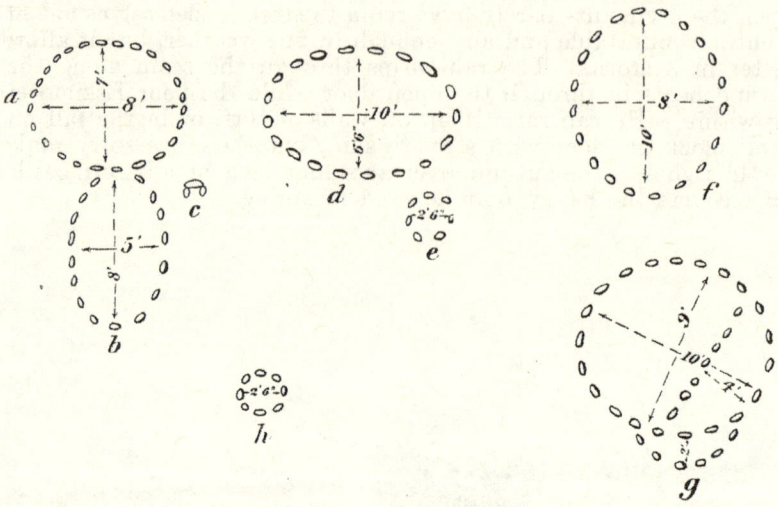

FIG. 29. Stone rings on an old camp site near Bernard harbour

down drying deerskins; others were plainly tent-rings, for there were hearth-stones close beside them.   Often not far away were large overturned boulders, to which the natives had fastened their dogs.   The plans and dimensions of some of those rings are given in Fig. 29.

[1]Cf . McClintock, p. 168, *et passim;* Parry, Vol. I, p. 70f.

CHAPTER VII

SOCIAL ORGANIZATION

The Copper Eskimos, like all the other branches of their race, have built up their society on the basis of the family, the term family being taken to mean a man, his wife and their direct descendants. There are certain peculiarities, however, in their conception of the family, and the angle from which they regard the various relationships, both within and without it, differs considerably from our own. This is evident from their kinship terms, a table of which is given below. As the vocative forms are never used in some cases, I have given throughout the forms for the 3rd person singular.

| Term | Relation to Male or Female | Meaning[1] | |
		Relation to Male	Relation to Female
(1) *atata*	grandfather (father's father?)		
(2) *atatsianga*	grandfather (mother's father?)		
(3) *ananga*	grandmother		
(4) *angota*	father[2]		
(5) *arna*	mother[3]		
(6) *nutara*	child		
(7) *irninga*	son		
(8) *pannia*	daughter		
(9) *kattangota*	sibling[4]		
(10) *angayua*		older brother	older sister
(11) *nukka*		younger brother	younger sister
(12) *alekka*		older sister[5]	
(13) *neya*		younger sister	
(14) *annia*		....	older brother
(15) *akalluanga*			younger brother
(16) *inrotata*	grandchild		
(17) *pangnaryua*	paternal uncle		
(18) *atsia*	paternal aunt		
(19) *anga*	maternal uncle	....	brother's child
(20) ?	maternal aunt....		
(21) *kangiganga*		brother's child	
(22) *oyorua*		sister's child	
(23) ?			sister's child
(24) *nuatkattia*	kinsman or relative[6]		

[1]The Rev. H. Girling has kindly confirmed the accuracy of most of these terms.

[2]Lit. "man", or "male".

[3]Lit. "woman", or "female". Little children often use *amama* as the term of address.

[4]"Sibling", a new word coined by American anthropologists, combines the meanings of both "brother" and "sister"; that is to say, it denotes common parentage without making any distinction in regard to sex.

[5]I have heard the word *agarulua* used once or twice instead of *alekka* but this may be due to the influence of Mackenzie river Eskimos. It is certainly not the usual term in Coronation Gulf.

[6]The Barrow (N. Alaska) word is *nunakattia*, which means "place-companion" or "fellow-countryman". Since all the Eskimos living in one place are connected in some way, either by affinity or consanguinity, the term naturally acquired the additional meaning of "relative" or "kinsman". The derivation of the Copper Eskimo word *nuatkattia* is uncertain.

Term	Relation to Male or Female	Meaning	
		Relation to Male	Relation to Female
(25) *uwinga*	husband		
(26) *nulianga*	wife		
(27) *arnakattia*	alternate wife (where two men interchange wives)		
(28) *angotaukattia*	alternate husband[1]		
(29) *ukkwanga*	daughter-in-law	older brother's wife	sister-in-law
(30) *ainga*	....	younger brother's wife	brother-in-law[2]
(31) *ningauga*	son-in-law	sister's husband[3]	
(32) *hakkianga*	parent-in-law	wife's brother[4]	
(33) *tiguanga*	adopted relative		

In this classification there are two important points that stand out clearly. The first is that the Copper Eskimos are more concerned with the nature of the relationship than with the sexes of the individuals themselves. Where we make a distinction between nephew and niece they draw the dividing line between a man's and a woman's brother's child, and a man's and a woman's sister's child (22, 24, 25; cf. 20-23). The second point is that in the case of siblings there are six distinct terms which differentiate according to age and sex (10-15). There are no separate terms for grandson or granddaughter, nor even a general word for parent, though this is found in some other Eskimo dialects (e.g. Barrow *anak*). Again there is no distinction of parallel and cross cousins; all are included together in the general term *nuatkattait*. Whether first cousins are allowed to marry or not is uncertain. The Rev. H. Girling thought that they were; on the other hand I know of a case where a girl would sleep indifferently with her brother or with her cousin, the latter a young man of about 17 years, though there was no question of marriage between them. Rink says that in Greenland the Eskimos disapproved of marriage between cousins.[5]

Adopted children are classed as real children; an adopted child, for example, may not marry the real child. The same rule naturally applies to half-brothers and half-sisters. The girl above mentioned eventually married her step-cousin, so there is a limit to the restriction in this case. An interesting point in regard to this marriage is that the step-cousin was also the adopted son of the girl's step-father.

Children, as they grow up and marry, form new and distinct families of their own. I have already spoken of the Eskimo family with which I spent the summer of 1915; the man Ikpakhuak, his wife Higilak, her daughter (by a former husband) Kanneyuk, and Ikpakhuak's adopted son Haugak (who was really his nephew, being the son of a deceased brother). Higilak's married son Avranna and his wife Milukkattak accompanied us all through our wanderings. Occasionally, for convenience, both families lived in a single snow-hut or tent, but nearly always each had its own. Kanneyuk generally remained with her

[1] Cf. Lacombe, Dictionnaire de la Langue des Cris, p. 671.
[2] *Ainga* is therefore the term for a "sibling-in-law" of the other sex, except in the case of the older brother's wife. It is difficult to understand the reason for this exception. There is no trace of the levirate; indeed a man is apparently not allowed to marry his deceased brother's wife.
[3] Possibly the same word *ningauga* is used also for "wife's brother" (male speaking), and so is a generic term for a "man's brother-in-law". See next note.
[4] No other term was found for this relationship, though perhaps *ningauga* may be used instead. *Hakkianga* is certainly used for other "-in-law" relationships, e.g., in place of *ukkwanga*, and is probably the general term for them all.
[5] Meddelelser om Grønland, Vol. XI, p. 23.

mother, but not infrequently she accompanied her brother and his wife on short excursions that lasted only a few days. The implements and household utensils of the two families, even their stores of fish and meat, were kept strictly apart, just as if no bond of kinship had united them; each woman, for example, had her own blubber pokes and her own racks of drying fish. In many little ways, however, family ties assert themselves. Milukkattak might often be seen dressing skins for Higilak, or helping her to pack before a migration; the same was true of Arnauyuk, an orphan girl whom Ikpakhuak had adopted shortly before her marriage. When either parent dies, the other finds a home with one of the married children, or lives with each in turn, while the orphaned child is always cared for by an elder brother or an uncle.

Fig. 30. Two summer tents joined together

Each family then has normally its own hut or tent, although on rare occasions, and under special circumstances, two families may share the same dwelling; in the latter case each has its separate half of the hut, though no fixed dividing line is set between them. Every inmate has certain definite duties to perform, and a definite place on the sleeping platform. The woman sleeps in the corner beside her lamp, and the little children lie between her and her husband. Outside of him sleep the older children, then any guest whom they may happen to entertain. One old man, however, would always change places with his wife at night after they got into bed, so that she would not disturb him when she rose in the morning to light the lamp and attend to her household duties. His position in the corner, too, had another advantage—it was less convenient for him than for his wife to turn out in the night when the dogs created a disturbance.

The custom of interchanging wives for a longer or a shorter period leads to a curious extension of the family[1]. The children of the two families are considered as brothers and sisters, *katangotit*, and marriage between them is forbidden. Apparently this is not due to any uncertainty as to their real parentage (a circumstance that must sometimes occur nevertheless), for the exchange may have been effected only once, and each family have two or three children. The head

[1]Cf. the discussion by Gilbertson in the Journal of Religious Psychology, Vol. VII.

of a visiting family will often connect himself in this way with the group that he is visiting; he ceases to be a stranger, and therefore a potential enemy, in his new community. A Kanghiryuak family, for example, arranged such an exchange with a visiting Puivlik family in the summer of 1915. Often, however, the same bond is found uniting two families that live more or less permanently in the same district. An exchange is then most likely to occur when they come together again after being separated for a few months[1]. Thus the Noahognik Eskimo Aksiatak who spent the summer of 1914 on the south side of Dolphin and Union strait exchanged wives for a night with the Puivlik native Haviuyak as soon as the two groups came together again in the fall. The exchange took place in the most casual and informal manner, without the slightest attempt at concealment. It was repeated a week later, although on the second occasion, instead of the women temporarily changing huts, it was the men who moved over. Similar instances occurred frequently later; in fact they were so usual that they passed almost unnoticed in the communities.

Occasionally there is some definite advantage to be derived from an exchange of wives. Thus a few weeks after the above-mentioned incident Haviuyak's wife accompanied Aksiatak to an Akulliakattak settlement on south-west Victoria island, because she wanted to visit her sister there; Aksiatak's own wife, of course, remained behind to keep house for Haviuyak. In many cases, however, lust seemed to be the only motive. The shaman Uloksak was one of the most influential men among the western Copper Eskimos; moreover he had three wives. In December, 1915, he sent two of them over to Avranna's hut one evening, and the latter had to send back his own wife Milukkattak in exchange, although she was then with child. The same thing happened again a month later. Milukkattak, in speaking about it afterwards, said that neither she nor her husband wanted to have any dealings with Uloksak and his family, but they were afraid of the shaman and did not dare to refuse.

The inhabitants of a settlement are all, or nearly all, *nuatkattait*, connected, that is, either by blood or by marriage.[2] Since no one person has any recognized authority over the rest, it is this bond of relationship that keeps the people united and maintains peace and harmony in the community. The vicissitudes of life, too, in these regions tend to prevent any discord, for there are many occasions, both in summer and in winter, when sickness or ill-luck in hunting will make a family dependent for a time on its neighbours. The *nuatkattait* owe special duties to one another. They must provide for each other in sickness, take care of the aged and infirm, the widows and the orphans, and support each other in the blood-feud[3]. This gives the community its solidarity. It has a corporate unity, and is called by a tribal name, the suffix *miut* added to the name of the region it inhabits, or to a prominent place in that region, such as a lake or river. Thus the Puivlirmiut is the group or tribe that inhabits the country of Puivlik, and the Kogluktomiut similarly the group that frequents the Kogluktok or Coppermine river.[4]

Strangers who come and attach themselves to the group try to connect themselves by marriage, or by establishing definite ties with individual members. Even temporary visitors do the same. When Kaksavik, the Pallik Eskimo from Hudson Bay, paid a three day's visit to the Dolphin and Union strait Eskimos, their foremost man Ikpakhuak made him his "dancing-associate", *numikattia*. In this way a permanent tie was established between the

---

[1] Dr. D. Neumann (The Eskimo, Nome, Alaska, March, 1919) says that in Alaska interchange of wives and adoption of children were not unusual at all reunions. Mr. Stefansson makes the same observation concerning the Mackenzie river natives (Anthrop. Papers, A.M.N.H., Vol. XIV, pt. 1, p. 164).

[2] Another word that is sometimes heard, *taukattait*, appears to be synonymous with *nuatkattait*.

[3] Aksiatak sprained his ankle in the early spring of 1915, and Ikpakhuak was ill for a week or more during the following winter. In both cases the invalids and their families were supported by the rest of the community.

[4] An individual of the tribe is designated by the addition of the suffix—*tak*, as *Puivlirmiutak*, "a native of Puivlik".

two men, to last till one of them died or a violent quarrel caused their estrangement. If at any time either should visit the other, he was sure of a dance of welcome and hospitable entertainment. In the same way when the Puivlik natives were welcoming the first Kanghiryuak family at Lake Tahiryuak Higilak adopted the visiting woman as her dancing-associate and Ikpakhuak adopted both the man and his wife. A few hours afterwards when the second family appeared a young Kanghiryuak man selected Milukkattak for the same honour. It is very common for a native to have two dancing-associates in a single community, one a man and the other a woman. Avranna, for example, found a married couple who were friends of this kind amongst the Kilusiktomiut, when we visited those natives in March, 1916. They gave a dance in his honour on the evening of his arrival. The dance-house was very small, there was no drum, and the whole settlement was on the verge of starvation, yet the welcome they gave him was none the less cordial on that account. They even made a special drum for him next day so that nothing might be lacking for his entertainment. It is by these two methods, then, by wife-exchange and by association in dancing, that the Copper Eskimo establishes friendships wherever he goes and travels from group to group without danger.

Often within a community one man will show special courtesy to another by sending him the hind flippers of every seal that he catches. This is a very delicate mark of attention, for the flippers are the parts that are most esteemed for food. The two men thus become *upatitkattik*, "flipper-associates," a relationship that is independent of kinship ties, and involves no other obligation than the return of the compliment in the same manner. It is never done with caribou, nor with anything but the common rough seal, since the bearded seal, *Erignathus barbatus*, is the property of all the hunters who are able to gather round the seal-hole when it is captured. Even with the rough seal a small portion is always sent over to each household, unless the settlement is too large for the meat to go all round.

Looser and more temporary ties are sometimes contracted. Two men will arrange to spend a summer together in a certain district, and naturally, during this period, a good deal of mutual assistance is required. A few rifles have now been introduced, and the natives keenly appreciate their superiority over bows and arrows. A man who possesses a rifle will sometimes associate himself with one who has none. This enables the two men to take turns in hunting, and while one with his bow and fishing gear wanders off after birds and fish, the other will take the rifle and scour the country for caribou. Each man, as far as possible, uses his own ammunition, but if one man's supply becomes exhausted he is free to use his companion's. The owner of the rifle naturally has more service from his weapon than his companion, who can make use of it, as it were, only by default. Still, it constitutes a bond of union between them, a not unimportant link in the welding together of the heterogeneous elements of the community.

DIVISION OF LABOUR.

The Copper Eskimos, like most hunting tribes, discriminate considerably between the work of the men and the work of the women. As a rule, the heavier tasks devolve on the men. They do most of the hunting, build the snow huts, and erect the heavy deerskin tents that are used in the spring and the fall. Their spare time is employed in minor work subsidiary to this, for example in making or mending their tools and weapons. During migrations the man does all the loading of the sled, his wife handing him the household goods through the doorway or through a hole in the wall. She helps him, however, to lash up the sled, while the children, if there are any, harness the dogs. On the trail the woman pulls ahead of the dogs, but the man hauls just in front of the sled, where he can urge on the dogs from behind; the son has a place beside his father, the daughter beside her mother. In the summer packing, the man generally carries the tent, with his tools and weapons on top of it; the woman has her own and her husband's sleeping gear, the lamp, if one is carried, and the cooking pot, while the children carry their own sleeping bags and their bows and playthings.

All the cooking and sewing fall on the women. In summer this often includes the gathering of fuel, though the children are usually sent out for this purpose. A man rarely condescends to gather fuel, and then only when he is alone with his family. Occasionally, in summer, he will cook a pot of meat if his wife is engaged for the moment in some other occupation, such as dressing skins, and he himself has nothing to do. The men often help their wives to scrape the skins, especially in the fall, when the daylight is short and new clothes are urgently needed for the approaching winter. Sometimes too they do a little sewing on their own account. An old man named Tusayok made a pair of water-boots for himself in the spring of 1915; the women were quite surprised at the excellence of his sewing, and talked about it for a long time afterwards.

Vice versa, a few of the women take part in the hunting and sealing. The eldest of Uloksak's three wives, indeed, was quite a noted caribou hunter. The same woman sometimes went sealing, as did also Milukkattak, Avranna's wife. The two of them went out together one day, leaving their husbands to mind the huts, and they often taunted the men with this afterwards. During my stay with Ikpakhuak the old man was teaching his little step-daughter to seal. She was only twelve years old at the time, and when she did finally transfix a seal in the winter of 1916 she had to call to one of the other hunters to help her drag her victim on to the ice. It is only the younger women, however, who go out hunting, though everyone, men, women and children, have to take part in the organized caribou-drive. Everyone, too, has to fish with rod and line through holes in the ice during the spring and fall. Even in their fishing, though, there are certain distinctions. Everyone uses the rod and line, but only the men as a rule employ spears. When the salmon are trapped in weirs during the late spring the men race about in the water jabbing at them with their spears, while the women catch them with their hands in the little stone caverns where they take refuge and string them on long seal-skin lines.

Very few women, I believe, can manage a kayak. Higilak attempted to paddle her husband's kayak one day, but she was unable to turn it round without capsizing it, and had great difficulty in making the land again. Few women too can build a snow hut, though all of them can make a perpendicular wall of snow five or six feet high. They know exactly how the hut should be built, however, even though they are unable to do it themselves. I saw an old woman directing a youth how to produce the spiral in the second tier of blocks, though the same woman, when called upon to make a short extension to the passage, was as awkward in fitting the blocks together as the merest novice.

PROPERTY.

Such a division of labour is naturally accompanied by a division of property. Roughly speaking three kinds of property may be distinguished, personal, family, and communal. Personal property comprises everything that is employed by the individual in his daily life. Most of these articles have been made by their owner, or else acquired by barter. In the case of a man they include his tools and his weapons, the tent and the sled, together with some or all of the dogs that drag the sled. The wife's property similarly comprises her household utensils and implements, the pot and the lamp with the boards and poles that support them (but not the table, it would seem), her knives, her fire-making apparatus, her sewing-kit, her fishing rod, and her walking stick. Some of these things she has received from her kinsfolk before she was married, others she has made herself or obtained by barter, while a few articles may have been made for her by her husband. One or more of the dogs, too, may be her property. Ikpakhuak had five dogs drawing his sled; three belonged to himself, one was Higilak's, while the fifth belonged to his step-daughter Kanneyuk. During the summer of 1915 Higilak's dog bore a litter of young ones. It was not possible to preserve more than two of them, and of these one was given to Kanneyuk; henceforward the girl had to take care of it, and carry it on the march until it was able to walk. Later, when she married, the dog would go with her to her new home. The same girl had a bow and quiver made for her by her step-father, who also made a set for his adopted son Haugak. Other things are given to children, and some they soon learn to make for themselves, such as marrow spatulæ and needle-cases. Clothing is always the property of the wearer. Articles picked up while travelling, like copper and pyrites, belong to the finder. Ikpakhuak found a large plank which had drifted ashore in Penny bay, and used it to make two fish-spears for himself. There was more wood than he needed in the plank, however, so he gave the rest to his kinsfolk.

The amount of property that may be accumulated in these ways by a single individual or family is considerable. It suffices for virtually all their needs, minor articles that they cannot make for themselves being obtained by barter with friends and relatives. How nearly self-sufficing an Eskimo can be is shown by a popular remark that is often quoted:—

"The man needs nothing but the heavy skin of the bearded seal for his boot-soles, and the skin of the young rough seal for socks."

Formerly everything except the stores of food and blubber could be carried on a single sled. The last few years, however, have seen a great increase in the amount of property each family owns.

When the expedition finally left this region in 1916, Ikpakhuak had acquired so many possessions that he was forced to convey them in relays whenever he travelled; and the same was true of other natives. Naturally they require more dogs now to drag their sleds; the problem of feeding them has been rendered a little easier by the introduction of firearms. When Mr. Stefansson first visited these Eskimos very few men had more than two dogs apiece[1]; now four and even five are not at all uncommon.

In cases of divorce the woman returns to her kinsfolk with all her property, and the man, who has generally no pot or lamp of his own, finds shelter with his people also. I do not know what becomes of the blubber pokes; probably, if they are filled with blubber, they are kept by the man. It is not unusual for friends and relatives to borrow from each other; the wife, for example, may often be seen wearing her husband's coat. If a woman has only one small lamp she will almost certainly borrow another from a neighbour to tide her over the winter. No payment is asked in such cases, although usually some trifle is given, or an extra portion of food sent over to the other hut. It is a curious thing, noticed also among Eskimos elsewhere[2], that if the borrower should lose or damage the article he makes no compensation of any kind; he merely expresses his regret at the loss and there the matter ends. Borrowed articles that have become damaged are usually not even mended before being returned to their owners. On the other hand, if an article, instead of being loaned, is offered as a gift, the recipient feels bound to make a return present of equal value, unless of course he declines to accept it altogether. At Lake Tahiryuak I shot three caribou which we were unable to take away with us, so, to prevent the carcasses from being wasted, I gave them to the two families of Prince Albert sound natives who were remaining there; each family visited me a few minutes later with an equivalent present. Normally among themselves a thing would not

[1]Anthrop. Papers, A.M.N.H., Vol. XIV, pt. I, p. 238.
[2]Boas, Bulletin A.M.N.H., Vol. XV, pt. II, p. 116.

be offered unless it was expressly asked for, and then the transaction would become ordinary barter. In the summer of 1915 two families separated from our party for about a month. I gave one of the women some matches, thinking they would serve both families until we met again. The woman kept the matches herself, and refused to give any to her companion. I questioned Higilak about it, but she thought the woman had acted quite rightly: "She is an Eskimo", she said, "and we don't give presents like you white men."

Disputes are liable to arise in hunting about the ownership of game, since two or three men may wound a caribou with their arrows. The hunter who inflicts the first wound is entitled to the booty, but, to prevent ill feeling, he generally gives some of the choicer parts of the meat, a whole saddle if he is generous, to his comrade. Avranna fired at a young caribou and grazed its leg. The animal was practically unhurt, and would have escaped us altogether had I not brought it down with a second shot. The deer nevertheless was Avranna's. If the caribou had made good its escape, though, and been brought down later, he would have had no claim. Ikpakhuak came upon a caribou that had been slightly wounded earlier in the day by another hunter. He shot it, and it was recognized as his property, all that the other man could claim being the arrow point that remained in the wound.

The family own all the food and skins that are acquired by any of its members, with this restriction, that all or some of the food must be shared with the neighbours. The amount that is kept by the family for itself depends on the quantity of food in camp at the time. If ten seals, for example, are caught in one day, and there are only six families in the camp, it is obviously unnecessary to send more than a tiny portion of the meat to each household. On the other hand, if only one seal is caught, the whole of the meat must be distributed, otherwise some of the people would go hungry. I accompanied Ikpakhuak on a sled trip to Penny bay in the spring of 1915, to bring back some caribou meat and fat which he had cached there the previous summer. On the return journey we stayed at a settlement of five Akulliakattak families. As soon as we arrived Ikpakhuak selected a little meat and fat from our load for each of the houses, enough for about one meal for one person in each house. That night we were one family's guests, and feasted on our deer-meat and on some seal-meat cooked by our hostess. Small pieces of cooked seal-meat were sent over to us later from each of the other houses.

In the winter, when each housewife cooks in her own hut, she can hide away some of the choicer portions of the meat for her husband and herself to eat after all the visitors have left; but in summer, when most of the cooking is done out of doors, everyone gathers round the pot to eat and no concealment is possible. Surplus food is the property of the family, and can be stored away for a future occasion. In summer innumerable caches of deer-meat and fish are strewn all over the country, each of which is the property of a single family. It is a serious crime to rob one of these caches, except under pressure of starvation.

Within the family the food belongs equally to all the members. The woman naturally takes charge of it,[1] but the husband and children may help themselves at any time. When a meal is in progress every stray visitor who looks in for a moment must be offered something, even if it be only a tiny morsel of meat or fat. The man may be exceedingly unwelcome, but his hostess would hardly dare to neglect him for fear of public disapproval; but in such cases the visitor himself will usually decline the food. I tried to conform to their customs as far as possible while I was living in their midst and when cooking rice, for example,

---

[1] If a woman received some hardbread or similar food from us she invariably kept a portion for her husband or child, though they might be miles away.

would leave a little in the pot for such Eskimos as happened to be present. Often their would be twenty natives and only one plateful of rice among them all, but everyone, even the smallest child, had to receive a taste of it[1].

Even children are regarded in some respects as the property of their parents. It is the parents, for example, who decide whether a newly-born babe shall be reared or not. If it is cast out alive another couple may recover it and rear it as their own child without payment, the parents having lost all claim; but in all ordinary cases of adoption the parents must be compensated before they

(Photo by G. H. Wilkins)

Fig. 31. Caches raised on stones to protect them from the foxes

will relinquish their rights. Ikpakhuak paid the father of Haugak (the mother being dead) a knife and a wooden dish for the boy; thereafter the father ceased to have any claim on him, and he became a member of Ikpakhuak's family. When a girl marries, the husband as a rule pays her parents nothing, because the newly-wed couple generally remain in the same neighbourhood, and the parents still have the benefit of the girl's (and the husband's) services whenever they are needed; but if the husband intends to take his bride away to another place he has to compensate her parents for their loss.

The land is the property of the community which uses it as a hunting and fishing ground. Strangers have no rights there unless they are accepted as members of the tribe for the time being, and conform to its customs in such matters as the sharing of food. No Copper Eskimo family, of course, would dream of

[1]When living with Ikpakhuak and his family I would take what I wanted of the food, then hand the pot to Higilak to serve her husband. She would set out his portion, and her own with it, then pass round the remainder among the visitors. It was very amusing sometimes to watch her fill the spoon, tell some full-grown man to open his mouth, then cram the spoon and its contents nearly down his throat.

holding itself aloof, because without the assistance and guidance of the local natives it might starve to death through ignorance of the best fishing and hunting grounds. Natives from the Coppermine river basin and even from Bathurst inlet remained in Dolphin and Union strait throughout the spring of 1916 in order to be near the expedition; but they joined the local natives at their fishing weirs as soon as the salmon began to migrate, and merged themselves for the time being into the foreign community. The expedition refrained from using these weirs as long as the natives were there, but after they had left we caught a number of salmon in them, and no objection was raised; nor did the natives disapprove of our using nets in their rivers, or shooting the caribou, but only because it was obviously to their advantage that the expedition should remain in their country. Had food been scarce at the time they would have expected us to share our food with them, or at least to refrain from diminishing their own supplies by hunting and fishing in their territories.

Even the drum seems to be regarded as in some degree the property of the whole community, though it may be made by the labour of a single individual. There was the frame of a drum in the hut of Uloksak when I visited the Coppermine river Eskimos in February, 1915. The natives decided to hold a dance in my honour, and for this purpose the drum was repaired. Uloksak supplied the membrane of caribou skin, and four of the natives fastened it over the frame. The drum was always kept in Uloksak's house, and carried on his sled during migrations; but it was at anyone's disposal for a dance, and there would have been much ill-feeling if Uloksak had refused to hand it over.

Certain intangible things may be classed as property; at least they can be bought, sold and inherited. The control that a shaman exercises over the spiritual world may be bought by an aspirant to the same profession.[1] Thus Uloksak paid a number of caribou to a shaman for teaching him how to obtain the command over certain spirits. A shaman too must be paid for his services in curing disease or in driving away bad-luck. Aksiaktak's son fell from the roof of the dance-house and broke his thigh, whereupon a local shaman offered to heal the leg if Aksiatak would allow him to adopt the boy. The parents naturally did not wish to lose their son, the support probably of their old age in years to come, but they could not refuse for fear that he might remain a cripple for life. A Mackenzie river youth whom I used for a time as interpreter gained the reputation of being a shaman through a simple trick with a piece of string that he learned from Mr. Chipman. One of the Copper Eskimos whose knee was troubling him presented the youth with some seal meat and with a pair of mittens, requesting that he exercise his magic power to heal his knee.

INHERITANCE

A portion of the property is always laid on the owner's grave; the rest is divided among his kinsfolk, the children receiving most or all of it. The distribution is decided after a peaceful discussion, the elder children, as far as I am aware, having no priority of claim. Implements and utensils of value that may be left on the grave are often recovered in after years by one or other of the survivors, when time has effaced the memory of their misfortune. In the fall of 1915 Kanneyuk found a small lamp lying on the ground, evidently deposited on a woman's grave. No one knew for certain whose grave it was, though there were several conjectures; but as we needed a lamp at the time, Higilak told the girl to bring it in to camp.

Of more intangible things the inheritance of shamanistic power is the most important. Higilak, for example, learned shamanism from her father, and Ilatsiak, the greatest living exponent of the profession, was teaching his adopted son. Yet it is not quite correct to say that the power can be handed down.

---

[1] Cf. Stefansson, Anthrop. Papers, A.M.N.H., Vol. XIV, pt. I, p. 369.

All that the possessor can bequeath is a knowledge of the necessary procedure, and what may be called his " good-will in the business." The actual acquisition of the power depends on other factors which will be discussed in a later chapter.

One of the most noticeable features in Eskimo society almost everywhere is the absence of chiefs, and the Copper Eskimos are no exception. A man acquires influence by his force of character, his energy and success in hunting, or his skill in magic. As long as these last him age but increases his influence, but when they fail his prestige and authority vanish. Although there were at least half a dozen shamans in Dolphin and Union strait, and Ikpakhuak himself professed no shamanistic powers, yet his personal dignity, his sagacity, and his prowess as a hunter won him the most prominent place among the natives of this region. He had no delegated powers, no established authority, but his counsels always carried the greatest weight and his advice was constantly sought in all matters of importance. On my first visit to the Puivlik settlement in 1914 I carried on a little trading in the crowded dance-house, and one of the natives attempted to rob me of a long machete. The rest looked on and watched the outcome. Only Ikpakhuak had the courage to interfere; he seized the man's wrist and forced him to give up the knife. Even Ikpakhuak's influence, however, could not always prevent stealing, or secure the restoration of stolen property, even among his own people. Two boxes of .30-30 cartridges which he had cached on the coast in the summer of 1914 were stolen, and it must have been one of his kinsmen who perpetrated the theft, since there were no other natives in the vicinity at the time. His nephew was robbed of a knife in the following winter and could obtain no redress. In the spring of 1916 a case of .30-30 ammunition was stolen from the expedition's cache at Bernard harbour; Ikpakhuak secured about 15 boxes from one of the thieves, but the remainder we had to recover ourselves by a display of force.

The shaman Uloksak, who was credited with wonderful powers of control over the world of spirits, was probably not more than thirty years of age. He was bolder and more unscrupulous than most of the Eskimos, and for a time had considerable authority among the natives around the Coppermine river; but a streak of cowa dice in his nature finally brought discredit on him and destroyed much of his influence. Farther east, however, in Bathurst inlet, there was one man, Ilatsiak, who might with justice have claimed the title of chief. His fame as a shaman had spread far and wide, and he had no rival in that sphere. The most extraordinary powers were ascribed to him—he could discover the past, foretell the future, and, more than any other shaman, control the supply of game and the elementary forces of nature. In all matters relating to everyday life his integrity was beyond question; he had never been known to abuse his influence, or divert it to his own selfish ends at the expense of his fellow-countrymen. In stature he was below the mean, and he was well advanced in years—his beard, in fact, was quite white—but he was still vigorous and full of energy, and his movements quick and decided. His pleasant and open countenance wore usually a somewhat grave expression, and his manner was calm and dignified, but there was no trace of arrogance in his demeanour. Natives in his presence would recount the most wonderful tales of his shamanistic feats, and he would listen quietly, without either assenting or denying. His small black eyes were shrewd and sparkling, indicating a personality far in advance of the average Eskimo's. The natives of Bathurst inlet seemed to obey him without question. Frequently he led them on their migrations; he brought about forty of them with him to visit our station, and without question they were the most honest and the best behaved natives we ever had dealings with. The Rev. Mr. Girling informs me that Ilatsiak is now the very best friend that the missionaries have in this region; all his influence is being exerted on their behalf. He possesses intelligence enough, it seems, to understand the new conditions created by the coming of the white men, and to try and adapt himself and his people to the change. Even Ilatsiak, however, will probably lose his authority when infirmity overtakes him, and when he is gone there will be no one to take his place. The Eskimo is intolerant of anything like restraint. Every man in his eyes has the same rights and the same privileges as every other man in the community. One may be a better hunter, or a more skilful dancer, or have greater control over the spiritual world, but this does not make him more than one member of a group in which all are free and theoretically equal.

LAW AND ORDER

In a society such as has just been outlined, without law-courts, judges or chiefs, without laws even save the time-honoured customs handed down from one generation to another, crime can be held in check only if the majority of the people of their own accord unite in punishing the wrongdoer. Direct action of this nature, however, can rarely be taken, because there is no common council wherein the will of the people can find a voice, no spokesman to give it public expression, and no leader to translate it into action. The shamans, who might be expected under certain circumstances to take the initiative, are rivals of one another. Moreover they are frequently men and women of little credit or standing even among their own people; they themselves are the victims of injustice quite as often as the rest. For minor offences, therefore, such as theft and abduction, there is no remedy unless the victim takes the matter into his own hands and exacts compensation or vengeance. In the summer of 1914 Uloksak saw something he coveted in the possession of another Coronation gulf Eskimo. He tried to induce the man to sell it, and when the owner refused Uloksak hacked him across the wrist and side with his knife. In February of the following year the same man was sitting in Uloksak's hut as though there had never been any feud at all. He had not forgotten the incident though, for it was he who first told us about it, apparently with the idea that he might prejudice Uloksak in our eyes.

Feuds may be settled occasionally by single combat. I have no record among the Copper Eskimos of the regular stand-up fight such as occurs among the Netsilik Eskimos farther east.[1] They know of the custom, however, for Ilatsiak told me of a Netsilik Eskimo named Nuliagyuk who was injured for life in such a combat. He had quarrelled with Kallahea, a native rather smaller than himself, and challenged him to single combat. Nuliagyuk struck the first blow and knocked his adversary down; but the latter quickly rose and gave Nuliagyuk such a buffet on the temple that he destroyed the sight of one eye and broke or dislocated his jaw-bone.

It is quite possible that similar combats happen occasionally among the Copper Eskimos also, for two men in Dolphin and Union strait settled a dispute by pelting each other with dog excreta. As a rule, however, the quarrel is either dropped or settled in a more deadly manner. A native who had a grudge against Ikpakhuak threatened to enter his hut one day when he was sleeping and shoot him, but as a hundred miles or more separated the two men, Ikpakhuak's tranquility remained undisturbed. In the winter of 1914-15 a Kanghiryuak woman named Keyuk taunted another woman of the same tribe with childlessness, and the latter stabbed her in the stomach with a knife and killed her. In the following year a man of the same people was sitting in his hut sharpening a knife that he had just made, when a neighbour entered and began to jeer at him,

---

[1] Mr. G. H. Wilkins witnessed a fight with fisticuffs in Prince Albert sound, but the combatants were merely youths.

saying that he did not know how to make a knife. The owner quietly continued
to sharpen his weapon until its edge was keen enough, then drove it into the
jester's stomach with the remark, "Now see if I can't make a knife."

In neither of these cases, as far as my information goes, was the murderer
punished. There is always the danger though that one day a relative of the
deceased may avenge him by driving a knife into the murderer's back. Usually
the danger is avoided by flight. A man named Ekkeahoak was stabbed near
Lambert island, about 1913, by a companion named Hitkok. The murderer
fled to the eastward, and in 1914 was living near Bathurst inlet. Ekkeahoak's
daughter in speaking of the affair expressed no bitterness towards Hitkok, and
probably if he had returned to Dolphin and Union strait he would have been
left perfectly unmolested. Such at least was the opinion that other natives
expressed; the murder had taken place long ago, they said, and no one wanted
to remember it or to wreak vengeance on the murderer.

Sometimes, even when the evildoer escapes scot-free, his purpose is frus-
trated by the rest of the community. Tamauyuk, an east Coronation gulf
native, coveted Kingollik, the wife of a man named Ailanaluk, so one day when
Ailanaluk was spearing fish Tamauyuk went up behind him and stabbed him to
death with his knife. The murderer then took the woman from her tent and
forced her to become his wife, but the other natives interfered and took her
away from him.

About 1908, at Asiak, east of Kent peninsula, a woman named Mittik was
accused of causing a man's death by sorcery. At once a quarrel arose, for this
was a straight charge of murder, and a man was stabbed with a knife. He ran
outside to get his rifle, but fell dead in the snow before he reached it. Another
man stabbed his murderer, then three men were shot, but none fatally. The
feud seems to have ended at this stage, no one being willing to carry it further.
An even more serious affray had occurred in the same region a few years earlier.
There had come to the settlement from Netsilik an elderly couple with three
sons, the eldest of whom brought his wife with him. An Asiak native wanted to
share the woman, but the young man objected to her having two husbands, and,
when he could not prevent it, stabbed his wife with a spear as she was stooping
down to enter her hut. The woman staggered outside and fell dead in the snow.
Her father then came up, and with the help of some of the other natives seized
the murderer and stabbed him to death. The second brother crept up behind
them and stabbed the father in the back, but the other natives pursued him and
stabbed him also. They now decided to put an end to the vendetta by destroying the whole family, so they killed the old father and wounded the third son
This boy, however, managed to escape, while the second son, who had been
stabbed with a knife, recovered through the care of his mother. Altogether
four people were killed and two wounded in this affair.

A somewhat similar incident occurred among the Ekaluktomiut. A man
named Savugaluk was stabbed in the dance-house one evening, but not killed
outright. For many years he remained an invalid, unable to hunt or to do any
work. Finally, as he was only a burden to the community, the Eskimos decided
to take his wife away from him and leave him to starve to death. Savugaluk then
stabbed his wife, so a man went into his hut and stabbed him. Thus both of
them perished.

Sometimes a native will resort to magic in order to wreak his revenge,
especially if he is afraid of adopting more open means. Two children died
among the Kilusiktomiut, and a man named Kavyektok laid the guilt at the
door of a Kanghiryuak family that was living in the settlement at the time.
Not long afterwards Kavyektok's hands became partly paralyzed, and he was
unable to work. The natives immediately put it down to sorcery; it was the
Kanghiryuak family, they said, that had taken this vengeance on him because
he had accused them of murder.

It is clear, therefore, that the maintenance of order in a Copper Eskimo community rests purely and simply on a basis of force. No man will commit a crime, save in the heat of passion, unless he believes that he can make good his escape until the affair blows over, or else that his kinsmen will support him against any attempt at revenge. Detection is certain; there is so little privacy in their lives that all the possessions and actions of a man are known to everyone around. Until recently, when firearms and steel knives and other articles of civilization were introduced, there was little inducement to steal, for practically all their possessions could be made or acquired without much labour. Murder, however, with its corollary, the blood-feud, has always been frequent, and nothing but external influence can prevent it. The natives came into conflict with civilized law for the first time in 1916, when a patrol of the Royal Northwest Mounted Police arrested and deported the murderers of the two French missionaries.[1] They learned then that the murder of a white man would inevitably lead to their paying the penalty at some time or another; but life will never be secured or progress possible to these natives unless swift and exemplary punishment is meted out for assassination within their own groups.

----

[1] Report of the Royal Northwest Mounted Police, Ottawa, 1916.

CHAPTER VIII

FOOD[1]

Fishing and hunting are the Eskimo's sole means of subsistence, and meat and fish are his staple diet. Neither the mainland in Coronation gulf nor the islands north of it furnish edible fruits or roots in any abundance. The only vegetable foods obtainable around Dolphin and Union strait are the sorrel, *kongulik*, (*Oxyria digyna*) and the watery alpine bearberry, *kovlut* (*Arctostaphylos alpina*); and even these are so rare and scattered that the wandering native rarely troubles to stoop down and pluck them. During the six months from May to October that I wandered with the Eskimos over south-west Victoria island, only once did I see a blade of sorrel eaten, and twice a few stray bearberries. The latter indeed often fail to reach maturity before they are overtaken by winter and covered with the falling snow, while most of those that do mature are eaten by the longspurs and the ptarmigan. Crowberries, *paunrat* (*Empetrum nigrum*) are sometimes eaten by the natives, but not cloudberries, *akpit* (*Rubus chamaemorus*), although they grow plentifully around Great Bear lake and perhaps in other places as well. Mr. Stefansson, in a letter commenting on this strange neglect of the cloudberries, says, " My western natives attempted to teach the local people the use of these berries. We found that some of the children picked it up rather readily, but some mothers were displeased at the idea of the children trying them and few of the women tasted them, though a good many of the men did."

The roots of *Polygonum* species—the *masu* that the Alaskan and Mackenzie river natives esteem so highly—are eaten only sparingly by the Copper Eskimos. The same letter of Mr. Stefansson that was quoted above contains a valuable note about this root. He states that it "is used to a slight extent for food in Bank's island by the Victoria island Eskimos when they are over there, and according to them it is used more extensively in the center of Victoria island, where the Prince Albert and Albert Edward Bay people used to meet. The first day we were at Rae River we joined the natives in a meal of *masu* roots and were told that they had been eating a good many for the preceding several days, for food had been scarce. We continued to eat *masu* during the summer, but we probably ate it oftener than would have been the case had I not had with me Alaska Eskimos who, I believe, commonly suggested it."

In seasons of scarcity, of course, the Copper Eskimos will resort to any kind of food. Thus several Kanghiryuak natives are said to have died through eating 'tea' (*niokak*) during a famine.[2] But the only vegetable food that enters their regular diet is the semidigested reindeer moss taken directly from the first stomach or rumen of the caribou. In summer when cutting up his deer the hunter usually eats as much as he wants of this and throws the rest away. Only occasionally is it taken to camp, where it is mixed with water till it has the appearance of spinach set out to soak. It is then left to stand for a few hours, and eaten cold. In the autumn, however, the stomach is allowed to freeze intact with the herbs inside and kept for the early winter, when it is cut into slices, distributed with the ordinary meat among the different families in

---

[1]Cf. for this chapter Stefansson, Anthrop. Papers, A.M.N.H., Vol. XIV, pt. I, p. 47 *et seq.*; and Dr. R. M. Anderson in the Ottawa Naturalist, October, 1918, pp. 59-65.

[1]This "tea" was probably a toadstool, called "tea" from a remote resemblance to the "tabloid tea" that was used by the expedition.

the settlement and eaten frozen.[1]   Mr. Stefansson thought that the natives never pour seal-oil on it because all their oil is cached on the coast in summer, and they have no opportunity of eating the two together; but this is not quite true, for the natives often take a small quantity of seal-oil inland with them in the spring, and in any case more reindeer-moss is consumed in the early winter, when the natives are living largely on seal-meat, than in summer. The real reason why the two are not eaten together is because there is a taboo against it.

The Copper Eskimos are predominantly eaters of fish and meat.   Collinson, who calls them a carnivorous race, says that for the most part they consume their food raw.[2]   This is not quite correct.   What Parry observes of the Eskimos of Igloolik is equally true of the Copper Eskimos, "they prefer to boil their food when they can obtain fuel."[3]   In winter, unless blubber for the lamps is unusually scarce, the principal meal of the day is always boiled seal-meat, but in summer the Eskimo often suffers from a scarcity of fuel and has to eat his food raw and unfrozen or merely sun dried.   Cooking under any circumstances is a slow and tedious process; using a lamp and blubber, it takes about an hour to boil the meat even after the snow has been melted.   In summer, using dry willow twigs for fuel, with the pot set on a small hearth of three stones (one on each side on which it rests and a third at the back to keep in the heat), the operation takes a little less time.   But willow is not always procurable; for example the Colville hills in many places contain neither willow nor its best substitute, heather, and the same is true of many places on the mainland.

In many places on the coast driftwood would supply the natives with a fair amount of fuel, if it were not deliberately avoided, as a rule, owing to the well-known Eskimo taboo against mingling products of the sea with those of the land.   Driftwood comes from the sea, so caribou, and fish that are caught in rivers and lakes, like trout and salmon, must not be cooked over a driftwood fire.   Seal-meat may, but seals supply their own fuel, while driftwood is scarce and impracticable in a snow hut.   The Eskimos frequently helped us to collect spruce sticks from the beaches so that we could cook our own seal-meat in a tent, on top of an iron stove.   They sometimes objected to our cooking caribou-meat when we were in their settlements on the ice, although we would point out that the taboos that applied to them were not equally applicable to us.   Once too they protested against our using cottonwood for cooking seal-meat; they said it would cause the weather to become very cold.   They have no scruples against cooking caribou-meat over a wood fire on land provided that the wood has not been washed up by the sea.   Generally they made shavings of any wood they used, because the pot, having string handles, could not be suspended over the fire, but had to be set on a stone hearth, which left only a small space underneath for the fire.   The taboo in regard to driftwood, however, seems to be dying out.   Dolphin and Union strait Eskimos would not cook over a driftwood fire even the salmon that were caught migrating up the streams to the lakes, though they had come directly from the sea only an hour or two before; but their scruples broke down when some Tree river natives told them that it was done at the east end of Coronation gulf.

In many places the only possible fuel during the summer is the *okauyak* (*Dryas integrifolia*), and this is an abomination.   Whenever it rains, or a dense mist covers the land, as often happens in the late spring and summer, the plant will not burn; while even if the weather is fine, but the wind a little boisterous, it is difficult to maintain a fire in the small half-open tent the natives use.   One day when I lay ill in my tent on Victoria island, the Eskimos detailed the little

---

[1]Dr. Anderson says that when the stomach contains woody grass fibre instead of the succulent reindeer moss it is usually discarded by the western Eskimos; whether this is true of the Copper Eskimos also is uncertain.

[2]Collinson, p. 285.

[3]Parry, Vol. III, p. 285. Cf. Murdoch, Am. Naturalist, Jan. 1887, p. 15.

girl Kanneyuk to stay behind and cook a trout for me while the rest went fishing. Kanneyuk lit a fire in the largest of our tents, but in the midst of her cooking a sudden gale of wind snapped the tent-pole and the tent collapsed on her head, upsetting the small pemmican can which served as a cooking pot. She moved to another tent and lit another fire, but it was not until three hours later that the cupful of water in which the fish was immersed approached the boiling-point, so feeble was the flame from the *okauyak* fire; by that time too the fish was so smoked that it was scarcely edible.

Fig. 32. Haugak bringing in *Dryas integrifolia* for fuel, Colville hills

It is no wonder therefore that the Eskimo frequently does not trouble to cook at all. Dried meat or fish gives him a satisfactory breakfast, and if he is fishing during the day he can always appease his hunger with the raw fish he catches. If the fish is large he will content himself with the intestines, if small he will probably devour it entire, sometimes not even excepting the bones. In winter the wife occasionally boils some seal-meat while her husband lies in bed, but frequently, more especially in the early half of the season when they still have a stock of frozen fish or caribou-meat on hand, they make their breakfast on that, after which both dress and the man goes off to his sealing while the wife stays at home and sews.

Owing to their manner of life there are no set hours for meals. Breakfast is eaten as soon as they wake, then usually nothing more till the day's work is over. In winter, when it is certain that the sealers will return as soon as it grows dark, each wife has always a substantial meal ready for her husband, and the smell of boiling seal-meat and steaming broth strike his nostrils as soon as he enters the hut. If the meat is not quite cooked he will often undress and eat in bed. In spring and summer, when the weather is mild and the daylight long, it is altogether uncertain when the husband will return. If the fishing is poor he will probably turn up as the sun reaches the west; if good, not until it is well in the north; while if he happens to be caribou hunting he may be absent twenty-four hours or more. The wife then cooks whenever she feels inclined, eats her meal alone, and puts some of the meat away for him so that he may eat the moment he returns. Woe betide the wife who keeps him waiting after a day spent in fishing or hunting! Even if the whole family has participated in the same pursuit the wife should return early, if possible, so as to have everything ready for the rest when they arrive in camp.

If the weather is inclement and the men unable to go out hunting they frequently spend much of the day in bed. The wife then cooks when she wishes, usually towards evening. A little food is often left on the table at night or beside the door of the tent close to their heads, so that they can reach out and eat, if they wake up, without stirring from their sleeping-bags.

The quantity of food consumed at one meal naturally varies according to the amount of fat it contains. Men and dogs will half-starve on a diet of lean caribou-meat, however plentiful, whereas half the quantity of blubbery seal-meat will satisfy their desires and keep them well nourished. The appetite of the average Eskimo is not abnormal; as Dr. Anderson has pointed out, it is no greater than that of a white man living under the same conditions on the same diet.

The fish and deer-meat dried in the summer, and the meat kept frozen from the autumn, are generally all consumed by the beginning of the new year. In these latitudes the sun disappears for the winter night about the beginning of December, and few seals are caught before the middle of that month. On December 6, 1914, "dinner" in an Eskimo's hut consisted of four courses, caribou-fat, frozen caribou-meat, a dried and very mouldy fish, and, last of all, a portion of boiled caribou-leg. The Eskimos were camped on the coast at the time, so the boiling of caribou-meat was not prohibited. They like to have a stock of caribou back-fat to eat with the frozen meat and to nibble at whenever they feel inclined. During the winter, however, seal-meat constitutes their principal, and for several months their only food. Small pieces of skin and blubber are frequently eaten both when cutting up the seal and later; especially is this the case with the bearded seal. A strip of blubber is usually left on the table inside the hut, and the visitor helps himself to a small cube of it about the size of a sugar lump. The liver and kidneys are always eaten raw, generally unfrozen, while the intestines of the bearded seal are considered a delicacy. So, too, are the flippers, both of the bearded seal (*Erignathus barbatus*) and of the rough seal (*Phoca hispida*). The blood is poured into a sealskin bucket, and kept for thickening the soup; generally it freezes into a solid lump.

To prepare a meal at this season the wife hangs the pot over the lamp, scours it out with her fingers, and fills it with crystalline snow, *anyu*, which she crushes with her ulo or more rarely with the horn snow-knife, *haviuyak*. The meat is placed in the cold water and slowly brought to a boil, when the surface is covered with a thick scum. It is then taken out, squeezed between the thumb and fore-finger to drain off the water, and laid on the table to cool. Seal blood, liquid or frozen, now takes its place in the pot; it too is allowed to simmer, then the steaming broth is dished out in musk-ox ladles (or any convenient dish) and handed round to everyone present.[1] A little raw blubber is nearly always eaten with the seal-meat, but most of it is consumed in the lamp or fed to the dogs. When migrating a little meat, either raw and frozen, or boiled on the previous day, is placed in a convenient place on the sled for lunch. In good

---

[1]For a fuller description of an Eskimo meal in winter, see Mr. Stefansson's excellent accounts, My Life with the Eskimo, p. 176 *et seq.*, and Anthrop. Papers, A.M.N.H., Vol. XIV, pt. I, p. 243.

seasons a considerable quantity of blubber is wasted until the warm days of spring, when it is carefully stored away in large bags and cached on the mainland or on an island near the shore for use in the following autumn.

Around Prince Albert sound and Minto inlet polar bears are almost as important an item of diet in winter as seals. The liver is said to produce sickness and is therefore never eaten. According to McClintock, the same thing is said in Greenland about the heart,[1] but whether this is so among the Copper Eskimos I do not know. Caribou are very numerous in the valley of the lower Coppermine river throughout the winter. In February, 1915, we saw at least two hundred in a single day, just above Bloody fall. The Copper Eskimos, however, never hunt them at that season, but spend all their days on the sea ice. One man said that their bows would snap with the intense cold; but this can hardly be true, for the Backs river natives, who remain inland all the winter, live during that season on caribou and musk-oxen, which they must formerly have secured with bows and arrows, though now many of the hunters possess rifles. In reality the Copper Eskimo is afraid to leave the ice in winter, because it is there alone that he can obtain an ample supply of fuel for his lamp. It is only in the Coppermine region that caribou are numerous enough to furnish the back-fat that might take the place of blubber, and back-fat in any case is a very poor substitute. The Backs river natives use it, but their existence in winter is characterized by the Copper Eskimos as cold and miserable in the extreme. Wood is found in abundance all down the Coppermine to within twelve miles of its mouth, but an open fire is impracticable in a snow hut, and unsatisfactory in a tent; the northern Indians in their tipis scorch on one side of their bodies while they freeze on the other.

In the early spring, when the caribou are moving across the straits northward, the Eskimos are still living on the sea ice. Occasionally they attempt to intercept the deer; but as a rule they have little success, because the level surface of the ice gives no cover to a hunter who must approach within twenty yards of his quarry before he can launch a shaft with any certainty of hitting his mark. Rifles, however, are changing this, and the Eskimos are beginning to hunt the deer on land and ice alike, both in the spring and fall. They welcome a change of diet just as we do, and after a long regime of seal-meat they look forward to caribou-meat and fish in the early spring just as much as they do to seal-meat at the end of summer. Eagerly the natives watch for the first sign of the migrating caribou; they even go shoreward at times to intercept the herds. In March, 1916, a band of natives moved close in to the shore off Cape Lambert just at the time when the caribou might be expected to cross the strait, and portions of the first deer they killed were conveyed by sled to the main camp near the Liston and Sutton islands. There the natives were expectantly awaiting its arrival. As the sled approached the settlement the hunter ran from side to side two or three times to announce his success, and immediately an excited crowd of natives turned out of their huts to welcome him.

Whether fish or caribou predominate in their summer diet depends entirely on the resources of the particular region in which they live.[2] Thus in 1915, in southwest Victoria island, sealing was definitely abandoned at the end of April. In May, when the main body of the caribou was migrating north across Dolphin and Union strait, the Eskimos ate more caribou-meat than fish, especially those parts of the animal that are less suitable for drying, such as the head, the chine, the shoulders and the thighs. In June caribou were less plentiful, so during that and the following month the people lived mainly on fish, moving about

[1]McClintock, p. 100.

[2]The introduction of rifles has naturally increased the possibilities of hunting and made caribou correspondingly more important. Fish-nets are slowing coming into vogue, but as long as the caribou remain numerous the Eskimos will always spend more time in hunting than in fishing, because the caribou furnish not only food, but skins for clothing and for tents, sinew for sewing and for small lashings, and bone and horn that can be worked up into implements of various kinds.

from one group of lakes to another and incidentally hunting any caribou that they might happen to encounter. By the end of July even the larger lakes were becoming free of ice, and jigging with hook and line or spearing with the long trident was no longer possible; besides it was necessary to obtain a supply of short-haired summer skins for clothing. So the Eskimos began their summer packing, scouring the land day after day, securing a caribou here one day, two or three there the next, then no more perhaps for several days. When their supplies ran low they would sometimes rock the stones on the edges of the lakes and spear the small fish that darted out, eating them raw; or they would draw on the little stock of dried meat or back-fat that they carried for just such an emergency. In the latter half of September the caribou began to straggle back to the coast, and wait for the sea to freeze over so that they could migrate south again. Those Eskimos who had rifles remained near the coast to intercept them, the others, after a few days, went inland again to the lakes to fish, trusting to buy later, from their more fortunate countrymen, the autumn skins that they required for clothing, paying for them with fish. The main body of the caribou had passed by the middle of October, although for several weeks after an occasional herd of stragglers still drifted by. Satisfied with the game they had already killed, three families now decided to return to the hills and obtain a few fish which they could keep frozen for consumption during the winter; but a fourth family, indifferent to the attractions of fish, remained on the coast. Throughout November all these natives were living on the stores that they had laid by during the preceding months; indeed it was not until well on in December that sufficient seals were caught to produce any noticeable change in their diet.

In the valley of the Coppermine river and behind Bathurst inlet caribou are even more numerous than in Victoria island. In other districts, again, they are comparatively scarce, and the Eskimos depend far more on fish. Thus very few caribou remain in Noahognik, on the south side of Dolphin and Union strait, during the summer months, after the spring migration is over. Natives who were spearing salmon here in June, 1916, went down to the Rae river in July for their hunting. For some distance east of the Coppermine river, too, most of the caribou disappear in the height of summer; it is only in the migrating seasons, in early spring and in autumn, that they are plentiful. Fish, on the other hand, are very abundant, and in certain areas squirrels; the fur of the latter is almost as valuable to the Eskimos as its meat.

In cutting up a caribou the Eskimo is careful to preserve every particle of fat, even that around the intestines. In summer and autumn indeed, when the intestines are coated with a thick lining of fat, they are eaten raw and intact, the black pellets of excrement being usually, but not always, squeezed out between thumb and finger.[1] The liver also, like seal liver, is eaten raw, while the kidneys are thrown away or fed to the dogs. The lungs are sometimes cooked and eaten, but they are little esteemed; the heart, however, is carefully preserved, to be split later into two halves, and either boiled at once or laid out on a stone to dry. The wall of the stomach, when emptied of its vegetable contents, is sometimes retained for dog-food, while the reticulum, which is shaped like a pouch, is cut off, filled with blood, and closed with one of the bone pins that a hunter always carries on his bow-case; the blood is used, like seal-blood, to thicken the bouillon after the meat has been boiled. Unborn fawns are skinned, and either dried, or cooked at once, generally for the children to eat; sometimes, however, they are thrown directly to the dogs. As a rule the first parts of a caribou that are cooked, besides the tongue and the heart, are the fore- and hind-quarters, the bones of which contain the much prized marrow; the tongue, according to Eskimo rules of cookery, should be boiled with the tip uppermost.

---

[1] Mr. Stefansson is mistaken, I think, when he says (Anthrop. Papers, A.M.N.H., Vol. XVI, pt. I, p. 61) that the intestinal and kidney fat are usually boiled by the Copper Eskimos. To my knowledge they were always eaten raw, though the back fat was often boiled. Alaskan and Mackenzie river Eskimos, however, frequently boil the intestinal fat as well.

After these parts come the ribs and the sternum, which are often coated with a layer of fat; the ribs are sometimes cracked between the teeth in order to extract the tiny quantity of marrow they contain. Last of all come the chine, the neck and the head; the last is split into four pieces, first down and then across, before being put into the pot, and the brains, as well as the marrow of the jaw-bones, are carefully picked out and eaten.

The marrow of the caribou, especially that of the leg-bones, is a great delicacy. The Copper Eskimo first scrapes all the meat and sinew from the bone with his knife; in autumn this is allowed to freeze and is eaten, sinew and all, in that condition; but in spring and summer the sinew is separated for making seal and fish lines. When the bone is clean the native takes two stones, one of which, the hammer stone, should have a rather sharp edge. With these he cracks off the knuckle at one end, then with the sharp edge of his hammer splits the bone down its shank, and picks out the marrow with a bone spatula, *saudlun*. On rare occasions, to vary the monotony a little, the bone is roasted in the fire before the end is cracked off, when the marrow will flow out like very soft butter.

Sometimes the Eskimos preserve all the bones that have contained marrow— the vertebrae, ribs, leg and feet bones— pound them to fragments, and boil them slowly over an open fire. The fat that separates out on the surface is skimmed off with a ladle of musk-ox horn and poured into some convenient receptacle, such as a bag or the pericardium of the caribou, where it solidifies to form a pure white tallow. This is esteemed more highly perhaps than any other food the natives possess. Mr. Stefansson says that the Baillie island natives never boiled down the bones for their fat until the whaling ships came out and they were taught by natives from farther west; among the Copper Eskimos, however, it seems to have been done from time immemorial.

For drying meat the Copper Eskimo rests a pole or board on two pillars made by piling flat stones on top of one another, or by setting up large slabs on edge. The meat is cut into thin slices and laid across the pole. Often these racks will not suffice to hold the quantity that accumulates in the camp, and the meat lies littered about in every possible place, on sleds, on seal-skins, and even on boulders on the ground. The dogs are always kept tied up at this season, and nothing save the flies can molest the meat. Fish are treated in the same manner. About a week of warm, bright sunshine is sufficient to dry either meat or fish, but if the weather is unsettled and the sky overcast two or even three weeks may be required. The Copper Eskimo never learned to smoke his fish, as the Eskimos do farther west.

Lake trout and lake salmon are the principal fish that the natives secure. Nearly all the lakes with which the country is dotted abound in both these species, and they bite readily at a hook jigged through the ice at the end of a line, either unbaited or with a strip from the fish's own belly as a bait. Many are speared with a long trident (*nuyakpak*), or a double gaff (*kakivak*), in the large pools that form on the edges of the lakes while the main portions are still covered with ice. Hundreds of salmon trout are caught in spring migrating up the rivers to the lakes, while a few sculpins are speared through the ice in the autumn at the mouths of certain creeks. Many tom-cod are caught with long copper hooks through cracks in the sea ice during the spring and fall, especially near Cape Krusenstern and around the islands in Bathurst inlet. Long ago, a native told me, the little bullheads about an inch long that are so common in the lakes and streams were quite an important item of food; now the natives seldom trouble about them, In Noahognik, where caribou are comparatively scarce but fish plentiful, the Eskimos resort to the lakes as soon as sealing is abandoned, and jig for lake trout through holes in the ice; then when the rivers and creeks break out in the late spring they go down to their mouths or to their exits from the lakes and trap the migrating salmon in stone weirs, both the large fish ascending to the lakes to spawn and the young

fry, two seasons old, that are making their way down to the sea. The migration
ends when summer begins, and the Eskimos then wander over the land in search
of caribou. Autumn finds them jigging again through the ice of the lakes.
Life varies somewhat with the different economic conditions; while one band
of Eskimos is hunting caribou or musk-oxen, another, fifty or a hundred miles
away, may be snaring squirrels, or gaffing salmon in the rivers, while still a
third is jigging for trout and salmon through the ice of the lakes. Thus at the
end of May, 1916, there was a settlement of natives on a small island off the
mouth of the Coppermine river, another at Cape Franklin on Victoria island,
and a third at Bernard harbour. In the first the natives were hunting caribou,
in the second they were both sealing and hunting caribou, in the third they
were hunting caribou and fishing inland in one of the lakes. The presence of
several traders and of a Hudson's Bay Company's post in the country since
1916, together with the introduction of rifles, has already caused a considerable
modification in the seasonal movements of the Copper Eskimos, with the exception of those round Prince Albert sound, and the natives east of Kent peninsula.

(Photo by J. J. O'Neill)
FIG. 33. Fish hung up to dry, Nulahugyuk creek, near Bernard harbour

The Copper Eskimos seldom take the trouble to clean their fish before
boiling them. The intestines are drawn out and eaten raw, the remainder
divided into large cross-sections and inserted into the pot. Many of the fish
are very fat, and the top of the water becomes coated with oil, which the natives
remove with the bottom of their horn ladles, and lick up with great gusto. The
head, too, is rather a dainty, especially the eyes, because of the fat that surrounds
them. Nothing is ever wasted; the Eskimos even suck the roots of the fins
in order to extract the last remnants of meat and fat. In the harvest season
of late spring, when as many fish as possible are dried and stored away, the
heads are often the only parts that are cooked. Every bone in them is taken
apart and sucked separately. The natives give them special names from
fancied resemblances to natural objects; there is the ptarmigan, for example,
the hare and the raven, while the five teeth in the front of the upper jaw are
"polar bear's claws."

Fish that are intended for drying are slit from the anal fin to the anus,
then from the gills along each side of the spine; finally they are severed at the
root of the tail. This leaves the two sides hanging from the tail ready to be
laid across a pole to dry, while the head remains attached to the spine. The

next step is to cut off the head for the daily meal, and to lay the spine out to dry on a stone or a seal-skin, together with any roe the fish may contain. The spines of small fish not particularly rich in oil may be thrown to the dogs with other scraps. The dogs fare rather badly at this season—the late spring and early summer—for they receive hardly anything but fish-bones and broth; much depends, however, on the quantity of food in camp at the time.

The diet of the natives, then, is normally restricted to caribou, seal and fish. These are supplemented in a few local areas by one or two other animals, by polar bears in western Victoria island, squirrels in the valleys of the Rae and Coppermine rivers, and musk-oxen in both north-west Victoria island and in the country round Bathurst inlet. The skin of the musk-ox is prized for bedding only, being too coarse and heavy for ordinary clothing when deer-skin is available; but for this fact the animal would probably have long since been exterminated in this region. Ducks are numerous in the spring and fall,[1] geese and loons are met with occasionally, while ptarmigan, though rare in winter, may yet be found in most places at all seasons of the year. The natives shoot a few from time to time, but the supply is too uncertain for them to go out of their way to look for them. Sea-gulls and hawks are sometimes eaten, though Europeans find them distasteful. The children often shoot small birds, such as plovers and longspurs. Their skins serve for hand towels, while their bodies, if the birds are of medium size, are cooked with other meat; but small birds like longspurs and snow buntings are either eaten raw, head, feet and all, or thrown away. Occasionally a rabbit, a wolverine, or a wolf is shot, and hardly a summer passes that the Eskimos on the mainland do not secure two or three brown bears. Now that traps are becoming numerous more foxes are caught then before; the meat of a lean fox is very rank, but one that is rich in fat is palatable enough. Generally speaking, however, it is in the nature of a luxury for an Eskimo to dine off anything but caribou, fish or seal.[2]

The Eskimos are as fond of the fat that is found in geese, loons and eider ducks as they are of caribou fat. They pluck the feathers from the body of the bird, but leave them on the wings and legs, The body is then skinned and the meat cooked in the usual manner. Later the skin is boiled, and the layer of fat that forms on the surface of the water is either drunk immediately or skimmed off into another vessel, when it congeals like lard. The eggs of these birds are sometimes boiled, but most of the Eskimos seem to find them distasteful. Near Bernard harbour there was a rocky islet which the eider ducks had made their nesting ground. Hundreds of eggs could be obtained there each spring, but the local natives never troubled to collect them. I have seen an Eskimo girl take an immature egg from the body of a freshly-killed ptarmigan and eat it raw, but the same girl was horrified when a western native ate some boiled duck's eggs which turned out, when opened, to have immature chicks inside them.

Cooking among these people is not an art that calls for much skill or experience. An Eskimo woman has many to cook for as a rule, and during their life on land the pot has usually to be refilled two or three times in order to provide a single meal. Hence the meat is cut into large portions and as much as possible crammed into the pot at once. It matters little if half of it projects out of the water, for as soon as the lower half is cooked each piece can be turned end for end. Sometimes the meat is served up half raw, more smoked

---

[1]Collinson, p. 285, says that the yellow top-knot of the male king eider was a favourite tit-bit with the Eskimos of Cambridge bay.

[2]Dr. Anderson (op. cit., p. 63) explains how the Eskimos procure the salt that is said to be so necessary for the maintenance of health in men and animals. He points out that the melted snow used for drinking water is frequently very saline, and that caribou meat, especially in the fall, contains a considerable amount of salt.

than boiled, but the Eskimo finds it palatable in any condition. A hunting party often dispenses with a pot altogether, and uses instead an improvised oven of stones. Ikpakhuak thus provided us with a good meal one day when he and I were hunting, and had shot a caribou about ten miles from camp. He collected a few flat slabs of dolomite for his oven and some dry willow twigs for fuel. Then he constructed a hearth in the shelter of a turfy bank about two feet high. First he made the windbreak, three stone slabs on edge along the top of the bank. Beneath these, at the foot of the bank, he set two slabs on edge about two feet apart for the sides of the fireplace. A slab laid flat on the ground between them made a good bottom for the fire, while another, resting on the two side slabs, formed the top of the hearth, the whole structure resembling very much a Dutch oven. He covered the top slab with a layer of moss, poured water over it, then laid slices of meat and back-fat on the moss and covered it all over with a large inverted grassy sod. A fire was soon made by setting one of my matches to a little dry grass, holding it up in the wind till it kindled to a blaze, then pushing it into the hearth and stoking willow twigs on top of it. As soon as the meat was cooked on the under side he rolled back the turf, poured a little more water on the meat, turned it over and replaced the turf. In about twenty minutes the steaks were ready. They proved delicious; the moss had given them a very slight flavour that was not at all unpleasant. Ikpakhuak at the same time roasted part of the liver and two of the leg bones in the fire itself, so that altogether we had an ample and varied repast.

Cleanliness or daintiness is not a characteristic of the Eskimos. In the fall of the year they casually cache their caribou without removing the stomach. The semi-digested vegetable contents ferment and taint all the flesh, but the Copper Eskimo relishes both the smell and the flavour, though his more sophisticated brother in the west pronounces them disgusting. I have seen a man take a bone from rotten caribou-meat cached more than a year before, crack it and eat the marrow with evident relish, although it swarmed with maggots. As a rule such meat is fed to the dogs, but not infrequently the natives cook it for themselves, especially when fresh meat is not available. Dried fish that have become covered with mould are considered hardly inferior to freshly-dried. The grubs of the warble fly, which bore through the skins of the caribou in the spring, are picked out and eaten, either raw or boiled. Small birds, like longspurs, are skinned and swallowed whole without being cooked at all, and it was not uncommon to see a woman transfer the entrails of a freshly killed ptarmigan to her mouth. Caribou droppings are eaten occasionally in the hunting field, but I never saw them collected, as Mr. Stefansson relates, probably because the natives were seldom short of food during the summer that I lived amongst them.

Their lack of cleanliness is shown also in their manner of eating. Every family has a stock of bird skins for use as towels and napkins. Theoretically ptarmigan skins are preferred when eating deer-meat, and sea-gull skins when eating seal-meat, but in practice any skins at all are used; the only discrimination the natives make is that the same skin should not be used for both kinds of meat, not because there is any taboo against it, but because seal-meat is so much more oily. The same napkin is used by everyone until it is worn out. Food that falls to the ground is picked up and eaten. The dishes are never washed, and are used for human beings and dogs alike. Instead of a dish-mop or cloth, the woman uses her fingers to drain the pot or to scour out a bowl or ladle. Much of their uncleanliness is undoubtedly due to the difficulty of obtaining water during the greater part of the year, but it extends far beyond anything that can be ascribed to this cause alone.

The only beverage of the natives, apart from water, is the broth in which the meat or fish has been cooked, thickened when possible with blood. Parry was surprised at the quantity of water the Eskimos drank when they boarded his ship. "It was often with difficulty that our coppers could answer this additional demand. I am certain that Toolooak one day drank nearly a gallon in less than two hours." [1] Avranna drank one evening three cups of soup, two of tea, and nine of ice-cold water, all within the space of three hours; the cup was about the size of a large breakfast cup. The reason for this abnormal thirst appears to be that meat, unlike rice and other vegetable foods, absorbs very little water, so the liquid sustenance that the natives require they must take into their systems as pure fluid. During the winter they obtain all their water from snow, being ignorant apparently of the fact that ordinary sea ice loses its salinity with age, and that an old cake of the previous winter will yield perfectly fresh water. They never use the sea ice themselves, and I never heard them remark on our use of it at Bernard harbour (perhaps they thought it was fresh-water ice), but the Rev. Mr. Girling tells me that they were astonished at the missionaries obtaining all their drinking water from it, and refused to believe at first that it would not taste saline. This ignorance is the more remarkable as they are well aware of the fact that fresh water can be obtained from the spongy ice found in old seal-holes during the spring. They came on such a seal-hole in May, 1915, when they were migrating to the land. It was only about a foot in diameter, and concealed beneath a layer of snow; beside it, but still under the surface of the snow was the small cavity or chamber in which the young seal had been nourished. Fragments of melting ice were floating on the surface of the water; the natives merely let them drain for two or three seconds, after which they tasted perfectly fresh.

In spring, when they are camped beside a lake, the Eskimos naturally fill their water-buckets from one of the fishing-holes. The hunter resorts to various devices. Often there are large boulders embedded in the ice on the margins of ponds, protruding a little above the surface. The stone is warmed by the rays of the sun and melts some of the ice around its edges, when the hunter has merely to chip away a little of the surface ice in order to reach the water. If there is too little for him to suck up with his lips he dips in a piece of snow, which will absorb the water like a sponge. This absorptive power of snow is utilized by the natives for removing fresh blood stains from skins and furs.

However much the Eskimo may look forward in summer and autumn to the winter life on the ice, with its comfortable snow-huts where the lamps, filled to the brim with seal-oil, reflect their light round the pure white walls, while beneath and behind the table the floor is littered with meat and blubber —winter, when the dance-house is crowded with friends and visitors who gather each evening to spend the hours in singing and dancing and in the performance of religious ceremonies—yet always at the back of their minds there is the lurking dread of hunger and of cold in those dark sunless days, when the huts perhaps are empty of food, the lamps extinguished for want of oil, and the people, driven indoors by the howling blizzards, huddle together on their sleeping platforms and face starvation and death. The winter of 1914-15 was a comparatively mild one; food was plentiful, and the settlements of the Eskimos were filled with rejoicing. But the following winter was more severe. From Christmas until the middle of March one blizzard succeeded another. Often the Eskimos, unable to find the seal-holes on account of the snow that had drifted over them, sat and shivered in their huts, with their lamps extinguished, or burning so low that the heat they gave out hardly lessened the prevailing cold. The stores of food they had collected in the summer and autumn were exhausted, and the seals they caught from time to time were all too few to satisfy the needs of so many hungry mouths, even though they ate the skins and blubber with the meat. Many of them ate the sealskin boots that they were keeping for the following spring, others the sealskin cases of their bows. Night after night

---

[1] Parry, Vol. II, p. 182, *et seq.*

their shamans would interrogate the spirits that they believed to control the weather, and try to appease their anger and bring about a cessation of the storms. Whenever they did abate in the slightest degree, and there was the faintest prospect of securing seals, every man and youth would sally forth, and search for hours in the bitter cold in the hope that he might at last find something to take home to his starving wife and children. There was not a man in a Kilusiktok settlement that I visited at the end of February whose face was not covered with great blotches where he had been severely frost-bitten. Even the women braved the weather, and fished for tom-cod through the ice behind the shelter of a few snow-blocks. Sometimes the natives would recall dreadful tales of years gone by, how, not a generation before, the Kanghiryuarmiut had chopped up the corpses of their dead and eaten the frozen flesh to save themselves from starvation. Away in the east, too, the Netsilingmiut had cut off a man's legs while he was still alive and tried to appease their hunger with his flesh. No one, so far as I know, actually starved to death in 1916, though the lives of two or three old people were undoubtedly shortened through the privations they had to endure. Fortunately, a change came over the weather about the middle of March. Before the month was out the crisis was over; the huts of the Eskimos were filled once more with meat and blubber, and the dance-house resounded with song and laughter.[1]

A few remarks may be added about the way in which these natives produce fire. The thong drill used by all other Eskimos is known to them, but they never employ it except in an emergency, because of the labour involved and the difficulty of obtaining suitable wood. They use in its stead two lumps of pyrites, which they obtain from the Kugaluk river on south-west Victoria island, from a creek a few miles east of the Coppermine river, and possibly from one or two other sources as well. Parry's description of the process will serve admirably; he says: " For the purpose of obtaining fire the Esquimaux use two lumps of common iron pyrites, from which sparks are struck into a little leather case, containing moss well dried and rubbed between the hands. If this tinder does not readily catch, a small quantity of the white floss of the seed of the ground willow is laid above the moss. As soon as a spark has caught, it is gently blown till the fire has spread an inch around, when the pointed end of a piece of oiled wick being applied, it soon bursts into a flame, the whole process having occupied perhaps two or three minutes."[2]

The Copper Eskimos use the seeds of the *Eriophorum* or cotton-grass more often than those of the ground willow for both tinder and lampwicks. Large quantities of these *Eriophorum* seeds are collected during the late summer and fall and are stored in small bags of one kind or another, often made from a loon's foot, or a squirrel skin, or the lining round the heart of a caribou or bear. The tedious process of stripping the stalks from the seeds is done by the women in spare moments in their houses. For the lampwick the *Eriophorum* seeds are dipped in the blubber, then drawn up on to the edge of the lamp and pinched into a low ridge all along its rim. Such a wick requires renewing every day, whereas a tinder bag will last for months. In winter, if the lamp expires in one house, a fire-stick dipped in blubber is kindled at a neighbour's lamp and carried over in a bag or other convenient receptacle. *Eriophorum* seeds are

---

[1]Mr. Stefansson, I think, gives too gloomy a picture of their life when he says (op. cit., p. 131): "At Cape Bexley and to the east there is apparently hardly a winter when the people do not have to subsist for considerable periods on seal oil alone . . . saved the previous spring and cached during the summer." At that time he had never visited the country except in spring and summer. I have already explained that this oil is stored away for their lamps in the fall, and generally lasts, with the food they collect in the summer, until about Christmas. January and February are the critical months in stormy winters, which occur, as far as my data allow me to judge, about once in every four years. Then they suffer from privation and want, but real starvation on any considerable scale probably happens not more often than once in every fifteen or twenty years.

[2]Parry, Vol. III, p. 284.

sometimes used in this way, but more usually a torch of matted moss roots dipped in blubber. During a migration, of course, every lamp is extinguished, so the natives have to resort to pyrites on such occasions.

In spring and summer the natives carry a little dry grass to catch the glow of their tinder instead of an oily stick. On old camp-sites fragments of charred wood may always be found which will serve the same purpose. For this reason the Eskimos are careful to cover the embers of their open fires with flat stones which convert some of the unburnt wood to charcoal. In blowing a fire they never purse the lips as we do, but curl the tongue along the lower palate so as to make a concave channel, thus giving the breath its direction.[1]

---

[1]In my preliminary draft of the report I had proposed to follow up this chapter on food with another on clothing. That idea has now been abandoned, for a detailed account of the styles and patterns of the garments worn by the Copper Eskimos, their methods of sewing and of dressing skins, will require a special monograph, and a cursory sketch of the subject seemed unnecessary here. The Copper Eskimos wear only fur clothing, most of their garments being made of caribou fur. The only changes caused by the seasons are the substitution of seal-skin for caribou-skin in certain portions of the foot-gear, and the wearing of water-boots and of older and lighter clothing during the summer months. There are certain differences in the garments worn by the two sexes, but only of a minor character.

CHAPTER IX

WINTER LIFE

There is a transition period each year in the lives of the Eskimos when they cease from their quest of food on land and yet are not prepared to begin the winter's sealing on the ice. Its length varies from about a fortnight to a month, and corresponds roughly with our month of November. The sea ice is still thin, and though it is possible to cross between Victoria island and the mainland, it is unwise to camp on it in most places. This is not an idle period for the Eskimos, however. During the dark days when the sun is absent no new deerskins may be sewn, so the women are now fully occupied in making all the clothes that will be required by their families during the next five or six months. The men, in the meantime, bring in their caches of deermeat, and dried or frozen fish, and the pokes of blubber that have been secreted in stone cairns on the coast since spring. They repair too their sealing implements, or make new ones, and scrape most of the skins that the women intend to use. Leisure hours are occupied in trapping foxes, or fishing in adjoining lakes.

(Photo by J. J. O'Neill)

Fig. 34. Tree river Eskimos descending to the sea at the approach of winter

All through the summer the families that compose each separate group or tribe have been scattered over various fishing and hunting grounds in the interior; but now they assemble once again at some well-known meeting place on or near the coast. The Akulliakattak natives gather at Lake Akulliakattak, the Noahognirmiut at Chantry island or at the fishing creek four miles east of Bernard harbour, the Coppermine river natives on an island off the mouth of the nearer Kugaryuak river, the Pingangnaktomiut on Hepburn island, and the Kilusiktomiut on one of the Barry islands in Bathurst inlet called Igloryuallik. The Puivlik natives have several places where they may assemble in the autumn. At the beginning of December, 1914, they had a large settlement a short distance from the mouth of the Kimiryuak river. There they were joined by two Noahognik families, who, through lack of food, had crossed the strait and foisted themselves for the time being on their more prosperous neighbours. There were then nine double houses in the settlement, but no dance-house, because the season for visiting was still far off and the men were sufficiently occupied in carrying out their various tasks. Accordingly, the dance they gave in honour of my arrival was held in the portico or domed interspace of one of the larger double huts. The natives remained about a month at this settlement; by that time their clothing was practically all finished, the ice in the strait was growing more and more solid every day, and everything was ready for their winter sealing. On December 11 about half the people moved down to a sandspit on the coast some four miles away. The remainder, who still had a little more work to finish, postponed moving till the following day, the women staying up most of the night to complete their sewing. I accompanied the later party, with my host and hostess, Haviuyak and Itokanna. We rose about 4 a.m. and breakfasted immediately on frozen deermeat; for the Eskimos, having no watches, could not tell in the foggy condition of the atmosphere how long it would be before daylight. We waited idly an hour and a half, then Haviuyak iced the runners of his sled and began to load up, removing the ice window out of his hut and receiving the household goods from his wife through the opening. We started at 9.45 a.m., Itokanna pulling in front of the dogs as usual, and Haviuyak behind, while his father Haviron, who had been ailing for some time, was carried on top of the sled. On reaching the new settlement Haviuyak immediately set about building a hut for himself and his family beside the huts that were already erected.

This migration marked the real opening of the winter life, for they began their sealing the very next day, although several more days elapsed before they had any success. It was forbidden to cook caribou and fish again until the spring, when the natives would return to the land, and the sewing of new deerskins was tabooed until the sun should reappear about the middle of January. A week later the whole settlement moved to a new sealing ground about ten miles south by east. Here too they remained a week only, then crossed to Putulik, one of the Liston and Sutton islands, where they amalgamated with the three Noahognik families that had crossed over from Chantry island.

In the autumn of 1915 the five Puivlik families with whom I spent the spring and summer in south-west Victoria island assembled at Okauyarvik, while others gathered near the Kimiryuak river; all of them crossed over to Bernard harbour at the end of November, or early in December, before commencing the winter sealing. Thither too flocked the Noahognik Eskimos, and others who had spent the summer round the Rae river. Some came from farther east, from the Coppermine and even from the Tree river. Such a commingling of the tribes at this season was due, of course, to the presence of the expedition and the facilities it offered for trade. Normally the different groups remain in their various assembling-places until it is time to move out on the ice and begin the sealing. They live during this transition period on the dried fish and caribou meat they have stored away in the summer, and the frozen meat and fish kept from the fall. Should the winter prove stormy they may have to fall back on these again later on, so they wisely begin their sealing before all their stores are exhausted.

Amundsen says of the Netsilik Eskimos that they "are not altogether without forethought for the future. Their stock of meat and fish will last over Christmas and a little way into the new year. According to their law, seal-catching must not commence before the middle of January, and even then it is carried on only on a small scale for some time, as the seals, which have very sharp ears, can hear the hunter's steps a long way off, while the layer of snow on the ground is thin, and consequently they can keep out of his way. Therefore, from the middle of January up to some time in February is their period of greatest privation."[1] The Copper Eskimos begin sealing early in December, as soon as the sun has disappeared; they would begin earlier still but for the necessity they are under of sewing new clothes, and the danger of living and hunting over

[1]Amundsen, Vol. II, p. 22 *et seq.*

thin ice which may be broken up at any time by a sudden storm. While the ice is still forming, indeed, they sometimes shoot bearded seals (with rifles now but formerly too with bows and arrows) as the animals bask on the surface of the ice off the mouths of streams and rivers.[1] For the Copper Eskimos too the period of greatest privation is from the middle of January till about the middle of March, because it is then that the coldest and stormiest weather usually prevails and they have least success in their sealing.

One of the first actions of a community after it settles down in its winter sealing ground is the construction of a dance-house. This is never a separate structure standing by itself, but a large dome covering the fore part of a single hut, or more usually the fore-courts or two or more huts. In this way it is kept warm by the lamps that are always burning in the dwellings, and is more fitted to fulfil its other function of a club-house.

On a normal mid-winter day the Eskimo hunter never stirs till about eight o'clock. His wife rises a little earlier to kindle the lamp, which usually expires during the night. Sometimes she lights it from her bed, but an energetic woman will always rise early and occupy herself with some task or other. Occasionally she boils a little seal-meat to warm up her husband before he goes sealing, but often he is content with frozen fish or deer-meat, or cold boiled seal-meat left over from the night before. The woman removes the snow-block from the door, and goes outside to look at the weather, and, it may be, to bring in a fresh supply of blubber for the lamp. Presently children appear, bringing food from other houses, and are sent away with corresponding portions to distribute among the neighbours. Any child, no matter whose it is, may be sent on such errands; and if there are no children, or the wife wants to pay a visit herself, she will take her own contributions of food. A man or two will now probably enter the hut, and the husband, who has eaten his breakfast in bed, turns out

Fig. 35. Eskimo hunters starting out for the sealing-grounds, Dolphin and Union strait

and dresses. "Are they starting out for the sealing-ground yet?" he asks, and if the answer is "Yes", he hurries forth, harnesses his dogs, and takes his sealing apparatus from the rampart that encompasses the house. With the breaking light all the men set out in a body for the sealing-ground, which may be from three to five miles away. As soon as they reach it they scatter and the dogs sniff about and smell out the holes where the seals come up to the surface of the water to breathe. The hunter watches them, searching about

---

[1] Early in October, 1915, when we were camped not far from the mouth of the Okauyarvik creek, Ikpakhuak shot one rough and three bearded seals on the surface of the ice. He had to stalk them on his hands and knees, and in so doing froze both his wrists so that they were black for days afterwards; but he merely laughed over his misfortune and considered it rather a joke. In the spring of the same year an Eskimo hunter in Coronation gulf stalked a large bearded seal on the ice and launched an arrow at it that missed by a hand's breadth only.

himself at the same time and probing every suspicious mound. Suddenly a dog begins to scratch in the snow. The hunter hastens to the spot and probes about with his long horn "feeler" until he finds the exact centre of the hole; then he carefully stamps the snow round the probe and draws it out, leaving only a deep hole about half an inch in diameter. Down this he pushes his indicator, a fine stick of bone or horn about as thick, but as long again, as an ordinary steel knitting needle. At the lower end is a small thin bone disc, and at the top an eyelet to which the short string of sinew is fastened that attaches it to another needle, shorter and discless. The indicator rests against the snow at the side of the hole, which keeps it from falling, but the slightest disturbance below will cause it to drop. The second needle is pegged into the snow above so that the indicator can be recovered afterwards. The hunter then places his deerskin or bearskin foot pad under his feet to keep them from freezing and remains perfectly still, holding the shaft of the harpoon in his right hand and the loop at the end of the line in his left. Every few minutes he stoops to examine his indicator, then straightens up again and scans the horizon around him. A slight quivering of the indicator gives him his cue. He stands with uplifted harpoon on the lee side of the hole—for the seal has a very quick scent—and when the indicator suddenly drops he strikes with all his might.

Sometimes a hunter will use another kind of indicator. Instead of the long bone needle with a disc at the end he has a flattened piece of caribou leg-sinew split nearly to the top. The two ends are then bent round till they lie some two or three inches apart; and each is split again a little to make them grip a wisp of down that is stretched between them, the down being taken indifferently from a duck, a goose or a swan. The sinew is now laid vertically in the hole without reaching to the water, and is held in place by a short needle pushed into the snow above, as with the other form of indicator. The seal, when it blows at the surface, causes the down to flutter up and down, and the hunter strikes as nearly as possible down the centre.

Often the hunter fails to strike his quarry. Sometimes the harpoon just grazes it, sometimes it penetrates but not sufficiently deep to hold the animal fast. But if it does hold a struggle commences, a very grim struggle indeed if the animal is one of the larger rough seals or a bearded seal. The usual method of killing the animal, after it has been dragged to the surface, is by stabbing it in the eye with the sharp handle of the scoop or ladle that is used for enlarging the seal hole. Not everyone can hold on to a large bearded seal, and only a very few can draw one up out of its hole. The hunter must call to his companions for assistance. Many Eskimos have great scars on their hands that testify to the enormous strain of holding a bearded seal on the end of the line, and many a stirring tale is told of the adventures of different hunters. Some have a tragic issue. Ilatsiak had seen a Netsilik Eskimo named Tutiktok whose mitten had dropped off during the struggle, and the line, dragging through his hand, had severed all his fingers. Another man, Ikpakhuak said, harpooned a bearded seal one autumn on the edge of the ice in Simpson bay. The animal immediately plunged into the water, and dragged the man in with it. From time to time the people saw it rise to the surface, blowing hard, and apparently still having the hunter in tow behind it.[1]

Most of the scars that cover the hunters' hands, however, are gained in a more inglorious manner. A rough seal is dragged home intact by one or more of the dogs, after a small piece of the skin and blubber has been cut off and thrown away as an offering to the other seals. A bearded seal, on the other hand, is cut up beside its hole. A great shout goes up whenever a man spears one of these animals, and all the hunters in the vicinity rush to his assistance.

[1]Cf. Stefansson, My Life with the Eskimo, p. 268.

Everyone crowds round as the seal is drawn to the surface in order to obtain a share of the meat. Heedless of the value of the skin, heedless even of each other's hands, they hack away, not infrequently cutting each other as each man in his greed tries to hew off as large a portion as possible. The Rev. Mr. Girling, writing in 1918, said: " There have been a great number of cases of maiming this winter arising from their ridiculous system of going temporarily mad when they strike an *ugyuk* (bearded seal) and all stabbing their knives in to get what they can grab; our surgical outfit has been kept busy." Yet they know that when they return home both the raw meat and a portion of what is cooked must be distributed amongst the other families, so that all they gain for their exertions is a strip of the skin. Even that is often eaten, so that the only outcome of their folly is a number of severe wounds.[1]

If the day is far spent when he strikes his quarry the hunter usually returns home without waiting for his companions; but if it be still early either he sends his dogs to camp with the seal, (a toggle is passed through the nostril and attached to the trace of the dog), or he drags it around with him until he finds another seal-hole, when the same performance is gone through again. Generally the whole party return together, and are met a little way out by the children,

Fig. 36. The return from the sealing-grounds, the dogs dragging home the seals

who fall on the seals and pretend to stab them to death, thereby bringing good luck, as they think, to the hunters. The dogs know their own huts, and each drags its burden to the entrance of the passage, where the housewife is waiting to receive it. The man puts away his sealing-gear, setting his harpoon upright in the snow wall outside the hut, while his wife drags the seal indoors and lays it on its back in the middle of the floor.[2] Sometimes she skins it herself, sometimes a little girl is allowed to skin it, and thus be trained in one of her duties in later life. First a little fresh water is poured into its mouth, for seals, these Eskimos say, have an intense desire for water, and bad luck would attend the hunter who did not administer to their wants.[3] Sometimes small pieces of the blubber are cut from the breast and handed round as tit-bits. The bulk of it, however, is stripped off in long slices, and thrown across the board that supports the table, or into the empty space at the back of the lamp. The skin is folded

---

[1] Mr. Stefansson's account (My Life with the Eskimo), p. 269, is not quite accurate, at least not for the Dolphin and Union strait Eskimos.

[2] On Dec. 6, 1914, a Noahognik native speared a large rough seal, the first that was caught that winter. His wife, who was standing at the entrance of her hut when he returned, merely remarked, *kowanna natsemmun*, "Hurrah for the seal", and went inside the house again. The dogs dragged it into the passage, and she unhitched them and drew it inside the hut. Before skinning it she cut a few small pieces of skin and blubber from its breast and gave each of us one as a tit-bit.

[3] I could find no definite belief concerning the rebirth of seals and their gratitude in the new life for the water they received in the old, such as Mr. Stefansson attributes to the natives of Baillie island and Point Atkinson (Anthrop. Papers, A.M.N.H., Vol. XIV, pt. I, p. 351). Nor do Copper Eskimos keep the bladder or nose skins, like their neighbours. The catching of seals in nets was unknown to them, as indeed were nets of any kind.

and laid against the wall, and the children are sent out to the various houses with portions of the meat. The husband enters, removes his heavy sealing coat, carefully beats the snow from it with the ",duster", and sits down beside the table to help himself to the steaming food that his wife has just cooked in anticipation of his return. Sometimes, though, if he is very tired, he will undress first and slip into bed, then roll over on to his stomach and eat his supper.

In mid-winter the women have usually very little to do while their husbands are away sealing. It is forbidden to sew new garments during the days that the sun is absent, but they may still patch old ones, and they can spend an infinite amount of t me in emptying out their bales of clothing and clearing away the snow that is always drifting inside. Such labour, however, is rather useless, for the next gale will bury them up again, and in midwinter there is no danger of the snow melting and damaging the skins. The most fruitful task is to go and gossip in the dance-house, or in the houses of neighbours, until the growing gloom brings warning that it is time to trim the lamp and put the pot on for the hunter's evening meal. Woe betide the woman who is slack in this respect; her husband will probably beat her, or stamp her in the snow, and may even end by throwing her household goods after her and bidding her begone forever from his house.

The children have even less to do. They run about outside, throwing each other in the snow, or playing hide and seek, or building miniature snow walls and snow houses. One of them, perhaps, will carve out a block in the shape of a rabbit and the rest will decapitate it. Every now and then a child will run inside to help itself to a little food from the table, then go off again to visit some other house or to resume its play outdoors.

Neighbours drop in after the evening meal to discuss the hunting and all the little events of the day. The hunter is lying in his sleeping-bag. They sit down beside him and chat for an hour or so, then one by one retire, remarking as they leave, " I am going out." By seven or eight o'clock the hut is empty, and everyone is preparing for bed. The inmates have another little snack of food, then undress and compose themselves in their sleeping bags, the wife first trimming the lamp so that the flame burns brightly all along its rim, and closing the door with a snow-block. The lamp grows dimmer and dimmer; often it expires altogether before morning, unless some one wakes and trims it again, or throws a little more blubber into the well. The dogs sleep quietly in the passage. Sometimes one prowls about outside, and climbs on to the roof among the bales of clothing. The crunching of its feet on the crystalline snow disturbs the house-wife, who yells at the dog at the top of her voice, " Won't you lie down? You dog, you're a confounded nuisance." Her husband rolls over mingling his voice with hers, and similar cries come faintly from a neighbouring hut. The crunching ceases for a moment, then recommences, and the woman, with a muttered " Confound it," slips on her clothes, picks up the snow-duster, removes the door and crawls out through the dark passage. Shrill yelps soon proclaim that the dog has received a well-merited punishment, and everyone heaves a sigh of contentment and settles down to sleep again. The wife comes in, readjusts the door, dusts her clothes, and crawls into her sleeping-bag again. Sometimes she brings with her an old headless harpoon, so that if the dog climbs up on to the roof again she can stab it through the snow wall without rising from her bed.

With the reappearance of the sun and the dawning of longer days the monotony of this life undergoes a change. Hitherto dances and shamanistic performances, with a little wrestling and gymnastics, have been their only diversions in the evenings and on days when terrific blizzards make sealing impossible. Undoubtedly these afford much enjoyment, and relieve to some extent the tedium of their sedentary existence; but still the nights are long and weary and half their life is spent in bed. Longer days mean travel, migrations to new sealing grounds and visits from friends in other communities. It is then, about February or the early part of March, that the Akulliakattangmiut combine with the Puivlirmiut and Noahognirmiut, and the Coppermine river natives come north to the neighbourhood of Locker point, whence some continue west and visit the Dolphin and Union strait Eskimos. Farther east the Pingangnaktok and Kilusiktok natives meet, and some of the Ekaluktomiut and Asiagmiut often visit them. Dances are held almost nightly in honour of both visitors and hosts, and a brisk barter is carried on. Both at this time and later the groups rearrange themselves, some of the local group returning with the visitors to their sealing-grounds, while some of the new-comers in turn stay with the group they came to visit.

A migration of a whole community is a wonderful sight. In the autumn, when the Eskimos are moving out to their sealing-grounds, they have to start with their sleds before daylight in order to reach their destinations before dark. Time is everything at that season of the year, and often half the journey is made in twilight. In spring, on the other hand, there is no need for haste, for the air is mild and pleasant, and the daylight as long as the darkness has been in the winter. No definite hour is set for the migration, no definite day even, for in a land where the only calendars are the seasons one day is no better than the next. The natives are not accustomed therefore to plan all their movements beforehand, and to carry them out with the exactitude of clockwork. Conversation usually simmers on the subject for several days before a migration takes place, and nothing is decided; then one evening a man will suddenly announce to his wife that he intends to move next day. The rumour quickly spreads from house to house, and others announce their intention of accompanying him. Next morning everyone is on the alert. Someone enters a hut and announces that so-and-so is packing up. Everyone begins to do the same, and soon the settlement is a hive of industry. Breakfast is finished quickly, or even forgotten in the excitement. The man goes out, takes down his sled from its stand, and trims the mud runners with his knife; his wife, in the meantime, crushes some snow in the pot so that when he re-enters there will be water all ready to pour over the mud. He carries it out, fills his mouth with it, streams it along the runners, and before it freezes quickly rubs it over with a pad of polar bear skin so as to leave a perfectly smooth coating of ice.[1] Finally the sled is ready; he turns it right side up, and lays on the bottom all the heavy bales that have been resting on the house wall. Then he cuts a great hole in the side of the house, or takes out the ice window behind the lamp, and calls to the inmates to pass out the things.

All this time the wife has been busily packing indoors. Odd garments, sewing material, knives, and other miscellaneous articles are hastily stuffed into bags. The pot is taken down and emptied, the lamp extinguished, and the blubber packed into a skin bag. Then while the children pass out the sleeping skins through the opening in the wall the woman herself scours out the lamp with her forefinger, carefully lashes it inside a sealskin, and thrusts it through the doorway into the passage, since it is generally too heavy to lift up through the opening in the wall. Its usual place on the sled is near the bottom, above the willow bed-matting or on top of the bales of clothing; here too the ice window generally finds a place. The drying-rack is taken out with all its contents, and the table and its supports; the ends of the latter are often frozen into the wall, and have to be chipped out with the ice-chisel.

The husband carefully packs all these things on the sled, while his wife indoors (or outdoors, if the weather is mild) changes her old grease-stained

---

[1] Polar bear skin is preferred to any other kind because water does not adhere to the fur.

house-clothes for the clean, warm, ornamented clothing that is kept for travelling and for ceremonial occasions such as dances. Both then lash everything tightly on the sled while the children harness up the dogs. Yet even when the lashings are all firmly secured the packing is not quite finished, for there is always a multitude of shoes, socks, sticks, poles, harpoons, tins, pots, scraps of skin too precious to throw away, and odds and ends of the most extraordinary kind which must be fastened in some way or other to the top and sides of the sled, either pushed under the lashings or tied on with threads of sinew. This after-packing, in fact, often takes longer than the first.

Fig. 37. A migration train near Cape Krusenstern

At last everything is finished, the yelping dogs are hitched to the sled, wife and husband hitch their harness on also, and the family is ready to start. Other sleds have already preceded them, and soon there is a long train extending over a mile perhaps, each sled, as a rule, following exactly in the trail of the one in front. Here a woman is pulling in front, with a daughter or niece at her side; behind her are the dogs, which she urges on with cries of *ha ha ha*. Then comes the husband, also in the yoke, steering the sled round hummocks, and heaving it over those unavoidable ones on which the sled threatens to stick. All three, husband, wife and daughter, carry walking-sticks to help them along. The man has another use for his; when his cry of *hok hok hok* fails to spur on one of the dogs, he seizes its trace, jerks it back till it comes within reach of his stick and smites it a stinging blow. Usually though the mere striking of their traces is sufficient to keep the dogs working. Suddenly the sled sticks. The man stoops down, lifts all the traces with one hand to make the dogs start together with a jerk, and heaves with all his might. If it still holds he knocks down the snow from the front of the runner and heaves to one side to set the sled swinging a little until finally it moves on again.

Behind this sled there is another with only one woman in front of the dogs and the husband behind, while a little boy clings to the side of the sled. On the next, father and son are pulling side by side, while the aged wife drags herself along by holding on to the lashings. The fourth has a curious sail-like apparatus on top. Only the man is pulling, his wife trudging along at the side of the sled; the queer-looking " sail " on top is a deerskin wrapped round the baby to protect it from the wind. So the whole train moves slowly along for two or three miles; then the front sled stops, the dogs are unhitched, and one or two taken back to help some kinsman far in the rear. One after another as they come up the natives unhitch their dogs and sit or stand around to rest. A little frozen meat is divided up for lunch, and the children run to and fro, playing hide and seek, or raven, or some other game that serves to keep them warm. Several of the men and women perhaps begin a skipping competition, using a dog-trace for a

rope, while the older people lean against the sleds and gossip.   Half an hour later
the journey is resumed, but by the time they have travelled eight or ten miles
everyone is tired out, and the leader begins to search out a suitable place for the
new camp.   He takes his snow-sounder, and prods about in the snow till he
finds a spot where it is firm and deep, then draws his sled up alongside it and
begins to build his hut (or, if the season is too advanced for a snow hut, he erects
his tent instead).   His wife and child unharness the dogs and unlash the sled, then
help him in making their home.   One by one the other families come up and do
likewise, so that two hours later a new settlement has arisen almost identical
with the one they have just abandoned.

Travelling of this kind is very hard work, especially for those who own
only one or two dogs. The natives perspire freely from the labour of dragging
their sleds, then when they stop to rest their bodies cool down and tend to
freeze all the more quickly.   Yet during a howling blizzard, when the thermometer registered –30° F. and the wind was blowing 30 miles an hour, I have
seen a woman squat down in the lea of her sled, draw her baby out from under
her hood and leisurely proceed to change its little garment, holding the naked

Fig. 38. A rest during a migration, near Cape Krusenstern

infant in the meantime fully exposed to the weather. Such was the severity
of the cold that day that several adults had their wrists badly frozen.   Then
again they often have trouble with the runners of their sleds if their course
takes them over the land.   In February, 1915, I accompanied a band of Coppermine river Eskimos on a migration near Locker point.   Among them was
the shaman Uloksak ; his two wives were hauling side by side, with six dogs
following them, while Uloksak himself was hauling behind.   The sled was
piled to its utmost capacity with all the miscellaneous articles of an Eskimo
household, and the big drum, with its membrane removed, was hanging from a
pole at one side.   Trailing behind was a smaller sled that was also piled high
with bags.   (Wealth is not always a blessing, even among the Eskimos;   it
doubles the labour on the trail.)   We were crossing the neck of land behind
Cape Krusenstern, and stones along the portage scraped some of the ice from
the runners of his sled, causing it to drag so heavily that he was compelled to
stop and re-ice them.   With a few shavings and some blubber he kindled a
small fire and melted some snow in the cooking pot;   then he took a box from
his sled and propped up one runner.   The younger wife filled her mouth with
the water and poured it over the bearskin mitten her husband was holding in

his hand, and while he rubbed it along the runner she filled her mouth again for the next application. Fully half an hour passed before their sled was ready to proceed again.[1]

As a rule Eskimos can travel but one or two days at a time, when they must stop and hunt seals, which are too heavy for more than one or two to be carried on the sled with the rest of the property. Nor do the natives travel very far in one day unless their sleds are light, for not only must they drag them themselves, but before it grows dark they must find a suitable camping-site and begin the construction of their snow huts. On the other hand, they have no cumbersome tent to carry, with its poles and ropes, at least not in winter. When spring does finally come and a tent must be carried, the weather is mild and the daylight long, so that there is no need for haste; at this period therefore a native with a light sled will often travel as many as thirty miles in a day. For convenience of transport the covering of the tent is usually rolled up in two bundles, which are joined together again before the poles are set up.

Abandoned camps are often reoccupied a few weeks later, generally by the same inhabitants returning from a visit to neighbouring tribes; a stranger, though he occupies the same site, will usually build a new hut for himself. Often, although the settlement is abandoned, there are clear signs that the inhabitants intend to return before very long. The ice windows are left in place, the door-ways are blocked with snow, and tent poles and other gear still remain planted in the walls. Looking through the windows two or three large bags may be seen inside filled with meat and blubber. One native made a cache of three sealskin bags, two containing blubber and one seal meat, in a square hole in an ice keg near the hut he was abandoning. He covered the bags with three sealskins, and closed the hole with blocks of ice. Three weeks later he came back and recovered his property.

Spring with its mild, sunny weather brings longer and pleasanter hours for hunting. Seals, though not more plentiful perhaps, are more easily discovered, and the camp is filled with meat and blubber. To the women this season means more work. The winter, provided food and fuel were not wanting, was almost a holiday time, but now each family requires spring boots that will not spoil in the melting snow. Some of the sealskins must be scraped and dried, partly for footgear, partly to make up into bags for clothing, meat and blubber. Such skins are scattered all about the camp, some pegged to snow blocks, others to the walls of the houses, others again stretched over the sleds. There is a general spring cleaning. The clothes that are ranged in bags on the ramparts of the houses must all be unpacked, shaken out and aired in the sun. A sharp eye is kept on the weather for the least sign of drift, and after every gale or snowfall the bags are emptied again, the snow brushed out before it melts, and the clothes carefully repacked. The tent now supplants the snow hut, and in place of closing up chinks in the walls and scraping the window, the wife now beats off the encrusting frost and snow. Surplus blubber is no longer thrown away, but diligently packed in large sealskin pokes to be sorted away for the autumn. At the same time many of their fine winter clothes are packed away, since it will be impossible in summer to carry them wherever they go. Migrations take place more frequently, and the men hunt nearer home, staying away eight or nine hours a day instead of four or five as in winter.

Now that rifles are growing more common many of the Eskimos abandon the ordinary method of sealing much earlier than in former years. Instead they wander along the coast to intercept the caribou as they migrate north, or to shoot the bearded seals that in certain well-known places, especially off the

---

[1] A quick way of re-icing the runners in the fall when travelling down a river bed is to dig a hole down to the water with the ice-chisel (a matter of perhaps five minutes when the river is frozen to a depth of only about two feet), pour some water over the surface of the ice, and run the sled through it before it freezes. The usual method, however, produces a more even surface.

mouths of creeks and rivers, crawl out on top of the ice to bask in the sunshine. Occasionally a native, having no rifle, will stalk the smaller rough seal as it lies beside its hole, and when there are no more ice-cakes to cover his approach, he will dash forward and try to harpoon it before it dives. Long before the snow has melted from the ice, however, (before the middle of May in an ordinary season) the majority of the Eskimos have cached their blubber and clothes on the shore, or on islands near the coast, and gone inland to fish and hunt.

A chronological record of the movements of the Dolphin and Union strait Eskimos in the winter and spring of 1915-16 will illustrate this account of their winter life. From December, 1915, to February, 1916, they were all united in one settlement of thirty-three snow huts, on the shore of Illuvillik, the most westerly island of the Liston and Sutton group. Some time during the first week of February they migrated in a body ten miles to the west and built new snow-huts on the ice. They remained here almost a month, then moved four or five miles south-southwest. Throughout March they were visited by large numbers of Coronation gulf natives, some from the Coppermine river basin and others from as far east as Bathurst inlet. On April 3, the settlement split up. One band of sixteen families made new homes ten miles farther west, four families migrated about the same distance north-northwest, and the remainder, save for two or three who left for Coronation gulf, moved eastward again and camped on the ice between the two eastern islands of the Liston and Sutton group, where they could seal in an area that had not been hunted over during the winter. The eleven families of this last settlement now set up nine tents to live in. The larger settlement to the west, on the other hand, consisted of snow huts only, the weather not being as yet so warm as to make these dwellings untenable. Their exact movements later I do not know, but by the end of April the members of the larger settlement had all moved away, some to Okauyarvik on the north side of Dolphin and Union strait, where they were hunting caribou, the rest to the mouth of a creek twelve miles east of Bernard harbour, where they were shooting bearded seals and trying to intercept the caribou. The natives who had camped between the two islands were slowly moving northeast at the same time towards the land, and by May had reached the shore not far from Clouston bay. In June there were nine families at the fishing creek four miles east of Bernard harbour, two at the other creek twelve miles east, and six at a creek that flows into a bay just west of Cape Krusenstern. The other natives who had wintered in Dolphin and Union strait were all lost to view in Victoria island, with the exception of those who had gone down into Coronation gulf.

CHAPTER X

SUMMER LIFE

A great change comes over the Copper Eskimo world each year in the month of May. The sun circles constantly round in the sky, never setting below the horizon. During the warmer hours of noon the snow that covers both sea and land begins to glisten and melt, then in the cooler hours of the night it freezes again, offering a firm resistance to the traveller's sled. Already in a few exposed places the ground shows brown and bare, but the streams and lakes are still ice-bound, and the valleys filled with soft, deep snow. The birds are returning. Throughout the winter a few ravens haunt the Eskimo settlements, and here and there is found a solitary snowy owl or one or two ptarmigan. But now the snow-buntings appear, and ptarmigan that herald the caribou, soon to be followed by ducks and geese and a multitude of other birds, both large and small. The seals emerge from their holes and bask in the sunshine on the surface of the ice, while from far to the southward come countless herds of caribou streaming north to their summer pasture grounds.

The Eskimo, too, feels the quickening of nature and bestirs himself to new activities. Tents and household goods are all overhauled, and new and lighter clothes brought out to meet the warmer weather. His outer boots are now of seal-skin, which will not spoil in the slushy snow; often, too, he wears a seal-skin coat. The season for sealing is now rapidly drawing to a close, and certain economic factors, varying from district to district, govern the movements of the natives as soon as it is over. One group will hasten shorewards and vanish immediately into the interior, while another will linger for several weeks along the coast. But before each group finally takes its departure inland it is careful to deposit on the coast all its surplus winter gear and clothing, as well as stores of blubber that will provide fuel and light when the summer days are over and winter grips the land once more.

The safest place for a cache is on an island close to shore, where foxes, wolves and wolverines cannot reach it in summer across the water. Wolverines, the most destructive of all the animals in the north, are fairly numerous at the mouth of the Coppermine river; consequently the natives of that region cache their goods on one of the Moore islands, and cross by sled to the mainland before the ice breaks up, which usually takes place some time in June. In the spring of 1914 some of the Noahognik Eskimos cached their possessions on Chantry island; and in 1916 Ikpakhuak and others used the island at the entrance of Bernard harbour for the same purpose. Ikpakhuak stored his blubber there while the ice was still solid, but left his clothing till June, when he ferried it across on his kayak. On the mainland the Eskimos choose as far as possible places that are least accessible to animals; for instance, in 1915, at Cape Wollaston, in Bathurst inlet, they left a cache on top of a huge crag so steep and high that not even a wolverine could scale its sides. Crags such as this, however, are rare, and most of the Eskimos' caches are simply built up with boulders, while articles of stone and wood, which cannot be damaged by beasts of prey, are left exposed on the surface. Thus in 1914 we found some caches of the Noahognik Eskimos at the fishing creek near Bernard harbour. There were four boards resting on the ground, and, on top of them, a soapstone lamp and a wooden bowl, the latter weighed down with stones to keep it from being blown away. Near them were three stone cairns. One enclosed a large poke full of blubber; in the second we could see only a few sticks. The interior of the third was not visible at all, but inserted upright between the stones were four sealing harpoons. A few yards away there were three coal-oil cans and a couple of sticks lying together on the ground. The sleds and heavy spring tents of these natives had been left at a lake a few miles inland.

Often the tribes partially break up as soon as their blubber caches are made, though the full disbandment does not take place till early summer. Many families even break off while the main body is still sealing on the ice, as there are many different hunting and fishing grounds, and every man is free to choose his own. In every region there are certain well-known highways that lead into the interior, and the native naturally makes his caches at the entrance to the one which leads to the particular district that he has chosen for his summer home; then in the fall he returns by the same route. The spring cache-sites therefore are often the same as the winter assembling-places. Thus the

(Photo. by R. M. Anderson.)

Fig. 39. A cache on top of a high rock at Point Wollaston

Akulliakattak natives cache their things at Lake Akulliakattak, and the Copper-mine natives on one or other of the islands off the mouth of the Coppermine river. But in some tribal areas there is more than one highway into the interior, and so more than one potential cache-site. Different families will then make their caches in different places, so the group splits up while the natives are still living on the sea-ice. In the fall the families usually return first to their caches, then, later, all unite in one common assembling-place.

In southwest Victoria island, for some reason or other, there is no great run of salmon up the creeks and rivers during the early summer, and the best fishing lakes are inland in the Colville hills. Consequently, the Puivlirmiut who inhabit this region have no inducement to remain on the coast after the sealing has ended. Already, while still on the ice, they have split up into smaller bands;

each of these now travels inland by sled, carrying the lamps and a little blubber to furnish them with fuel until the snow has partly melted and they can gather the wretched *okauyak*. By slow stages, with many stop-overs at different places to fish, they finally reach some well-known lake, the centre of a fruitful fishing region. There they remain until early July, when the ground is growing bare of snow, and travelling by sled, or even with its substitute a polar bear skin, is no longer practicable. There, then, they cache their sleds and lamps, together with their heavy tents and all their surplus clothing. The band splits up, the families radiate, one going north perhaps to a lake to fish, two others east, two others again perhaps southwest. Thus they wander about in July from one lake to another, sometimes uniting for a few days to enjoy each other's company, then scattering aga n. Fishing is their main pursuit, and as long as the lakes are covered with ice they continue to accumulate trout and salmon, which they dry in the sun and store away in caches for consumption during the fall and early winter. Caribou are plentiful in June, but in July, when the migration has ended, the herds break up and the deer are few and scattered. The Eskimos, as long as they had only bows and arrows, gave little attention to hunting them at this period, for their flesh is lean with long travelling, and their fur useless for clothing until they gain their summer coats, which is not until early in August.

In other regions, where the salmon migrate in numbers, the natives usually gather in July and spear them as they make their way up the streams. Sealing ends, as a rule, towards the close of May, when cracks develop in the ice and the seals no longer need to resort to the holes they have kept open all the winter. From this date, then, until the appearance of the salmon the natives linger near the creeks, and either fish for tom-cod through the sea-ice, or go inland a few miles to fish in the lakes, although a few hunters, having rifles now, remain on the shore and intercept the bands of caribou as they pass north. In July, as soon as the salmon begin to run, the natives gather at their salmon weirs, which are either at the mouths of the creeks or near their outlets from the lakes. Sometimes a whole tribe will reassemble at these fishing-weirs; more often the different families spread out over different creeks so that each may secure a greater individual toll. The three creeks where the Noahognirmiut spear salmon have been mentioned already. Farther east there are other well-known "salmon-ponds"; the cascade about eighteen miles up the Rae river, below Bloody fall on the Coppermine, at the rapids near the mouth of the Tree river, and, in Victoria island, on the creek that flows into Cambridge bay.[1] Hearne and Franklin both came across natives below Bloody fall. The former remarks that the salmon were "so numerous that when a light pole armed with a few spikes, which was the instrument the old (Eskimo) woman used, was put under water and hauled up with a jerk, it was scarcely possible to miss them. Some of my Indians tried the method, for curiosity, with the old woman's staff, and seldom got less than two at a jerk, sometimes three or four."[2]

By the end of July the salmon run is over, and the ice has melted from all except the very largest lakes. The caribou in the meantime have grown fat with peaceful grazing, and their skins are now in their prime. The Eskimos, leaving safely stored away in stone caches whatever fish they have caught, and packing their light tents and a few spare articles of clothing on their backs, wander off to hunt. Wherever the country is barren and reindeer moss scarce, the deer are scattered and far apart; then the Eskimos too must scatter out to cover as wide an area as possible. On both sides of Dolphin and Union strait, therefore, the traveller will find scattered families roaming about from place to place, here today and gone tomorrow in their restless search for game. Days

---

[1]See Collinson, p. 279; Rae, Journ. Royal Geogr. Soc., Vol. 22, 1852.
[2]Hearne, p. 183.

of feasting alternate with days of fasting according to their failure or success. No fowl of the air, no creature of the land, no fish in the water is too great or too small to attract their notice at this time. They knock down ptarmigan and longspurs with stones or arrows, they shoot the ducks on their nests and carry off the eggs, they spear or catch with nooses the squirrels that burrow in the ground, and they spear or catch with their hands the tiny fish that hide under the stones on the margins of the lakes. With their bows and arrows they fearlessly attack brown bears and wolves, while polar bears they run down on foot with the help of their dogs and stab them with improvised pikes. In 1915, for example, an Eskimo named Komak spent the summer months in the country between Dolphin and Union strait and the Rae river. Two other families kept him company; sometimes the party separated out for a few days, then joined together again. They caught a great quantity of fish, some with spears, others by jagging with long rakes; in addition they killed a wolf and a brown bear, several caribou, and a large number of squirrels. The squirrels they caught with nooses, which were sometimes set to operate by themselves, sometimes operated by hand; but many, too, were killed with improvised spears, made by lashing points of caribou antler to walking-sticks.

Even in summer, however, the caribou wander in large herds occasionally in some of the more fertile valleys and plains. The Eskimos congregate there also, and organize hunting expeditions in concert. If the natives have kayaks they drive the caribou into the lakes and spear them in the water (this is the commonest method inland between Bathurst inlet and the Coppermine); but if kayaks are lacking the deer are driven down a hastily improvised compound towards the hunters, who are concealed in pits in the narrow pass at the end. In such regions six or a dozen families may stay together all through the summer. More often, however, the Eskimos break up into smaller parties and move along a few miles apart, the approximate location of each party being known to all the rest. Then they can all unite again whenever an exceptionally large herd is encountered and concerted action promises greater booty.

Their hunting often takes them long distances. In recent years the presence of white men has caused the natives of Coronation gulf to gravitate more and more towards the north end of Great Bear lake. Even the Eskimos of Bathurst Inlet make their way overland to this region, along a chain of lakes where caribou and musk-oxen abound during the summer months. Rivers and large lakes are crossed in kayaks, which serve the natives also for their hunting.[1] Caribou have always been plentiful around Great Bear lake, but it is only within the last few years that this region has become the common hunting ground for natives from every part of Coronation gulf. Probably half a century ago the Pallirmiut kept as a rule to the Rae river basin, and the Bathurst inlet natives to the country north of Backs river and east of the Coppermine, while the natives of the Copper-mine basin itself kept for the most part to the lower reaches of the river, and only ascended as far as the Dismal lakes when they wanted to procure timber for making their sleds and tables. Fear of the Indians kept them away, and hence the early explorers, Franklin, Richardson, Dease, and Simpson, saw no traces of them south of Bloody fall. As soon as white men settled on Great Bear lake, however, the natives flocked thither from all directions, not only in mid-summer during the regular hunting period, when they packed their possessions on their backs, but even in the spring, as soon as the sealing season ended, while they could still travel inland by sled. The Eskimos who visited the Roman Catholic priests at Lake Rouvier in 1913 had travelled by sled from the mouth of the Copper-mine in the late spring, and they returned in the same way in the fall. In June, 1916, again, a large party of natives from various tribes, anticipating

---

[1]See Stefansson, Anthrop. Papers, A.M.N.H., Vol. XIV, pt. I, p. 81.

a profitable trade with some white men at Great Bear lake, congregated at the mouth of the Coppermine and travelled across by virtually the same route, accompanying Mr. K. G. Chipman and a police patrol.

Hunting carries some of the Kilusiktok natives in summer as far south as Backs river, even after they have spent the spring fishing for tom-cod round the Barry islands. As a rule, however, those who intend to spend the summer far inland leave the coast in spring and travel a large part of the journey by sled, as the Puivlirmiut do farther west. Little is known of the more northern natives. Apparently the salmon do not run in their country either, so there is nothing to keep them on the coast after the sealing is over. Their fishing and hunting grounds are some distance inland, hence they naturally make the journey by sled; such at least was the case with the two Prince Albert sound families that I met at Lake Tahiryuak in the summer of 1915. They had just finished their sealing, cached their blubber on the coast and travelled south by sled. The majority of their tribe, they told me, had gone northeast in the same manner to another lake named Tahiryuak, some thirty miles, perhaps, from the head of the sound.

The first snow-fall in September and the gradual freezing over of the lakes warns the wandering Eskimos that it is time to retrace their footsteps and return towards their caches. There they recover their heavy tents and warm clothing, and either fish again through the ice of the lakes or intercept the caribou as they migrate south. In October the reappearance of ptarmigan in numbers heralds the coming of the caribou, which gather along the south shores of Victoria island until the ice in the straits is solid enough for them to cross. Small parties of Eskimos often wait near the coast for them, laying in a stock of willow twigs for fuel and building low sod walls round their summer tents. Others go back to the lakes where they have cached their sleds in the spring, hoping to encounter at least a few of the caribou in the hills. The natives on the mainland also gather in bands on the coast and intercept the deer as they come off the ice. Some families still live in their summer tents, burning driftwood or willow for fuel; others collect their caches and re-erect the same heavy tents that they had used in the spring, with the stone lamps burning blubber inside. There is no unanimity in their actions. Almost invariably, however, they all move into snow huts as soon as the snow is deep and firm enough, for a snow hut at this season of the year is far more confortable than a tent that is constantly covered with frost. Hunting and fishing absorb all their energies until November, by which time the caribou migration is usually over, and the Eskimos must redeem all their caches and prepare for the winter's sealing. Then the bands that are still inland come down to the coast and join their tribesmen at the assembling-place.

Such, in brief outline, is the life of the Copper Eskimos on the land. As no other traveller has accompanied them all through this period, and observed the influence of the economic conditions on their social life, a brief diary follows of the seven months, from April to November, 1915, when I lived with some Puivlik natives on south-west Victoria island as a member of one of the families. When I joined them, on April 13, they were living in spring tents on the ice about fifteen miles northwest of the Liston and Sutton islands. I found a home in the tent of Ikpakhuak and his family, which consisted of his wife Higilak and two children, Kanneyuk and Haugak. Avranna, Higilak's son, and his wife Milukkattak, lived in the same tent for the next two days; then, as it was rather crowded, they set up one for themselves.

April 14: Several of the natives went sealing.

April 15: Kanneyuk and her cousin Kesullik freighted some blubber and my dog-pemmican towards the shore in preparation for a migration the following day. One native and his wife left the settlement to join the Eskimos on the mainland. Most of the men went sealing.

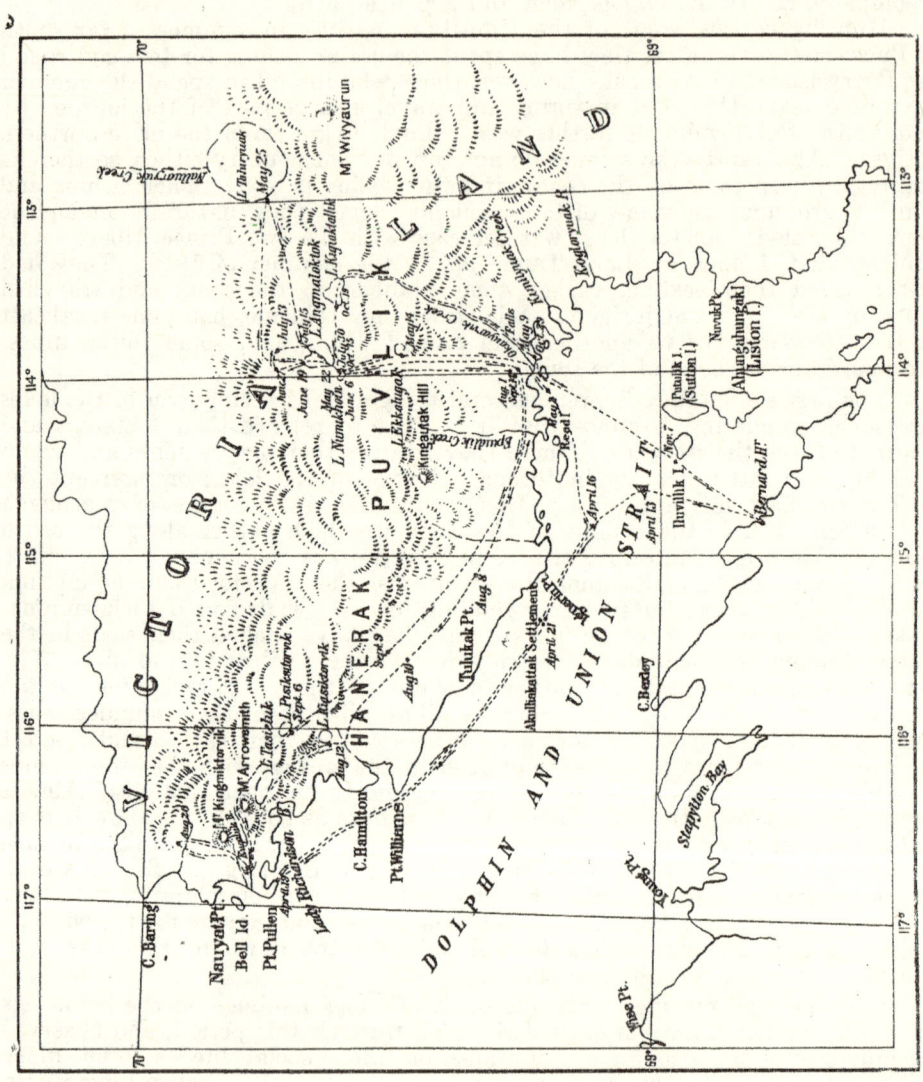

Map 1. Sketch map of south-western Victoria island showing wanderings of Puivlik Eskimos from April to November ,1915

April 16: The whole settlement migrated about ten miles north by east, and re-erected their spring tents, with the exception of Ikpakhuak, who intended to send his shorewards the next day. He therefore built a circular wall of snow-blocks instead, which he roofed over with two musk-ox skins and one of my cloth tents.

April 17—23: Ikpakhuak and I made a trip to Penny bay to bring back some deer-meat and deer-fat which he had cached there the previous summer. We carried no tent, for Ikpakhuak proposed to make a snow hut each night for us to sleep in. Near Ingnerin we found the settlement that the Akulliakattak natives had built the previous winter when first they crossed over from Cape Bexley and began sealing. It was now deserted, save for a single family who gave us a lunch of seal meat. Four days later, on our return, we found five families there, all living in their old snow-huts again for a few days before crossing over to Cape Bexley and the mainland.

April 23: Ikpakhuak and I reached our old settlement again. We had lived for four days on rotten deer-meat and deer-fat, save for two meals of seal-meat provided by the Akulliakattak natives. Ikpakhuak had found the diet quite agreeable. Our camp was littered with clothes of all descriptions that had been set out to dry in the sun; some were suspended on sticks, others laid out on bags. Caribou were sighted for the first time crossing the straits from the south.

April 24: Most of the men went sealing. Two families left us and camped ten miles to the west. There was another camp about six miles south-east.

April 25: The blubber and pemmican that had been freighted forward on the 15th were brought in to camp. The Eskimos went sealing, and with them Avranna's wife Milukkattak. The clothes were set out again to dry.

April 26: Our blubber was freighted ahead again about six miles by some of the natives, while the rest went sealing.

April 27: Stormy weather, so everyone remained in camp.

April 28: We migrated again [towards the land, travelling slowly, with many halts, during which the snow had to be kicked up round the sled-runners to prevent the iced surface of the mud from melting. About noon some of the Eskimos made a little shelter of snow-blocks and melted some snow for drinking water, using shavings for fuel.

April 29: All the men went sealing.

April 30: A strong east wind in the morning caused the snow to drift. The wind died down before noon, and the women hurriedly unpacked their bales of clothing and beat out the snow before it had time to melt. The men went sealing.

May 1: All the men went sealing, save two, who were freighting blubber one stage forward. Higilak held a shamanistic performance in the evening.

May 2: Two families left us and went towards Epiullik; two others joined us from another camp and we all moved to a point on the ice about four miles from Okauyarvik.

May 3: The other Eskimos went sealing, while Ikpakhuak, Avranna and myself went over to Read island and shot some hares and ptarmigan. The two families that left us yesterday joined us again in the evening.

May 4: Caribou hunting. Two herds were sighted crossing the ice, and several of us went over to the mainland and intercepted them, securing three.

May 5–6: Stormy weather kept everyone in camp except Avranna, who went caribou hunting.

May 7: Some of the natives went sealing, others caribou hunting. A caribou fell through a crack in the ice and was speared by one of the sealers. This was the last day that the natives went sealing until the fall. Our little party, as now constituted, remained together more or less all through the summer; we were the only inhabitants that year of all the country south of the Colville hills and west of the Kimiryuak river. Altogether we numbered 20 persons, divided into five families, as follows:—

1. Ikpakhuak, his wife Higilak, her daughter (by a former husband) Kanneyuk, who was about 12 years old, and Ikpakhuak's nephew and adopted son Haugak, a boy of about 8 years of age. I was also included as a member of this family.
2. Avranna, Higilak's son, and his wife Milukkattak.
3. Tusayok, Higilak's older brother, his wife Hakka, and their son Kesullik, a youth of about 17 years of age.
4. Okalluk, his wife Kullak (an adopted daughter of Higilak), and their son Ukpik, who was perhaps 8 years old.
5. Tutsik (Ikpakhuak's nephew), his wife Mikinrok and her son (by a former husband) Kimaktun, a boy of about 13 years of age.
6. Pissuak (a kinsman of Ikpakhuak, though the exact relationship I have not recorded), his wife Itkellrok and their baby girl Hanna. With this family lived a widower, Ivyarotailak, a brother, I think, of Itkellrok.

May 8: Avranna went hunting, while the other natives conveyed their blubber pokes to Read island and cached them. Okalluk left for the Kimiryuak river to bring back some deer-meat that had been deposited there the previous autumn.

May 9: We migrated to Okauyarvik, where Ikpakhuak recovered his large spring tent which he had sent ahead a fortnight before. Milukkattak put on the coat and mitts of her husband Avranna, who was away hunting, and built a circle of snow-blocks as a base for their tent; Ikpakhuak then helped her to set it up. Higilak gave a shamanistic performance in the evening, to enquire into the prospects of food during the coming summer.

May 10: Avranna went off alone to hunt, while Ikpakhuak and I climbed a ridge to watch for caribou crossing the strait. Ikpakhuak made a low semi-circular wall of snow on top, sufficient to shelter us from the breeze without obstructiong the outlook; later in the day he emptied one of his old caches. The other men filled in the time at various occupations round the camp.

May 11: Ikpakhuak feathered some arrows for Haugak, then gathered together such of his possessions as he intended to cache in this place. Avranna began the day by filing down some large primers to make them fit Ikpakhuak's .44 Winchester rifle that he had been using; later he joined Tutsik and myself hunting. The women were busy drying clothes in the sun; Milukkattak towards evening went off to visit two fox-traps that she had set the day before. The children wandered away with their bows and arrows to hunt for ptarmigan. They joined Tutsik and myself just after we had secured a deer, and were sent home with the head and hind-quarters.

May 12: The Eskimos proposed to migrate inland the next day, so everyone was busy packing up and laying aside whatever was to be left behind. Each family had its own separate cache, though all the caches were situated close together on the side of a low ridge. The goods were piled on the ground in a heap and covered with skins, weighted down around the sides with a few stones. Ikpakhuak cached his sled here, and piled his goods above it, while my cases of pemmican were laid underneath; on top of the pile he laid his kayak. Caribou were sighted in the evening, and some of the natives went in pursuit of them, but returned a few hours later unsuccessful.

May 13: We migrated north about 12 miles over an undulating plain interspersed with small lagoons. Ikpakhuak carried his things on Avranna's sled, as he had left his own at Okauyarvik. No caribou were sighted but some ptarmigan were seen; the Eskimos tried to shoot them with arrows, but missed. The sun was now so warm that skins had to be hung over the sides of the sleds to keep the runners from melting. In the evening the other Eskimos raised their tents on snow-blocks; but Ikpakhuak found a place where the snow was very shallow, so he cleaned it away and pitched his tent on bare ground. Milukkattak cooked some deer-meat outdoors over a small wood fire, sheltered from the breeze by some snow-blocks that Avranna set up for her.

May 14: Caribou were sighted early in the morning while we were loading the sleds, and Ikpakhuak and I went in pursuit of them, leaving the others to break camp and trek to Lake Ekallugak, in the Colville hills. We spent the whole day in an unsuccessful hunt, then about 8:30 p.m. began to look for the camp. About a mile from the lake we came upon three snow-blocks arranged in line about twenty yards apart; our people had set them up to guide us to their new camp. They had already begun to fish through the ice, and had caught enough trout for supper.

Fig. 40.   Ikpakhuak jigging for fish in Lake Ekallugak, Colville hills

May 15: The men divided into three parties and went hunting, Milukkattak accompanying her husband Avranna. Two caribou were shot. The skins were carried back to camp, but the carcasses were left to be brought in later on a sled. The women and children fished all day in the lake, and caught about two dozen trout.

May 16: Most of the men were away hunting, the others fished with the women and children in two or three different lakes. Higilak and Kanneyuk went out with a sled and brought in the two deer that were shot the day before.

May 17: The children shot two ptarmigan with their bows and arrows; the adults hunted and fished as usual.

May 18: We migrated north, about six miles as the crow flies, though, as we had to wind in and out following the line of the lakes, we actually travelled about ten. Many ptarmigan were seen on the way, and the Eskimos frequently launched their arrows at them, but invariably missed. In many places the snow was soft and deep, and one of the sleds capsized three times.

The Eskimos avoided the glare ice as much as possible, for their sleds would slide in all directions on it, then stick on the merest patch of snow, from which it was difficult to start them again as both the dogs and the Eskimos would be standing on smooth ice. We stopped to camp beside a small lake. The men, as soon as they had set up their tents, went fishing, leaving the women to unload the sleds and prepare the evening meal.

May 19: Hunting and fishing occupied the natives all day. For the first time this spring Higilak was able to cook a pot of deer-meat over an *okauyak* fire. Hitherto the woman had used their stone lamps and blubber, as in winter; but as their tables and lamp-supports had been left on the coast, they used to set up their lamps on snow-blocks, and rest a stone on each corner to support the cooking-pot. We had an exciting chase after a weasel, which finally disappeared down a hole in some rocks.

May 20: Pissuak and his family, who had left us about a fortnight before, rejoined us at this place. Pissuak owned a rifle, which he shared with Ivyarotailak just as Ikpakhuak shared his with Avranna. Everyone went hunting and fishing as usual. Ikpakhuak left in the early morning, and did not return until long after midnight. The weather was now so warm that the women did most of their work out of doors.

May 21: A repetition of the preceding day.

Fig. 41. The return from a caribou hunt, packing the game, Colville hills

May 22: The whole settlement moved to Lake Numikhoin, where Ikpakhuak and others had met some Prince Albert sound families the previous summer. The natives proposed to cache their sleds here, as they had done the year before. Accordingly they dragged them up on to bare ground where the mud runners, exposed to the sun, soon began to crack and break off. As soon as the tents were erected Ikpakhuak and others went off to bring in some caribou he had shot two days before. As the hills in many places were bare of snow they took a polar bear skin instead of a sled; most of the meat was wrapped inside the skin, which the dogs dragged home to camp, while the Eskimos packed the remainder on their backs. No caribou were sighted, but Ikpakhuak shot two ptarmigan.

May 23: Some of the men went hunting, others fished near the camp. The women were busy all day cutting up caribou meat and setting it out to dry, scraping skins, and feasting. Meat was lying all about the camp, on sleds, stones, boards and sealskins; wherever meat was absent there were dogs tied by their traces to large boulders. Just before our last migration Milukkattak had made a tent from the skins of the caribou her husband had killed; here at Lake Numikhoin Pissuak's family shared it with them. At this period it was usually midnight when we went to bed, and noon before we rose. Higilak held a shamanistic performance on the evening of this day to discover whether we would find any Prince Albert sound natives if we went on to Lake Tahiryuak.

May 24: The whole party set out for Lake Tahiryuak, with the exception of Tusayok, his wife and the little boy Haugak, who were left behind to look after the drying meat. Besides my own sled, which was an ordinary European sled shod with steel runners, there were two others, stripped of their mud shoeing but protected by runners of whale's bone. Okalluk's family carried all its possessions in a polar bear skin drawn by three dogs. Several ptarmigan were shot during the day and one caribou. Our camp in the evening was rather unusual. There was a lean-to under which four of the natives were huddled in their sleeping bags, one ordinary summer tent of deer skins, and my own light canvas tent in which Ikpakhuak and Higilak slept also. Some of the natives had no shelter at all. We had left our lamps and blubber at Lake Numikhoin, and there was no fuel of any kind in the neighbourhood, so the Eskimos satisfied their hunger with raw meat.

May 25: We reached Lake Tahiryuak in the evening, after killing three caribou and some ptarmigan on the road. Everyone began to fish as soon as camp was made. About 1 a.m., before we had turned into our sleeping-bags, Higilak held a séance to discover whether any of the Prince Albert sound natives would visit us. As the weather was mild and our tents too small to hold all the company she held her performance in the open air.

May 26—31: Everyone was engaged in hunting or in fishing. One or more of the women each day went out to collect *okauyak* for fuel; it was rather scarce in this locality, or at least difficult to find under the snow that still covered the ground in most places. We were given one meal of cooked meat each day, and for the rest ate semi-dried meat and fish. Higilak divined on the evening of the 28th to try and discover whether the Prince Albert sound natives were coming or not.

June 1: About noon a Kanghiryuak (Prince Albert sound) family arrived travelling by sled across the lake. It consisted of a man Kunana, his wife Allikammik, their little baby, and a young man named Imerak. A dance was held in their honour, but while it was still in progress a second sled appeared, with three more Kanghiryuak natives, Nilgak, a cripple, his wife Utuaiyok, and a boy of about 11 years named Akoaksiun. This second family joined its tent to Kunana's, making the open end of the latter's tent a common entrance for both. Higilak held a séance in the dance-house, after which some of the natives amused themselves with drumming and singing, while the others crawled into their sleeping-bags. Several natives slept in the dance-house during the next few days, as the skins which they had brought for shelters had been used to form its roof. Each morning they rolled back their sleeping gear against the wall out of the way of the dancers.

June 2: A ceremonial dance was given in honour of Nilgak and his family. A good deal of sporadic trading now took place between the Kanghiryuak and the Puivlik natives.

June 3: One or two natives went hunting. During the day the Kanghiryuak families gave a return dance to express their appreciation of the welcome that they had received. Some of the Eskimos retired to their tents about midnight, and were visited by others who were anxious to learn the new dance-songs they had just been hearing. Nilgak and his wife Utuaiyok taught Ikpakhuak's people a Kanghiryuak song,[1] and were taught a Puivlik song in return.

Fig. 42. Dressing for a dance, Lake Tahiryuak, S.W. Victoria island

June 4: Food being plentiful, the natives spent the day in camp, gossiping. Most of them went into the dance-house in the afternoon and held an informal dance.

June 5: A farewell dance was held in the morning, after which the Puivlik natives loaded up their sleds and set out on the return journey to Lake Numikhoin. Kanneyuk and another child were asleep when we left, and did not overtake us till the evening. Ikpakhuak went off to fish as soon as the tents were erected, though the other natives tried to dissuade him saying that everyone was too tired. Higilak divined again in the evening, the Eskimos being perturbed because one of my dogs had barked suddenly without any apparent reason; they feared that it foreboded some one's death.[2]

June 6: We continued our journey to Lake Numikhoin, stopping at Lake Angmaloktok to fish. Avranna and Pissuak turned aside to hunt and secured two caribou. We reached Lake Numikhoin late in the evening.

June 7—18: Up till now we had lived largely on caribou meat, but from this date until the fall caribou were comparatively scarce. Only one more herd was seen migrating north. Accordingly, during the next few weeks the Eskimos gave most of their attention to fishing, making Lake Numikhoin their centre. We would rise about noon, and after a light meal of semi-dried

---

[1]This song is included in a collection of phonographic records brought back by the expedition; it is hoped to publish them in a later volume.
[2]Cf. Stefansson, Anthrop. Papers, A.M.N.H., Vol. XIV, pt. I, p. 343.

fish or meat gather up our fishing-gear and start out for some lake, seldom returning before 9 p.m. If one lake yielded nothing we crossed the low dividing ridge and fished in the next. The dogs were kept in camp, tied to boulders, and fed on fish broth and on bones that had already been gnawed clean by the natives. The children often spent whole nights in wandering about, shooting at birds with their bows and arrows, and jigging for trout and salmon in the lakes; they would return to camp in the morning and sleep all through the day. Three or four caribou were shot, and a few birds, and a sea-gull was caught in a fox-trap. The women used *okauyak* for fuel whenever they cooked, as there was neither heather nor willow in the neighbourhood. One day Higilak used her stone lamp, burning some of the seal blubber she had brought inland with her. But in summer the lamp seldom burns well owing to the draught inside the tent, for the front is partly open and the roof half agape, while the sides are often full of rents. Two shamanistic performances were given during this period. Everyone was busy on the 18th packing up the things that lay scattered all round the camp. Whatever was not absolutely essential during the next three or four months, such as skins, sinew, spare clothing, and various tools and implements, was cached on top of the sleds, while the dried meat and fish were piled up in heaps and covered with boulders.

June 19: Packing everything we needed for the summer on our backs, and on the backs of the dogs, we crossed Lake Angmaloktok, and camped beside a small bay named Kauwaktok at the northwest extremity of the lake where fish were said to be very plentiful. The distance was about five miles. Okalluk's pack, which was exceptionally heavy, must have weighed over two hundred pounds. The Eskimos went fishing as soon as camp was made. The songs that they had learned from the Kanghiryuak natives two or three weeks before were very popular about this time, and every night they were sung in one tent or another.

June 20—26: Fishing was carried on as usual. Avranna went hunting one day, using Ikpakhuak's rifle. In his absence Ikpakhuak sighted a bull caribou and wounded it with an arrow, but it escaped. A few loons and ducks and ptarmigan were shot. The natives made lard from the fat of the eider ducks we shot to carry along with them. By the 26th we were threatened with a shortage of food, for our daily catch of fish was very small and the reserves of dried fish and meat that we had brought with us were nearly exhausted. Accordingly the party decided to spread out, and Tutsik and his family moved on this day to a lake a few miles farther north.

June 27: Okalluk and his family moved off to the northeast, Tusayok and his wife and son to the southeast, while the families of Ikpakhuak and Avranna, with myself, went north by west. On the way we stopped at two lakes to fish, then camped towards evening on the edge of a third lake. Our whole catch for the day was only two small salmon trout and two lake trout.

June 28: We moved again about two miles north to a lake called Sagsagiak laid down our packs, tied up the dogs, and began to fish. This day we had more success. The women abandoned the fishing before the rest of us in order to tidy up the camp.

June 29—July 2: The weather was very foggy during the greater part of this period. Caribou were sighted on the 29th while we were fishing, so the next day most of us went hunting. Ikpakhuak, Avranna, Milukkattak and Kanneyuk went north, but a heavy fog settled down soon after they left and they were unable to find their way back to camp for three days. During this interval they fished in various lakes with considerable success, and shot two deer. At night, having neither tent nor sleeping skins, they huddled together on the ground under the shelter of some bank. This little adventure in no way dampened their spirits, however; they were as cheerful as ever when they returned, though somewhat tired from lack of sleep. Higilak was greatly perturbed by their absence. She knew they would return as soon as the fog lifted, but she was afraid that her little daughter Kanneyuk would be very cold and miserable; consequently, she held a séance to try and dispel the fog.

July 3: Two causes brought about a further division in our little party. The first was the probability of finding caribou farther east, the second the apparent abundance of fish in a certain lake to the north. Accordingly Ikpakhuak and his family went east, while Avranna and his wife, with Kanneyuk, went north. Higilak and Haugak were left to transfer all our things to Lake Kullalluk, some four miles away, while Ikpakhuak and I went hunting. We secured two does and two fawns, an eider duck, a ptarmigan and two lake trout before reaching camp again at one o'clock in the morning. A light south breeze was blowing and the weather was warm and clear, so Higilak left our tent behind at the old camp. During the next three days therefore we slept in the open.

July 4: Ikpakhuak and I left about noon to hunt, while Higilak and Haugak fished near camp. Early in the afternoon we met Tutsik. He and his family had experienced very little success in their fishing, so we sent him to our camp to have a feast of deer-meat. He arranged to join us the following day with his wife and son, as Higilak had caught a large number of fish in the lake beside our camp. Our hunting was again successful; we secured two fine bulls. The skins, heads, and legs, with one shoulder blade, we carried back to camp, a distance of about six miles, leaving the remainder for Higilak to bring in later.

July 5: Tutsik and his family joined us about midnight, and, according to custom, produced a little food for us to eat as soon as they arrived, they themselves eating later. The fishing this day was very successful, 38 trout and 2 salmon.

July 6: Higilak went to bring in the remainder of the caribou we shot on the 4th, but could not find it. In the meantime Ikpakhuak and I packed some meat over to our last camp to deposit in a cache. There we found Avranna and his family, who returned with us to our camp. We brought back our tent with us, rather fortunately, for rain came on in the evening. Avranna and Tutsik made rude shelters of caribou skins for themselves and their families, using their walking-sticks and the handles of ice-chisels and fish-spears for tent poles. During the day Tutsik caught a trout by jigging a line through a crack in the ice and spearing it when it came to nibble at the hook.

July 7—12: Higilak and Kanneyuk, with two dogs, found and brought in the caribou we had shot on the 4th. Ikpakhuak, Avranna and Milukkattak went hunting, carrying a cooking-pot but no tent. They were absent till the 12th, and secured five deer, besides a considerable number of fish. The rest of us fished near camp. On the 8th two loons settled in a lane of water on a lake; Kanneyuk and Kimaktun raced up and down on the ice along the water's edge, frightening them under the water as soon as their heads emerged so that they had no time to take breath and fly away. Tutsik meantime was vainly shooting at them, and when his arrows were exhausted, he bestrode a raft of floating ice, poled along with his fish-spear and re-covered them one after another; finally we shot the birds with the .22 automatic rifle. On the 10th Tutsik and his family departed for their old camp, where they had left their tent and some drying fish.

July 13: Avranna and his family gathered up their fish and meat at Sagsagiak and moved to our old camp at Kauwaktok. Ikpakhuak at the same time conveyed his things to Lake Nanitak, about three miles north of Kauwaktok, where Higilak, Haugak and I joined him soon afterwards with the camping equipment. Tutsik, we found, had moved here also.

July 14: The day was spent in fishing. The children caught a longspur with
a noose of sinew. Mikinrok in the evening boiled some old deer-meat; it
was full of maggots, but the Eskimos ate it with great content.

July 15: We moved again to a bay at the north end of Lake Angmaloktok.

July 16—19: Mosquitoes bothered us a great deal; the Eskimos flapped them
from their faces with loon skins. We secured a fair number of fish at this
place. Early in the morning of the 18th Higilak went to examine a fox-trap
she had set for sea-gulls, and saw several fish swimming in a large pool
where a stream from the hillside entered one corner of the lake. She returned

FIG. 43. Avranna repairing his bow, Colville hills

and told Ikpakhuak and Tutsik, who seized their spears and waded in after
them, securing six. The following day, with Avranna, who had arrived
with his family in the meantime, they repeated the process in another lake
and speared 15. The water could not have been above 32° F., for all but
this corner of the lake was still ice-bound, yet they waded about in it for
fully half an hour, often immersed as high as their hips. It was impossible
not to admire their endurance, for their skins were blue with the cold.
During the last three or four weeks only the heads of the fish were ever
cooked (except for me), the bodies being dried and stored away for the
winter. Higilak divined on the 16th.

July 20: We moved to Kauwaktok again.

July 21—29: The Eskimos fished every day in Lake Angmaloktok, the only lake in this neighbourhood that still remained completely ice-bound. Higilak held another shamanistic performance on the 29th.

July 30: The camp was moved to Lake Numikhoin. As soon as we reached our destination the children stripped and played about in the water all the evening.

July 31: After caching a little more meat and fish, we moved south about three miles. Then a caribou was sighted, and the caravan halted to allow us to stalk it. As soon as it was killed Ipkakhuak climbed a ridge and signalled our success by running to and fro three or four times. Thereupon the women pitched the tents, while the children brought over our pack-straps and we carried the carcass to camp.

August 1: We trekked south again. About five miles from the sea was a curious outcrop of dolomite; it resembled in some respects the floor of an old temple, for it was almost level and the stone was cracked into more or less rectangular blocks. Formerly a kayak had been cached here on two pillars made by piling some of the blocks on top of one another. The kayak was gone, but the pillars still remained. A caribou was sighted, so we pitched camp and tried to stalk it, but the animal winded us and fled. Every one returned to camp except Ipkakhuak, who followed after it and returned early the following morning with the news that he had shot two caribou.

August 2: We moved west about four miles, then camped close to the caribou that Ipkakhuak had shot. Some of the natives went hunting. Willow and heather were plentiful in this coastal region south of the Colville hills, giving us far better fuel than the *okauyak* that we had been using. The weather was fine and warm, so Ipkakhuak, instead of setting up his tent, slept out in the open with his wife. However, it rained in the night, and he had to set up his tent after all.

August 3: The rain lasted all through the morning, so we spent an idle day in camp. In the evening three of the Eskimos bathed in a creek; they could "dog-paddle" for short distances, but had no idea of the art of swimming.

August 4: Several of us went down to Okauyarvik to cache some meat and fish. Ipkakhuak and Avranna separated from us there, and went to look for caribou and birds' eggs. On our way back we raised two ptarmigan with their fledgelings among some willows. The Eskimos caught the young ones and made them cry in order to attract the parents and bring them within easy range of their arrows; but they succeeded in shooting only one of the birds. We made a slight deviation from our course in order to visit a cache of caribou meat that Ipkakhuak had made the previous summer. The meat proved to be full of maggots, but the dogs had a good feast, and the Eskimos cracked the bones and ate the marrow.

August 5: We packed westward, following the coastline at a distance of about four miles inland. Ipkakhuak and Avranna joined us again just before we made camp.

August 6: We travelled west again and met Okalluk and Tusayok and their families, whom we had not seen since out party broke up on June 27. They joined us in our trek westward. About 5 p.m. two caribou were sighted, so we laid down our packs and went in pursuit of them, leaving four women to make camp. There were no ridges to conceal our approach, so the natives held a council and planned a drive. Milukkattak and Kanneyuk made their way round behind the deer while the men set up a row of stones to fence the deer off on one side, capping the stones with black turf so that they resembled the heads of hunters lying half concealed. On the other side there was a cliff that formed a natural barrier. Between the stone fence and the cliff the hunters concealed themselves at short intervals from each other, Ikpakhuak with his rifle at one end of the line and myself at the other, while the rest of the natives, armed with bows and arrows, were spaced between us. When all was ready Milukkattak and Kanneyuk howled like wolves behind the deer to set them in motion towards us, but the animals broke back past them and fled in the wrong direction.

August 7: The Eskimos had run out of food, so we broke camp breakfastless and trekked west. Coming to a swift-running stream about three feet deep, the natives removed their trousers and footgear, tucked up the long tails of their coats and waded across. Some brant were sighted in a lake and the natives shot six of them with their arrows. Part of the meat, raw though it was, they ate immediately, having fasted since the day before; the remainder was kept for the evening meal. After camp had been made Higilak held a séance to find out why the caribou were so scarce.

August 8: After a breakfast of back-fat and a little raw brant we broke camp and moved westward again about fifteen miles. As soon as the tents were pitched the men went hunting in different directions, but without success. Tutsik saw an old-squaw duck swimming in a pond with its young, so he took off his trousers and waded about in the water, shooting arrow after arrow till at last he transfixed it. The young birds he scorned to trouble about.

August 9: Avranna and his wife, who had moved along parallel to us the day before two or three miles farther inland in order to scour the country more thoroughly, brought some cooked deer-meat over to our camp about 9 a.m. I had given him a ·22 automatic rifle and he had shot a caribou with it. All the men went hunting during the day and secured a large bull.

August 10: Pissuak and his family, who had separated from us in the middle of June, joined us again this day, so our little party was once more united. Pissuak and his people had been very successful in their hunting and fishing, and had left two or three caches of food in the Colville hills and one on the coast. The whole party moved west again after this union. The weather was very sultry all day and our packs heavy, so when we reached a lagoon of clear sparking water most of the natives stripped and bathed. This was the only occasion during the whole summer on which the adults bathed, though the children often played in the water.

August 11: We moved west again, Avranna and Okalluk keeping a mile or so north of the main party. A caribou was sighted after a few miles, so we made camp and most of the men went hunting. Three small deer were killed. During the day Itkellrok, Pissuak's wife, carried not only her usual pack, but her little girl Hanna as well, sometimes astride her bundle, sometimes across it. This must have brought the weight of her load up to more than 100 pounds.

August 12: We broke camp and began to move west again, despite a westerly gale. Crossing a broad sandy plain named Kiasiktorvik, we sighted a herd of fifteen caribou grazing quietly on a grassy slope. A drive was organized and eight of them shot, Avranna securing four, and Ikpakhuak and myself each two. Pissuak fired several shots at the deer with his rifle, but always missed. He was so disappointed that he would have gone out hunting again immediately if his wife and the other natives had not dissuaded him. Avranna and his wife, on the other hand, were greatly elated, and maintained a constant chorus of congratulatory remarks with each other in their tent.

August 13—14: We remained at this place (beside Lake Kiasiktorvik) for two days, the meat we had accumulated being too heavy to carry along with us. On the 13th the men went out hunting again, and Pissuak and Avranna each secured a caribou. On the 14th everyone stayed in camp and feasted. During the day the natives set up a clod of earth for a target and shot at it with their arrows. The children played about, bathing in the lake and shooting at imaginary deer from miniature pits.

August 15: We divided into two bands and moved westward again. Ikpakhuak, Avranna, Tusayok and their families travelled along three or four miles in from the shore, while the rest went farther inland. Our party (Ikpakhuak's), after securing three caribou, camped for the night beside a lake called Tasieluk, about three miles long and a mile wide, situated directly below Mount Arrowsmith, which the natives call Annorillit.

August 16: Instead of migrating this day the Eskimos went hunting, but they obtained nothing except a brown crane.

August 17: We packed west to the Kugaluk river, securing one caribou after the camp was pitched. While travelling the natives caught three small fish from 4 inches to 6 inches long that had come up the river from the sea. These they ate raw, though heather and willow were plentiful all around us.

August 18: We had now accumulated so much green meat that the Eskimos determined to dry it, thereby both preserving it and making it lighter to carry. Early in the morning therefore they strung it across some poles in the sunlight, and left it in charge of Hakka, Tusayok's wife. Her husband left her his tent, taking for himself and his son only a few caribou skins. We then packed northwest across the stream Attautsikkiak to a huge crag named Kunuamnak on the forward slope of Mount Kingmiktorvik. A yearling caribou was sighted about noon and shot by Avranna, who cached the meat under some stones. Another caribou was shot near our evening camp.

August 19: Three caribou were sighted from the camp in the morning and a drive was organised, but only one of them was secured. Ikpakhuak then went down to the shore to look for driftwood, and returned in the evening with a large board studded with nails, and with several smaller pieces of wood. The board had probably dropped overboard from a whaling ship and drifted ashore at this place.

August 20: Snow fell in the night, but it changed to rain in the morning. The Eskimos stayed in bed till it ceased, singing, playing, gossiping and sleeping. Later in the day Ikpakhuak and Tusayok split up the plank to make fish-spear handles.

August 21: A gale was blowing and snow falling at intervals during the morning. We broke camp nevertheless and trekked north, for our food supply was running low again. About 1 p.m. we were stopped by a blinding snowstorm and had to pitch camp and dine on raw meat and back-fat, as it was impossible to light a fire. Raw meat to the natives is about the equivalent of a bread and butter diet to us, while caribou back-fat, raw or cooked, is a luxury corresponding to jam.

August 22: We packed north about two miles, when we sighted caribou. A drive was organised and three killed, one by Tusayok with an arrow; it was the first caribou he had secured the whole summer. The sky cleared during the day and the snow melted rapidly, but the wind was very keen. Higilak, who had brought only one coat, improvised a second one out of Kanneyuk's sleeping bag; she ripped out the stitches in the morning before we began packing and sewed the skin up again at night.

August 23: We moved a few miles north again, securing three caribou. Higilak and Milukkattak were the only women in our party, and the latter spent much of her time in hunting. Nearly all the cooking therefore fell on Higilak, who found her work rather strenuous. The children, Kanneyuk and Haugak, generally gathered the fuel for her, willow twigs or heather, whichever was nearer to hand. Besides the cooking she had to mend the footgear of the whole family, five persons including myself. This in itself was no light task, since the seal-skin soles of our boots used to wear right through after two day's trekking over the stony ground. Milukkattak had only Avranna's boots and her own to mend, though later I induced her to mend mine also, thereby relieving Higilak of a little work. The skins of the deer we shot were scraped by both the men and the women, after which they were laid out on the ground to dry.

August 24: We trekked north again, securing one caribou.

August 25: We trekked north for about three miles, and shot two polar bears, a mother and her cub.

August 26: Our camp was moved about four miles north to the place where the carcass of the mother bear was lying. Here we remained four days, feasting on the bear until the greater part of it was consumed. The dogs were so satiated with meat and fat they they could scarcely move. Meanwhile our caribou skins were drying, so that by the time we came to trek again they had lost half their original weight. Caribou were sighted on the 27th, and we secured four as the result of a drive. The skins, sinew, back-fat and leg bones were taken back to camp, the remainder was cached in stone cairns for the use of the Eskimos in the following summer. Tusayok and Kesullik departed on the 29th to return to our old camp at Kugaluk, where they had left Hakka with their tent.

August 30: We started back for the Kugaluk river, carrying with us a large quantity of bear-fat to take the place of seal-blubber in our lamps when we should reach Lake Numikhoin again. Our packs were very heavy, so we camped early in the afternoon after travelling only about five miles. Avranna had found a plank on the shore two days before while he was away hunting, and had trimmed it a little to make a sled-runner. He and Ikpakhuak now went down to the beach and brought it in to camp.

August 31—September 1: The natives decided that a new sled-runner was not needed, so Ikpakhuak split the plank to make tent poles, using an antler for a wedge and a large stone as a mallet. The chips came in useful for fuel, since both willow and heather were scarce in our immediate vicinity. The natives went hunting on the 31st, and killed two yearling caribou. The rest of the time was spent in feasting. There was a lake near the camp almost divided into two by a long sand-bar. Round its margin numbers of young salmon trout, from an inch to an inch and a half long, were hiding under the stones and boulders. Milukkattak and Kanneyuk idled away several hours in catching them; all that they caught they devoured immediately.

September 2: We broke camp and travelled south about 14 miles to the Kugaluk river, where we rejoined Tusayok and his family. Kesullik had caught a few lake trout in the river, and Hakka boiled them for our supper.

September 3—4: The women boiled down all the caribou back-fat that we had accumulated, and ran the tallow into bags so that the dogs could carry them on their backs. Rain fell each night and morning, but the sky cleared before noon. Near our camp the river had cut through a bed of dolomite running southeast by northwest at right angles to its course. The gorge thus formed was about 300 yards long and from 50 to 100 yards wide, with perpendicular cliffs about 40 feet high. The Eskimos jigged their lines from a ledge half way down the face of the cliff, and caught about a score of lake trout from the deep pool below. Just below the gorge, from the bed of the river, they gathered several lumps of pyrites, which they kept for striking fire.

September 5: Our plan now was to return to Okauyarvik and intercept the caribou as they migrated south. We therefore trekked east on this day, and camped after about eight miles beside a lake on the north side of Mount Arrowsmith. The Eskimos caught a few fish here by rocking the boulders that lay one on top of another near the margin of the lake, and spearing the fish as they darted out from under them. Kesullik used a small double gaff for this purpose, but the rest of the natives merely lashed broad pieces of antler to their walking-sticks. The fish varied in length from 3 inches to 1 foot.

September 6: We continued our journey southeast for about seven miles, and camped beside a large lake named Pisiksitorvik, where many of the Hanerak natives had fallen sick and died several years before. Our stock of food was running low again, though we still had a good supply of lard. All the men went hunting as soon as the tents were pitched, and shot three caribou about three miles away. It was then almost dark, so the hunters left most of the meat to be picked up next day, and carried only the skins and two shoulders to camp.

September 7: We moved to where the caribou lay, and the women cut up the carcasses. Some of the meat was cooked at once, the remainder was stored away in bags for future consumption. The short summer season was now at an end and all the smaller lakes were beginning to freeze over again.

September 8: While Higilak was cooking some deer-meat for our breakfast several of the Eskimos went fishing; half their breakfast therefore was made up of raw fish. We packed southeast again, camping at dusk in the bed of a dried-up stream where willows were plentiful.

September 9: We packed east again through a meadow clothed with *Eriophorum* seeds, which the women gathered for their lamps. No caribou were seen all day, consequently the dogs had to go hungry. We ourselves had a little dried meat and some lard for supper.

September 10: There was a heavy fall of snow in the night, and a blizzard raged throughout the day. We had to move on nevertheless, for our supplies were running low again. There was no hope of sighting any caribou through the clouds of driving snow, and as the weather was cold and our packs heavy we camped early, about 4 p.m.

September 11: We moved east to Tipfiktok, though the weather continued very stormy. Two small caribou were shot during the day. All the smaller lakes were frozen over by this time.

September 12: We packed east to Epiullik, where Pissuak's people had cached their goods in the spring. To reach it we had to cross a lake named Tunungeok, which was covered with glare ice about 3 inches thick. The Eskimos laid down their packs and dragged them across the lake, placing their walking-sticks underneath to act as sled-runners. Higilak proposed to divine in the evening, to discover why caribou were so scarce, but for some reason or other the performance did not take place.

September 13: Pissuak and the other natives who had left us on August 15 made their appearance today; they had travelled back to Lake Angmaloktok to fish. Higilak's divining performances, postponed from yesterday, took place this evening.

September 14: The whole party had intended to remain at Epiullik to intercept the returning caribou, but Ikpakhuak now changed his mind and determined to go to Okauyarvik instead. He and his family, therefore, myself included, packed east again, and camped about three miles inland beside a small lake from which we could obtain water.

September 15—October 13: We remained at Okauyarvik for nearly a month caribou hunting. On the 15th Higilak went down to our caches on the coast and brought back, among other things, a sealskin tent which could be used as a kitchen. During the next few days she gathered a large quantity of willow twigs for fuel, before the winter snow had completely buried them. She gathered too some *Eriophorum* seeds for lamp-wicks, and tufty moss roots, *mannik*, for torches. Her real lamp was at Lake Numikhoin, in the Colville hills, but she improvised a lamp from a hollow stone about 4 inches in diameter; at first she burnt bear-fat in it, but later, when Ikpakhuak shot a bearded seal, she used the ordinary blubber. During the first days of our stay Ikpakhuak made a semi-circular stone shelter on top of a ridge near the camp which would command a wide view over the surrounding country; every day one or other of us would spend several hours there watching for caribou. He speared a few salmon, too, in one of the lakes. They were bright red at this season, and mating; one could see them chasing each other round boulders under the ice. On the ice off-shore he shot four bearded seals. Idle hours in camp were spent in helping Higilak to scrape the caribou skins. On the 21st Tutsik, Okalluk and Tusayok with their families came over from Epiullik and camped beside us. They left us again on October 3 to return to Lake Numikhoin, for there was very little chance of their securing any caribou in our vicinity, seeing that they had bows and arrows only, while both Ikpakhuak and myself were using rifles. We gave them, however, some of the carcasses and skins for helping to discover the deer and pack the meat. Ikpakhuak and Higilak secured a few sculpins at the mouth of the Okauyarvik creek early in the month; Higilak had no proper spear, but she lashed one of my forks to the end of her walking-stick and stabbed the fish with that. The weather became rapidly colder, so on October 5, she took down the cloth tent in which we had been sleeping since the spring, and wrapped it round our sealskin kitchen; outside of this again she laid several deerskins. The sealskin tent lay in a hollow, banked round with a low wall of turf, so our new dwelling, though small, was warm and comfortable. Avranna and his wife joined us on the 10th. By the 13th the caribou seemed to have all disappeared, having migrated apparently to the south-east. All the deer we had shot (about thirty-five) were cached under the stones wherever they had fallen, for we intended to gather them up early in the winter, just before the sealing season opened. The skins, the back-fat and the sinew we cached on the shore, where Ikpakhuak now recovered his sled. Its wooden runners were quite bare, for their mud shoeing had dropped off during the summer, and the runners had never been shod with whale's bone.

October 14: We set out for our old camp at Lake Numikhoin to gather up our caches there and to fish again in the adjacent lakes. Everything was loaded on Ikpakhuak's sled. Numerous patches of bare stony ground made it drag heavily; even on the snow it was hard to pull along, because it had no mud shoeing. At dusk we found a deep snow drift, and Ikpakhuak was able to make a circular wall of snow-blocks, which he roofed over with our tent skins; Avranna did the same for his family.

October 15: We broke camp early in the morning and reached Lake Numikhoin shortly before dark. Okalluk and the other natives had left the place a few days before, so we utilized two of their deserted snow huts. Higilak immediately recovered her stone lamp from one of the caches and warmed up our dwelling.

October 16—18: Ikpakhuak and Avranna dismantled their caches and covered the runners of their sleds with mud shoeing. We fished in various lakes at odd times and caught a few trout.

October 19: The sleds were loaded up at daybreak and we travelled east by south for about five miles to Lake Kigiaktallik, the source of the Okauyarvik creek. Here we found the rest of our party, except Pissuak and his family, who were still at Epiullik. The natives were living in snow huts on the margin of the lake and steadily fishing each day through holes in the ice.

October 20—21: The women and children fished near camp, while the men collected the dried fish and meat from their various caches and fished in lakes
more remote. By the 21st we were ready to start for the coast again.

October 22—29: We entered the Okauyarvik creek at the south-east corner
of Lake Kigiaktallik and followed it down to its mouth. Caribou were
sighted after a few miles, and we camped to enable Ikpakhuak and Avranna
to go in pursuit of them. The first night we slept in snow huts, the second
in tents with snow passages, as the snow was too shallow for proper houses.
We halted one day, the 24th, to fish in a lake. The other natives continued
the journey on the 25th, but Ikpakhuak and his family stayed behind to
enable him to go hunting. He shot a caribou, so his family stayed over
another day while he brought it in to camp. We overtook the other natives
at Okauyarvik falls, about four miles from the mouth of the creek, on the
28th, and reached the coast on the following day.

Fig. 44. An Eskimo autumn encampment at Lake Kigiaktallik, S.W. Victoria island

October 30—November 8: This was the transitional period between the summer
and the winter life. Pissuak and his family joined us on the 6th, so that
our whole party was united again as in the spring. The women were busy
making our winter clothing; one or two of them had already begun the
task in the hills, but they had been too busy fishing and travelling to make
much progress. Higilak went out one morning with her husband's ice-
chisel and chipped a rectangular block of fresh-water ice from a lake to
make a window for the hut and give her more light for sewing. One or
two more deer were shot while we were bringing in the carcasses of those we
had killed and cached a few weeks before, and the pokes of blubber that had
been left on Read island in the spring were collected again and brought in
to camp. Ikpakhuak replastered the runners of his sled, for the mud
shoeing he had put on at Lake Numikhoin had been badly chipped by
stones when we descended the Okauyarvik creek. He made too a new head
for his harpoon, and in odd moments scraped several skins for Higilak.
By November 7 the strait was frozen solid, so early the next morning he and
I started out with a light sled and crossed over to Bernard harbour. The
others followed us a week later, and remained beside our station till the
end of the month, when they crossed over to the Liston and Sutton islands
and commenced sealing.

There is a theory, advanced by M. Mauss, that not only does the economic life of the Eskimos undergo a complete transformation from summer to winter, and from winter to summer, but that their social organization and religious life also are so profoundly modified as to be radically different at the two seasons. M. Mauss, for example, says, " La vie sociale des Eskimos se présente donc à nous sous deux formes nettement opposables, et parallèles à leur double morphologie. Sans doute, entre l'une et l'autre, il y a des transitions: ce n'est pas toujours de façon abrupte que le groupe rentre dans ses quartiers d'hiver, ou en sort; de même ce n'est pas toujours d'une seule et unique famille qu'est composé le petit campement d'été. Mais il n'en reste pas moins d'une façon générale que les hommes ont deux manières de se grouper, et qu'à ces deux formes de groupement, correspondent deux systèmes juridiques, deux morales, deux sortes d'économie domestique et de vie religieuse. A une communauté réelle d'idées et d'intérêts dans l'agglomération dense de l'hiver, à une forte unité mentale religieuse et morale, s'opposent un isolement, une poussière sociale, une extrême pauvreté morale et religieuse dans l'éparpillement de l'été."[1]

Fig. 45. Digging for water through the ice of Okauyarvik creek, S.W. Victoria island

Now as far as the Copper Eskimos are concerned the brief sketch that has been given of their life during the two seasons suffices to disprove this theory. Changes in their environment, it is true, produce marked changes in their economic life. At one season they are dispersed into small bands that seek their sustenance on the land by hunting and fishing, at another they are assembled into large communities on the sea-ice and live by sealing. But their social organization and their religious life continue unchanged during both periods. They have different dwellings at the two seasons, tents in summer and snow huts in winter; but it is only because nature compels them to make the change; for, whether on land or on the sea, they prefer to live in snow huts whenever it is at all practicable. Given snow and ice and the possibility of procuring

---

[1] L'Année Sociologique, 9me Année, 1904–1905, p. 124.

seals in mid-summer, many of the natives would live at that season exactly as in winter; the skins they require for clothing they would obtain by trade with their neighbours. Contrarily, if trapping for foxes ever becomes profitable, and the natives are assured of fuel and food apart from seals, nothing in their social organization or their religious beliefs will prevent them from abandoning their winter life given over to sealing, exactly as their kinsmen have done in northern Alaska. The introduction of rifles, and the stimulus it has given to the hunting of caribou on land, has already shortened the period of sealing on the sea-ice. In fact there is really no fundamental change in their lives at the two seasons, but merely an external difference occasioned by, and directly reflecting, the difference in their climatic and economic environment.

CHAPTER XI

HUNTING AND FISHING

On the land, as we have seen, the whole life of the Copper Eskimos is devoted to hunting game animals, and fishing for lake trout and salmon in the lakes and streams. Naturally the natives have adopted many curious devices in their endless quest for food. Their principal hunting weapon, apart from the harpoon used in sealing, is the bow. Back says that the inland natives make a most effective use of the sling.[1] I never saw a regular sling amongst the Copper Eskimos, though the children often use their tump-lines, *kakautak*, for throwing stones at birds; they call a sling *illuktak*. Some of the natives have seen the bolas among the inland people; they described it correctly enough, but could not say how it was used. All their own hunting on land, whether for big game or for small, is done with the bow. Collinson thought their marksmanship was very good; he states that "on one occasion the natives were induced to show their skill by shooting at the mast-head vane from before the windlass. I did not see the practice, but was told it was extremely good, the vane being hit three or four times, although it was unsteady."[2] Parry found the natives

(Photo by R. M. Anderson)

Fig. 46. A Bathurst inlet native shooting with bow and arrow

of Wager inlet tolerable archers. "We tried their skill in archery by getting them to shoot at a mark for a prize, though with bows in extremely bad order on account of the frost, and their hands very cold. The mark was two of their spears stuck upright in the snow, their breadth being three inches. At twenty yards they struck this every time; at thirty, sent the arrows always within an inch or two of it; and at forty or fifty yards, I should think would generally hit a fawn if the animal stood still."[3] Mr. Stefansson says that "tolerable accuracy, such as is needed in shooting birds, is not secured beyond a range of twenty five or thirty yards. Against caribou the effective range varies with

---

[1]Back, p. 381.
[2]Collinson, p. 275.
[3]Parry, Vol. IV, p. II.

different archers, generally between seventy-five and ninety yards, and is probably not over one hundred. At thirty or fifty yards members of our party have repeatedly seen an arrow pass through the thorax or abdomen of an adult caribou and fly several yards beyond."[1] In another passage he says, "Two bows were brought out at our request. The range seems to be about one hundred yards, and at twenty-five yards they hit within a foot of the target bull's eye about four out of five times. Doubtless these two were the best bowmen. Evidently the bow is a more satisfactory weapon for deer than I had supposed, yet it surprised me that they should have given up the method of spearing, which has everywhere, so far as I know, been the mainstay of deer-hunting."[2]

My own observations led me to a less favourable conclusion. Ikpakhuak was reputed to be one of the best bowmen in Dolphin and Union strait, and the maximum distance he could send an arrow was about 125 yards. Even at a fixed target his marksmanship was indifferent. During the summer of 1915 the natives set up a clod of earth about a foot square for a target. They went back forty paces and tried their skill, but only about one shot in twenty hit the mark. The men seemed to be no more accurate than the children, though, their bows being stronger, their arrows flew with more velocity. Two of the women joined in the sport, using their husbands' or their children's bows; they acquitted themselves hardly less creditably than the others. I frequently watched the men shooting at ptarmigan and water-fowl, and without exception their marksmanship was poor. It was no better even with larger game. They could hardly fail to hit a caribou at fifteen or twenty yards when the animal was stationary, but I have seen them miss a running deer at this range. They themselves admit that the bow is of little use at distances greater than about thirty yards. It is worth noticing that one of the best archers in the whole country used a single-piece bow; probably it was more reliable than the usual three-piece weapon.

What he lacks in weapons, however, the Eskimo makes up for in craft. All the precautions and tricks of the European hunter are known to him. The moment a deer is sighted he examines the country to discover the best means of approaching unseen. He tests the direction of the wind by pulling a few hairs from his mitten and letting them float in the air. Stealthily, with soft footsteps if the snow is hard and crystalline, he approaches his quarry, and if he cannot draw near enough under cover he patiently lies down and waits for hours till the deer comes close of its own accord. When there is no cover at all he imitates the deer itself, drawing his peaked hood up over his head and stooping as he walks. In one hand he holds up his walking-stick, in the other his bow, so that from a distance they resemble the horns of a caribou. Two men will walk side by side in this fashion, when the deer is on a flank, or one behind the other when the deer is straight ahead. Sometimes it takes no notice, conceiving the hunter to be only another animal of its own kind; the man then wanders to and fro as though grazing, but always drawing a little nearer, until suddenly he drops on one knee and launches his shaft. More often the deer grows curious and runs towards him, then stops, stares hard for a minute and pretends to go on feeding. Let the man forget his part for an instant, or make a single mistake, and the deer will dash away at full speed; but let him pretend to graze also and keep his distance, and the deer will probably come nearer still. It seldom comes close enough for the man himself to shoot, but nearly always there is another hunter concealed close by for whom the first acts only as a blind.

Indians often stalk as close as possible to their game, then race forward at full speed, trusting to get near enough to fire a shot before the animal has recovered from its amazement and turned to flee. The Copper Eskimos occasionally

---

[1] Stefansson, Anthrop. Papers, A.M.N.H., Vol. XIV, pt. I, p. 96.
[2] Ibid., p. 242.

adopt a similar method when the caribou are migrating across the ice in spring and fall. They lie in wait with their sleds; the moment the deer appear the dogs dash after them and sometimes carry the hunter close enough for him to launch a shaft successfully. This method was seldom attempted as long as they had only bows and arrows, but is naturally coming more into vogue now that many of the natives are supplied with rifles. As a rule, though, the Copper Eskimos prefer to stalk their game, and will wait several hours if necessary till the animals draw near of their own accord. The patience of the natives is extraordinary. In May, 1915, Ikpakhuak would spend 12 or 14 hours at a stretch watching from the top of a ridge for the caribou crossing the strait; now and again he would snatch a little sleep with his head resting on a boulder, then wake and resume his watch. In June of the same year Avranna, Miluk-kattak and I went hunting, but had gone only about five miles when a heavy snowstorm came on, with a cold driving north wind. It was useless to look for caribou through the blinding clouds of snow, so we decided to wait where we were until the atmosphere cleared again. Avranna and I sat with our backs

(Photo by R. M. Anderson)

Fig. 47. An Umingmaktok Eskimo hunter at Cape Barrow

to the wind, and Milukkattak huddled in partial shelter between our feet. Thus we sat for half an hour. I found it bitterly cold, but Avranna was quite accustomed to it and merely dropped his head on his chest and fell fast asleep.

Many signals are used in hunting, as might be expected from such a people. "Caribou or musk-oxen in sight" is indicated by alternately throwing up the arms and stooping down. If the game is near the outstretched hand is lowered towards the ground several times, palm downwards, as a sign to keep quiet.

Our "tsh" is *attaho* or *atta*, the latter being used also towards dogs. If the other hunter is some distance away the Eskimo sometimes croaks like a raven to put him on his guard. For "come quickly" the hunter holds the forearm vertical and moves it rapidly up and down as in our military signal "double march." Waving the coat over the head upward means "come", downward towards the ground "go back." The hunter announces his success by running from side to side two or three times,[1] often following this up by waving his coat upward, when the women or children go over with the sled or pack-straps and carry home the meat. To answer a signal, showing that it has been observed, bow two or three times towards the ground. The two animals that are considered the most dangerous, polar and brown bears, have a special signal. The hunter capers first on one foot, then on the other, waving his arms or his coat above his head.[2]

Signs or landmarks, *nakkatain*, are often erected to guide the hunter back to camp, or to point out the spot where meat has been cached. Thus a hunter who is unable to carry home all his spoils will erect two triangular or rectangular snow-blocks about a hundred yards apart, on rising ground if possible, so that the person sent out to bring in the meat will sight their broad surfaces from a distance, and know the direction of the cache. In summer, when there is no snow on the ground, large stones are used in exactly the same way; the Eskimos often cap them with black turf to make them more conspicuous. Ikpakhuak and I killed two caribou one day, and, not being able to carry all the meat back to camp, we piled most of it in a heap on top of a ridge, and surrounded it with five stones capped with sods, so that Higilak might find it more easily the next day. On another occasion we were returning to camp after a day spent in hunting, and came upon three fresh snow-blocks in line with one another and about twenty yards apart. They pointed directly toward the tents of the Eskimos on the other side of the ridge, and had been set up expressly to guide us thither, for the camp had been moved during our absence.

The same word *nakkatain* is used for the stones that a hunter often places on the spot where he has killed his quarry. They are found most frequently near pits, *tallut*, where the archers have lain concealed during organized deer drives, and from which they have launched their shafts. On the site where a caribou has fallen the victorious hunter places a small black stone on top of a larger white one, or vice versa, the main object being to make it conspicuous. The stones vary in size according to the size of the caribou killed, large ones for a bull and small ones for a fawn. Sometimes one finds three or four such marks near a single pit, and then the suspicion arises that some wandering hunter, lighting on the pit, has left these supposititious records by way of a joke. Ikpakhuak was doing this one day in the fall of 1915; he set up *nakkatain* beside every pit that we came across in our hunting. Such records therefore are not to be relied upon. Yet there is one point in connection with them that is worth noticing; they rarely lie more than twenty paces from the pits, showing how close the Eskimo needs to be before he can launch a shaft with any certainty of success.

As long as the natives used only bows and arrows comparatively few caribou were shot by individuals hunting alone. The majority were obtained in drives, when the animals were either herded through narrow gaps where the archers lay concealed in shallow pits, or were driven into the lakes and speared while swimming. Richardson saw this latter method carried out on the Rae river. "The more active of the natives," he says, "go at this season to the meadows which we had crossed the previous day, and gradually drive the

---

[1] The same signal is used to announce the arrival of friendly strangers. Cf. Stefansson, My Life with the Eskimo, p. 280.
[2] Boas, Bulletin A.M.N.H., Vol. XV, 1907, p. 266, gives an illustration of this signal from Hudson bay, but calls it the musk-ox signal.

animals to the inlet, hemming them in and compelling them, with the aid of their dogs, to take to the water. As soon as this takes place, the rest of the party, who are lying in wait in their kayaks, paddle towards the herd and spear as many of them as they can."[1] Lines of stones, with here and there a stick to which a coat or a flat resonant board is attached, are run down each side of the valley from the deer to the lake, where the hunters lie concealed in their kayaks.[2] The women and children behind the deer howl like wolves *hu-u-u-u hu-u-u-u*, and the startled deer move down between the lines until they reach the water. There they stop irresolute, afraid to dash off to a flank on account of the barricade of stones and streamers. The "wolves" draw nearer and nearer until the frightened deer one after the other rush into the water and try to swim across the lake. Then the kayakers dash out, each man armed with a short knife lashed on the end of a pole. One after another the helpless caribou are stabbed in the nape of the neck, nooses are thrown over their horns and their carcasses dragged to the shore.

Scores of caribou are killed in this way every summer on the mainland south of Coronation gulf. Farther east, round Bathurst inlet, the slaughter is greater still. In November, 1917, a Royal North West Mounted Police patrol visited the mouth of a small river that flows into Gordon bay, and found deer carcasses strewn all along its banks under the snow. Evidently the natives had speared them that summer and taken only the skins, leaving the meat to be devoured by the wolves and ravens.[3]

In Victoria island kayaks are rarely used. Instead, the natives make shallow pits, *tallut*, across the neck of the barricades and shoot the deer as they are driven up. These drives call for a considerable amount of strategy and the careful utilization of topographical features. The caribou may be grazing at the end of a plain a quarter of a mile wide, bounded by a low ridge on one side and a lake on the other. Then the hunters will set up their turf-capped stones at intervals of thirty or forty yards along the top of the ridge, and probably swing the line round across the plain to within a hundred yards of the water's edge. Where the ground is low and stones would not show up with sufficient clearness walking-sticks are driven into the soil, and coats, or laths of wood shaped like a bull-roarer, only broader, are fastened to their ends. The fluttering of the coats in the wind deters the caribou from breaking through the line; in the case of the laths a child is stationed near by to hammer them with a stick.

Between the end of the barricade and the lake each hunter digs a shallow pit, using for his adze a sharpened antler. He stabs this into the turf, pulls the clod up with his hands and lays it round the edge. In a few minutes he has made a saucer-shaped depression faced with turf and stones or snow to make it as inconspicuous as possible. Here he lies, face downwards, with his bow and arrows by his side, waiting for the deer to be driven within range. The women and children, in the meantime, have gone to windward, and the deer either catch their scent and move off down the wind, or are set in motion by wolf-howls. If the women are not in sight the caribou usually reach the hunters walking or slowly trotting, at intervals one behind the other, so that often the first is shot before the rest are yet in sight. Sometimes, as they dash back after the first animal is shot, an Eskimo will utter a sudden loud shout, when often they will stop amazed for a moment and allow him to launch another shaft,

---

[1]Richardson, p. 188; cf. Dease and Simpson, Journ. Royal Geogr. Soc., Vol. 8, p. 218; Russell, p. 227; Stefansson, Anthrop. Papers, A.M.N.H., Vol. XIV, pt. I, p. 385, etc.

[2]Douglas, p. 131, mentions barricades of trees thrown across a river near Great Bear lake, apparently for a deer-drive.

[3]Report of the Bathurst Inlet Patrol, Ottawa, 1917, p. 40.

Generally, though, the hunter still tries to keep in concealment, and the caribou, meeting the women as they run back, return again. I have seen them driven backwards and forwards in this way three or four times before the remainder of the herd broke through the lines past the archers and galloped away. Small herds of four or five deer are occasionally exterminated, but usually some of them escape, while not infrequently the deer break back past the women at the very

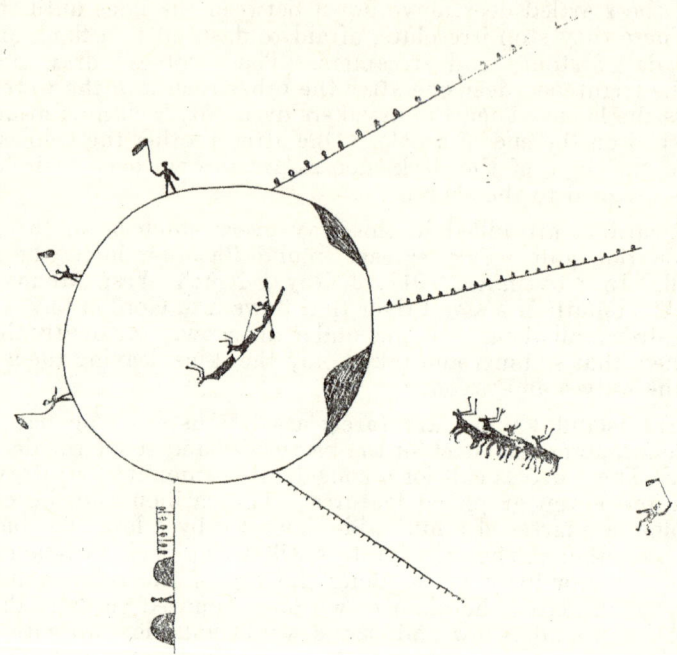

Fig. 48. A representation of a caribou drive, drawn by an Eskimo of Northern Alaska

beginning and never approach the hunters at all. Natives who have only bows and arrows, however, much prefer this method to simple stalking, even in the case of a single caribou, because they are much more certain of securing a shot at close range.

Although the caribou is not as dangerous as the moose during the rutting season, yet there have been cases in which a bull has turned and gored his hunter. The fathers of two men, Kaiyaryuk and Karitak, whom I met in Dolphin and Union strait, were living together one summer on Victoria island, their wives being sisters. One day, while they were fishing in a lake, a large bull caribou suddenly came into view. Kaiyaryuk's father caught up his bow and concealed himself, while his companion went round behind the animal and tried to drive it towards him. The bull turned on him, however, and gored him several times before his fellow-hunter had time to race up and despatch it with his arrows; but the man was injured so severely that he died a few hours afterwards.

Similar drives are organized for musk-oxen, though I never witnessed one myself. The natives say that these animals, unlike deer, will not flee at the sight of a human being, and in consequence are often driven right up to the camp before being despatched. The women utter a more prolonged wolf-howl for musk-oxen than for deer, but I was never told the reason. The natives have a story that an inland hunter named Kernet once ran down a musk-ox, sprang upon its back and ripped open its flank with his knife. These inland natives between Bathurst inlet and Hudson bay dig pits, *karigittak*, for caribou in deep mounds of snow, and plant knives with upturned points at the bottom, concealing the hole with grass and snow. Sometimes they set up snow-blocks beside the pits and urinate on them, so that the deer will be attracted by the odour, break through the crust, and be impaled on the knives at the bottom. A Puivlik Eskimo who made a similar pit near the mouth of the Coppermine river in 1915 caught two wolves in it.

Fig. 49. A representation of a caribou drive, drawn by the Copper Eskimo Ikpakhuak

Deadfalls for foxes were common enough when we entered the country, for during the three preceding years Captain Bernard had given a great impetus to trapping by trading mainly for skins. I saw a very typical deadfall on Victoria island. It was made of snow-blocks, and had a small rectangular doorway leading into a square chamber with a snow-block roof. The roof was weighted with a stone and supported underneath by a perpendicular stick, itself pivoted on another stick that pointed inwards and was baited on its inner end, about an inch and a half from the ground, with a piece of blubber. The fox had to enter the chamber before it could seize the blubber; in so doing it displaced the upright stick and brought the roof down on top of itself.

Wolves, rabbits, foxes and brown bears are shot from cover in the same way as caribou. From the top of a low knoll one day Ikpakhuak saw a fox down in the valley below him. He kept carefully under cover and made a squeaking sound with his lips like the cry of a young bird. The fox ran straight up the side of the knoll and came within twenty yards before it noticed the man and fled. I have seen Ikpakhuak try to quiet startled rabbits in the same manner, by emitting a smacking sound with his lips such as the rabbits themselves make. Once, too, after shooting a doe, he tried to attract its tiny fawn by "chucking" after the manner of its mother.

The brown bear is far more dreaded than the white bear, apparently because it is more ready to turn on the hunter when brought to bay. We saw one man with his thumb torn off, another with his head badly scarred, and in each case the injury had been inflicted by a wounded brown bear that had turned and mauled the hunter before he could deliver the death stroke with his knife. A Dolphin and Union strait Eskimo named Taligvak had a startling experience with a brown bear. He and the natives of his settlement saw two or three flashes of lightning one day, and retired in alarm to their tents. Taligvak fell asleep, but was suddenly awakened by the sound of fighting outside, and before he had time to rise a brown bear ripped open the side of his tent and broke the poles. Taligvak seized his knife and delivered a blind thrust at the animal. He missed it, but the bear, quite as startled as the man at the sudden collapse of the tent, turned round and fled, tramping down in its terror the racks of meat that the Eskimos had set out to dry.

Polar bears are run down on foot, usually with the help of dogs, and are then speared with harpoons, or with knives lashed to the ends of long poles. We ran down a mother and its cub close to Cape Baring in 1915, after a chase of about five miles. The natives have many stories, of course, about their experiences with these animals. One seized the leg of a woman as she was entering the passage of her hut. She screamed, and a man rushed out and shot it with his bow. Another bear trampled down a snow hut and carried off a woman who was sleeping inside, although there was a man on each side of her. A polar bear attacked a boy who had lingered behind his people during a migration. He thrust his harpoon into its throat until it retired, when he fled and told his people; several of the hunters then returned and killed the bear. A rather humorous story is told of a native in south-west Victoria island, near Cape Hamilton, who heard a noise outside his tent one night and, thinking his dogs were fighting, seized his snow-duster and went out to punish them. In the darkness he faintly discerned an animal in front of him, so he caught hold of it and began to thresh it. To his horror it proved to be a polar bear, but with great presence of mind he caught up his bow and shot it.

There is very little that calls for notice in the methods by which birds are secured. A native who comes on a flock of ptarmigan will circle cautiously round it until he can shoot at two or three birds in line, when there is naturally far less chance of his missing. Some of the natives have even tried to line up two caribou in this way, and the hunter who has succeeded in bringing them both down with one shot will boast of it for months afterwards. In the early days of spring loons and other water-fowl settle in small pools of open water and dive down in pursuit of fish. The Eskimos wait until the bird dives, then rush up and the moment it emerges shoot it with their arrows or stab it with their fish-spears. Snares are employed for squirrels and for small birds like sand-pipers, larks and snow-buntings, but never for ptarmigan or for caribou. In the case of birds the noose is set over the nest and the end made fast to a stick. Snares for squirrels, on the other hand, are usually operated by hand.

FISHING.

Primitive as are the methods of fishing that the Copper Eskimos employ they are nevertheless in most cases very effective. The fish-net, so universal among the Eskimos of the Mackenzie river and of northern Alaska, is here unknown, or was until the last few years. Often the Copper Eskimos practise the most primitive of all methods, catching the fish with their hands as they lurk beneath boulders on the edges of lakes or streams. It is but one stage in advance of this when they rock the boulders with their feet, and stab with improvised spears at the fish as they dart out from underneath. But their commonest method of fishing is with hook and line through holes or cracks in the ice with which the lakes are covered during the greater part of the year.

The hook, *karyok*, was originally made of copper, but iron, beaten into the same shape, now frequently takes its place. Of whichever metal it is made, however, the hook is always barbless; even if given an ordinary European hook the natives will immediately file away the barb. This may be due in part to mere conservatism, but mainly to the fact that lake trout and lake salmon, which are the principal fish the natives catch, seem rather to nibble round the bait than actually to swallow it. At any rate, on the two or three occasions that I have set lines over-night most of the bait was nibbled away, but no fish was caught on a hook. Trout and salmon must be jagged in the lip as they come to nibble, and hauled up rapidly before they have time to escape. The barb is thus a disadvantage, for often it merely tears the lip and lets the fish drop off; moreover it is more difficult to disengage a barbed hook, especially in cold weather.

Having no eye, the hook is riveted to an oval piece of bone or horn, *tivyak* or *karyoksak*, which acts also as a sinker. The line, *ukkwak*, is attached through a hole, or two holes, drilled at the upper end of this sinker. Most lines are made of plaited sinew taken from the leg-bone of the caribou, but sometimes, especially in Dolphin and Union strait, one comes upon a line made wholly or partly of baleen; I was told that these baleen lines are used chiefly for tom-cod, but did not discover the reason. The Eskimo's fishing-rod, *aulezzuk*, is usually a short piece of wood with a deep notch at one end, forming as it were two thumbs, *kuvlokuk;* the other end is spliced to a curved horn handle which also has a deep notch close to the end, the two notches being used to wind up the line. The rods vary in length from eighteen inches to two feet or more. Often one or two small bone pins, *naigliglarvik*, are inserted along the stick to enable the line to be shortened a little while fishing. For bait, *mikkigak*, the native generally uses a strip of skin and flesh from the belly of the fish, though sometimes he uses the oesophagus. Some fishermen take pains to conceal the hook, but others are quite careless in that respect; it really appears to make very little difference, as the fish will nibble in either case, and often indeed the natives use no bait at all. The fisherman's outfit further comprises a copper or iron chisel, *turk*, mounted on a long stout wooden pole,[1] a small wooden scoop, *ilaun*, with a bone "free-board" to protect the edges,[2] a seal-skin water-bucket, *kattak*, and a seal-skin bag or haversack to hold the fish, *ungellak*. In the later days of spring, and also in the fall, the man usually carries also a trident, *nuyakpak*, or a double-gaff, *kakivak*.

The lakes freeze in winter to a depth of from five to six feet. As many of them are shallow and freeze right to the bottom, while others, though deep in most places, have shallow bays, the fisherman needs some guide to show him where to dig his holes. So wherever an Eskimo has found successful fishing he sets up two stones about a dozen yards apart on a ridge overlooking the spot, lining them up so that they point exactly to his fishing-ground. Every lake of any considerable size has landmarks of this kind, which are given the same name, *nakkatain*, as the stones set up by the hunter to mark the direction of a cache. A native who is unfamiliar with the region always searches out these fishing-guides, follows their direction out on the ice for a hundred yards or so and digs his hole.

It takes a man nearly half an hour to make a hole of from 12″ to 18″ diameter at the top and from 4″ to 6″ diameter at the bottom. The chips of ice are baled out with the scoop, which, in the early days of spring, must be lashed to a long pole in order to reach to the bottom of the hole; later in the season the hole automatically fills with water from the melting surface of the lake, or the fisherman can pour water into it, so that the fragments of ice will float to the surface. The line is lowered until it touches the bottom of the lake, then raised two or three inches and kept constantly jigging. If the lake is very deep the line, unless it is exceptionally long, is lowered to its full extent, then, the moment a bite is felt, it is given a jerk, and, if the hook catches, pulled up

---

[1]The natives prefer copper as a rule, because in shallow lakes or streams the chisel often strikes a stone on the bottom. An iron blade will chip and is difficult to sharpen again, whereas a blade of copper merely burrs. For the same reason copper knives are still used occasionally for building snow huts on land.

[2]Sometimes the broad base of an antler is used in place of a scoop.

as quickly as possible so that the fish has no time to wriggle itself free. The Eskimo uses the back of his hands, or the wrists, in pulling up the line, hand over hand, instead of grasping it each time in the fingers; it is really a much quicker method. If the line is very long, however, it may become tangled in its own folds, or the fish may drop off before it reaches the surface; the native therefore runs back with his rod from the hole, and gradually slows down to a walk as the fish approaches the under-surface of the ice.

(Photo by G. H. Wilkins)

FIG. 50. Jigging for fish through an ice-crack in a lake near Bernard harbour

A hole is usually exhausted in about an hour, for the fish become cautious and keep away from the hook. The fisherman has therefore to dig four or five holes, as a rule, in the course of the day. A small lake yields almost nothing on the second day. Lake trout must find plenty of food during the winter, for many of them are very fat in the spring even before the ice round the edges of the lakes has begun to melt. They seem to stay near the bottom at this period. Lake salmon lie more dormant, and are smaller than those that have access to the sea. We caught none at all in the Colville hills until water had formed round the edges of the lakes. Both trout and salmon appear to love the sunlit pools into which the streams from the hills pour their waters. In one such pool a woman caught twenty-nine trout and two salmon in the space of four hours, while three of us who had dug holes not a hundred yards away could hardly raise a bite. The next day, however, only four fish were caught in the same pool.

When a fish bites, but is not hooked, the native cries *keuk keuk*, "Come again" or *keuk allaralumik kannakoktumik*, "Come again, another one; there are plenty down there." After the fish is drawn up, it is killed with a sharp rap on the back of the head from the fishing-rod, and laid with its mouth towards the hole. The natives could give me no reason for this, but merely said that "it had always been their custom" (*pitkuherigaptigut uvagut*) to point the fish towards its hole; there seemed to be an idea, however, that other fish would

approach the hole to keep it company   After one has been caught, the fisherman
will often say, as he lowers his line again, *taki, taki, taki aiperlugo*, ' Come, come,
come, give me another;" but expressions of this kind have no magical significance.
Sometimes an exceptionally large trout is caught on the hook, too big to be
drawn up through the hole.   The fisherman then holds it firmly against the
under surface of the ice to keep it from dropping off, while a comrade runs up,
lowers his own line, and jigs his hook also into the fish.   The two men then
steer it carefully through the narrow opening, or one holds the fish while the
other enlarges the hole with the chisel.

A crack in the ice materially lessens the labour of digging a hole.   In the
later days of spring the surface of the lake becomes perforated with holes, and
an ice-chisel is no longer needed.   As the cracks widen and pools of water form
round the edges the men make more and more use of their spears.   They jig their
hooks a foot or two below the surface, and impale the fish on their tridents as they
approach the bait.   I have already described in the previous chapter how they
wade about in the water at this season and spear the fish at the corners of the
lakes.   In summer, when the lakes are free from ice, they sometimes employ
another curious method, should any fish be seen close in to shore.   The Eskimo
will cast his line as far out as it will reach, and slowly draw it in again (*ekkasaktok*
is the name given to the process); sometimes, but not often, the fish will bite
as the line is being drawn in.

Now and again a simple form of gorge is employed in the lakes.   One
woman slit a piece of bone about six inches long from the tibia of a caribou.
She whittled one end to a sharp point and drilled a hole in the other to attach
her line.   This gorge she concealed inside the body of a small trout, and set it
over night in a lake.   In the morning she drew in a fine trout weighing about
ten pounds—the lake trout apparently devours the young of its own species.
Another woman removed the spine from a small salmon trout and inserted in
its place a number of short sharp-pointed bones.   She then tied the fish together
again, fastened a line to its tail, and set it overnight through a hole in the ice of
a lake.   I was away hunting the next day, and omitted to enquire whether
she caught anything or not.

Trolling proper can be done only from a kayak.   The fisherman holds his
rod in his mouth with the line trailing behind him in the water.   He paddles
round and round until a fish is hooked, then makes for the shore as fast as he can,
since he dare not draw in his line at once for fear his kayak will capsize.   As
soon as the boat touches the beach he jumps out, hauls in the fish and knocks
it on the head with his fishing-rod.   This method, as far as I know, is seldom
practised outside of the region around Bathurst inlet, where kayaks are much
in vogue for summer caribou hunting.

The salmon trout that come up from the sea are sometimes speared in the
autumn as they pursue each other round the boulders on the margins of the
lakes.   This is their mating season, and their colour changes to a bright red.
The natives are well aware of both these facts, and further that the salmon at
this time will never bite at the hook.   The few that Ikpakhuak caught in the
fall of 1915 were all speared with the double gaff.   Large numbers are speared
in the spring as they migrate up the streams and rivers.   The use of a rake for
this purpose has already been described.   The Eskimos construct stone dams,
isikat, across some shallow reach, either near the mouth of the creek or at its
exit from the lake.[1]   Usually there are four dams at intervals of twenty-five
yards or so from each other.   The lower three have narrow gaps through which
the fish can pass, but the upper one is complete and blocks their passage altogether.   As soon as the shoal has all entered through the third dam the natives
rush in with their spears and slaughter them, throwing them out on to the
bank or stringing them on long seal-skin lines.   Sometimes they take the pre-

---

[1] Cf. Boas, Bulletin, A.M.N.H., Vol. XV, p. 475.

caution to close the entrance to the first dam with a boulder, sometimes one man merely stands guard over it and spears any fish that try to escape.   In some weirs small blind caverns of stone are made in the dam where the fish can hide when frightened by the splashing and shouting of the natives.   There the women catch them with their hands and string them on thongs of sealskin, using a rough bone needle about four inches long to pierce their bodies.   It is very seldom indeed that a fish escapes when once it has entered a properly constructed weir. So simple and efficient a method of fishing naturally means a very pleasant and lazy existence for the natives as long as the migration lasts.   They lie about in their tents all day waiting for the fish to appear.   From time to time some one goes down to examine the weir, and gives a shout if any salmon have made their appearance, when everyone rushes out, clothed or unclothed, grasps a spear and races into the water.

At Nulahugyuk creek near Bernard harbour the natives had two series of weirs, one for the larger salmon migrating upstream, and one for young fry, two seasons old, migrating down to the sea.   The latter are only about 8 inches long and weigh perhaps a third of a pound, whereas the adult salmon averages two feet in length and eight pounds in weight.   Sometimes, as in June, 1916, the two are running at the same time; more often perhaps the young fish make their appearance two or three weeks later.   Mr. G. H. Wilkins, who took a number of moving pictures at this place in 1915, describes the scene as follows:—

" The men and sometimes the women would run into the water with their spears and jab and poke at the fish as they swam around.   Some of the women would run to the walls of the weir and catch the fish as they stuck in between the stones in their attempts to get away.   By this method the fish would soon get thinned out and there would be great competition for the remaining few. Eight or ten people would sometimes be spearing for the same fish with the result that some one or other's toe would suffer.   I never saw any argument as the result of this, but the injured one would retire from the fray for a moment or so and rub his toe.   Soon the possibility of getting the fish would induce him to try for it between the other people's legs, with the frequent result that another would be delayed for a minute or so to rub his toe or shin.   All the knocks were taken good-naturedly and they would discuss their injuries after the fray without any sign of ill feeling.   When a fish was caught either by the men or women, they would run it through with a bone needle threaded on a string with a cross piece at the end, and drag the fish about with them in their endeavours to secure another one.   Sometimes when the pond was almost cleaned out they would stop to kill the fish by knocking it on the head with a stone picked up r om the river bed before threading it on the line.

. . . " Their fishing was not restricted to the spearing of the big fish that were making their way up the river to spawn, but they also caught hundreds of the small fish as they came from the lake to the sea.   Indeed it is surprising that the supply of fish in the lake keeps up so well, for it would seem as if the weirs that they build would entirely block the fish from getting up stream and the small ones would entirely block the young ones from getting from the lake. It is certain that few escape that once get into the trap, but I have noticed numbers of the small ones hesitating to go through the narrow entrance to the trap. The Eskimos had noticed this, and before they went to clear the trap of the small fry, several of them would go some distance up stream and splashing through the water and waving their arms would 'shoo' the fish down stream.   This ruse was fairly successful, and at times the trap would be a seething mass of young salmon trout about six inches long.   The disposal of these would be mostly left to the women and the children, although sometimes a man or two would join in with the rest.

" If there were more of these fish than the fishermen could conveniently eat as they caught them, they were strung on a line in a similar manner to the

larger fish, but as a rule the majority of these young fry were eaten alive, as
one might say. A man, woman or child as the case might be, would catch a fish
in the rocks, and would pop it into his mouth head first and chew up the head;
the body quickly followed, convulsively protesting with its tail until that disappeared from sight and was crushed between the teeth. In most cases nothing
more was seen of the fish, but if there were a few people there, and the haul was
likely to be large, then some of the people would take the trouble to spit out
the skin or else bite the head of the fish and then strip the skin off by catching
hold of it with the teeth and sleeving the fish, eating the body afterwards and
throwing the skin away."

Just as fish caught in the lakes must be laid with their heads towards the
hole, so salmon that are killed going up-stream must be placed facing the lakes,
and those going down-stream facing the sea. If they are split in two and hung
up to dry the dorsal fins must face the lakes, or the sea, as the case may be;
other salmon will then follow in their wake as though the previous shoals had
continued their journey unmolested. The same regulation applies to the fish-
spears; their points must face upstream or downstream according to the direction
in which the fish are running. Bows and arrows (and guns) must not be used
within a hundred yards or so of the stream lest the fish should be frightened
and cease to migrate; and when the salmon are running up-stream no iron
utensil or weapon must be dipped into the water lest the fish should object to
its taint.[1]

Tom-cod are caught through the sea-ice in the same manner as lake fish
except that a much larger hook is used and lures of bone are employed instead
of regular bait. Sometimes, instead of a hook, the natives merely jig a bear's
tooth with two or three smaller teeth or pieces of bone dangling around it. The
tom-cod are attracted by the white gleaming teeth and are speared with the
double gaff. The rod is usually a straight piece of wood notched at each end
so that it resembles a very long netting needle. Similar rods are sometimes
used in lake fishing, but there the preference is for a curved handle.

---

[1]Back (p. 381 *et seq.*) says that the Eskimos of Backs river caught white fish and small trout in an
eddy below a waterfall and kept them alive in specially constructed ponds. Probably they had weirs
like the Copper Eskimos into which the fish entered of their own accord and were then unable to escape

CHAPTER XII

MARRIAGE, CHILDBIRTH, NAMING AND TREATMENT OF CHILDREN

In the eyes of the Copper Eskimos, celibacy in either sex is a contemptible condition. A man is the natural complement of a woman, a woman of a man; neither is complete without the other. There are no crafts or professions among them, no food stores or clothing establishments where they can barter for what they need. A woman is dependent on a man for shelter and for food, and a man needs a woman to dress the meat and skins of the game he kills, to cook his food and make his clothing. Every boy and every girl therefore expects to marry at no very distant period in life. Owing to the preponderance of males over females, and to occasional instances of polygamy, a man may sometimes be unable to find a wife until he is well in his prime; but every native marries sooner or later in life, unless he is a cripple and cannot support a wife or is disqualified in some other way. In the settlement at Bernard harbour in November, 1915, thirty-eight out of the forty-six men were married, two of them to one woman; of the eight unmarried men four were widowers and two mere boys hardly old enough to marry. Thirty-nine of the forty-two women were married (one man had three wives), two of the others were widows of forty-five years or more, and the third was a young girl who had just been divorced and was about to marry again. A settlement at Tree river about a month later consisted of eleven married couples and their children and one unmarried young man.

There are no early contracts among the Copper Eskimos. A woman may sometimes say that she will marry her daughter to a certain man, but a few weeks later she may change her mind, or the girl herself when the time comes may refuse to accept her mother's choice and select her own husband. Boys cannot marry until they are able to perform the duties that devolve on the head of a household; that is to say until they can build a snow-hut without assistance and possess the strength and skill that are requisite for hunting seals and caribou; they seldom begin to look for wives therefore until they are at least seventeen or eighteen years of age. Girls, on the other hand, have simpler duties and often marry before they reach puberty, though they bear no children until three or four years later.[1] Higilak, for example, was a wife before she was really of age, and Hakungak, the last of Uloksak's three wives, could not have been more than thirteen years old when she married her first husband Kikpak. During the summer of 1915 Higilak would frequently urge Kanneyuk to marry the following winter, though the child had not yet reached puberty.

No ceremony marks the attainment of puberty by either girls or boys. The first significant event in a boy's life is the killing of his first caribou or seal. His mother usually makes a pair of trousers for herself from the caribou skin; in the case of the seal practically all the meat is cut up and distributed among the other families in the settlement.[2] By either method the parents make public pronouncement that their son has attained the first stage of manhood and has become a productive member of the community. The second significant event in his life, and the first in a girl's, is marriage. Even marriage, however, is marked by little or no ceremony. The contracting parties make their own arrangements, though they are naturally influenced by their parents. If the

---

[1] D. B. MacMillan (Four Years in the White North, p. 274) says that in Smith sound girls usually marry at the age of twelve, but are unable to bear children before they are eighteen.
[2] Cf. Stefansson, Anthrop. Papers, A.M.N.H., Vol. XIV, pt. 1, p. 340.

bride is to be taken to another settlement the bridegroom makes a small payment to her parents; they then give a farewell feast in her honour, and she is led away, weeping because she is leaving her familiar surroundings and going out into a new and unknown world. No payment is made if the new couple intend to remain in the same district; the bridegroom merely sets up his hut or tent and the bride moves over to it without any ceremony, taking with her a lamp and a few household things. A well-bred maiden should show some reluctance, however willing at heart she may be, and often the bridegroom has to lead her across with a show of force. In 1915 Mr. Wilkins, the photographer of the expedition, was travelling in Coronation gulf with an Alaskan Eskimo named Natkusiak. Natkusiak wanted to take a wife back with him to Banks island, and made overtures for a young girl named Tupik, offering her father and her brother a rifle in payment for taking her away. They gave their sanction to the match as soon as the brother had tested the rifle and found it satisfactory; but at the last moment the father stipulated that Natkusiak should spend the first year in Coronation gulf, on the ground that the girl was too young to be taken so far away from home at once. Natkusiak, however, had to return with Mr. Wilkins the same summer, so the negotiations came to nothing. Natkusiak then made overtures to the relatives of a middle-aged widow named Kaulluak, but no decision was reached. Mr. Wilkins was about to leave the settlement when suddenly Kaulluak's brother appeared and held a short conversation with Natkusiak. A few minutes later the brother walked calmly away with the rifle and a youth was sent to bring out the woman; she came, and at the suggestion of some of the natives took her place in front of the sled and began to run ahead of the dogs, accompanied for a short distance by several of the young men. Mr. Wilkins gives an amusing picture of their farewell. "They would frequently stop, and one or other of the youths would grasp Kaulluak round the waist and press his nose against hers . . . Our dogs were always on the heels of the people running ahead, and with the frequent stops were getting tangled up, so I told Kaulluak to come and ride on the sled. Here one of the youths sought to engage in a long nose push, but the load of the two of them on the sled was too heavy, so I made them get off. He ran beside for about a quarter of a mile, but soon got tired and dropped behind. Several times during the day she pretended to run away, and Natkusiak had to bring her back with his arm round her waist. They were not very serious attempts, for once when Natkusiak was several miles ahead and she could have escaped had she wished she followed steadily in his trail. She disappeared in the morning, and Natkusiak had to search for an hour before he found her on a small island near the camp. After one or two more pretences at escape the claims of modesty were satisfied and she settled down quite cheerfully as his wife." In the end, however, she did not go to Banks island, but left Natkusiak and returned to her own people.

Real "marriage by capture" is not infrequent, though only, I believe, with women who are or have been already married.[1] A man would hardly dare to carry off a young girl against her own wishes and those of her parents. On the other hand he might with impunity carry off a widow who was only a burden to her kinsmen, and he might even deprive another man of his wife. Uloksak, who had two wives already, took a fancy to Hakungak, Kikpak's young wife. Kikpak was only a youth with no one to back him up and Hakungak was either not adverse to being transferred to so influential a man or afraid to offer any opposition. At all events Uloksak made her his third wife, leaving Kikpak with none. The change did not benefit the girl very much, for she became the drudge in her new household and lost her good looks before the year was out.

---

[1] The "scrimmage for wives with deer-antlers", which the Baillie island natives told Mr. Stefansson was the custom among the Nagyuktogmiut (My Life with the Eskimo, p. 159), is half-legendary.

Ikpakhuak adopted an orphan girl named Arnauguk, or Kila. In the spring of 1915 she married a young man Aiyalligak with whom she lived until the winter. For some reason or other he divorced her, and she fell back on Ikpakhuak's hands again. Ikpakhuak married her three or four weeks later to the young divorcée Kikpak. One evening, as she was returning from the dancehouse, a man who already had a wife of his own tried to drag her to his hut and force her to spend the night with him. She struggled to release herself, and, with the assistance of two other girls tumbled him into the snow and escaped to her hut. Kikpak divorced her after they had been married only a fortnight, and for many months she remained single again, though several natives made overtures to her. Finally she married a western Eskimo from the Mackenzie river delta.

The old shaman Ilatsiak told me of a bigamist Anengnak who was living with a band of other natives near Cape Krusenstern. He was tall and heavily built, and his teeth, like those of old Eskimo women, were worn right down to the gums. In the same settlement was another man named Norak who was not nearly as big as Anengnak. Norak, being unable to obtain a wife elsewhere, laid hands on Anengnak's second wife one day and began to drag her away. Anengnak caught hold of her on the other side, and a tug of war ensued, but finally Norak, though the smaller of the two, succeeded in dragging her away to his hut and made her his wife. The Rev. Mr. Girling tells me that in the winter of 1917-18 an Eskimo in Coronation gulf tried to carry off another man's wife, and the woman was injured so severely that she died shortly afterwards.[1]

For the first year or two at least a marriage is considered a kind of trial in which the young couple discover whether they can adapt themselves to each other and live together harmoniously or not. The girl may leave her husband at any time and return to her parents taking, with her all her possessions; but in that case the bride-price, if any has been paid, must be restored to her former husband. Natkusiak's rifle, for example, was returned to him when Kaulluak deserted him and went back to her own people. An interesting case was that of a widow named Kullahuk who married a young man named Agluak, but quarrelled with him the very next morning and was severely beaten and dragged in the snow. Immediately she gathered up all her belongings, transferred them to the house of another man named Utugaum and became his wife instead.

It often happens that a girl is divorced, or divorces herself, two or three times within a year. On the other hand instances of genuine affection are not at all uncommon, even before a child is born to cement the union. Avranna and Milukkattak might often be seen stretched out on the bed-skins in their hut pressing noses and caressing each other, wholly oblivious of the presence of other natives around them. Milukkattak would go out hunting with him, and sealing too at times, so that they might not be separated for a single hour. In February, 1916, Avranna accompanied me on a visit to the Bathurst inlet natives. Milukkattak wanted to go too, but as her time of delivery was near it was thought advisable for her to remain behind. She entreated me to look after her husband, not to allow any eastern woman to seduce his affections but to bring him safely back again. We were absent only a few weeks, but Avranna was worried about his wife all the time; he was certainly the happiest man in all the country when he joined her again and saw a little baby face peering over her shoulder.

I never knew of any instance where a couple separated after a child was born to them. It does occur, though very rarely. One reason perhaps why it seldom happens is that the wife can still claim to be supported by her husband. Even in childless marriages, if the man divorces his wife and takes another, the

---

[1] Two women from Kittigaryuit, the big settlement in the Mackenzie river delta, told me that similar contests were not infrequent among their people also in the days before the coming of the white men. Cf. for parallels from other, mainly Greenland, Eskimos, the authorities cited by Gilbertson, Journal of Religious Psychology, Vol. VII, p. 53 *et seq.*

first wife still has a claim upon him. Some years before we entered the country Ikpakhuak divorced his wife Kitiksik and married the widow Higilak. He did not see Kitiksik again for many years; in fact he might have forgotten her existence altogether if Higilak had not reminded him occasionally by pouring ridicule on her or inducing others to make jests at her expense. Kitiksik, however, had not forgotten, and when the rumour spread that Ikpakhuak was now a wealthy man she made up her mind to share his prosperity, whether he wanted her or not. Accordingly, in the early spring of 1916, she journeyed westward, and at the beginning of April I found her living alone in a small hut that Ikpakhuak had built for her adjoining his own and Higilak's. Kitiksik was old and ugly, as Higilak had said, and even more voluble than Higilak herself. It was clear that Ikpakhuak and his people did not welcome her, but she had a claim on him which he could not honourably overlook. She rarely entered his hut unless there were other natives present with whom she could converse, for Higilak always affected to ignore her presence, while Ikpakhuak never addressed her except when it was absolutely necessary, and then only in the briefest possible manner. Yet whenever the camp was moved he always made a separate dwelling for her, and was careful to see that she lacked none of the necessaries of life, such as clothing and bed-skins and blubber for her lamp. Higilak too had to send over some food for her each day. It could hardly be expected, however, that Ikpakhuak should support her indefinitely, so towards the end of spring he paid her relatives to take her east again.

Very few men have more than one wife each. Polygamy increases their responsibilities and the labour required of them; moreover it subjects them to a great deal of jealousy and ill-feeling, especially on the part of men who cannot find wives for themselves. The Eskimo polygamist, therefore, must be a man of great energy and skill in hunting, bold and unscrupulous, always ready to assert himself and to uphold his position by an appeal to force. Such a man was Uloksak. He had two wives when we first encountered him, but later he took a third wife from Kikpak. Uloksak was more intelligent than the average native; he was strong and capable and energetic, possessing all the prestige of a skilful hunter increased by his repute as a shaman to whom was ascribed the most extraordinary powers over the spirit world. There was a great deal of bluff in his character, but the bluff was successful as long as he had only his own people to deal with and did not come into opposition with any white men. His first wife well supported the dignity of her husband's position; she was a quiet kind-hearted woman of much sense and judgment, an excellent housewife, and a successful hunter of both seals and caribou. Uloksak much preferred her to both his other wives, but she had one failing—hitherto she had borne him no children. His second wife was reputed to be one of the best-looking girls in the country, but there her good qualities ended; she was bad-tempered and idle and merely a burden to her husband. He married her, he said, because she was good-looking, and he needed some one to help in the summer's packing and in dressing the meat that he brought in to camp. Possibly he would have divorced her again had she proved childless, but she bore him a son, and a son is the delight of every Eskimo household. He kept both his wives, therefore, the good one and the bad, and took a third, Hakungak, who became the drudge of the family. It is not easy to say what the ultimate outcome will be, especially if Hakungak bears him a child also. Sooner or later he is sure to lose one or more of his wives. Some younger rival will forcibly take one from him, unless Uloksak has already forestalled the event and unburdened his household of some of its superfluous members. He was the only native we actually encountered who had more than one wife for any long period, though in several instances a native took a second wife into his house for a few days and sent her away again as soon as he grew tired of her.

In one case a woman had two husbands for about a fortnight. Her first husband was a quiet good-natured man with whom she had lived quite peacefully for many years. Moreover they had one child from their marriage, a boy of about eight years. What induced them to admit a second man into the privacy of their married life I do not know; it may be that the woman desired a change, and induced her husband to gratify her whim for a period; or, more likely, the husband was offered some valuable object as a bribe, and the wife was forced to submit. The result, as might have been expected, was not a happy one. The two men became jealous of one another and vented their spleen on the woman. One day the second husband gave her a beating. This brought matters to a head, and after a violent altercation he had to take his belongings away and find refuge in another house. He married a young divorcée soon afterwards and went away to another settlement. This was the only instance of polyandry that ever came under our notice.

Marriage involves no subjection on the part of the woman. She has her own sphere of activity, and within that she is as supreme as her husband is in his. All important matters, such as the migrating to another settlement, are discussed between them before any decision is taken. Both within and without the house she behaves as the equal of the men. Her voice is heard in the dance-house when any deliberations are in progress, even in the hunting field when caribou are sighted and a drive is to be organized. Some of the women are shamans, and so obtain a considerable influence in the communities to which they belong. Yet they can never attain to a full equality, because from the physical weakness inherent in their sex the heaviest tasks must be left for the men to perform, and these tasks, the procuring of food and the construction of a home, are precisely those that are the most vital to their existence. Nevertheless woman meets with far more consideration and respect among the Eskimos than falls to their lot among most races. Quarrels between husband and wife are not of course uncommon, but they are usually soon patched up and as quickly forgotten. In the summer of 1915 Avranna and Milukkattak had a quarrel. Milukkattak wept long and loudly, and refused to go fishing with the rest of us. She fasted all day and would not listen to her husband when he tried to make peace with her in the evening; but next morning they settled their quarrel, and everything went smoothly again.

A more exciting quarrel arose one night in Ikpakhuak's hut. Something struck me on the head as I lay asleep and awakened me. In the middle of the floor was Ikpakhuak, thrashing Higilak with the back of his tomahawk, while she was stooping down and butting her husband in the stomach. Fearing that the woman might be injured I sprang up to stop the fight, but Ikpakhuak threw his tomahawk into a corner and scrambled back into bed again. He cast a wink at me before rolling over in his sleeping-bag, then pretended to be sound asleep. His wife, after looking at him in silence for a few minutes, relieved her feelings by expressing her plain, unvarnished opinion of his conduct, then slowly undressed and crawled in beside him. Next morning they were both joking over the quarrel. It seems that one of the dogs had climbed up on the roof during the night and awakened the old couple by scratching on the hard snow. Their yells and curses having no effect Ikpakhuak had finally ordered Higilak to get up and drive it down. It was a bitterly cold night, and Higilak's vexation at having to turn out of her snug sleeping-bag was doubled when she found that the dog had ripped to pieces one of her finest garments. She came inside and blamed Ikpakhuak, saying that he had built the wall too low and adding a few more remarks of a very uncomplimentary nature. This enraged the old man; he sprang out of bed to punish her, and their scuffle had awakened me.

These two had another quarrel in the spring of 1916. Higilak was an inveterate chatterer, and her strident voice could be heard long before she was near the door of our station at Bernard harbour. But one day she came in very quietly, closed the door behind her, and leaned her back against it without saying a word. We were wondering at her unusual silence when suddenly we noticed that one of her eyelids was badly swollen and surrounded with a large black ring. I asked her who had caused her black eye, and she said "Ikpakhuak, with his fist"; but when I asked her why, all she would say was that he was angry, and that she herself had done nothing to cause his anger. She was afraid to go back to her tent, so I went over to see Ikpakhuak and hear his version of the matter. The old man was whittling a stick in his tent, and looked rather sullen when I entered, for he knew that Higilak had been over to our house. We talked about the hunting for a while and the chances of more caribou appearing, then, suddenly changing the subject, I asked him why he had struck Higilak in the eye. "Oh, she talked too much," he answered, with a look that implied, "You know what a chatterbox she is." The affair was over as far as he was concerned, and Higilak might safely return as soon as she wished. Half an hour later the two of them were laughing together in their tent and Higilak was making fun of her attractive appearance.

Jealousy is probably the commonest source of trouble. Higilak was very proud and jealous of her husband and would ridicule her possible rivals on every conceivable occasion. Generally speaking, though, the women are well treated by their husbands, and the longer a couple has been married the less they tend to quarrel. It is the widows who have the hardest lot. Their kinsmen are bound to support them and provide them with a home, but naturally a man with a wife and children of his own to take care of has no desire to be burdened with a widowed sister any longer than he can help. Friction, too, may arise at any time between sister and wife. Sometimes the widow becomes a public harlot; she will offer herself, that is, to any man who wants her for a day or a week, in the hope that some one will finally keep her permanently; should she give birth to a child no one will ever reproach her. Young widows never have any difficulty in finding new husbands, but the middle-aged often have to wait a long time, if they re-marry at all. The people have a proverb about them which runs: "She had no property. She was an old woman when she finally remarried, an aged woman".

All travellers have remarked on the small number of children in the average Eskimo family. Parry, for example, says that "the women do not appear in general very prolific. Illumea had borne seven children, but no second instance of an equal number in one family afterwards came to our knowledge; three or four is about the usual number."[1]

M. Mauss even goes so far as to say that the maximum is four to five, and thinks that there may have been an error of observation in the only case he knew of where more were mentioned—a family of eight children reported by Captain Comer from Hudson bay[2]. Holm, however, says that among the Ammassalik Eskimos of East Greenland the average number of children that each woman bears seemed to be about three or four, counting only those who survived, while seven or eight children were by no means uncommon. My own data tend to show that among the Copper Eskimos from four to five children are born, on the average, to each woman, and three survive, while there are

[1]Parry, Vol. IV, p. 42. Cf. Hall, Arctic Researches, p. 101.

[2]L'Année Sociologique, 9ième année, 1904–05, p. 61, note 2.

occasional instances of both lesser and greater fecundity. The following statistics will illustrate this:

Women	Age (approx.)	Tribe	Children living	Children dead
Apattok	40	Coppermine R.	4	?
Arnauyuk	35	"	3	1
Ungahak	28	Puivlik	3	?
Mannigyorina	25	Pingangnaktok	1	3 (miscarried)
Hattorina	45	"	5	?
Milukkattak	25	Akulliakattak	1	4 (miscarried)
Kormiak	35	Puivlik	3	1
Hoka	(dead)	Kilusiktok	5	3
Higilak	45	Akulliakattak	2	1 (possibly more)

I knew of two cases among the natives farther west where an unusually large number of children were born to one family. One was at Kittigaryuit in the delta of the Mackenzie river, where a woman bore five sons and five daughters. Four of the sons were still living in 1915, one being my interpreter Palaiyak; of the daughters three were dead. A North Alaskan woman, the wife of a man named Teriglu, had two boys and three girls, and was pregnant again in 1914. These were exceptional cases, however, for as far as I had means of judging the average in these regions too seemed to be from four to five.

Sexual intercourse takes place at all seasons. It seemed to me that more children were born during the winter then at any other time. Of the births between 1914 and 1916 in the vicinity of Bernard harbour two occurred in December, one each in January, February, March and October, and one in either May or June; it must be remembered, however, that the natives are more scattered and less under observation during the summer months, so that complete information of this nature is difficult to obtain. Kohoktak, a Tree river native, and his wife, Mannigyorina, were employed by the expedition during the summer of 1915. They built a hut beside our station in November, and in the following month the woman gave birth to a child. Much anxiety was felt while she was in labour, for she had already suffered three miscarriages[1]. Two married women attended on her, but her delivery was long and painful. Her husband was hurriedly sent out to invoke our assistance, but the child was delivered almost as soon as he left the hut. About a quarter of an hour afterwards Mannigyorina was kneeling on the sleeping platform inside her hut (she was not allowed to sit), and holding the unwashed baby underneath her coat against her breast. The following morning Kohoktak presented a slab of sinew to Dr. Anderson, in payment for his (supposed) services in driving away the malignant spirits that had hindered his wife's delivery. We visited his hut, and found Mannigyorina attending to her lamp with the baby dressed in deerskin clothes sleeping on the platform. Its little feet were curled up, so the mother pulled them gently out to make them straight, then allowed her proud husband to take his first-born into his arms.

There is no seclusion of women among the Copper Eskimos either before or after child-birth.[2] The mother is delivered in her own hut in the presence

---

[1]Dr. Daniel Neumann. the Health Officer of the Bureau of Education in North Alaska, expressed the opinion that the frequency of miscarriages among Eskimo women is due to the intense cold.

[2]Mr. Stefansson noticed among the Akulliakattak natives that a young woman whose child died soon after birth had a tiny tent to herself. (Anthrop. Papers, A.M.N.H., Vol. XIV, pt. I, p. 248). There was no seclusion or isolation of the mother in any case that came under my notice. Possibly this woman's husband was absent from camp at the time, when she would naturally be living alone. Cp. Boas, Bulletin A.M.N.H., Vol. XV, pt. I, p. 117.)

of her husband and of one or two married women who act as mid-wives, sometimes too of a shaman whose aid is solicited to give her an easy delivery. The mother does little or no work for a day or two, and the husband also remains idle as a rule. I could discover no taboos in reference to food or clothing beyond the necessity of obtaining another bed-skin for the babe to sleep on; the usual custom, apparently, is to exchange a bed-skin with a neighbour. The woman is confined to the house for one or more days according to her health. If the parents decide to preserve the child a relative is called in to massage it within a few hours of its birth. On the last day of the year 1915, about four o'clock in the morning, Ikpakhuak and Higilak were roused by a woman who came to announce that the old man's niece Kaiyoranna had just given birth to a child. Both dressed immediately and went over to see it. Ikpakhuak "worked" it, *savaktok*, pulling out its legs to make them grow big and strong, exactly as Higilak and Avranna had "worked" their pups the preceding summer. They came back to their own hut about an hour later bringing Kaiyoranna's bed-skin, in exchange for which they sent over their own. The following day Ikpakhuak refused to chop up a frozen deer carcass, on the ground that, as he had "worked" the baby only the day before, some harm might come to it if he used his tomahawk. Higilak many years before had "worked" her nephew Kesullik in the same manner. Ever afterwards the child is considered as the foster-child of all who assisted at its birth, whether they acted as mid-wives proper or merely administered the ceremonial massage.

Parents frequently massage their own children while nursing them, as our own parents do. They twist up their fingers and draw out their arms and legs so that they will grow strong and beautiful, stroke their bodies, and pinch their noses to make them straight. The ceremonial massage, however, is always performed by some other person. It is never a very gentle process, but far less severe than the ceremonial massage that young pups have to undergo.[1]

Often the parents are unwilling to rear their children, for a baby involves much hardship to the mother, especially in the summer when all the household goods are packed on the back. The child is only an additional burden to the mother up to the age when it can make a long day's journey on its own feet; she has to carry it on her back over and above her full share of the household effects. Moreover, since the diet of the natives is confined to meat and fish, she must suckle the infant up to three or four years, and sometimes even to five. Nik, the wife of Aksiatak, was still occasionally suckling her son Nakitok, though the boy was certainly five years old and she had a baby of two or three months. It is little wonder therefore if the younger women in particular refuse to rear some of their children. Sometimes another family will adopt the babe, though more usually it is an older child that is adopted, since the new-born infant requires its mother's milk. Early in 1914 Higilak arranged to adopt the little daughter of a man named Wikkiak, whose wife was then on the eve of giving birth to another child; the parents received a pot and a knife as the

---

[1]In the summer of 1915 one of Avranna's dogs had a litter. One pup he kept for himself, another he gave to Tutsik. Each man took his pup into a tent and massaged it. Avranna, placing his poor little victim between his knees, pulled out its legs one after the other to make them grow big, and twisted its tail so that the dog would always hold it curved over its back, which the Eskimos regard as a mark of beauty and of health. Next he held the pup up to his face and expanded its nostrils by blowing into them; it would thus become keen-scented and able to follow a trail and to discover the seal-holes under the snow. In order that so important a quality should not be left to chance he expanded the nostrils again with the eye of a needle. Then he stretched its body to make it grow big, and fastened round it a miniature harness that had been made for the occasion by his wife. Holding the trace in his teeth and the pup in his hands he pulled the line taut several times, thereby ensuring that the dog would be a good worker when hitched to the sled. To make it strong for packing loads in summer he placed his heavy tool-bag on its back and forced it to execute a kind of march. It should be swift in pursuit, so he rubbed an arrow along its belly between its legs; and fierce in attack, so he bit its head and body and feet till the poor animal writhed and howled with pain, and its mother outside nearly ripped the tent to pieces in a frantic effort to rescue her offspring. Last of all it should be quick to pounce on seals, so he knocked its mouth against a strip of blubbery sealskin. At each stage of the operation he murmured into its ear, exhorting it to grow big and active, to pounce on seals, and to do and become everything that befitted a perfect Eskimo dog.

price of the adoption. After the baby was born, however, they decided to keep all their children, and rather unscrupulously went back on the agreement without restoring either of the articles, the pot or the knife.

Frequently the parents settle their problem by simply suffocating their baby and throwing it away. Even a mother will do this, for apparently she has no spontaneous affection for her offspring at the time that it is born. In the autumn of 1915 a Pingangnaktok native travelled westward with his wife and joined the Dolphin and Union strait natives at the Liston and Sutton islands. There, on January 22, the woman gave birth to a girl. Neither of the parents wanted to have any children at the time, for their companions were intending to return to Tree river the following day. They were both young still, they said, and in all probability would have at least one more child later, a boy perhaps who could take care of them when they grew old. The woman therefore suffocated her child and laid it out on the ground a few yards from the camp, where it was soon covered by the drifting snow. Only a year or two previously this couple had similarly exposed another little girl baby. There were three other cases of infanticide that winter in the vicinity of our station, more than the average number, probably, owing to the severity of the weather at this

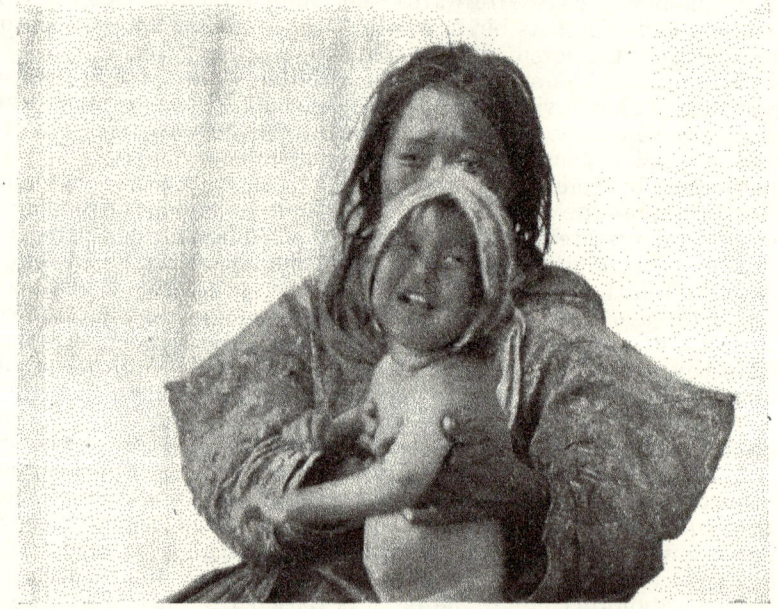

(Photo by G. H. Wilkins)

Fig. 51. Kalyutaryun and her baby Okomik

time and the shortage of food. One woman exposed a child about three years old; it was bewitched, she said, and only a burden to her. The child was probably defective, for, though it had grown in size, it had not developed properly and could neither stand alone nor walk.

Where twins are born one at least must either be killed or given away, for an Eskimo woman cannot possibly rear both children at the same time. If one is a boy and the other a girl, it is invariably the girl that is made the victim. Boys, in fact, are seldom exposed, for they will support their parents when they grow up. The utmost callousness is displayed in the matter. One woman laughed over a baby girl she had killed two or three years before, and said that it had provided the foxes with a good meal. Very rarely some other woman in the settlement takes pity on the helpless infant; thus, when a Dolphin and Union strait woman named Keyuk exposed her baby without first suffocating it, another woman rescued it and reared it as her own child. The mother seems to forfeit all claim to it in such cases even when the child grows up. One thing these natives have to their credit, however—they never resort to pre-natal infanticide; I am not sure whether it is known even, although a native who quarrelled with his wife when she was pregnant threw her down in the snow and rolled his foot on her stomach.

Within two or three days of its birth a child that escapes exposure is given a name, or rather two and sometimes even three names. These are often suggest-ed by relatives, but the decision rests with the parents. Usually there is very little choice, for it is customary to name the child after a near kinsman who has recently died; nevertheless differences of opinion do occasionally arise when two or three kinsmen have died within the space of a few years. All the names of the kinsmen descend to the child, or to the young dog, for the same rule applies to dogs also. Aksiatak called one of his dogs Itaiyuk after his dead father; later, when his wife bore him a son, he named him Itaiyuk also. Higilak, again, held a discussion with Ikpakhuak as to the name she should give to one of their pups; finally she called it Nerialak after Ikpakhuak's elder brother who had died two or three years before. A few months later her grandchild was born and received the name Nerialak also.

Distinctions of sex never enter apparently into the question of names The dead Nerialak above mentioned was a man, while the baby that was named after him was a girl. Higilak's daughter was named Kanneyuk, and there was a man Kanneyuk in a neighbouring group. I do not know in this instance whether they were both named after the same person, in which case their other names would be the same also. Such a thing is not uncommon however; there were two Puivlik children, for example, both boys, who were called Utuallu Taipanna after a common kinsman.

The majority of the people seemed to have two names, though some had only one and a few three; but the third was usually a nickname. Where a native had two names one would often be used for a few months, then the other would supersede it for a time without any apparent reason for the change. Thus, when first we entered the country, Ikpakhuak's wife was always known as Taktu. In the summer of 1915 her second name Higilak gradually took its place, and during our last year the name of Taktu was seldom heard.[1] It was used sometimes nevertheless, so that plainly there was no taboo concerning the matter. A Noahognik boy had two names, Taptuna and Hahra, but hardly anyone used the second name except his father.

A child often receives another name later on in life, a sobriquet from some peculiarity in its appearance or an event in its career. Sometimes this nickname entirely supersedes the proper names. Thus a Puivlik Eskimo who possessed an unusually big nose was always known as Kingalokanna, "Big Nose". Another man who had both his feet amputated as a result of frost-bite was called Iti-gaitok, "Footless", and a Kanghiryuak native for a similar reason was called Nilgak, "The Limper". Higilak's elder brother received the name of Kaulak when he was born, but one day when he was out hunting, he said, he heard some wolves talking about him, calling him Tusayok "The Listener", so he immediately changed his name and was always called Tusayok afterwards. In recent years

---

[1] Mr. Stefansson was misled by this use of the second name without any explanation, and consequently over-estimated the number of the Hannerak group. The Puivlik natives told him of the family Tak-tukkut (i.e. Taktuk's family), and of a man named Avranna (Anthrop. Papers, A.M.N.H., Vol. XIV, pt. I, p. 250). Now Avranna was Taktuk's son, and Taktuk, or Taktu, was Higilak, the woman who had travelled to Tree river and composed a song in commemoration of the journey, *ibid.*, p. 34).

one or two children have been named after notable visitors; thus, a Coppermine river girl was called Issumatak "The Thinker" or "The Leader", which was David Hanbury's title. Hanbury's companion Darrell was honoured in a similar manner; and a Puivlik child was called Tannaumik after the Mackenzie river youth who accompanied Mr. Stefansson on his first visit to the Copper Eskimo country.

In introducing himself a man usually gives both or all his names, but if he is asked his name he will often give only one. Sometimes he will make a joke about it; Kingalokanna, for example, would usually point to his nose and laugh.[1] Unlike the Mackenzie and Alaskan natives, these Eskimos have no hesitation whatever in telling their own names; nor is there any taboo against mentioning the names of the dead, though the speaker will usually remark that the person referred to is dead and seems to expect that the matter will be dropped as having no further interest. Despite the inheritance of the names I could find no trace of any belief in the reincarnation of the souls of dead ancestors or relatives, a belief that is held by the Eskimos farther west.[2] Frequent enquiries indeed have convinced me that the doctrine is unknown to the Copper Eskimos, though now that the western natives are entering their country they will probably soon acquire it, their minds being very receptive of such ideas.

(Photo by R. M. Anderson)

FIG. 52. Eskimo mothers and their children on the trail

Not only are there no taboos on the names of the dead, but, under ordinary circumstances, no taboos in respect to the killing or eating of any animal, bird or fish whenever a person happens to have the same name. Thus Taktu, "Kidney," would eat the kidney of either the seal or the caribou, and Tutsik had no scruples about eating the old-squaw duck, *ahangik*, though his own second name was Ahangik.[3]

A parent seldom addresses his child by its proper name, but simply calls it *nutarara*, "my child", or more simply still *nutarak* "child", which is the term that other adults employ towards it. If the child be an adopted one, *tiguara* "my adopted relative" is often used instead. Once the danger of exposure is

[1] Cf. Stefansson, Anthrop. Papers, A.M.N.H., Vol. XIV, pt. I, p. 247.
[2] Cf. Stefansson, Anthrop. Papers, A.M.N.H., Vol. XIV, pt. I, p. 357 *et seq.*; also Crantz, Vol. I, p. 201.
[3] Exceptions to this rule are given in the next chapter.

over it receives all the care and attention that its parents can lavish on it. The mother carries it everywhere on her back underneath her coat, and whenever it cries she rocks it backwards and forwards, patting it on the back and singing some popular song to lull it to sleep; if this fails to quiet it she walks with it up and down along the floor in front of the sleeping platform. Often, if you push back her hood, you may see the infant sleeping soundly on her back. Sometimes she lays it on the bed, covering its face with a skin in summer to keep off the flies. Little charms are attached to its clothes; a bone from the fore-flipper of a rough seal on its shoulder, or the penis bone of the seal on its wrist, will make it a good sealer, while scraps of caribou skin on the other shoulder will make it a good caribou hunter[1]. Aksiatak's wife Nik wore a short flap of deerskin on her own belt to make her baby a good hunter in after years. As the child grows older, and can bear stronger food, the mother masticates small pieces of meat and puts them into its mouth. The father too takes great pride in his offspring and will often play with his baby inside his hut, nursing it in his arms or dandling it on his knees; for an Eskimo seldom rests a child on one knee, as we do, but lays it on his lap between his knees, with its feet pointing forward.

A casual visitor might gather the impression that children are badly cared for by their parents. Both boys and girls run about in the most wretched clothing, full of gapes and rents, often cut down, indeed, from the worn-out garments of their elders. Even their footgear is of the same description, and often it is soaking wet. It must be remembered, however, that these are their oldest clothes, and that there is always a good warm set of garments carefully stored away for special occasions. Our children do not wear their Sunday clothes at school, nor do the Eskimo children wear their cleanest and finest garments when playing about in the greasy snow in and around their houses. If a child's feet become wet and cold it can always run inside the house and put on other boots, leaving the old ones to dry on the rack above the lamp.

Eskimo children show little respect for their elders in the manner to which we are accustomed. They address them as equals, and join in any conversation that may be taking place, not hesitating to interrupt or even correct their parents. Often they have nicknames for their elders which they will use to their very faces; thus Kanneyuk would sometimes call her mother "the woman with the wide mouth". Yet they do show a certain amount of deference, and a child will generally do what it is told, however unwilling. If it disobeys, some elder is sure to chide it and lecture it on the duty of children; the shame of public disapproval is sufficient in most cases to produce submission. Boys are more apt to be spoilt than girls, probably because they are more errant and come less directly under their parents' influence. Corporal punishment is never resorted to, though a child may receive a thump with the fist or a blow from the snow-duster in the passion of the moment, when it will often try to retaliate. Thus Kanneyuk was vexed one day when Higilak told her to do something, and sulked in a corner of the hut. Her cousin Kesullik jeered at her behind her back, so she turned round and hit him in the eye. He began to cry, and Higilak poked Kanneyuk two or three times with the snow-duster, causing her to cry also. The quarrel was soon over, however; the same evening the two children went off together to sleep in a little tent by themselves. Many similar incidents might be recorded. Aksiatak's boy Nakitok received a sharp slap on the side of the head one day because he knocked some things off the table; and a Coppermine river native named Huputaun knocked his little daughter violently against the wall because she was quarrelling with her younger brother. It is only natural that the children should often quarrel among themselves and knock each other down, but no one takes any notice. Generally speaking, boys and girls grow

---

[1] This is, of course, sympathetic magic of the usual type. Similarly Higilak once wrapped the body of a live bumble bee in a shred of cloth and tied it round a pup's neck to make the animal fierce and bold like the bee.

up like wild plants, without much care or attention from the time they can run about till they approach puberty. A girl receives a little elementary education in cooking and sewing and in dressing meat. She is encouraged to make dolls and to mend her own clothing, her mother teaching her how to cut out the skins. Both boys and girls learn to stalk game by accompanying their elders on hunting excursions; their fathers make bows and arrows for them suited to their strength. One of their favourite pastimes is to carry out, in miniature, some of the duties they will have to perform when they grow up. Thus little girls often have tiny lamps in the corners of their huts over which they will cook some meat to share with their playmates. In summer they love to sleep out-of-doors together, or to set up house in an empty tent. So the days pass happily enough until they reach manhood and womanhood and take up the responsibilities of life in real earnest.

The Rev. Mr. Girling tells me of a very touching custom that he witnessed on two or three occasions. He was travelling along the coast with an Eskimo from Bathurst inlet when the native met his aged mother, whom he had not seen for many years. The old woman lifted up the front of her coat, exposing her breast, and her son reverently stooped down and touched it with his lips. However rude and uncultured these Eskimos may be, the bond that binds the mother to her child is an enduring one, lasting as long as life itself.

CHAPTER XIII

SICKNESS, DEATH AND BURIAL

Melancholy thoughts of death seem to be always hovering in the penumbra of the Eskimos' minds. Especially is this true of the older people, for the young, here as elsewhere, are little troubled by its imminence. During the summer of 1915, when the natives were formulating their plans for the future, even though it might be for but a month ahead, Ikpakhuak or Higilak would often say "Granting that we are still alive," and add "Evil shades are constantly assailing us." Not infrequently, too, some such expression as "People are continually dying here" would fall from their lips. Yet in their minds there seemed to be no anxious dread of death weighing them down, no passionate clinging to life, only a profound resignation and melancholy calmness in the face of the inevitable issue. Generally they lowered the voice and assumed a mournful tone when speaking of dead relatives or friends, though occasionally one heard the remark, half jest, half earnest, that "The foxes have eaten so-and-so," or "So-and-so's remains retained no semblance of a man." They seldom mentioned the dead by name, but seemed rather to try to forget them, as though they would fain banish every unpleasant memory from their minds.

For the forerunners of death, accidents and sickness, the Eskimo knows of only one cause, the malignant activities of evil spirits or of the shades of the dead. Many of Higilak's séances in Victoria island were held for the purpose of propitiating or intimidating these shades and dispelling their influence. The natives have no knowledge whatever of medicine, and very little of surgery. A head-ache is sometimes cured by bleeding, broken limbs are set in splints and frozen members are amputated. Aksiatak, for example, dislocated his ankle while wrestling in the dance-house; he pulled it back into place, covered it with a long deerskin sock and laid three splints around it, one on each side and one at the back, keeping them firmly in place by means of a raw-hide lashing; a second cord running from his hand to the sole of his foot enabled him to raise his leg without bending it. A year later his son Nakitok fell from the roof and broke his thigh; the Eskimos set his leg in splints also. Both accidents were ascribed to the machinations of evil spirits and the shamans were asked to appease them. A painful swelling on the arm of the old shaman Ilatsiak was cured by lancing. For snow-blindness the natives use counter-irritants, flooding the eyes with the smoke of burning heather or of the *Dryas integrifolia*, or tying a louse to a thread and letting it scratch the sclerotis. Complaints that are considered magical in their origin, however, find their surest remedies in counter-magic, so a shaman is usually called in at once to diagnose the cause and prescribe a cure. In most cases he discovers that some taboo has been broken, or that the patient has committed some action which offended a certain dead person's shade. The latter was the interpretation given to the illness of the Noahognik Eskimo Hitkok, who killed his dog in a fit of anger because it refused to follow him to the sealing ground; in this case the resentful shade was the dead relative after whom the dog was named.[1]

In most cases of sickness the diagnosis alone is considered sufficient to arrest the evil, especially if it is reinforced by an abstinence from such articles of food as the shaman may ordain. Even if it fails no discredit falls on the shaman, for the forces of evil are many and great, and his powers after all are limited.

---

[1] There was no conception of the dead man's soul residing in the dog; Hitkok had merely shown disrespect to him by killing his namesake.

The soul is the mainspring of a man's vital strength. A dead man, or more accurately his shade, *tarrak*, may steal the soul of a living man, who will then pine away and die. In the winter of 1915 a Puivlik Eskimo named Wikkiak and the little boy Haugak were both ill at the same time. Wikkiak recovered soon after I visited their settlement, whereupon a shaman announced that his soul had been carried away by the shade of a dead man, but that my dog Jumbo had brought it back. Higilak therefore tied a strip of white deerskin round Jumbo's neck, thinking that perhaps he might be grateful for its warmth and bring back Haugak's soul also. The boy recovered, but a few months later

Fig. 53. A Tree river Eskimo wearing a fillet of caribou-skin around his forehead to cure a headache

Higilak fell ill herself, and Jumbo had to come to the rescue once again. In the eyes of the Eskimos he was clearly not an ordinary dog, but possessed an unusual amount of vital force. On this occasion, therefore, Higilak rubbed his saliva over her forehead in order that some of this force might enter into her and overcome her sickness. Jumbo's reward was another neckband of white deerskin.

Sometimes a friend will lend some of his vital force to drive away a disease. For example, if a man has stomach trouble, a comrade will often spit on his hand and rub the afflicted part, thereby instilling some of his own surplus strength to aid in the patient's recovery.[1] The calves of Avranna's legs were sore one day, and the natives asked me to rub them with my saliva. On another occasion Avranna bound my belt around his head to cure a headache; my vitality communicated itself to my belt, passed into his body and effected a cure. A charm too will often keep off an ailment. The bill of the yellow-billed loon (*Gavia adamsi*) will help to ward off snow blindness, so in spring some of the natives wear them on their shoulders or carry them in their hands. An old hunter, Aiyallik, who had his thumb torn off by a brown bear, used

---

[1] Cf. Rasmussen, p. 145; Egede, p. 198.

to wear it as a charm in a small skin bag suspended round his neck, but whether it was intended to give him good luck in general, or to ward off some specific danger or sickness, I did not discover.

Not infrequently a malady is conceived of as something concrete implanted in the body by an offended soul. The shaman then has to extract the object, which he does by the aid of his familiar spirits. To prove his success he displays to his audiences pieces of bone, or worms, or similar things that he has secreted on his person beforehand. The laxatives that we occasionally administered answered the same purpose. Both sickness and ill-luck can be embodied in physical objects and carried away. Haviuyak had a boil on his arm which he pricked with a needle as soon as it came to a head, squeezing the pus on to a piece of caribou meat. He asked me to let him give it to Scotty, the biggest dog in my team, who would carry the contagion away with him when I left. One of his own dogs snatched at the meat, but he kicked it away and anxiously watched till the whole morsel had disappeared down Scotty's throat. To propitiate the dog he tied a band of white deerskin round its neck. Some days later he was asked how the boil was progressing, and answered, "It has all disappeared, thanks to the dog." Another Eskimo, Kaiyoranna, made me a present of two bone pins fastened to the outside of a small deerskin bag. I wanted to look inside the bag, but he checked me and tried to draw my attention to the fine workmanship in the pins. Later, after I had left the camp, I found only four old scraps of skin in the bag. I showed it to some of the natives, and they explained that Kaiyoranna had fastened some one's illness or ill-luck in the bag, and added the pins as a bribe to induce me to take it away.

A woman must abstain from sewing, and usually from fishing and hunting, whenever her husband or brother is ill. A shaman sometimes enjoins on her certain food restrictions as well. Thus Higilak was forbidden to eat either the liver or the kidney of a seal when her brother Tusayok was ill. In this particular instance the prohibition was suggested by her second name Taktu (Kidney). Sometimes the malady itself suggests it, as when Ikpakhuak was forbidden to eat the stomach of the caribou when he himself was suffering from stomach trouble.

Tales of people dying and coming to life again are so common among these Eskimos that one is almost tempted to believe that catalepsy may not be at all infrequent. In the majority of cases, of course, the story has arisen from the difficulty of distinguishing the unconsciousness of an invalid from death. Milukkattak told me that her grandfather died on the trail one day. His sons wrapped him in his sleeping bag, laid all his possessions on the ground beside him, and went on and made camp. In the midst of their weeping the old man suddenly appeared with his sleeping bag still wrapped round his shoulders. He wandered around the camp for a few minutes noting the arrangement of everything, then took his fishing rod and went off to fish in a lake near by. Several times afterwards he died and came to life again, but at last he died and never recovered.[1]

There are numerous tales of this nature. A man named Okalluk died and was laid out by his relatives in the usual manner, wrapped in a deerskin. Four days afterwards he came to life again, cut the lashings of his deerskin wrappings and followed the trail of his kinsmen, whom he found fishing in a lake. They laid hands on him and conveyed him to one of their tents, where the shamans held a séance and restored him to health again. Again in Bathurst inlet a woman named Allanak died one winter and was laid out on the sleeping platform of her hut, covered over with skins; she too came to life again five days later and regained her usual strength. In the same region Inernek or Ikpakusaluk, for the man had two names, fell ill, and was left in his house

---

[1] Cf. Stefansson, Anthrop. Papers, A.M.N.H., Vol. XIV, pt. I, p. 222.

supposedly dead. He recovered after seven days and became in consequence a very famous shaman. There is also a story of a native named Iyillik who announced that he would die and recover at the end of four days, but when his people laid him out on top of a rock an animal with the body of a wolf and the head of a polar bear came and devoured his corpse; so his prophecy came to naught. Strangest of all is the tale of Akarak, a Kilusiktok Eskimo. A spirit or the malignant shade of a dead man struck him on the nape of the neck while he was hunting south of Bathurst inlet. He fell dead into a swamp and his face was buried in the water. There at sunset his son found him; his face was blue, his hands were frozen stiff and his body was cold and dead. The son caught hold of his ring finger with one hand and extended the arm, then laid his other hand on Akarak's shoulder. Forthwith the latter's soul returned to his body and he was restored to life again. Then his son tied his quiver round him and helped him to his feet. Stiff and sore he staggered home, leaning on the younger man's shoulder. As soon as they arrived in camp the shamans invoked their magic powers and restored the hunter to health again. Akarak had been a fairly powerful shaman before this adventure, the natives said, but afterwards his prestige was greatly augmented.

It so happened that I never witnessed the actual death and burial of a Copper Eskimo. The natives of Bathurst inlet and farther east leave the corpse inside the hut or tent and abandon the camp immediately. In 1913 two white men, Radford and Street, were killed close to one of the small islands in Bathurst inlet; thereafter the natives avoided this side of the island and camped instead on the opposite side, fearing the white men's shades that still lingered round their death place.[1] In the Coppermine region and in Dolphin and Union strait the Eskimos also leave the body inside the tent in summer and move on to another camping ground. In winter, however, they lay the corpse out in the snow, and build a wind-break of snow-blocks around it to protect it from the weather. Usually it is conveyed to the land a few days later and deposited on the beach above highwater mark, though sometimes it is simply left neglected on the ice. The relatives remain in their dwellings and mourn the day after the funeral, then resume their ordinary occupations and try to forget their loss. Probably certain taboos are observed, but my enquiries on the subject failed to yield any information.

Some or all of the dead man's implements are broken and laid on the ground beside him for his use in the future life. The man is dead, the natives say, and wants to have his implements dead also. Should he die outside his tent the survivors build a wind-break of stones and sods around his corpse to keep it warm, like the wind-break of snow in winter. In the summer of 1915 we found an old camp site in south-west Victoria island where a woman had died many years before. The tent had disappeared through the ravages of time, but its broken poles were still lying on the ground. Near them was the woman's knife, a hunter's bone pin for fastening the reticulum of the caribou when filled with blood, a needle case and the toggle of a woman's belt. I would have taken two of the tent sticks to use for fuel, but my companions protested that the dead woman needed them to keep her warm.

In a few places stone cairns are found protecting the corpse from the ravages of birds and animals. Captain Bernard unearthed human bones and a few implements from some cairns on Bell island in south-west Victoria island, where he noticed also the ruins of houses built of wood and sods. Mr. Stefansson discovered other cairns at Cape Parry and in Langton bay.[2] Dr. Anderson tells me that he never saw or heard of them farther west than this, logs of drift-wood taking their place; he considered Langton bay as their western limit. The Copper Eskimos, as far as I could learn, never cover their dead, so these

[1] Report of the Bathurst Inlet Patrol, Ottawa, 1917.
[2] Anthrop. Papers, A.M.N.H., Vol. XIV, pt. I, p. 212, etc.

stone cairns are probably the relics of that earlier tribe that peopled the coast from Baillie island to Dolphin and Union strait. The six "stone graves" that Mr. Stefansson noticed between Clouston bay and the Colville hills were almost certainly meat-caches, hundreds of which are scattered about the hills and valleys of this region.[1]

The only recent burial we saw was that of one Puivlik Eskimo, Haviron, who died in April 1915, after an illness that had lasted all the winter. His body was conveyed to the mainland near Cape Lambert and deposited on the shore just above high-water mark. Mr. Wilkins, the photographer of the expedition, examined the body a month or so later and furnished me with the following description. "The corpse was on a point about twenty-five yards from the

(Photo by G. H. Wilkins).

Fig. 54. The grave of Haviron

water and three or four feet above high-water mark. The coast hereabouts was a mass of broken rocks and an occasional boulder. The corpse was placed on the rocks, but no rocks had been placed on or around it. It was lying on its left side with the head towards the east, the right arm doubled across the chest, the left stretched along the body slightly to its front. It was dressed in a simple suit of inner deerskin clothes, attigi (i.e., coat), pants, socks, and mittens, and had on a pair of sealskin slippers. The right eye was open, the left closed, and the mouth closed. The corpse was loosely tied in two deerskins, and its head rested on a pair of folded outer pants. An outer attigi was noticed a few feet

[1]Anthrop. Papers, A.M.N.H., Vol. XIV, pt. I, p. 301.

away, presumably blown there by the wind.   About twelve feet to the south (inland) and parallel to the body had been placed the following articles:—

One fish-hook attached to a small stick, 6 inches long, by a short length of braided sinew.

One brass seal-spear head.

One pair of scissors (made of bone, tin-lined).

One battered lard-pail.

One pair of outer boots.

One broken bow without string or sinew lashing.

Two arrows with bone heads, in good order.

One bone-handled iron-bladed knife (snow knife).

One worn-out whittling knife, with a bone handle and an iron blade.

The most interesting of the ancient graves was one discovered near Bernard harbour by some western Eskimos who were serving the expedition.   There were no bones, but they brought me a fishing rod, a woman's knife with an iron blade, a drill with an iron point, a marrow-spatula, two horn points and pieces of the shafts of a child's arrows, and two skewers for pinning up the blood-bag. The local Eskimos did not know whose grave it was; they thought a whole family must have been laid there, for while the arrow-shafts suggested a boy, the knife indicated a woman and the drill a man.   Some of the natives protested against our removing the objects, but suggested that if we really wanted them we ought to leave their equivalent on the grave.   Following their advice, therefore, we deposited a cartridge for the use of the man, some needles for the woman, and a small trinket for the boy.

Often the relatives of a dead man will retain his more valuable property and place only miniature copies on his grave.   This is done more particularly with the water-boots, but sometimes too with the bow and arrows.   The dead man is able to enlarge the miniatures if he wants them, so there is no necessity to leave the genuine articles.[1]   Captain Bernard found a grave in Richardson bay on south-west Victoria island where miniature water-boots had been substituted for the real ones. He described to us, too, a funeral in which the same substitution had taken place.   A native named Ekkeahoak was stabbed by a companion near Lambert island in the spring of 1913.   His kinsmen wrapped the corpse in caribou skins and conveyed it by sled to the mainland, where they deposited it on the ground with its back to the north and its head to the east.[2] They laid his possessions in a row by his side, piece by piece, the various tools, the bow and arrows, the sealing-harpoon broken into two pieces, and all his spare clothing, each garment neatly folded in a separate bundle; in place of the real water-boots, however, they left a miniature pair about an inch long. As soon as the corpse was thus disposed of all the people returned to their seal-ing-ground.[3]

---

[1]The Rev. E. J. Peck says that in south Baffin island: "In the case of a woman's death the articles she had been accustomed to use, such as needles, circular knife, etc., were placed at her grave by female relatives and friends, but in the case of a man's death his hunting implements were placed by his male relatives and friends by the side of his grave. These did not always consist, in either case, of the full sized articles, but miniature things made to resemble the larger were often used instead."

[2]Haviron's head also pointed toward the east, but I do not know whether this is the universal practice.

[3]The following extract is taken from Dr. Anderson's diary of his first expedition—the Stefansson-Anderson Arctic Expedition—under date July 28, 1911:—

"On the western side of cliff (a little east of Point Williams, Victoria island) found part of old seal-spear, bone head, copper-riveted, also shaft of human femur (ca. 15 years). On top of rock, Tanaumirk found fragments of oblong stone pot and shaft of human ulna. I went up and found epiphysis of femur, and two phalanges of toe. No sign of grave about. About 30 yards W. of cliff I found old iron knife, long bone handle. About 100 yards inland Tanaumirk found remainder of stone pot, and about 100 yards from this the runners of a sled—very old. Two or three hundred yards W. found old tent site (stones in circle), a few broken arrows, sealing implements, etc. About 25 yards from house saw a little circle of stones on ground (about 2 feet across). In centre, half buried in moss and dirt, found quite a set of miniature implements, child's toys, bows, 3 copper-headed arrows (about 6–8 in. long), copper ice-pick, drill, fire-stones, knife (tin riveted to bone handle), caribou hunting accessories, etc.—all diminutive, much weathered."

These miniature implements may have been a child's toys, as Dr. Anderson thought at that time, but I strongly suspect that they were placed on a grave instead of the real implements.

Although there is a universal belief among these natives in an existence after death, their conception of that existence is very vague and indefinite. The names of the dead are not tabooed, though a certain natural reluctance is felt in pronouncing them. The soul, *nappan*, apparently ceases to exist altogether, but the shade, *tarrak*, is believed to linger for a time round the place where the body was laid.[1] Thus the spot where Haviron was buried was always spoken of afterwards as "Haviron's place," and the context often implied that his shade still existed in that locality. Ikpakhuak's eldest brother died in the Colville hills in 1912, and his body was laid on a ridge-top. Three years later, when passing near the place, Ikpakhuak began to mourn aloud, and all the natives in our party wept in sympathy. A few days later, at the end of a long day's fishing, he went to visit the grave, accompanied by Avranna and Milukkattak. Higilak, in camp, wept all the time they were absent, and Milukkattak would only speak of their visit afterwards in hushed tones. They seemed to think that the shade of the dead man still hovered round his remains despite the ravages the foxes had committed on them.

Direct questions as to the fate of the individual after death invariably received the answer *nauna* "I don't know". Occasionally, when pressed more closely, a native would say, "Perhaps he is still alive in some other place, we have no knowledge." One woman told me that the dead sometimes go to the moon. Higilak once asked me whether I had ever seen her first husband Nerialak among the western Eskimos; he had been dead for several years, she said, but she had been told (by some shaman probably) that he was still living over in the west. On another occasion she asked me whether I had heard that her father was dwelling among the Kanghiryuarmiut. Many summers before he had gone out hunting and had neither returned to camp nor left any traces to show what had become of him. Finally a shaman discovered that the malignant shades of some white men had carried him off to the country of the Kanghiryuarmiut. Nowhere, however, could I find any trace of the belief (existing more or less vaguely at Barrow and elsewhere)[2] that the souls of the dead are reincarnated in their descendants, or in the children of friends and relatives.

Known graves, even those of relatives, are usually avoided by Eskimos travelling alone, even when death was due to natural causes. Very few natives will voluntarily visit alone the place where a man was killed by violence; they are afraid lest his shade that still hovers in the vicinity may wreak its vengeance on his survivors. When the two Roman Catholic priests were killed near the mouth of the Coppermine river in 1913 the murderers ate small pieces of their livers, believing that this would prevent their shades from taking revenge.[3] An Eskimo broke into two caches belonging to Uloksak and another man, and stole a number of their skins; afterwards the thief hung himself, fearing the owner's revenge, and his corpse was laid out on the ground about a mile from the settlement. The natives hoped that the animals would quickly devour it, and Uloksak set some fox-traps near by. Instead of two foxes, however, he caught two wolves, but one of them gnawed off its foot and limped away. Uloksak, following its track, could see it running in the distance. Suddenly it changed to a man and waved a hand to him, beckoning him to follow, then instantly reverted to a wolf again. He chased it up a cliff and shot it, but the moment the bullet struck its body the wolf gasped "ah", and a voice from inside the cliff cried, "You too shall die and many of your people." Uloksak cut off

---

[1] The word *tarrak* has at least three meanings: (1) a low ridge that offers cover to the hunter, and so generally any low ridge; (2) the shadow of any object cast by the sun or the moon; (3) the "shade" of a dead animal or human being.

[2] Stefansson, Anthrop. Papers, A.M.N.H., Vol. XIV, pt. I, p. 363 *et seq.*; Crantz, Vol. I, p. 201.

[3] The same belief existed in Greenland. See Rink, p. 45; Rasmussen, People of the Polar North p. 297, 300; Cf. also Nelson, p. 328.

the wolf's legs and crushed its head to make certain that it was dead, then returned to camp, leaving the carcass on the ground. The first news that greeted him was that his wife was dead, and subsequently many others of his party died also.

The Copper Eskimo hardly knows the comforting doctrine that the souls or shades of the dead hover round their living kinsfolk like guardian spirits and protect them from every harm. The shade to them is a malignant being, at least potentially, and its activities know no bounds of time and space. Some remain harmless always, especially the shades of those who worked no evil in their lives; others change to *tornrait*, and are identified more or less closely with those malignant spirits that never had a normal human existence, though they sometimes assume a human form. Unseen, save when of their own accord they render themselves visible or are revealed to a shaman through his familiar spirit, they haunt the hapless natives night and day, ever ready to seize a favourable opportunity to work them harm; the shade of a man who died in one place may cause the death of another man a thousand miles away. In some vague manner too these shades control the weather and the supply of game. Often a shaman will discover and name the particular shade that is responsible for a man's sickness or ill-luck, or for the scarcity of caribou or seals; then it will be petitioned or intimidated and made to cease its evil machinations. The Eskimos try to preserve the good will of the shades in various ways. Whenever a caribou is killed scraps of its liver and kidney (and sometimes of its other intestinal organs as well) are thrown to them as an offering with the exclamation *tamaizza*.[1] So too when a seal is killed a small piece of blubber is left for the shades on the ice.[2] Dease and Simpson noticed that the Copper Eskimos regularly offer an oblation at mealtimes. "(Mr. Dease) took them into his tent and gave them food to eat. A small piece was first broken off, as a sacrifice or oblation, and the remainder made the circuit of their faces before passing into their mouths."[3] Before drinking, too, the native often tips his bowl and with the prayer *tamaizza* pours out two or three drops for a libation. These offerings are often omitted at mealtimes, but never in the hunting field when the game is being cut up; and though sometimes the Eskimo may make them only half-consciously, following a stereotyped custom, yet occasionally there does seem to be some faint sense of gratitude to those unseen powers on whom he believes himself dependent for his daily food.

---

[1]Cf. Crantz, Vol. I, p. 207.

[2]This was the usual interpretation of the custom. One native, however, said that it pleased the seals, so that others would allow themselves to be caught. As the shades of the dead are supposed to be able to control the supply of seals the two interpretations come to almost the same thing.

[3]Simpson, Discoveries, p. 349.

CHAPTER XIV

RELIGIOUS BELIEFS

A flat unbroken expanse of land and sea—the earth— covered over during the greater part of the year with snow and ice; of undefined limits, but stretching farther than any man knows; at each of its corners a pillar of wood holding up another unbroken expanse, the sky[1]; above that, on its surface, another land, abounding in caribou and other animals like our own earth; wandering across this upper expanse semi-spiritual beings, the sun, the moon and the stars— such is the conception that the Copper Eskimo possesses of our universe. The sun and the moon are semi-human, or at least the abodes of semi-human beings, the sun being a woman and the moon a man. The mountains of the moon are the man's dogs, according to one account; according to another, they are a woman with her dogs behind her, for once she came down to the earth and the shamans tied a rope round her and hoisted her up to the sky again. The weather, *sila*, spoken of as a man, but conceived apparently as some mighty power, moves along the sky, and as he walks the sun goes down; hence the disappearance of the sun each evening. In summer the sun draws near the earth and warms it, but in winter it goes far away under the sea. On the 9th of January 1915, the first day of its reappearance after the winter night, the natives heard its hiss as it set again in the ocean. Its face is covered with black at eclipses, *siriapaluk*, and then the Eskimos know that it is trying to kill people and the shamans have to wipe away the black. The appearance of two mock suns, (parhelia) is ominous to travellers and hunters, who will be cut off by sudden death and never reach their homes again.[2]

The stars were human beings or animals before they ascended into the sky. The three bright stars of Orion's belt were three sealers who never returned to their camp, so the Eskimos call them *tupigat* "The sealers", or *tubaryuit* "The early risers"[3]. Long ago a polar bear was being hunted by a man and his dogs. It fled into the sky, and its pursuers followed after it. We can still see the bear, *nannoryuk*, in the sky, and behind it the hunter and his dogs, always pursuing but never overtaking it[4]. One native pointed to the Pleiades and called them the bear, while Aldebaran and some stars near it were the hunter and his dogs, *agleoryuit* "The pursuers"; but the more usual name for the Pleiades is *Agietat*, the meaning of which I did not discover[5]. Two stars in the Great Bear (β and a faint star near it) are *tuktuyuin*, "The caribou", while Venus is the "Big Star," *uvloreahugyuk*. Arcturus when high in the heavens ushers in the sealing season, and hence has been given the name of *sivulik* "The leader". Other stars which I was unable to identify are *agiatsiak* (perhaps the same as *agietat*), *kuttoryuk* and *agyuk*. Falling stars are the *annak* (feces) of larger ones, but bright meteors are called fire, *ignik*.[6] The rainbow is *aiyakutak*, the same name that Mr. Stefansson found for it at Barrow, where the word means "The prop that keeps the sun from falling."

---

[1]Cf. Crantz, Vol. I, p. 131; Nelson, p. 498.

[2]At Barrow two mock suns, one on each side of the real sun, are said to be its walking sticks, *aiyopiak*. The sun holds them out to steady itself when a gale is imminent. Cf. Peary, Northward over the Great Ice, Vol. I, p. 243.

[3]In Greenland they are called *siektut*, "The bewildered men." (Crantz, Vol. I, p. 232, Egede, p. 209), but the legend is the same.

[4]At Barrow the name is *tubatsiat*, which also means "The sealers."

[5]At Barrow they are called *sakopsakkat* "The ones that close their eyes."

[6]So too in the Mackenzie river delta (Stefansson, Anthrop. Papers, A.M.N.H., Vol. XIV, pt. I, pp 327, 341.)

If the Copper Eskimos see a rainbow while they are out hunting they throw a small piece of skin from the belly of a deer toward it, to win its favour and give them good luck. They call the aurora *ahanik*, and believe it to be a manifestation of the spirits that bring fine weather. Rain comes from snow that goes up into the sky when the weather is warm, while lightning is due to a being named Asiranna shooting his arrows. Not all of the natives, however, agreed to this interpretation, for some called it fire, *ignik*, and thought that it was caused by the sky, *kilak*, or by the shades of the dead. The winds, *annorait*, issue from two holes in the sky. In stormy weather the shamans sometimes tie them all together with a cord of fur taken from the throat of a caribou and push them back into one of their holes. Then the Eskimos enjoy fine weather until the malignant spirits of the dead, *aggioktun tarrain inyuin*, desiring the destruction of people still living, untie them again and let them loose. The old shaman Ilatsiak, however, confessed that he did not know what became of the winds in calm weather; nevertheless he knew certain things that would cause them to blow hard, for example, "if the women sewed new deerskin clothes during the dark days of winter, or if in spring and summer the Eskimos lingered too long round the lakes and islands, or ate the lungs of the cariboo."

Even the solid earth is full of mystery. Many a strange and only semi-human race surrounds the Eskimos, and is known through the spirit-flights of their shamans or through ancient tales of adventurous wanderers of other days. The Indians perhaps are human, but beyond them are white men, *kovlunat*, a people whose customs and manners are altogether strange.[1] After we had been in their country for over a year Higilak announced as a great discovery one day that the white men were no different from the Eskimos. Then there are numerous dwarfs, *inyuorligat*, so short that their bows trail behind them on the ground, yet so strong that many of them can carry the largest caribou on their backs. Somewhere far away perhaps there are giants still, for they existed in olden times in the Eskimo land itself. Then there are *tornrin*, a race that once lived above the ground in the days when Eskimos were few, though afterwards they were driven below by the shamans. The *tornrin* used to hunt caribou but not seals, and one may still pick up an occasional arrow point that they have dropped. It was they, too, who built the stone huts like the one near Locker Point. We saw a large rectangular "sleeping place" behind Cape Lambert; it was made of slabs of dolomite set on edge, and was about 8 feet long by 4 feet wide and from 12 inches to 18 inches high. The Eskimos were quite convinced that it must have been a house of the *tornrin*.[2] Then there is a tribe of Amazons; another people with four eyes in their heads; a third with no eyes at all; and yet another whose mouths are in their chests.[3] Away at the back of beyond, *avalirmi*, there is a country where seals grow no longer than a foot, and the hunters put them in their footpads and sling them on their backs. Many other strange and wondrous things the earth contains, and no tale is too marvellous to win belief.

Birds and animals too have extraordinary faculties and powers. Some of the shamans know their speech and can converse with them. Many animals have changed to human beings before the very eyes of the hunters, and changed as quickly back again. They can be offended by scornful words, and the hunter who mocks the caribou, for example, or the seal, will suddenly find himself stricken down by sickness or afflicted with constant ill-luck. A Tree river Eskimo who served the expedition for a time told us that his brother Annarvik

---

[1] The Siberian belief about the teeth in white women (Jochelson, Jesup N. Pacific Expedition, Vol. VI, pt. I, p. 377) is current also among the Copper Eskimos.

[2] Cf. the discussion of the *tornit* by Thalbitzer, in Meddelelser om Grønlad, Vol. XXXIX, p. 687 *et seq.*

[3] Cf. Stefansson, Anthrop. Papers, A.M.N.H., Vol. XIV, pt. I, p. 302.

went hunting one day with another Eskimo named Angivranna. They sighted a brown bear on the opposite bank of a river and began to cross over towards it, but they had hardly reached half way when the bear's ears began to enlarge and gradually cover its whole body. Annarvik turned and fled to shore; when he looked round again a man had sprung out from beside the bear and entered the water. It disappeared below the surface, and presently the terrified Angivranna disappeared also, pulled under by his adversary. No sooner had he sunk than the brown bear vanished into the ground, but on the same spot appeared the mysterious man. Annarvik fled to his camp and told his companions of Angivranna's fate. The brown bear had killed him, the natives said, because he was too good a hunter.

Quite recently another hunter met with a similar fate, according to local tradition. In the summer of 1914 a party of Eskimos was travelling about in the country south of Bathurst inlet. One day they saw a wolf and one of the men cried, "Shoot it." His gun, however, failed to explode, and the wolf seized him by the wrist and dragged him to the ground. Another hunter shot it with his bow, but as the arrow pierced its body the wolf cried "Oh" exactly like a man. Time went on, and the hunter's wrist slowly healed. One day he shot a caribou, and went on farther to look for more game. That night he failed to return to camp, nor was anything seen or heard of him for many months. The shamans held a séance and discovered that the evil shades of the dead, *aggioktun*, had murdered him. Finally, in the spring of 1915, his body was found with a wolf lying dead beside it. The wolf had been wounded by his bullet, but before it expired it had succeeded in killing the hunter; so the animals had their revenge.

It behoves the Eskimo therefore to be very careful in all his actions. Not only must he propitiate the shades of the Eskimo dead, lest they should become offended and strive to slay him and to convert him into a *tornrak* like themselves; but he must never forget to propitiate also the animals he kills. Every seal that is dragged inside his hut must have a little water poured into its mouth, or a little lamp oil instead, for seals are thirsty animals and have a great craving for water (or blubber). Caribou would be given the same, the natives say, only they have not the same strong desire. Geese and other waterfowl, and ptarmigan, all have a longing for oil, so before an Eskimo skins or plucks such a bird he rubs a little fat or blubber on the head, the wing-joints and the feet; but birds of other species have no desire of this kind. Propitiation must be offered to the shades of all fierce and dangerous animals, that is to say of polar and brown bears and of wolves. We shot a polar bear and its cub in the summer of 1915, and Ikpakhuak made a tiny bow and arrow to leave beside the mother's head; he called it a hunting weapon for the bear's shade, and said that a similar gift should be made to the shade of every bear or wolf that is killed. No sewing was permitted on the following day. Moreover, on the last day of the same year, Kesullik, who had been in our party when the bears were killed, captured a seal which he handed over to Ikpakhuak; it was the first seal that had entered Ikpakhuak's house since the slaying of the bears. Now polar bears are like the Eskimos in this respect, that they, too, live largely on seals. Accordingly, when Ikpakhuak had cut off the flippers of the seal and laid them at the back of the hut, his wife stripped off a little of the skin so that he could drive his knife into the animal's belly. This would please the polar bear, he said, and give him success in his sealing; if he had not done this they would have been angry with him and kept all the seals away. According to Milukkattak the usual custom is to lay a miniature bow and arrow beside only the male bear or wolf; beside the female the hunter places a strip of sealskin or deerskin which the shade of the animal can use as a needle-holder. They are like human beings, Milukkattak went on to say, and have need of the same things, the male of his hunting weapons, and the female of her needle-case.[1]

[1]Cf. Rasmussen, p. 111; Stefansson, My Life with the Eskimo, p. 57, and Anthrop. Papers, A.M.N.H., Vol. XIV, pt. I, p. 353; Boas, Bulletin A.M.N.H., Vol. XV, pt. I, p. 124.

Nature has ordained that certain animals shall live in the sea and others on the land. The Eskimo therefore must follow the same distinction, and keep the products of the two regions separate. He is a little vague as to who enforces the taboo. Sometimes he says that the animals themselves would be offended and avenge themselves on the trangressors, who would then die of starvation; sometimes that the shades of the Eskimo dead would take offence, and wreak their vengeance by sending terrible storms or a plague of sickness and death, especially when the natives are living on the sea ice; at other times again it is a deity who dwells at the bottom of the sea and controls the supply of seals, or another living in the sky, or one of the many spirits that dwell in cliffs and tide-cracks and similar places, in so far as they have any fixed abode. But whatever the manner in which he thinks the taboo will be enforced,—and the same Eskimo will believe in every one of them—there is no doubt whatever in his mind that punishment will inevitably follow disobedience. Woe betide the Eskimos if they fail to observe the due restrictions; sooner or later misfortune will overtake them in some form or another, and then the sin, however secret, is sure to come to light. Even if the wrong-doer does not confess immediately, as often happens, yet the shamans will soon discover his transgression when they invoke their familiar spirits and enquire into the cause of their misfortunes. Long ago certain people broke the taboo against cooking deer-meat on the ice, and the ice cracked up and every one was drowned. Such a result may happen again if the taboo be broken.

The caribou and the seal are the two most important factors in the economic life of the natives. The one lives on land, the other in the sea, so the doctrine that the products of the two regions should be kept separate ought to apply more strictly to these two animals than to any others. As a matter of fact even in their case it is only partially observed. Thus seal-meat, raw, frozen or cooked, may be eaten at any time of the year, whether on the land or on the sea ice. In summer, of course, when the Eskimos are usually wandering inland, practically no seals at all are caught, but many are secured in the spring and autumn while the natives are living on the sea-shore; most of the meat is consumed at once on the coast, but a little is often taken inland. Caribou meat again may be eaten, raw or frozen, at any season and in any place; but it must not be cooked on the sea-ice. The natives may cook it on shore at any time, even on the very edge of the ice; some of them did not hesitate to cook it at the Liston and Sutton islands during the winter, though the shamans reproved them for it and attributed a series of blizzards to their violation of the taboo. The prohibition applies only to caribou killed in the previous summer and autumn, not to those that are secured in the winter, or in the early spring when the animals. are migrating northward. It is hard to find any reason for this distinction. If the caribou migrating north across the ice in the spring are to be regarded as sea-animals for the time being, they should equally be so regarded in the autumn when they are migrating south again; but the natives of west Coronation gulf and of Dolphin and Union strait observe the taboo in the one instance, and not in the other. Some of the people, however, were more scrupulous than others, for I noticed one family that would not cook fresh deer-meat on the ice in spring, though other families were doing it in the same camp. This particular family did not condemn the others; on the contrary, it thought it was probably quite legitimate to cook the meat, though it preferred to be on the safe side itself. Some Bathurst inlet natives said that the only deer-meat they refrained from cooking on the ice was meat that had been cached in stone cairns on the land; if meat of this kind were cooked, the cold stones, for some not very evident reason, would make the weather cold.

There is one taboo, however, that is universal in its application, and must not be broken on any account. Products of the land and of the sea must never be cooked in the same pot at the same time. Accordingly, when the natives are living on the land and have stocks of both deer-meat and seal-meat, one is cooked in the morning and the other at night. Nevertheless, both kinds of food may be eaten at the same time; in fact the normal evening meal in the early part of the winter consists of boiled seal-meat and frozen venison. Mr. Stefansson states that "some families said that caribou and seal-meat should not be cooked in the same pot unless the pot were suspended over the lamp by a fresh cord when the caribou meat was to be cooked; but most people paid no attention to even this prohibition."[1]

The polar bear is a sea animal, *tarreomiutak*, and must be treated like a seal. I wanted to fry some caribou liver on the same fire on which Higilak was boiling some bear-meat. She was not at all sure whether it was right to cook the two at the same time, the bear being a denizen of the sea and the caribou of the land. She asked her older brother Tusayok, but he did not know either. Finally I told her that as we had killed the bear on the land, it was plainly, in summer at least, a land animal; further, that I was a white man, and in consequence Eskimo taboos did not apply to me. The arguments seemed to satisfy her, for she raised no further objection.

Similar taboos, based on the same general principles, apply to the cooking of other animals and to fish. Thus tom-cod which are caught in the sea, may. be cooked, like seals, on either land or ice; but fresh-water fish, even salmon

FIG. 55. Pegging out caribou-skins to dry in the sun, Bernard harbour

migrating from the sea, must be cooked only on land. Some natives will not use driftwood thrown up by the sea for cooking either caribou or fish, but others pay no attention to this and use whatever fuel is most available. Mr. Stefansson says that seal blood is used for splicing arrows[2], but the natives told me that this was strictly tabooed, and whenever I saw them making or mending arrows they invariably used caribou blood, if they used blood at all. However, seal blood might be employed by a hunter who intended to use his arrows for shooting seals on the ice. It is only the blood of the seal that is tabooed in this connection, for the skin is always used for the back bracings of the bow.

Sewing as well as cooking is subject to the same general prohibitions. Thus sealskin may not be sewn at the fishing creeks while the salmon are running. I wanted a woman to sew up the ends of a sealskin dog-pack to make it waterproof. She was uncertain whether it was right to do it while the salmon were still migrating up the creek near which the natives were encamped, and on

---

[1]Anthrop. Papers, A.M.N.H., Vol. XIV, pt. I, p. 48; Cf. My Life with the Eskimo, p. 266.
[2]Anthrop. Papers, A.M.N.H., Vol. XIV, pt. I, p. 92.

asking an old man was emphatically told that it was prohibited. Even at our station, four miles from the creek, she was afraid to sew some red sealskin bands on a dancing-cap, though I tried to assure her that it was not forbidden so far away. However, the natives have been compelled to modify this taboo in the case of their foot-gear, which at this season of the year, the late spring, requires mending every two or three days; they may sew sealskin patches therefore on worn-out boot soles, but must not steep them in the stream. Whether it is permissible to make new sealskin shoes on the land, the shoes that are worn in winter over deerskin socks, I am not quite certain. At all events, a woman refused to make me a pair one autumn when she was preparing my other winter clothes, though she promised to make them after we migrated out on to the ice.

It is possible that the prohibition against the sewing of new deerskin clothes on the ice during the dark days of winter also had some connection originally with this differentiation between products of the sea and of the land. At the present time, however, the taboo is in force for very little more than a month, since the natives are usually still sewing on the coast when the sun disappears, and do not migrate out on to the ice until later. The sun is visible again in the middle of January, after which time they may sew as many new clothes on the ice as they wish. Old clothes may be patched at any season of the year. The women would even make new clothes for us all through the dark days, provided that they were allowed to sew them at our station on the land. This may possibly be another instance, like the repairing of boots at the salmon creeks, where necessity has forced the Eskimos to modify the full application of a taboo that in its origin was much more general and far reaching.

Certain other taboos may be mentioned here, although they probably arose from different causes. Stone lamps and pots must not be made during the winter:[1] nor must cottonwood be burnt then, otherwise the weather will grow very cold. There is an idea, I imagine, that dislodging stones of any kind is liable to have this effect; it will be remembered that the Bathurst inlet natives gave this as their reason for not cooking on the ice any deer-meat that had been cached under stones. Cat's cradles are tabooed at most seasons of the year; it is only during the dark days when the sun cannot see them that the natives are allowed to play the game, for the sun may come down and tickle them at any other time, as tradition says it tickled a man long ago. The taboo is not very rigidly observed, however. The natives taught me some figures in the summer, although they took the precaution to close the door of the tent so that the sun could not see them. Some natives believe in a special spirit of cat's cradles that punishes them if they violate the taboo.[2] Mr. Stefansson says that it is only during the dark days that the natives tell stories,[3] but Ikpakhuak and his people had no hesitation about narrating them in the summer. There is a curious regulation about dances; they must never be held out of doors, lest the songs of the natives should be wafted abroad and the singers die. Throwing the scrapings from deerskins on to the floor of a snow hut is alleged to be tabooed, though the natives frequently do it. Farther east the Netsilingmiut are said to have a taboo against making new knives on the ice before the young seals are born, but the Coronation gulf Eskimos have no scruples in this respect. Avranna on one occasion refused to allow his dog to eat any part of the skin or meat of a rabbit that he had shot, saying that it was 'dry meat' and the dog would fall ill and die. It may have been a taboo, or only a particular fancy of his own.

---

[1]Cf. Boas, Bulletin, A.M.H.N., Vol. XV, p. 149.

[2]More details concerning the superstitions relating to cat's cradles will be found in a volume of Eskimo Cat's Cradles to be published in one of the later reports of this series.

[3]Anthrop. Papers, A.M.N.H., Vol. XIV, pt. I, p. 244.

The Eskimos must be just as careful in their conduct when the caribou are migrating south in the fall as when the salmon are migrating up stream in the spring. Higilak checked me from throwing a marrow bone to a dog one day, saying that it was tabooed in the place where the deer had been killed. I saw Ikpakhuak do the same thing a few days later, and when I told him of Higilak's objection he said that the bones he had given his dog were from caribou killed a long way off (actually it was about five miles), and that only the bones of caribou killed in the immediate vicinity were under the ban. In skinning such caribou it is forbidden to cut off the ears at the roots, as is done at other seasons of the year; the skin must be pulled off them. None of the contents of the stomach, again, must be allowed to escape and taint the ground in the path the caribou are taking, *kalgini*, otherwise the shades of the dead Eskimos, it was said, would be offended and keep the deer away. For the same reason Higilak would not make me a deerskin dog harness at this period, but waited until the migration was over. Ikpakhuak had bad luck in hunting one day, and Higilak discovered through her familiar spirit that she had been sewing too much deerskin clothing, while Ikpakhuak had also been at fault by hammering too much on the stones when loosening them for caches, neither of which things should be done to excess on the path of the migration.[1]

Mr. Stefansson's western Eskimos were responsible for the introduction of a new custom in 1910. They told the Copper Eskimos that if they did not cut off a fragment from every skin they sold to the white men to be taken out of the country, the animals would follow the skins and leave the country also. This applied particularly to the caribou, the natives said, which for this reason had almost disappeared from Alaska and the Mackenzie river delta. Hence some of the Copper Eskimos now cut a corner from each deerskin garment and an ear from each skin that they sell to the white men, lest their country too should be denuded of its game.

Mr. Stefansson says that in Coronation gulf every man, woman and child is forbidden to eat the muskrat. In another place he says that "the Akulliakattangmiut and others kill a few muskrats, but they use neither the skins nor meat, but only use the tails for charms."[2] The only place where muskrats are found is in the vicinity of Great Bear lake, and even there it is probably only within recent years that they have made their appearance; I very much doubt therefore whether the Copper Eskimos have any real taboo in regard to them.

Mr. Stefansson's discussion of *aglirktok*, again, the condition wherein an individual labours under a taboo with regard to certain things, is much more applicable to the Alaskan and Mackenzie river Eskimos than to those of Coronation gulf. I hardly know what the word would imply to the Copper Eskimos, for I never heard them use it. Its derivative, *aglenaktok*, however, is almost daily in their mouths, and there can be no doubt as to its meaning. It is a prohibition against doing something, for example against cooking salmon on the sea ice. If they disobey, the supernatural powers which surround them— the shades of the dead, *inyuin tarrait*, or the spirits, *ornrait*—will surely be wroth and punish them. How the prohibitions arose in the first case they do not know, but they are binding nevertheless on every human being. Taboos binding on particular individuals are common enough, but they are only temporary restrictions due to special circumstances; a sick man, for example, will be prohibited from eating certain foods. They are weaker taboos that issue as a rule from the injunctions of some shaman, and last no longer than the patient's illness, and not always as long as that; sometimes, indeed, a native will disregard them altogether. They really have more resemblance to the "taboos" of our medical men when they forbid their patients certain foods. Thus the shamans

---

[1] I do not know whether any of these taboos are observed in the spring while the caribou are migrating north.

[2] Anthrop. Papers, A.M.N.H., Vol. XIV, pt. I, pp. 244 and 59.

frequently forbid all sewing the day after they have held their séances, and tell the people it is taboo, *ag enangman*, and that they will die if they disobey; but if the particular shaman be a man of little repute the women will often disregard his command and sew as usual. There seems to be a tendency, indeed, among the Copper Eskimos to limit restrictions and taboos as far as possible; they say themselves that they do many things now that were forbidden in former days. Certainly they have no such intricate and far-reaching system of taboo as Mr. Stefansson describes, however true his remarks may be of the natives farther west.

The supernatural agencies with which the Copper Eskimo has to reckon are not confined to the shades of men and animals, *tarrait*. Over and above these are the *tornrait*, spirits that never had a normal life like human beings, though they are semi-human in their form. They live in isolation, as a rule, though divided into male and female. Whether they intermarry or not, and have children, the native never thinks of enquiring, and opinions even differ as to whether they can die. The shamans often assert that they cause them bodily harm, and sometimes claim to have killed one, but certain spirits at least the natives maintain it is impossible to kill. At times some little peculiarity in their appearance distinguishes them from human beings, for example, extraordinarily long hair; but they can change their forms and appear or disappear at will. Some have definite homes in hillocks or in tide-cracks or in old stone houses, but they are not altogether confined to these places; on the contrary, they are as free as other spirits to roam wherever they will.

The natives say that the shades of the dead, *inyuin tarrait*, often become spirits, *tornrait*, and in fact malignant shades that work the Eskimos harm are often called by this name.[1] The machinations of evil shades or spirits, *aggioktun*, is the explanation of every untoward circumstance and of every inexplicable phenomenon, whether it be sickness or stormy weather, an unaccountable sound or the movement of the compass needle. Mannigyorina, for example, had difficulty in her delivery, and the people said, "The shades of the dead are angry." Kanneyuk again heard a strange noise one day when she was inside her hut, and she rushed out crying, "Evil shades"; similarly, on another occasion, Higilak, who heard a sound as of something scratching on a skin while she was cooking outside her tent, whispered apprehensively, "Surely *aggioktun*." The men are as credulous as the women. Thus Avranna heard a whistle one day when he was leaving our station[2]. He knew it could not have issued from either of the two men who were there at the time, but thought there might be some one in one of the tents. However, as no one had ever been seen living in the tents he concluded with the other natives that it must have been a spirit haunting the station. The Eskimos believed that there was a spirit, *tornrak*, in the electric battery, and another in the phonograph. I induced a man to sing into the phonograph one evening, then changed the needle and reproduced his song. He was greatly alarmed, and asked whether some spirit were not boxed up in the machine. We told him to look down the horn and see for himself. Sure enough, he asserted he could see the spirit that had reproduced his song, a diminutive being like a man, but only about an inch and a half high. When a woman's voice was reproduced the spirit he saw resembled a woman, and when his little boy's song was played over for him he saw the figure of a little boy. Several other Eskimos could see the same spirits when they looked down the horn, but, curiously enough, the man's wife was the one sceptic in the party.

Spirits, *tornrait*, are liable to be encountered everywhere. They are especially dangerous in solitary places, and to natives wandering alone in the dark. A woman who had to take the usual portion of food one evening over to a house some thirty yards away ran the whole distance for fear of spirits. It is partly

[1] This belief exists also at Barrow, in North Alaska.
[2] Copper Eskimos never whistle, except to signal when hunting.

for this reason that the natives prefer to go about in company. Higilak became quite alarmed one day because I was absent from camp for about twelve hours, hunting in the Colville hills; she was afraid lest a spirit that was known to live in the vicinity had carried me off, just as one had carried off her father many years before. The Eskimos declare that long ago the ice suddenly cracked off Cockburn point and caused the drowning of a number of people who were encamped there. Then a spirit, a *tornrak* named Kalyutaryun, appeared in the crack—it was he who had caused the disaster. A man named Asiranna— the being to whom the Eskimos now ascribe the lightning—attacked the spirit with his harpoon, but Kalyutaryun disappeared beneath the ice again. In the winter of 1915-16 the natives told my interpreter Patsy that there were spirits in the rough ice near their settlement; Patsy said he would like to see a *tornrak*, and suggested that they should all go over and look for them, but the natives were horrified at the mere thought of it. Not a month later one of them saw a spirit issuing from a hole in the wall of an abandoned dance-house; he rushed for his rifle and fired a shot into the house, while the children fled in terror to their huts.

I was told that in Bathurst inlet the opening of the sealing season is marked by a pitched battle between the shamans and the many little *tornrait* that live on the ice. The shamans, it was said, hold a séance in the dance-house and summon their familiars; then with their snow-dusters they pursue the spirits, fighting them like dogs, so that often both the mouths of the men and the ends of the snow-dusters are covered with blood. The spirits of course are always defeated; but unless they were got rid of in this manner they would drive away all the seals, and the Eskimos would starve during the winter.

From generation to generation, from *inyuit sivulingni*, "Men of the first times," as the natives say, various incantations, *akeutit*, have been handed down to appease or drive away the malignant spirits. The incantation is usually sung by all the people, with one of their shamans standing in the centre of the ring; and as they sing their bodies sway from side to side, though their feet remain stationary. At the conclusion of the refrain the shaman invokes his familiars, and with their aid produces the desired result. Children are generally excluded from these performances. Many of the incantations are very old and have lost whatever meaning they had originally; but this does not lessen their potency. I heard one sung during a snow-storm in the late summer of 1915. Tusayok and Kesullik had no tent, so they improvised a rude shelter by stretching some skins between two crags; but since in spite of this they were very cold and uncomfortable, Tusayok chanted an incantation and repeated it over and over again for about an hour. There were only about half a dozen words in it, and each taken by itself was intelligible enough, but no one had any clear idea of what the whole song meant. Tusayok thought, however, that the mere singing of this incantation, even though he was not himself a shaman, might have the effect of driving away the evil shades or spirits who were causing the storm and produce fine weather again. Literally translated the song ran:—

I come again, I, again.
I come again, I ,again. Do you not know?
I come again, I, again.[1]

About an hour after this had happened Kesullik tied a cord round his face so that it wrinkled up his nose and distorted his features, giving him a most grotesque appearance. He then sallied forth with a knife in his hand and defied the weather. Almost the same thing had occurred a month or two earlier when Ikpakhuak and a hunting party were lost for three days in a fog. Higilak distorted her features with a cord and confronted the fog, brandishing a knife in one hand and a set fox-trap in the other; *ilanakhotin* "You are angry", she

---

[1] A spirit is supposed to be speaking all through.

shouted, and Haugak and I —one on either side of her pretending to hold her back—echoed her cry. We all had to laugh immoderately, to mock, it would seem, the shades or spirits that were responsible for the fog. Finally, with the cry *mammienaksilekpakpok* "Its a confounded nuisance", she flung her fox-trap down on the ground, making it spring off and thereby intimidate the hostile powers.

The greatest of all the spirits, *tornrait*, is Kannakapfaluk, who lives in a snow hut just like the Eskimos, with a lamp and sleeping-platform and all the usual household paraphernalia. But Kannakapfaluk's hut is at the bottom of the sea, and her dogs are two bears, one brown and one white. There is a dwarf who lives with her, a man about three feet high whom the Eskimos call Unga because of the cry he utters when the shamans drag him up to the surface. If the Eskimo women sew too much on the ice, or break any of the taboos in reference to either sewing or cooking, Unga gathers all the seals inside the hut, and the Eskimos in consequence have no success in their sealing. The shamans then hold a séance in the dance-house and lower a long rope through the floor with a noose at one end of it. All the people gather round the rope and sing this incantation, which is known from one end of the Copper Eskimo country to the other:—

> The woman down there she wants to go away.
> Some of the young sea-gulls I can't lay my hands on.[1]
> That man[2] he can't right matters by himself.
> That man he can't mend matters by himself.
> Over there where no people dwell I go myself and right matters.
> He can't right matters by himself.
> Over there where no people dwell, thither I go and right matters
>   myself.[3]

As soon as the song is ended the shamans are supposed to slip a noose over Kannakapfaluk's wrists and haul her up until her head is just below the level of the floor. They must not draw her any higher because she would be very angry if the people in the dance-house saw her. The shamans talk to her, telling her that the people are starving for want of seals and asking her to release them again; Unga in the meantime remains below guarding the seals. Kannakapfaluk is now lowered again, and at once orders Unga to release some of the seals. Then the Eskimo hunters are successful again and the community prospers.

Another method is said to be adopted occasionally by the shamans. One of them will dive down through the water and enter Kannakapfaluk's hut. Unga, the guardian of the seals, tries to escape, but the shaman tucks him under his coat and carries him up to the dance-house, holding him carefully concealed so that the people may not see him, though they hear his cries. Unga is then told to let out the seals and sent back to report to Kannakapfaluk.

Kannakapfaluk has other powers besides this one of hoarding the seals. She can send bad weather in winter, and so keep the Eskimos indoors till they starve; or she can break up the ice and drown them. Long ago she used to put people inside the breast of her coat and crush them to death. There were many taboos that the Eskimos of olden times had to observe, the natives say, but the majority of them have now been quietly dropped. Occasionally, however, in stormy weather the shamans will revive one or two for a short period. The two that should never be violated are the prohibitions against sewing new deerskin clothing on the ice during the weeks when the sun never rises, and cooking on the ice deer-meat that was obtained in the preceding summer and fall.

---

[1] One native said that when Kannakapfaluk cannot shut up the seals she shuts up sea-gulls instead. More probably "sea-gulls" in shamanistic utterances means "seals."

[2] "That man" refers to the shaman in the dance-house, but whether another shaman is supposed to be speaking or not is uncertain.

[3] The chant is then repeated from the third line.

These taboos are rarely, if ever, violated by the natives of Dolphin and Union strait and of west Coronation gulf as long as they are actually living on the sea ice, although they may sometimes disregard them when their huts are built so near the shore that it is doubtful whether ice or gravel lies under the floor.

In Bathurst inlet the myth of Kannakapfaluk as told by the shaman Ilatsiak is slightly different.[1] There are two women living under the sea, one of whom, Arnakapfaluk, is very big, while the other woman, who may be her daughter— Ilatsiak had forgotten her name—is much smaller. Two men live with them, Ikparyuak and Hitkoktak, and all the seals are gathered in their hut where the smaller of the two women keeps guard over them. The women would like to keep them away from the Eskimos altogether, and are therefore perpetually quarrelling with the men, who are friendly towards the Eskimos and would let them kill all the seals they need. Arnakapfaluk, whose hair streams above and behind her whenever a blizzard is raging, is especially wroth if the Eskimo women sew too much during the time that the sun is absent. When seals are scarce the shamans hold a séance in the dance-house, and after singing the incantation given above they haul Arnakapfaluk up to the surface, when the small woman down below immediately throws out some of the seals for the Eskimo hunters to kill later.

It is worth noting that among these Bathurst inlet natives there is no rigid prohibition against sewing new deerskin clothing during the dark days of winter; the women are allowed to sew provided they keep within reasonable limits. The reason given by the local natives was that the sea ice is much more solid in their region than it is farther west, where strong currents open up huge cracks even in mid-winter. It is possible that we have here an example of a taboo, based on or upheld by fear, dropping out as soon as that fear is removed.

Sila, the being who lives in the sky and makes the sun go down when he walks along, also holds a high place in the Eskimo cosmology. Sila is often hostile to human beings and carries one off; but sometimes he is gracious and will cure a sick man by imparting to him some of his own vitality. More important, because more dangerous, is Nigsillik, another spirit who lives in the sky; the Eskimos are very much afraid of him, for he carries a great hook, *nigsik*, which he stabs into his enemies. Like Kannakapfaluk, he too is wroth if the women sew new deerskin clothes during the dark days, and will break up the ice and drown the natives. On one occasion, they told me, he broke up the passage leading to a dance-house. The inmates said, "There is someone outside;" but one of them was skeptical and said there was no one. Nigsillik immediately entered the hut and drove his long hook under their armpits, killing them all. Now and again the Eskimos hear him break up the passage of a hut; then they frighten him away by driving a knife through the snow wall at the edge of the window, or by pouring water through a hole in the wall or throwing it out into the passage. They must keep perfectly silent, otherwise Nigsillik will enter and kill them, as he did the people in the dance-house.

According to Ilatsiak there are two spirits living in the sky both of whom are called Nigsillik; one of them carries a great club, the other an immense antler. A shaman named Arluna, he said, was once holding a séance in a crowded dance-house when these two spirits came down and began to batter on the wall; but Arluna drove his knife through it and frightened them away before they could reach the people within.

The Eskimos were terrified one night because my half-breed interpreter Patsy scratched on the ice window of one of the huts. They earnestly entreated him to stop, lest a spirit called Poalleritillik, "The one with the snow shovel,"

[1]Cf. Boas, Bulletin A.M.N.H., Vol. XV, p. 492. For other versions of the Sedna myth see Miss Wardle in Am. Anthropologist, N.S., Vol. II, 1900, pp. 568–580.

should come down from the sky and kill them all. Higilak then told us that a man was once talking to her uncle in a hut, and declaring that no such spirit as Poalleritillik existed, when suddenly they heard the scraping of his shovel on the window as though he were trying to make his way into the hut. Higilak's uncle, however, was a shaman, and through the power of his magic he was able to drive the spirit away.

Not many years ago what seems to have been an epidemic of some kind carried off a great many Eskimos in and around Bathurst inlet. Ilatsiak told me that close to the shore there was a large rock set up by men long ago among a number of smaller ones. Round this rock he fastened a line, attaching the other end to his belt. Then he spoke to the stone, saying that he did not wish to die, and asking it to preserve his life. When the prayer was ended he gathered six pairs of mittens—two for himself, two for his wife, and two for his adopted son—and with these in his hands he approached the rock and tied them round it as an offering. In consequence he and his family were preserved when others perished. I omitted to ask him whether the rock was the home of a *tornrak*, but almost certainly it was.

The religious doctrines of the Copper Eskimos, then, bring them little or no comfort. Life would be hard enough if they had none but natural forces to contend with, forces that they could see and estimate. But mysterious and hostile powers, invisible and incalculable, and therefore potentially all the more dangerous, hem them in, as they believe, on every side, so that they never know from day to day whether a fatal sickness will not strike them down or a sudden misfortune overwhelm them and their families—from no apparent cause, it may be, and for no conceivable reason, save the ill-will of these unseen foes. Young and old, the good and the bad, all alike are involved in the same dangers, and all alike share the same fate. Death rolls back the gate, not of a happy hunting ground, or of a heaven of peace and happiness where friends and lovers may unite once more, but of some vague and gloomy realm where, even if want and misery are not found (and of this they are not certain), joy and gladness at least must surely be unknown. It is little wonder therefore if the mind of the average Eskimo is deeply tinged with fatalism. Life would be unbearable indeed with this religion did he not possess a superabundant stock of natural gaiety and derive a joy from the mere fact of living itself. The future holds out no golden promise, not even the hope of a life as cheerful as the present one; so the native banishes as far as possible all thoughts of a distant to-morrow, and drains the pleasures of each fleeting hour before they pass away for ever.

CHAPTER XV

SHAMANISM

The mediators and intercessors between the living Eskimos and the super-natural world of shades and spirits are the shamans, *angatkut*. Mr. Stefansson has given an admirable account of their methods among the Mackenzie river Eskimos, and much that he says of the natives there applies also to the Copper Eskimos.[1] But the ideas and practices of the eastern natives are much less definite and precise, just as their religious beliefs are far more hazy and indeterminate. Accordingly, despite some necessary repetitions of Mr. Stefansson's remarks, it will be better to give a full description of shamanism as it is known and practised in the regions around Coronation gulf.

A shaman's powers are due to the control he presumably exercises over certain spirits, which are either the spirits (the shades?) of certain animals or the shades of the Eskimo dead. One or two shamans were reputed to control also certain white men, but whether it was their shades or their living powers was never stated; in any case they were remote enough to count as dead. The familiar spirit is called either *tornrak* or *tupilek*, usually the former; the word *keyugak*, which is the usual term in the Mackenzie delta, seems to be unknown, and even *tupilek* may be a borrowed word, although I hardly think so. A shaman inspired or possessed by his familiar is said to *onipkaktok* (which farther west means "to tell a story") or *tornraktok*. The Copper Eskimo makes no sharp and definite destinction between the shades of the dead, the spirits that have never been men or animals, and the spirits that the shamans control; there are separate names for both the first and last; but all alike may be, and usually are, called *tornrait*.

Control over any familiar may be obtained by purchase, as I have men-tioned elsewhere; Uloksak, for example, bought his power from a shaman in Bathurst inlet. This statement, however, is only partly true, for all that the owner can impart is his good-will, and a knowledge of how to approach and summon the particular spirit that he has sold; the rest depends on the spirit itself. The aspirant must go out to some lonely place and summon the spirit, which may or may not appear. Sometimes, however, a spirit will come to a man without being invoked, and tell him that henceforth it will accompany him everywhere and place its powers at his disposal. Thus Uloksak, after his purchase of certain spirits, used to go hunting all alone and summon them to come to him. For a time none came, then one day when he was alone on an island several appeared one after the other. They forbade him to eat any part of the stomach of the caribou, but to eat plenty of its brains; if he obeyed them in this respect they promised to attend him and bestow on him magical powers. After giving him these injunctions they knocked him roughly about and changed him into a white man. In this condition he returned to camp, where other shamans held a séance over him and restored him to his proper form. He then became one of the most noted shamans in the country.

The case of the old man Ilatsiak was very similar. He was fishing for tom-cod, all alone, when a spirit first appeared to him. It resembled a young man in appearance, and was accompanied by other spirits, but these Ilatsiak could not see. He was terrified when it approached him, and asked it whether he was going to die, but the spirit answered that he would live for many winters and reach old age before he died. It caught a tom-cod and made him eat it, and the

---

[1]My Life with the Eskimo, Ch. XXVI; Anthrop. Papers, A.M.N.H., Vol. XIV, pt. I, p. 126 *et passim*

eating of this fish gave him magical power. The spirit accompanied him back to his camp, conversing with him, and giving him various injunctions; thus he was forbidden to eat the intestines of any animal, only the meat and the fat. The spirit disappeared as soon as they reached the camp.

Higilak gained her power in very much the same way. Her father had been a shaman and had two familiar spirits. After his death these came to her one day when she was all alone in the camp. In appearance they resembled two men, and they told her that as they had attended her father in his life-time so now they would attend on her. She too was forbidden to eat of certain foods, in her case the stomach and the skin of the salmon, on pain of losing her magical power. The spirits then disappeared, and when the other Eskimos returned to camp Higilak was already holding her first séance.

As a rule the shaman's spirits are nameless, though the two that came to Higilak were called Kitafoa and Kingmitok. As their attachment to their owners is voluntary, so they can desert them at will. If the shaman for example should break the food prohibitions his familiars have enjoined on him they will leave him immediately. Such a fate befel a man in Coronation gulf quite recently, the natives said, when the people were feasting on the meat of a caribou that some one had shot. Two shamans, a man and a woman, began to hold a séance, but in the midst of it they drank a little of the blood of the deer, although this had been prohibited to them. The man's familiar immediately left him, and he lost all his shamanistic powers. The woman, whose name was Mittik, walked away towards the sun up the side of a ridge. Suddenly she disappeared into the ground, and a moment afterwards a dog sprang out from the same spot; then the dog disappeared and the woman took its place again. This occurred three or four times in the sight of all the people, then finally Mittik walked back to the camp in her human form, but with her faculties impaired. Other shamans laid hands on her, and with the aid of their familiars restored her to her senses.[1]

How and where the familiars live, and what becomes of them after the death of their owners, the Eskimos never trouble to consider. They still continue to exist, for Higilak could inherit her father's familiars. Obviously it would redound to the credit and influence of an Eskimo if he could say that he had control over the same spirits as some famous shaman of earlier days, even though he himself never acquired the same reputed skill and power. The shaman's power, in fact, depends rather on his own personality than on the familiars he controls. A man of weak character who models his life on those around him and is easily swayed by public opinion never attains to any great repute as a shaman. On the other hand a shrewd, strong-minded man, capable and success-ful in all the ordinary affairs of life, a leader of public opinion rather than its servant, may easily attain to the greatest influence and be credited with the most extraordinary shamanistic powers.

Shamans always, or almost always, have more than one familiar. Uloksak claimed to have many, including a white man, a polar bear, a wolf and a dog. I never heard of any bird familiars; they do exist perhaps, but not often, for birds are unimportant in the economy of the Copper Eskimos and therefore attract but little attention. One of Higilak's familiars was the shade of a dead relative, but she had besides this a polar bear and a wolf. Some shamans assign different functions to different familiars, using one, for example, in cases of sick-ness, and another for producing an abundance of seals. In this way one might be ranked as more important than the rest: for instance the familiar that was used for seals might be regarded as of more service than the one used to drive out a disease. But this specialization of functions is neither necessary nor usual. Every shaman probably has a preference for some particular familiar, and

---

[1] Kaksavik, the Pallik (Hudson bay) shaman who visited our headquarters, was prohibited from eating the liver, the lungs and the pancreas of the seal.

employs it more than the others he claims to control; for a certain amount of acting is necessary in shamanistic performances, and naturally a man may find one rôle easier than another. According to the belief of the natives a shaman will often change his form and take on that of the animal by which he is possessed, or will assume at least some of its characteristics.[1] This metamorphosis may even take place in the presence of spectators, though sometimes it can occur only when the shaman is alone. Thus Ilatsiak said that when his grandmother was a child there was a shaman named Makettak who could change into a polar bear. He would bend down to the floor of the dance-house, resting his hands on the ground. Slowly his hands would change into polar bear's feet, then his arms become legs, and finally his whole body and head would assume the shape of the bear. In this state he would go out of the dance-house and visit the neighbouring houses, saying to the children in each as he entered, "Stand up against the wall beside the door and then I shall not eat you."

(Photo by R. M. Anderson.)

FIG. 56. Women wading ashore from ice in a fishing-lake just south of Bernard harbour, July 3, 1915

The natives have numberless stories of such transformations and believe implicitly in their truth. Higilak's father could change into a polar bear, but only when he was alone. Uloksak claimed the power of transforming himself into a white or a brown bear, a wolf and a white man. Ilatsiak's wife, who was a shaman like her husband, put her fingers into her mouth on one occasion; gradually her hands became the feet of a wolf, then her head and body began to change and finally only her legs remained human. Even Higilak, according to her daughter Kanneyuk, had the same power; Kanneyuk had seen her change into a polar bear. I was present myself at one of her transformations, and in view of the interesting questions it raises regarding the psychology of these Eskimos, I shall describe the incident in detail.

---

[1]In 1916, when Ilatsiak visited our station, he chose me as his associate in magic, because, as he asserted, I could change into any form I wished.

We were living at Lake Numikhoin, in the Colville hills, and had been considering the advisability of travelling to Lake Tahiryuak to look for the Prince Albert sound natives.   Higilak accordingly gave a séance to discover whether we could safely make the journey there and back by sled before the snow melted.   The séance was held about midnight (it was at the end of May, when the sun never sets below the horizon), and all the Eskimos save the little children gathered inside the tent.   Higilak was sitting at the back, in a corner, and her husband Ikpakhuak was slightly in front of her, while I was sitting in the corner opposite Higilak.   She began by delivering a long speech setting forward the whole question at issue.   Suddenly she uttered cries of pain and covered her face in her hands.   Dead silence followed for a few minutes, a silence that was only broken by an occasional remark uttered in a low tone by some one in the audience. Presently Higilak began to howl and growl like a wolf, then as suddenly ceased and raised her head, when, behold, two canine teeth, evidently a wolf's, were protruding one from each corner of her mouth.   She leaned over to Avranna and pretended to gnaw his head, then began to utter broken remarks which her audience caught up and discussed, though very little of them could be interpreted.   Every now and then she had to put her hand up to her mouth to keep the teeth from falling out, and once she slyly pushed them right inside out of sight, pushing them out again a few minutes later.   After about a quarter of an hour spent in this manner she suddenly broke out into cries of pain again and concealed her face in her hands behind Ikpakhuak's back.   Then I saw her carefully drop one hand towards her long boot, into which she apparently slipped the teeth, for a moment later her face reappeared without them.   This was the critical moment, the moment when the wolf's spirit inside her body gave its answer to the question at issue.   A few broken words issued from her, uttered in a feeble falsetto voice that was almost inaudible.   Her audience was bending eagerly forward drinking in every syllable.   In about two minutes it was all over, and Higilak, after a few more cries of pain (the familiar was leaving her) followed by two or three gasps, resumed her normal bearing.   The séance was now concluded, but some of the natives lingered for a few minutes to discuss the oracle that had been delivered to them.   Higilak herself professed to be ignorant of it, for a shaman should not be conscious of utterances given under the inspiration of a familiar; accordingly she had to question some of the bystanders to find out what she had said.   In speaking of this séance some time afterwards the natives stated as an incontestable fact that Higilak had been transformed into a wolf.

To a critical and unsympathetic outsider it may seem that a séance of this type is simply a case of palpable fraud on the part of the shaman, and of almost unbelievable stupidity and credulity on the part of the audience.   A little very amateurish ventriloquism, a feeble attempt at impersonation, and a childish and grotesque blending of the human and the animal, all performed in full daylight before an audience incapable of distinguishing between fact and fancy, between things seen and things imagined, or at least so mentally unbalanced that it reacted to the slightest suggestion and hypnotised itself into believing the most impossible things—that perhaps is all there may seem to be in Eskimo shamanism.   But let us examine its functions a little more closely and consider a number of other séances before we give our final judgment.

In the first place the Copper Eskimo shaman, whether man or woman, has no distinctive mark or dress of any kind, not even during the séances.[1] There is absolutely nothing in his appearance that would suggest to a stranger the possession of special powers or functions.   The shamans are not priests in any ordinary sense of the word.   They may be of either sex, are self-appointed and act separately without forming a distinctive class or caste; further, they

[1]They differ from Mackenzie river shamans in this respect. See Stefansson, Anthrop. Papers, A.M. N.H., Vol. XIV, pt. I, p. 366.

perform at any time and in any place according to their fancy. No sanctity attaches to them, nor are they given special privileges. They resemble doctors rather than priests, doctors who give their services free in any public cause, but are paid for treating individuals. Thus the shaman receives no reward when he placates the spirits that cause the blizzards, or induces Kannakapfaluk to send the Eskimos plenty of seals; but if someone is ill and a shaman is called in he must be paid for his services, whether they are successful or not. Like a doctor, too, the shaman may abuse his powers and employ them against the interests of the community. He then becomes a malefactor like any common murderer, and is liable to the same fate.

Let us take concrete instances of each of these points. There were eight shamans in Dolphin and Union strait during the winter of 1914. Three of these, Kimaiyok, Higilak and Arnauyuk, were women, the remaining five, Anauyuk, Agluak, Utugaum, Kuniluk and Kamingok, were men. Every one of them gave séances at one time or another and so testified to their possession of shamanistic powers; but for this nothing would have marked them off as different from the other natives. Ikpakhuak and Aiyallik, who were perhaps the two most influential men in the region, were neither of them shamans. In Coronation gulf, on the other hand, the two most influential men, Uloksak and Ilatsiak, were both shamans. Séances were held most frequently in winter when the concentration of the families in a single camp gave more intensity and fervor to social and religious life. The nights at this season are long and tedious, and the people seek distraction in the dance-house, where singing, dancing and drum-beating key them up to the proper pitch for religious or magical rites. Their religion is not dropped, however, with the winter, and séances may be given in the open air in broad daylight at any season of the year, and in any place. When we first entered the country our Mackenzie river native, Palaiyak, met the shaman Anauyuk hunting on the tundra. This was the first warning that any of the Copper Eskimos had received of our presence, so Anauyuk immediately went into a "trance," invoking his familiar spirit to find out whether Palaiyak and the white men with him were friendly or not.[1] The same Anauyuk held a séance during a migration on December 19th, 1914, just at the commencement of the sealing season. It was concerned both with the supply of seals during the coming winter, and with the presence of white men in the country. Kimaiyok held another immediately afterwards, to discover the reason for a certain man's illness. Both of these séances took place in the open beside the sleds, with the natives standing in a ring around their shamans. Higilak held several séances in Victoria island during the spring and summer, some inside the tent, and some outside. In July, 1916, a native Tokalluak gave a performance beside the fishing creek near Cape Krusenstern. Clearly therefore the shaman is not bound by any restrictions as to time and place.

It was stated that the shamans are public servants to some extent, comparable to our doctors. Whenever anything goes wrong—the weather is unusually stormy, or seals are scarce, or a number of people become ill—the shaman are asked or themselves volunteer to discover the cause and remove the evil. I have already mentioned how in Bathurst inlet at the beginning of the sealing season they kill or drive away all the little spirits that live on the ice and would prevent the Eskimos from catching seals. In March 1915 Uloksak, who had just come from Coronation gulf, was asked by the Dolphin and Union strait natives to kill or drive away a certain evil spirit that was threatening to destroy them all; already, they said, one Puivlik and two Akulliakattak natives had died, and they feared that others might follow them. Uloksak's familiar, a

---

[1]Cf. Stefansson, Anthrop. Papers, A.M.N.H., Vol. XVI, pt. I, p. 252.

dog, drove the hostile spirit into a dance-house where the séance was taking place. One of the spectators—for it was visible to the people—said that it had the form of a human being, but was only about two feet high and had unusually long hair. Uloksak's familiar, though invisible, could be heard yelping inside the shaman's body. A long contest took place between the two spirits, but finally the dog drove the evil one outside the house and killed it in the snow. Thus the community was rid of its pest.

It was Uloksak who told me of a case where a shaman abused his power and brought disaster on his community. The story is fanciful, of course, but not without its significance, since the natives believed implicitly in its truth. A succession of blizzards one winter had prevented the Akulliakattak Eskimos from sealing, and reduced them to the point of starvation. Finally one of the natives died, and the shamans held a séance concerning the misfortunes that had overtaken them. Now Uloksak's father-in-law, who was one of the principal shamans in the settlement, had a grudge against the other people because they had killed one of his relatives, so with the aid of his familiars he knocked down one of the two poles that were erected by men in the earliest times to hold up the heavens. The sky fell, and many of the Eskimos were killed. The man then left the settlement and went east to Bathurst inlet. After he had departed the Akulliakattak shamans divined that the pole had been knocked down by some shades of the dead, so with the help of their familiars they erected it in place again.

In the examples just given the shamans' services are employed for the benefit or otherwise of the whole community; but they can be used to serve individuals equally well. Thus when Ikpakhuak had a headache one evening, Higilak divined over him. She borrowed my coat (*attigi*), rolled it into a bundle, and fastened her belt-cord around it. Then she summoned a shade into the bundle and asked it various questions, judging of the answers by the weight of the coat, "Yes" if it seemed heavy to lift and "No" if it seemed light. After a series of questions and answers she discovered that a dead sister-in-law of Ikpakhuak had bewitched him, so she appeased the wrath of the shade with soothing words until it promised to cease its baneful influence. This ceremony took place in Ikpakhuak's tent where there was no one present save himself and his wife. Lying in my sleeping-bag in a tent adjoining I could hear her questioning the bundle, but no one else was aware that she even intended to hold a performance. It is hard to believe that Ikpakhuak, who had lived with his wife for years, could have been deliberately deceived by her unless she was deceived herself at the same time.

The same magic powers that the shaman normally employs for the benefit of his fellow-men can equally well be used against them. Two natives carried off the wife of Anauyuk's father and tried to ferry her across the Rae river in their kayaks, which were lashed together to enable the woman to lie across the bows; but by the power of his magic, Anauyuk's father made the kayak capsize and their occupants were drowned. Similarly Uloksak threatened to use his magic power against me because we ejected him from our station one day; he told his fellow natives that the next time I crossed over to their settlement at the Liston and Sutton islands he would make me stumble and fall every few yards. In the same way Anauyuk, who was refused admittance to our house because he had robbed one of our caches along the coast, threatened to deprive us of our strength and make us waste away and die. Two shamans who were holding a seance together at the Liston and Sutton islands in December 1915, announced that they would cause some of our party to fall over a cliff and perish, in revenge for some offence that we had given them. The women were forbidden to sew on the following day lest they should all perish, and the children were told not to play too long out of doors for fear that an evil spirit might seize them. Of course, it is a dangerous thing for a shaman to let it be known that he practises witchcraft against his fellow-men, for some one is likely to end his career with a knife. It is often attempted, however, when the passion for revenge is strong enough to overcome the dictates of prudence.

I was told that rude human figures are sometimes made from the bark of the cotton-wood tree, *ningok*, and used in connection with magic; both the bark itself and the figure that is made from it are called *kaisalluk*. The shaman holds the figure in his hand and calls his familiar into it, then asks it questions. Sometimes, it is said, the fetish by its own might will clothe itself in clean white deer-skin garments, much whiter than any the Eskimos themselves ever wear. I believe that various ceremonies are carried out with it, for example, that it is sometimes stabbed with a knife, but my enquiries brought me very little information. I am not certain, therefore, whether the fetish served the purposes of legitimate magic or was used in connection with witchcraft.[1]

(Photo by J. J. O'Neill.)

FIG. 57. An Eskimo in his kayak, Port Epworth

The most extraordinary feats and miracles are ascribed to shamans when under the inspiration of their familiars. They swallow fire, fly through the air, change into animals, sink into the ground or water, kill and restore to life again and discover things that are hidden from ordinary sight. Once they were able to visit the moon, but the modern shamans have lost that power. On returning from a trip to Coronation gulf in March, 1915, I was handed a little note written by our Mackenzie river native Palaiyak describing what the shamans in Dolphin and Union strait had done in my absence. Translated it ran: "I shall relate what I was told about the shamans. Well, a man cut off both his legs and his arms. While he was holding this séance the children were forbidden to go outside; if they went out they would die. Once he killed a strong man (who left the dance-house during the séance). He exchanged his familiar spirit with Uloksak (*i.e.*, the two shamans sent their familiars into each other's bodies). Uloksak too forbade the children on pain of death to go outdoors while he was holding a séance. Some of the people were stricken with sickness (one of the patients was Uloksak's own wife Kukkilukak) and the shamans extracted some bones and worms from their bodies."

[1]Cf. Nelson, p. 494.

In May, 1916, two of our western Eskimos, both Christianized, witnessed a séance that was held by a woman at Tree river. Invoking her familiar, they said, she began to converse with it; feeble sounds issued in reply from the woman's stomach in which the spirit was lodged. After a few minutes some of the natives told our two Eskimos to look out over the land. There, protruding above the ground, they saw two heads, a man's and a woman's, which appeared and disappeared several times, then finally disappeared altogether. Our Eskimos went over to examine the spot and found that the ground was all overturned. They fully agreed with the Copper Eskimos that it was the shaman who had caused the phenomenon.

Innumerable stories are current of the wonderful powers that the shamans possess, and no native entertains the slightest doubt as to the literal truth of every incident. I shall narrate a few of them as they were told to me by eyewitnesses, since they throw considerable light on the mentality of the people.

Not many years ago, it was said, a certain shaman used often to fly through the air. He would hang his bow on his left shoulder and fly off like a ptarmigan. After a few yards he would settle and walk along the ground for a short distance, then rise in the air again. The people had often witnessed this. Ilatsiak was frequently credited with the same power, but he denied it himself, saying that he was not a bird. It is curious that I never saw or heard among these Eskimos of the so-called spirit flights, in which the shaman, after being lashed from head to foot, sets free his soul and travels through the air, finally returning to his body and releasing it from its bonds.[1]

Ilatsiak was dangerously ill while he was yet a boy, and all the professional attentions of the shamans failed to cure him. At last they told him to go outside and die, but instead of dying he recovered. Clearly the spirits favoured him, so he became a shaman, the most celebrated one in the country. While he was still but a youth he summoned some white men, who made their appearance in the dance-house before the astonished eyes of all the Eskimos. Maffa, a Tree river native who served us for a year, told us how Ilatsiak once threw a line out into the passage leading into the dance-house and roped in a number of spirits, *tornrait*. Maffa peered down through the door and saw them all in the passage. Ilatsiak spoke to them, but his language was strange, and all that Maffa could understand was that he was telling them to protect the people and to banish all sickness from their midst.

Ilatsiak's powers were derided by his cousin, who was also a shaman, so Ilatsiak clapped his hands and fire shot up from the floor. His cousin, nothing daunted, went outside and disappeared down a squirrel hole, re-emerging again from the ground a long way off. In the same way, the natives said, Ilatsiak himself once sank down through the snow floor of the dance-house, growing smaller and smaller till he vanished from sight altogether. A few minutes later he came up through the floor of another hut right beside some men who were sitting on the sleeping platform. Uloksak could remember when he was a boy how white men had appeared in the dance-house at Ilatsiak's command. The people sent Uloksak outside, and when he went back again he was amazed to see that Ilatsiak had cut off a leg and an arm and thrown them to the back of the hut. He was sent out once more, and when he re-entered Ilatsiak was whole again. Uloksak even claimed to have done the same thing himself at one of his séances.

Ilatsiak was a prudent old man and never boasted of his miracles. He asserted that he was totally unconscious of his actions when inspired, and only learned of them afterwards from the spectators; hence he was not able himself to guarantee the truth of everything that was said about him. We noticed that he always listened with an air of detachment to the tales of all his miracles

---

[1] See Boas, Bulletin A.M.N.H., Vol. XV, p. 491; and Bur. of Ethnol, Vol. 6, p. 594.

as though they concerned someone else. On one occasion, his kinsmen told me, he and three other shamans gave a séance together. The four men held their hands behind their backs and stretched out their necks, holding their mouths wide open. Gradually their teeth changed to polar bears' teeth, then as gradually changed back again. On another occasion when two Netsilik shamans were terrifying the people by driving their knives through their stomachs so that the points protruded from their backs, Ilatsiak went into an empty hut alongside, changed himself into a polar bear, and, going back into the dance-house, so frightened the two Netsilik men that they fled from the settlement. On still another occasion Ilatsiak had sunk down through the floor of his hut into the sea below without making even a hole in the ice. Another Bathurst inlet shaman had once remained five days and five nights under the water, wetting only his ankles and a small spot on his back.

Uloksak, having lost his seal-spear one day in a seal-hole, went home and summoned his familiars; the latter immediately made the spear come up through the floor of his hut. A still more remarkable story is told of Ilatsiak's younger brother. His wife lost her knife in the fall of the year, and in the following spring her husband resolved to find it. Going inside his hut he disappeared into the ground, and while the people were searching all about for him a large flat boulder suddenly came up through the floor, cracked in two, and ejected the knife on one side, and the shaman on the other. The man was rather dazed from his experience, but the shamans soon made him right again. Reminiscent of a well-known conjuring trick was a feat of Ilatsiak's, who drove a knife into the back wall of his hut, then stood out in the middle of the floor, removed his coat and picked up his knife from the ground at his feet. Another shaman took it and threw it out into the passage, making it come in again through the window. All these events took place in Bathurst inlet, where the shamans are reputed to have much more skill than those farther west. It was in the same region that some people threw their knives into the water through a hole in the ice, and the shamans made them float on the surface. Then they threw in their ice-chisels, and the shamans brought them to the top also.[1] The Hudson bay native Kaksavik was overheard telling Uloksak how he once laid some matches on the ice and told them to fly to a settlement where the people were in need of them. His familiars then carried them away, and the natives found them near their huts.

Some natives were once mocking a Bathurst inlet shaman named Pannaktok, saying that he had no real power. He took off one of his mittens and laid it on the floor; presently it stood up on end and changed to a tiny man, who turned around and gazed on all the audience. Pannaktok stooped down and picked it up, and it changed to a mitten again. Then he laid both his mittens on the palms of his hands and held them out toward the spectators. First they changed to polar bear's claws, then two tiny bears jumped down and began to scratch on the floor; again they changed to mittens when he picked them up.

This same Pannaktok, according to native accounts, told a man to stand upright against the wall of the dance-house, then drove his seal-spear right through his chest and threw the weapon to the back of the hut. The natives had to hold the man up to keep him from falling. The shaman then made the spear return through his chest, leaving the man whole and unharmed. On the last day of 1915 three shamans, Koeha, Agluak and Anauyuk, held a séance in Dolphin and Union strait to dispel the baneful influence of some malicious shades. Agluak breathed on his hand and struck three of the spectators on the chests. They fell to the ground dead, but he took them by the hands and they came to life again. I did not witness this performance myself, but heard about it the following day.

---

[1] Cf. Stefansson, Anthrop. Papers, A.M.H.N., Vol. XIV, pt. I, p. 293, and *My Life with the Eskimo*, p. 180.

Uloksak described a séance at Bathurst inlet in which he had taken part. A woman, stripped to the waist, swallowed a snow knife till only the handle projected from her mouth. Another shaman took hold of it and pulled it out of her stomach. A third shaman, a native of Ekaluktok, then swallowed a mitten and made it come out of Uloksak's stomach, whereupon Uloksak himself swallowed it and made it come out of the stomach of a man named Manneratsiak. Manneratsiak immediately went outside, and when he entered the dance-house again all the upper half of his body had changed to a musk-ox while the lower parts remained human. In this state he walked about the dance-house for a little while, then went outside again and returned in his proper form. Meanwhile a woman named Allanak was looking after her hut some distance from the scene of these marvels. The shamans threw a line out into the passage of the dance-house, and began to haul it in again; the spectators then saw that the end was fastened around Allanak's neck. The woman herself knew nothing about it until she was told some time afterwards.

Kuniluk, a Puivlik shaman, professed to have changed to a white man on one occasion. He was crossing Dolphin and Union strait, he said, on his way to our station, when a fog came up and he lost his way. He summoned one of his familiars, which changed him temporarily into a white man and enabled him to find his way again without any difficulty.

Many a shaman lays claim to clairvoyance. In the spring of 1915 when a number of Eskimos were encamped beside our station this same man Kuniluk was accused by Uloksak of stealing two boxes of cartridges. After Kuniluk had left the camp Uloksak entered the station and announced that he intended to recover one of the boxes. He rolled up his sleeves like a conjuror, waved his arms about in the air, rolled his eyes, and finally, diving down into a dark corner of the room, brought forth a box. The trick was rather too transparent, for plainly he had left the box there earlier in the day. Our cook immediately accepted the challenge, and, knowing of another box that lay in a corner out of sight, he went through a similar performance and 'discovered' it. Uloksak was astounded, and could not make up his mind whether the cook's 'discovery' was a genuine one or simply a fraud like his own.

In December, 1915, a woman shaman prophesied that some people to the eastward would fall over a cliff into a hole and perish. During the same performance she announced that evil spirits were threatening the lives of certain natives in the community. One of them was Avranna, so she forbade his wife Milukkattak to sew on the following day. Milukkattak had promised to make a sleeping bag for me, but in consequence of this prohibition she had to postpone it.

Many of the shamans' "discoveries" are made in dreams. Two fox-traps were once stolen from my sled; Higilak told me a few days later that in her sleep she had seen a hand and fore-arm stealthily abstracting them, but could not identify the person. On another occasion I lost a tin full of matches, and a shaman discovered in a dream that a certain woman had stolen them. Ilatsiak asserted that his familiar often visited him in his sleep and revealed what was about to happen. Whenever he dreamed of small knives he knew that some children were sick. Sometimes the knives lay broken on the ground and he would rivet them together; then the children would grow well again. One morning he heard that a little boy, the son of a Mackenzie river woman in our service, had taken suddenly ill; immediately he announced that during his sleep he had repaired a knife that lay broken on the snow, so the boy would recover. The very next morning he entered our house and reported that during the night his spirit had told him that something had gone wrong on our schooner; it was the thing, he said, that made the vessel move. We thought that he must mean the propeller, for we had put a new one on during the winter and had to keep the ice open around it. By a strange coincidence, however, we discovered during the day—what Ilatsiak could hardly have been aware of—that a boom we were using to roof our provision cache had snapped during the night owing to the weight of the snow above it. Two days later Ilatsiak announced again that in his dream he had seen a sled falling over a cliff, and expressed the hope that none of our sleds would meet with such a mishap during the spring.

These stories of shamanistic séances and miracles are from hearsay only, but Mr. Wilkins, our photographer, personally participated in a performance at the fishing creek near Bernard harbour. His interpreter for the occasion was the half-breed Patsy Klengenberg, and the account he gives is as follows:—

"On another occasion I visited a camp and there had been very few fish caught for the last two or three days. They had all waited all that day and there had not been a sign of any fish making a run. About nine o'clock at night they thought they should hold a séance to try and induce a few to come along, for although they had a quantity of dried fish they did not care to use that up. A fellow called Igluhuk had arrived at the camp that evening and he had the reputation of being a great shaman. We were all standing about outside watching for signs of a run when one of the men asked me if I would help in a séance to try to make the fish come up the creek. I agreed to do my best, and they all crowded into the largest tent in the village. I was given a seat next to the shaman which had been reserved for me, although I was almost the last to come in, and there was not room for any others to sit down after and some of them had to lean in and look through the door. At first it seemed as if they had forgotten their object, for the conversation was general and was mainly about the fishing at other seasons and on other days and at other creeks that season. After about thirty minutes of this, the shaman seemed to be doing most of the talking and gradually everyone else remained quiet.

"He seemed to be warming to his subject and would at intervals demand corroboration from one or other of the audience. Presently he started off in a kind of sing-song and the audience chatted to each other in whispers or nodded to each other across the tent. At intervals the shaman would address somebody in a language that they could not understand, and they would turn inquiringly to someone else for an explanation, but none would be forthcoming; no one seemed to know what it was that was asked. Then two or three would ask if it was so-and-so that was meant, or suggest something else, but the shaman would shake his head violently and repeat the question in the unknown jargon. After several fruitless attempts to make himself understood, and when the brows of the audience were wrinkled with thought, and most of them were bewildered in their efforts to understand, the old man gave a shout and clapped his hands to his forehead. Shutting his eyes, he started swaying backwards and forwards. He kept up the monotonous sing-song of an un-understandable sound for about an hour, while the other people talked intermittently about several things, sometimes looking at the performer and shaking their heads and whispering to each other. Presently the shaman gave a shout and uttered some intelligible sounds and I was requested to hold on to his hand.

"An old woman sitting next but one to him searched around and found the copper head of an ice spear, and while I held his hand on one side and the owner of the tent held his shoulder on the other, she gave him a smart tap on the left side of the head with a lump of copper. At this he released his hand from his forehead and opened his eyes. Huge drops of perspiration stood out all over his face and his eyes were wild and bloodshot. We released our hold and he kept his backward and forward swaying motion but with renewed vigour. He was now talking intelligible language, but so fast that most of the people in the audience could not understand him and they would repeatedly shout questions to him or ask him to repeat things. He took no notice of them and soon began to point to one or the other of the audience and, fluttering his fingers to indicate that the fish were swarming in the river, would prophesy that such and such a person would catch a number of fish.

"He kept this up for about half an hour, pointing mostly to two or three people who were, by the way, always successful in the contests when there were any fish to be caught. The whole performance had now lasted about three hours, and during that time no one had been keeping a look-out on the creek for fish, except perhaps the children who had been playing about outside. They paid an occasional visit to the door of the tent but did not stay long, as they were evidently not interested in the old man's performance. The shaman's movements began to become normal at last, and although he was still frothing at the mouth, his questions and exclamations became less frequent and finally subsided altogether. There was now a hurried whispered consultation amongst the audience, and the old woman took a copper spear-head and gave the old fellow a smart tap on the right side of the head, and he looked round the audience in a dazed sort of way, as if he had just come out of a hypnotic trance. One of the men near the door gave a shout and, jumping up, ran for his spear and towards the creek, with the others following as fast as they could. None of them were prepared for fishing in the ordinary way by having taken off some of their clothes or put on long water-boots, and as they ran towards the creek, some of them slipped off what clothes they could, while others rushed for the water in what they were dressed in. It was apparent at first sight that there were a number of fish in the trap, and within a few minutes they had caught sixty, a big haul in ordinary times, and now an extraordinary one for it had seemed that the fish had stopped running the day before. Whether the old man's performance had anything to do with it or not the Eskimos fully believed that it had; but I am rather inclined to think that the success was due to the fact that while they were listening to the shaman they were not outside making a noise and frightening the fish from coming into the trap, and that during the three hours' séance a number of stragglers had collected in the trap.

"The Eskimos were overjoyed at the success. The ones that the shaman had pointed out had surely caught the most fish, but then they always did when there were any fish to be caught. The man who had caught the most, and in whose house the séance had been held, after making a display of his catch to the people, cut a section from between the ventral fins of the largest fish and gave it to the shaman. He then cut a similar section from the next biggest and gave it to me. As these sections were only about an inch long and half an inch wide and as thick, and I noticed the shaman had swallowed his, I did likewise, to the evident satisfaction of the people. The only explanation of this that I could gather through the interpreter was that it was a present for making the fish come into the trap."

In regard to this séance the interpreter, Patsy—who, by the way, was thoroughly sceptical of all Eskimo shamanism—told me that Igluhuk (or Iglisiak as he should be called) had prophesied that a certain boy Hogaluk would capture three fish, and that Patsy himself would get only two. In both cases his prophesy proved true.

CHAPTER XVI

SHAMANISM (Continued)

Of the many séances that I witnessed myself among the Copper Eskimos at one time and another, a few are worth describing because of the light they shed on the psychology of the natives and on their religious beliefs. Among the earliest was a performance by Kaminggok at the Liston and Sutton islands in January, 1915. The people had been singing and dancing after their usual custom in the dance-house when he entered the ring on his own initiative and announced that he would hold a séance. He began in the orthodox manner with an oration, then suddenly uttered cries of pain and covered his eyes with his hand as though he were in the greatest agony. Soon he raised his head again, looking round with wild staring eyes, trying to speak apparently but unable to utter a sound. The audience questioned him, suggesting whatever they thought he was trying to say, and he nodded eagerly to the native who guessed correctly. In this way he told them that two men to the eastward had just died, one of them having been killed by the spirit of Cat's Cradles.[1] Again he uttered cries of pain and slapped his hand to his forehead, then began to speak in a weak falsetto voice about two of the local Eskimos and their lack of success in sealing. Something they had done with a hatchet, he said, had frightened the seals away, but he (*i.e.*, his familiar spirit) had removed the hatchet so they would soon kill more seals again. A third time he cried out in pain, then said in his natural voice, but in a low and rather husky tone, that he could see some dogs stealing fish. A native suggested that it might be my dogs, but he said, "No". Several of us then left the dance-house to find out whether what he said was true, and we discovered that the natives' own dogs had stolen some fish belonging to an Eskimo woman. How Kaminggok could have known about it I have no idea, for no one else had heard any noise. His performance was almost over by the time we returned. He closed his eyes suddenly and began to stagger; his soul, *nappan*, was returning, my Mackenzie river native whispered to me, or perhaps it was his familiar leaving him. A by-stander laid his hand on the back of the shaman's neck, and another man laid his on the side of it, while, at the request of a third native, I rapped him on the head with some matches. The first rap had no effect, nor the second, so, by the natives' advice, I placed my hand on the side of his head. Immediately he opened his eyes and gazed at me with an uncomprehending stare, then smiled, pulled himself together, and began an ordinary conversation with some of his audience. Throughout his performance there had been nothing so strange as to suggest an abnormal state of mind; the whole affair had resembled rather the trick of a fairly clever impostor. Palaiyak, however, my Christianized Mackenzie river interpreter, thoroughly believed in his inspiration, asserting that several familiars had successively entered his body and that he was really a great shaman.

A few days later Kaminggok gave another performance in the dance-house. I was projecting a journey to an Akulliakattak settlement on the morrow, with Kaminggok and another native as my guides; the séance was held to discover what fortune we would have. It resembled very closely his earlier performance: first, the oration, then the cries of pain, a period of dumbness during which the audience made guesses at what he was trying to say and he answered by nodding,

---

[1] The natives of North Alaska and of the Mackenzie delta believe that the opening stage in certain cat's cradle figures, or a development from it called "Two Labrets," has the power of driving away this spirit if performed more rapidly than the spirit itself can perform it. The man who had just died, it was said, had been defeated by the spirit in the contest.

a moment's gasping excited talk in a falsetto tone, more gasps, a glance at the roof and a sharp cry of pain as his soul returned to his body (or his familiar left him), and the performance was over. Anauyuk, who held a séance immediately afterwards, was much more normal in his actions. He spoke in his natural voice, though a little abruptly once or twice, and told the Eskimos that the shade, *tarrak*, of a dead man had stolen the soul, *nappan*, of Wikkiak, a native who had been ailing for some days. Wikkiak would now recover, however, for my dog Jumbo had brought his soul back again.

A young man named Agluak held a séance on December 20 of the same year, to discover why seals were so scarce and to bring them back to the Eskimos' hunting ground. After the usual dance he took his place in the centre of the ring and delivered a short preliminary oration, in which he confessed that he was not very expert in shamanistic matters. The audience encouraged him to proceed nevertheless, so he began a second and more elaborate harangue, this time about the absence of seals. Suddenly he stopped—he was invoking his familiar spirit. His breathing became hard and loud, his eyes wild and staring, and his features grim and distorted. Turning this way and that he gesticulated with his hands, and nodded whenever one of his audience guessed the proper interpretation. The women, we learned, had been making new deerskin clothes, and boiling caribou meat, both of which were tabooed at this season. A sudden inspiration struck him on seeing me standing outside the ring with my pipe in my mouth, and he told us by gestures that the seals refused to rise

FIG. 58. A Tree river native harnessing his dog in preparation for the day's sealing

to the surface because of the taint of my tobacco. For all these reasons the Eskimos had experienced no success in their sealing. Once he pointed at me and waved his arm to the west, but no one could understand what he meant. A few minutes afterwards he made similar gestures in reference to Uloksak, who simply shook his head and turned away with studied indifference, remarking that he could not understand. Agluak then told us in pantomime how many seals various people in the ring would capture. He would point to a man, go through the motions of spearing a seal in its hole, then hold up one or more fingers to indicate the number killed. He seemed to be rather sleepy, however, for once or twice he passed his hand over his forehead as though to revive his faculties.

Up to this stage he had maintained an absolute silence. Now broken words began to drop from his lips, elucidated by gestures, but the words were hardly more intelligible than the gesture language that had preceded them. Once he ejaculated "What's this? Something being cooked, caribou meat." We gathered that the seals were sleeping and that he had to go and stir them up. Further, that he should be given liberal portions of any seals that might be caught, because of his services in bringing them back to the hunting grounds. At last he said *taima taima* "Enough, enough," passed his hand across his forehead and terminated his séance.

In the general conversation that ensued Agluak reaffirmed that if the women would refrain from sewing the men would have good luck again in their sealing. But his shamanistic powers were not regarded very seriously by most of the natives. He had dropped his mittens during the séance, and was looking around for them when it was over; some one at the back of the hut threw them into his face, causing a general laugh. The women resented his prohibition against sewing and for the most part disregarded it. At least one of them too had no scruples about boiling more caribou meat the very next day (the house was built on the shore of one of the islands, and had gravel, not ice, beneath the snow floor, so that she could say they were camped on the land, not on the sea ice). Uloksak seemed to treat the whole matter as a joke, but then he was somewhat of a free-thinker, at least as regarded some of his fellow-shamans. With reference to my smoking, I told the natives that just as the smoke floated up into the air, so the seals would float up to the surface, and they quite agreed with this interpretation.

Another shaman, Kuniluk, held a séance about half an hour after Agluak, but I had left the dance-house. A month later he held another. The weather had been very stormy all day, and the Eskimos, unable to go out sealing, had spent most of their time in the dance-house. Kuniluk began in the usual manner with an oration, followed by a sudden cry of pain. He clapped his hand to his forehead and uttered a few more cries as his familiar, a dog, passed into his body. Now he gazed wildly round the ring and began to jabber meaningless syllables, accompanied by elaborate gestures of explanation. Once or twice he was heard to say *naukun naukun* "Which way, which way", but no one could understand what he meant. Occasionally he would direct his gibberish to some definite individual, and the rest of the audience would tell that person to assent. These proceedings lasted for about ten minutes, then suddenly Kuniluk uttered some cries of pain, stooped down and howled like a dog, his familiar. After a few howls he began to jabber again, still stooping. Thus he continued for perhaps a quarter of an hour, then, with a few cries of pain, he straightened up, and, speaking in his natural tongue, told the people that their ill-luck in sealing was due to some of them having played cat's cradles after the return of the sun, while others had sewn deerskin fringes on their coats during the dark days. He then uttered a few more cries of pain as his familiar left him, and the séance terminated. It had lasted altogether about an hour, and left the man quite exhausted. Uloksak, who stood near me in the audience, murmured in my ear just before it commenced, "Kuniluk is no shaman"; and when it was ended he wanted me to tell Kunilik to give a real séance, as though all that we had just witnessed were only the prelude.

After Kuniluk had brought his performance to a close a woman named Arnauyuk entered the circle and proposed to give a séance. The people encouraged her to proceed, so she began her preliminary oration; but before she had proceeded very far she broke down in self-conscious laughter and the audience laughed with her. She pulled herself together and began again, and again she broke down, so, after one more unsuccessful attempt, she retired to the ring. Her familiar, the natives said, had refused to take possession of her.

The winter of 1915-16 was unusually stormy, and for days at a time the Eskimos were confined to their houses and prevented from sealing. On February 3rd, a man named Utugaum held a séance with the object of petitioning Kanna-kapfaluk to stop the blizzards and let the people go sealing again. He opened with a long oration—about two ducks in some place or other, a giant fish in Lake Akulliakattak, two men living near some islands, another man at Uming-maktok (Kent peninsula) who had knocked down two poles, and about some

Fig. 59. Tokalluak, a Coppermine river shaman

one in the moon. He used vague and mysterious words, and his audience had to puzzle out his meaning, partly from his words, and partly from the gestures that accompanied them. In this case, as often, no one had any idea of what he was talking about. His oration lasted fully twenty minutes, then he stooped down and began to speak in a thin piping voice, quite unlike the strident tones in which his oration had been delivered. He now said that he was no longer a man, but an animal (my notes do not say what animal). He was searching for Kannakapfaluk, he said, so that he might drag her up to the surface, but he could not find her. Thus he stood for about two minutes, then straightened up, pressed his hand to his forehead, heaved a few sighs and closed the performance. There were a few interesting features in connection with it. At the commence-ment all the little children were sent to the back of the dance-house. My inter-preter Patsy was playing and laughing with them till the old shaman Anauyuk turned around and scolded them, saying that they should on no account laugh during a séance; however, they appeared to take very little notice of his warn-ing. I moved to leave the dance-house as soon as the performance was over and one of the natives stopped me, saying, "You mustn't go out while the shaman is performing"; but when I pointed out that Utugaum had finished he waived his objection. Uloksak had been telling the people earlier in the evening about the two pillars that hold up the sky, and Utugaum probably had these in his mind when he spoke of the two poles that a man had knocked down. There is a special incantation that is generally sung before a shaman goes in search of Kannakapfaluk, but for some reason or other it was omitted on this occasion.

Tokalluak, a Coronation gulf native, held a séance at the fishing creek near Cape Krusenstern in July, 1916, when a band of natives had gathered together to spear the salmon. He invoked his familiar and uttered some brief remark, then laughed and hid his face in his hands. His laugh, however, had caused his familiar to leave him and he had to recall it. This happened repeatedly, for he seemed to be unable to control his laughter whenever any of his audience laughed. He spoke of a boy whose legs were too long (Patsy, my interpreter), and of a man with long whiskers (myself) whom he called Patsy's father, and accused of frightening away the fish by dipping an iron cup into the creek. (Unluckily for Tokalluak's credit, the Eskimos had just caught a phenomenal number of fish that day). Finally he tabooed all sewing on the following day and terminated his séance.

Higilak held several séances during the spring and summer of 1915 in addition to the one that has been described already. The most interesting of them all took place at the end of July at a time when I was seriously ill in the Eskimo camp. I do not know what familiar possessed her, except that it was the shade of some Eskimo long dead. She began in the usual manner with an oration. There was a strained look in her eyes as she spoke, and a tension in her face, as though she were concentrating herself for a great effort. Suddenly she emitted several deep ventriloquistic cries, followed by shrill falsetto utterances from her head. Then she began to gabble in high falsetto, first about the scarcity of fish, for which some dead person was to blame, then about my sickness, for which another dead person she named was responsible. Suddenly she cried *aggioktok*, "A malignant shade is troubling me", and bowed her head, concealing her face in her hands. Avranna asked ,"Who is it?" and in a faint voice she replied, "Arnaktak" (Arnaktak was a relative of Ikpakhuak who had died in the previous winter). Ikpakhuak struck her on the head, and drove away the obstructing shade. Almost immediately another obstructed her, and Avranna asked of it again, "Who are you?" The shade, instead of answering the question directly, merely said, in faint accents issuing from Higilak's lips, "Here I am", and added some further remarks which I could not hear. Milukkattak now struck Higilak on the head and drove it away. A third shade took possession of her and Avranna held a long conversation with it. It finally promised to be good, *nagoyok*, whereupon a sigh of relief went up from the audience, and Higilak, after one or two gasps, came to her senses. A short discussion followed the performance, after which everyone retired to bed.

When Arnaktak, the native just mentioned, had died, I was a hundred miles away in Coronation gulf. Nevertheless some of the Eskimos accused me of murdering him, because, as they said, he had perpetrated some petty theft on me. There was some disagreement, however, so Uloksak, the most famous shaman among the western Copper Eskimos, was asked to find out what precisely was the cause of his death. The séance took place in a dance-house beside our station, and, having rather a personal interest in the matter, I went down to see it. Our cook, Sullivan, was present also, though from first to last he had no idea of what was happening. The people arranged themselves in a ring and began to sing, rather to while away the time than from any other reason, for their singing was very half-hearted and they did not trouble to bring out the drum. Uloksak sat outside the circle on a sleeping platform, leaning against his second wife and apparently quite unconcerned with what was taking place. Suddenly his whole frame drooped heavily against her, and gasping cries broke from his lips, while a quiver ran through his audience. He staggered into the centre of the ring and motioned for me to stand beside him; of Sullivan, who was on the other side of the dance-house, he took no notice. A torrent of wild gibberish flowed from his lips for about five minutes. His father, who was standing beside me, said that it was white man's language, and asked me whether I did not understand it. Uloksak heard the question and paused, looking at me with an expression that I interpreted to mean, "Back me up in this matter"; I therefore replied that it resembled the speech of white men, and nodded my head in understanding whenever he seemed to address his gibberish expressly to me. Almost immediately afterwards he dropped into his proper language, and speaking a few words about the dead Arnaktak, said that another of his familiar spirits, a dog, would take possession of him. Thereupon he crouched down like a dog, pushed his head into another man's stomach, and growled. In broken and only half-audible tones he told them how Arnaktak had come to die; a white man far away had killed him by sorcery, stealing his soul, while we, the white men who were living amongst them, were friendly and meant them no harm. Again he rose erect and with wild eyes poured forth a stream of gibberish— the language of white men, comprehensible to myself alone. Naturally we soon arrived at a mutual understanding; he would jabber at me for a minute, and I would answer in the first words of French that came into my head, using French so that Sullivan might not understand. After a time Uloksak turned to the natives and dropped a word or two in Eskimo. They had to guess at his meaning, and he nodded whenever they guessed correctly; his gestures indeed were almost lucid enough to make words unnecessary. In this way he repeated that Sullivan and myself and all the other members of our expedition were friendly towards them and sought them no harm, and that Arnaktak's death was due to another man far away. Then once again he crouched down and gasped a few times, while an Eskimo on one side and I on the other caught hold of him and kept him from falling. His familiar, the dog, now left him, and a moment afterwards he stood up and smiled.

The séance was over, but Uloksak was too shrewd a man to lose his opportunity. His audience was in the proper mood to be deceived by any fraud, and here was a rare opportunity of enhancing his prestige. He renewed his gibberish talk, and I nodded comprehendingly, throwing in occasionally a word or two of French, which he of course understood equally well; thus an animated conversation was carried on between us for a time. He next began to dance after the manner of the Bear lake Indians, and invited Sullivan to join him, which he did, much to the enjoyment of the spectators. This Indian dancing bears a considerable resemblance, if indeed it is not derived from, some Scotch dances, so that Sullivan had no difficulty in keeping up his part. Uloksak then dragged two women into their dance, one of them being his second wife. Whenever he wanted Sullivan to do anything, he jabbered at me in his gibberish, but took care to explain by his gestures so that I could understand and interpret. The strain on both of us, however, was rather too heavy; moreover there was a danger of the fraud being detected if we prolonged the performance too much. I pleaded weariness therefore, and moved to leave the dance-house. Uloksak immediately assented and preceded me outside, intending to speak to me; but as two of the Eskimos followed us he had to make use of his gibberish again, pointing first to our station, then to his house, as much as to say, "Go back now, and let us meet later in my hut." I replied in French, dropping the one Eskimo word *akago*, "to-morrow", and motioning towards his house. He at once nodded and retired, while I went back to our station.

The outcome of this séance was eminently satisfactory to both of us. Uloksak had vastly increased his prestige in the eyes of the natives by this proof that he understood the language of the white men; while I was acquitted of an unpleasant charge of murder, which might have endangered my work, if not my life, among these Eskimos. The following day I presented Uloksak with a cast-off Burberry snow-shirt, a very valuable garment in his eyes. The account that Sullivan gave of the séance to the other members of the expedition was rather amusing; the only words he had understood, of course, were the directions I gave him during the dancing. He was greatly alarmed at one period, he said, for he thought that Uloksak was urging the natives to kill us; then when Uloksak talked gibberish and I answered in an equally unknown tongue he thought that I had been hypnotized.

The greatest of all the shamans among the Copper Eskimos was Ilatsiak. In March, 1916, he guided a large band of Bathurst inlet natives to our station at Bernard harbour and camped beside us for about three weeks. Seeing us record one or two songs on the phonograph he asked to be allowed to summon his familiar spirit, Kingaudlik, and under its inspiration to speak into the machine. He was rather short of stature, so we had to raise him on a box to bring his face level with the horn; perched on this box he protruded his face into the bell of the horn and nervously kicked his legs out behind him, one after the other, in the manner of a person skipping over a rope. The usual preliminaries of a shamanistic performance were omitted; he merely paused a moment to collect his wits (or to give his familiar time to enter him), then said what he had to say and stood down. Some of the words are scarcely audible in the record owing to his jumping. As usual too, it is difficult to attach any meaning to them, but the literal interpretation of this first oracle was, "Where? Give me liver, liver; it is excellent. I hear speech"—a remark that Ilatsiak's adopted son understood to mean that his father's familiar Kingaudlik was asking for some liver.

This séance not being very satisfactory, Ilatsiak was requested to give another similar to those he habitually gave in the dance-house. When everything was ready he came forward and asked for a cup of water. He gazed into it very intently for a few seconds, then said that something was wrong on our schooner; some one on board was going to be drowned. He then drank the water, solemnly shook hands with all the white men present, stepped up to the phonograph and, at the word *takki*, "Begin", delivered the oracle that is translated below. Mingled with his words are the remarks of his Eskimo kinsmen, especially of his wife, whose voice, though she sat quite six feet away from the machine, can be heard quite distinctly on the record; for the natives regarded the séance as a perfectly genuine one, and tried to interpret Ilatsiak's utterances, and enlarge on them, just as they would have done in the dance-house. Ilatsiak gave a gasp at the conclusion and breathed very hard for a moment or two as his familiar left him, after which he sat down and enquired of the natives what he had said. Later in the day he invoked another of his familiars, Annakok, and we recorded yet another oracle.

It was not considered advisable to allow Ilatsiak to hear his own records, but after he had returned east two natives from the same region who had heard the oracles delivered helped me to reduce them to writing and to translate them into English. In many places the words were quite unintelligible even to them, for, as they took pains to remark, it was not the shaman himself who was speaking but the spirit that possessed him, and spirit utterances are not easily understood by the laity. Neither séance was in any way fictitious, either to Ilatsiak himself or to his audience. Even the Eskimos who heard the records only discussed them as real oracles, and had implicit faith in their verity.

The first oracle was as follows:—

".   .   . Did you do it? Did you do it? It is terrifying. Himiamin,[1] did you do it? The fish's eyes, the fish, they say. Did you do it? The fish, they say, ate the people. It is terrifying. The fish ate the people, it swallowed

---

[1]Himiamin was said to be the name of a woman shaman in Bathurst inlet.

them, they say; people afar off, it destroyed them all, they say. People here, the fish, the salmon, the thing that moves them, it is going to eat them, it is dangerous. These people unhappily it ate, it ate; those unhappily it terrifies; these people, dangerous, these, unhappily, the fish, these, it is going to eat them down there. Ukumarauta's shade, it seized him, him, out over the sea, Ukumarauta, the big island, intending to eat him, its shade, out over the sea, seized him."

Fig. 60. Digging fishing-holes through the ice, Lake Angmaloktok, Colville hills

(Here there are some indistinct words in the record, the comments of Ilatsiak's wife in the background. Ilatsiak continues:—)

"These people, these people, yes. How is it? These people, it seized out over the sea."

(Again there are constant interruptions by the audience, and Ilatsiak continues:—)

"Yes, Ukumarauta, the people, it, the fish, it seized, seized, it, the fish. The dogs, the dogs, these, these people, these, these people, their kinsfolk, those away over there, the Indians too, it kills with its heavy weight, it eats them, destroying them without difficulty. Yes, it seized, it seized that one, it seized, it seized, yes. But I speaking plainly I think I am."

(At this point the voice of his wife is distinctly audible, saying, "Speak plainly, speak out.")

"Yes, from the sea, the salt sea, it seized, hu, hu, yes, they are going to eat, yes, next summer, they are going to eat, hu, hu, hu."

Only the general drift of the meaning is distinguishable from these broken utterances. With regard to the first part the natives explained that there is a huge salmon, as large as an island, which swallowed two kayaks once with their occupants, and almost devoured two others at the same time. This was in a lake somewhere beyond Bathurst inlet where the Eskimos secure caribou, not with bows and arrows, but with pit-falls. The salmon is frightened and hides when the shamans hold a séance and talk about it.

The passage about Ukumarauta refers to a large stone of that name in a country to which the daylight never reaches. The stone is sometimes called the "Big Island," sometimes "The Heavy One," *ukumaura*. Occasionally a shaman will summon it to come and have a feast; then it falls unseen from the sky and kills many people with rocks, and other shamans (Higilak was instanced as an example) have to drive it back again. A shaman too will sometimes make it drop on an approaching kayaker and kill him, though it is sometimes affirmed that the magic stone uses a small spear to kill its victims. The stone can sing like a man, and the shamans have a special incantation or invocation, *akeun*, for it, but my informants did not know the words. A Bathurst inlet shaman, the Pannaktok who has been mentioned already, uses the stone for one of his familiars. In the present oracle the stone proposed to "eat" the expedition when it left Bernard harbour. The final portion of the record is a protestation by the familiar that it is speaking only the truth.

The second oracle that Ilatsiak delivered was equally obscure. The first part of it had reference to the thefts that some of the local natives had perpetrated on us during the period of Ilatsiak's visit. Then he spoke of his joy at my promise to pay him liberally for relating some of the old traditions of his people. The last portion referred to a great fish that had swallowed a ship, and would swallow our schooner also unless our magic was strong enough to prevail against it. The oracle concluded, like the previous one, with an asseveration by the familiar that it spoke nothing but the truth. Ilatsiak was about to step down after this performance when he suddenly recollected (or so it seemed to us) that he had omitted the usual gasps aud grunts when his familiar left him; accordingly he turned back to the phonograph and finished in the orthodox manner.[1]

In all these séances, except those of Uloksak and Higilak, my own limited knowledge of the language was supplemented by the services of an interpreter, either the Mackenzie river native, Palaiyak, or the half-breed Patsy Klengenberg. In every case the familiar spirit was supposed to have entered the body of the shaman and to have used the man as its medium. But there is an altogether different type of séance, divination by lifting,[2] of which I have already given one example. I saw only one shaman, Higilak, employ this method, and never had an interpreter at any of her performances. My knowledge of the ordinary conversational language was very imperfect, and shamans in their séances make use of old or semi-poetical expressions that greatly increase the difficulty of understanding them; a seal, for example, may be referred to as "the thing that has blubber." For my interpretations in this class of séances therefore I had to depend rather on my own observations at the time and the subsequent explanations of the spectators or of Higilak herself. It is not at all impossible that I may have missed the correct interpretation in some instances, but by describing a number of these séances a fairly correct idea can perhaps be gleaned of the religious notions that lie behind them. All except the last one took place on Victoria island during the summer of 1915.

On May 9, all the adults of our party gathered in Ikpakhuak's tent a little before midnight. Ikpakhuak himself was sitting at the back of the sleeping platform, with Higilak in front, while I sat opposite her at the outer end of the platform. Higilak rolled her coat into a bundle, made a running noose of her belt, and slipped it around the head of the coat. The loose end of the cord, with its toggle, she kept in her left hand, while the four fingers of her right hand rested on the coat under the noose, and the thumb on top of it. Her familiar spirit, in this case her *atatsiak* (mother's father?), was summoned

---

[1] Cf. Boas, Bulletin A.M.N.H., Vol. XV., p. 156 *et seq.*; Stefansson, "My Life with the Eskimo," p. 291 *et seq.*
[2] Cf. Crantz, Vol. I, p. 210 *et seq.*, 214; Boas, Bulletin A.M.N.H., Vol. XV, pp. 135, 512; Stefansson, Anthrop. Papers, A.M.N.H., Vol. XIV, pt. I, p. 360 *et seq.*

into the bundle, and made its presence known by the increase in weight when Higilak tried to lift it. Both Higilak and the spectators then asked it various questions, and the answer "Yes" or "No" resulted according as she found it heavy or light; if the bundle was heavy the answer was "Yes," if light, "No." Once Kesullik wanted to test it after Higilak had said that it was heavy, but she would not let him. She yawned several times during the performance, and once or twice the conversation drifted off on to other topics, but no one seemed to be credulous of the answers that were given. As far as I could gather their questions were all concerned with the prospects of securing an abundance of fish and caribou during the next few months. A coat when tied up and used for this ceremony is given the special name of *kila*.

On May 26th Higilak questioned the *kila* again, this time to discover whether any Prince Albert sound natives would visit our camp at Lake Tahiryuak. The ceremony took place out of doors, because the air was warm and our little tent was too small to hold all the audience. The *kila* affirmed that they would come to us, but I gathered that Higilak was not altogether satisfied with the reply, for the next morning when no one was near she asked the same question of me. Two days later she borrowed my two coats (the outer and inner *attigi*), and divined again. I was told to say to the bundle that being a "white" man it was to be heavy for an affirmative answer and light for a negative. (This was contrary to the usual regulations.) Higilak and the audience then asked it one question after another, and at each one she tested its weight. I noticed that whenever the *kila* was light she drew it straight up, but whenever it was heavy she gave a slight twist to her hand so that the back of it was pressing down on the bundle while the fingers and wrist were ostensibly trying to raise it. I gathered that the spirit in the *kila* on this occasion was one of my familiars, not one of Higilak's.

The following evening, not seeing Ikpakhuak in the camp, I asked Kanneyuk whether he were fishing on the lake; at least that was the question I intended to ask her, but through a slight grammatical error what I actually said was "Has he caught a fish?" It so happened that about that time Ikpakhuak did catch a large trout at a fishing-hole a few hundred yards away. Some of the natives therefore thought that I must possess second-sight, and wanted to know whether the Prince Albert sound natives were not already on their way to visit us. Even Ikpakhuak, when he returned a little while afterwards, supported their request that I should allow Higilak to tie a cord round my head or my foot and divine, as with the *kila*, by lifting it and testing its weight; however, when evening came, she used my coat instead. In the meantime Kesullik pretended to hold a séance on his own account; he asked various questions of an old tobacco can, rapping it with a stick for "yes" and not rapping it at all for "no".

Higilak held an interesting performance when we were returning from Lake Tahiryuak to Lake Numikhoin. The immediate cause was a sudden, apparently spontaneous, bark from one of my dogs. The Eskimos had been much concerned about it, fearing that it foreboded someone's death, and Milukkattak had asked me whether the dog *tornraktok*, i. e., was acting as a medium for its familiar spirit. (Even a dog, it seems, may have its familiars).[1] Higilak therefore borrowed my coat after I had turned into my sleeping-bag, and, making a *kila* of it, began to ask it questions. First she demanded, "Is there anyone in it?", and after a minute or two the *kila* became heavy—a spirit had entered. Through a series of questions she elucidated the fact that one of us was in danger of death, and after testing two or three names it was finally fixed on Tusayok. Higilak now addressed herself to me and asked whether Tusayok had been successful or not in his fishing, for he had remained behind at Lake Numikhoin a fortnight before when the remainder of the party went on to Lake Tahiryuak. I said ,"Probably not," on the presumption that as

---

[1]Cf. Stefansson, Anthrop. Papers, A.M.N.H., Vol. XIV, pt. I, p. 342.

we had all been rather unsuccessful before we left Lake Numikhoin, so Tusayok afterwards would probably have met with little better luck. This appeared to be the answer she wanted. She then said that a man had entered the *kila* and asked me whether I saw him, but I tried to avoid the question and asked her instead if she had. She said "No, I was the only person who had", an assertion she made on her own account, or possibly judging by some expression on my face. Next she asked whether it was a white man, and I told her to question it; the answer was "yes." One or two other questions were addressed to it, then she turned to me again and asked whether the 'man' had not gone out of the *kila*; when I said, "There is no one in it" she requested me to put him back in again. I told her to continue her divining, and the *kila* immediately became heavy again—'the man' had re-entered. She now wanted to know whether it was a kinsman of mine, and I told her it was not. Again she questioned it about our fortunes, and the answer, as she finally announced it to us, was, "He is going to be friendly towards the people." After addressing a few more remarks to the *kila*, the meaning of which I could not follow, she found that it had become light again, indicating that the 'man' had left it. Accordingly, after requesting my permission, she removed her belt from round it and terminated the ceremony. The theory of the natives seemed to be that as it was my dog that had barked—the dog of a white man—it must be a white man's shade that was trying to do them harm, and I should be able to help them to deal with it; further, that the man, or rather the shade that was conceived to enter the *kila*, if not a familiar spirit of mine, was yet to some extent at least under my control. It was for this reason that Higilak had sought my cooperation.

Avranna had a headache one day, and borrowed my belt to tie round his head. It drove the pain, he told us later, from the front to the back of his head, but did not dispel it altogether. Higilak then borrowed my coat to hold a divining performance and discover the cause of her son's malady. As usual she slipped her belt round it and enquired who was inside the bundle making it heavy. Through a number of questions she discovered that it was a kinsman of mine. Then she enquired who it was that was threatened with sickness and death, "Was it Avranna?" "No." "Tusayok?" "No." "Ikpakhuak?" "Yes." "From whom? From a white man?" "No." "From someone near at hand?" "No." "Someone afar off?" "Yes." "The Prince Albert sound natives?" "Yes." "How? Through the stone pot she had bought from them and was using for cooking fish?" "No." "Was it through" (this question I could not understand). "Yes", "Who was causing it? Was it Nilgak?" "No." "Kunana?" "Yes." Here was our answer then; Kunana tried to kill Ikpakhuak at Lake Tahiryuak by some kind of sorcery, but failed. A general conversation among the audience followed this statement, during which Higilak addressed a question now and then to the *kila*. The upshot was that Avranna's headache did not presage a fatal illness and he would soon be well again.

When Higilak came to borrow my coat for this performance I suggested that perhaps the *kila* might lie to her. She was not in the least offended or disconcerted, but argued quite logically that it had proved true on other occasions, for example when it predicted that we should meet with the natives from Prince Albert sound. Ikpakhuak was fishing all the time she divined, but she told him about it when he returned. During the performance itself an incident occurred that is well worth remarking. Higilak had announced that the *kila* was heavy, and she told Avranna, who was sitting beside her, to take hold of the cord and test it himself. He caught hold of the cord, but told her to take away her own hand, which she had kept on top of the bundle. I imagine that she was not expecting this sudden request, but she kept her countenance very well and removed her hand. Avranna then said, " It's light," the very opposite to what she had stated. "Take hold of it here," she told him, fidgeting the bundle about a little, possibly to place it in such a position among the bed-skins that it would be less easy to lift. "Now it's heavy, isn't it?" she asked, and he said "Yes, it is a little." "Take hold of it here lower down," she directed him again, "It's heavy now, isn't it?" "Well, just a little," he replied. This appeared to satisfy her; she took the cord in her own hands again and weighed it. "It is heavy", she said, and went on with her question-ing. No one seemed to think that there might be any fraud on Higilak's part. Avranna's doubts related not to her good faith, but rather to her interpretation of the weight of the *kila*, just as we might sometimes question the accuracy of a doctor's diagnosis.

I understood rather less of what was said at a divination that was held just a week later. There was no definite reason for this performance as far as I could learn. When I asked Higilak why she was holding it, she merely said *aggioktoraluk*, "the shades of the dead constantly beset us." My coat was used again for the *kila*, and two shades appeared to enter it at once, for Higilak said *tamna aiparivaga ukumailivaktok* "the one accompanying him is making it heavy." Mikinrok thumped the sides and head of the *kila* to drive it out, but without effect. I was then asked to thump, and this time the result was satisfactory. Higilak asked me who it was that had entered the *kila*, and when I suggested at random that it might have been "Charlie", the natives immediately identified it with a white man of whom they had heard (Captain Klengenberg?). Another shade entered the *kila* after "Charlie" had gone; this time it was "Joseph." "Charlie" had announced that Ikpakhuak was threatened with evil, but when he had been driven out, and after him "Joseph", everything seemed to be propitious again. A fortnight later Higilak again used my coat for divining, and this time the only spectators were the little boy Haugak and myself. The other natives of our party had all gone out hunting with Ikpakhuak, and a sudden fog that descended over the land had prevented them from finding their way back. The fog was due, Higilak thought, to certain shades of the dead which entered the *kila* one after another. Some were the shades of white men, so I was asked to name them—"William, May" etc.—and to tell them that we were good people without evil intentions. Others were the shades of Eskimos, one being Nerialak, Higilak's first husband, and another Arnaktak, a relative who had died the previous winter; these, her fellow-countrymen, Higilak propitiated as I had mine. The majority of them were readily appeased, for they left the *kila* immediately. Others refused to go, and the *kila* remained very heavy, although by Higilak's direction I thumped on its sides and head; finally she had to slash the top of the coat with her knife in order to eject them. When all the shades had thus been disposed of in one way or the other the *kila* announced that the fog would lift on the morrow, and that Ikpakhuak and his party would be able to find their way back to camp.

I was taken very ill shortly after this, and my condition remained serious for several weeks. Ikpakhuak and Higilak became greatly alarmed, and the latter held a "consultation" over me. She used my coat to divine with, though she made a pillow for it out of her foot-gear. First she orated about the dis-agreeableness of being ill, how it made everyone unhappy, with other remarks in the same strain. Then, addressing the *kila*, she enquired whether my system was out of order of its own accord, and the *kila* replied "No." "Who caused it then? Was it a white man?" "No." "Some one from Great Bear lake?" "No." "A western Eskimo?" "Yes." I was told to enquire his name, and suggested Aiyakak. The *kila* answered "Yes." "What are you doing here," said Higilak, "Jenness is not here, he's a long way away. What do you want here?" [1] and Ikpakhuak, at her signal, struck the *kila* with the edge of her

---

[1] Apparently a malignant shade may be fooled or deceived as well as propitiated or intimidated. Why the human breath should drive it away I did not discover.

knife. This disposed of one shade, but almost immediately the *kila* became heavy again through the entrance of another, Alak, as I suggested. Ikpakhuak tried to evict it in the same manner, but failed. Then a man suggested that Higilak should breathe on the bundle, and this was successful. "It's heavy again," she said a moment later. Ikpakhuak caught hold of the cord and said, "No, it's light." "Heavy, surely," she replied, not too well pleased, I fancied, at her husband's interference. "Go on," said a woman spectator. Higilak did not trouble to enquire the name of the shade this time, but merely said "Go away," and struck the *kila* with her knife and breathed on it. The bundle at once became light; all the malignant shades had been disposed of, and nothing remained presumably to prevent my recovery. A year later Higilak reminded me of this performance, and claimed that she had been instrumental in curing me of my illness.

FIG. 61. Ilatsiak, the most important shaman among the Copper Eskimos

Of the other divining performances that Higilak held at various times one has a certain interest for our purpose. It took place in August, at a time when no caribou had been sighted for several days and our food supplies were running low. Besides myself and Higilak there was only Ikpakhuak in the tent, and he was sound asleep. Higilak divined with my coats as usual, but when she found that the shade of a dead kinsman of Ikpakhuak was recalcitrant and would not leave the bundle she roused her husband from his sleep to propitiate it with fair words and induce it to leave us.

The last instance of divination that I was to witness was tinged with pathos, and would alone have dispelled any doubts I might still have possessed as to Higilak's good faith in these performances. I was paying the old couple one of my final visits before we left their country. Late in the evening Higilak sent the children away to another hut, and she asked me to let her divine by lifting my head. I was lying in my sleeping bag, and Ikpakhuak, the only other person in the hut, closed the door to keep out all visitors. Higilak slipped her belt round my head, and told me to close my eyes. Then they both questioned me, and Higilak lifted my head from time to time for the answers. The whole ceremony lasted perhaps a quarter of an·hour. I could understand very few of their questions, partly because my knowledge of the language was imperfect, partly also because, as in most shamanistic performances, they employed a different vocabulary from that in every-day use. Immediately afterwards, however, she told me the reason for the ceremony. The great shaman Ilatsiak had warned them that their son Avranna was threatened with grave danger, and had advised them to obtain help from me. She entreated me, therefore, and Ikpakhuak supported her request, that after I had left their country and was no longer within reach of an ordinary message, I should send my familiars, *tornrait*, to their aid whenever they or their kinsmen were in danger or distress. *Tusarialutilli*, "Hearken to our call," they urged me again and again. I told them that sometimes perhaps I should not be able to hear them, and with a sigh Higilak responded, "Yes, sometimes one can do nothing."

We have now laid the foundations on which we can build our theory of Copper Eskimo shamanism. Let us consider first the séances, where some familiar spirit is presumed to enter the body of the shaman and to take possession of him, the shaman himself being only the medium. All the utterances are those of the familiar, though they come, as the natives will say themselves, from the lips of the shaman. First it is to be noticed that the man has little or no opportunity for conjuring tricks, seeing that he performs in the open daylight or under the bright light of the lamps in the dance-house; moreover, there are natives all around him so close that they can put out their hands and touch him at any moment. He has to depend therefore on creating the proper "atmosphere," both in himself and in his audience. The important séances given by shamans of credit like Uloksak and Ilatsiak always evoke in the spectators a feeling of tense emotional excitement. Usually their minds are keyed up beforehand to the proper pitch by singing and dancing, and especially by the booming notes of the deep-toned drum. The shaman himself is in a condition of hysteria, or of something that nearly resembles it, brought on at the commencement of his séance by the straining of every muscle, the rolling of his eyes and the ejaculation of cries and strangled gasping sounds. Long practice in self-hypnosis, combined at times perhaps with organic weakness and an inclination towards hallucinations—Ilatsiak had gone through a serious illness when a boy—help to induce the condition more readily. So intense is the strain that the man nearly faints with exhaustion at the close of the performance. The insertion of the teeth of the animal familiar, or the wearing of garments made from its fur, serve, like stage scenery, to increase the illusion. The shaman is not conscious of acting a part; he becomes in his own mind the animal or the shade of the dead man that is deemed to possess him. To his audience, too, this strange figure, with its wild and frenzied appearance, its ventriloquistic cries and its unearthly falsetto gabble, with only a broken word here and there of intelligible speech, is no longer a human being, but the thing it personifies. Their minds become receptive of the wildest imaginings, and they see the strangest and most fantastic happenings. If the shaman ejaculates that he is no longer a man but a bear, forthwith it is a bear that they behold, not a human being; if he says that the dance-house is full of spirits they will see them in every corner. It is in this way, apparently, that most of the tales arise of shamans cutting off their limbs, or flying through the air, or changing to bears and wolves. There may be conscious fraud in the early stages of a shaman's career, in some cases perhaps all through it. Uloksak's séance when he acquitted me of the charge of murder was almost certainly fraudulent from beginning to end; yet even he firmly believed in the genuineness of the shamanistic powers of Ilatsiak and of Higilak. Even if a shaman begins by consciously deceiving his audience, the constant repetition of the action, combined with auto-suggestion and a belief that others have done what he is pretending to do, must inevitably lead in most cases to his deceiving himself. He will accept as true the wildest tales that are told about him by his audiences, tales that are magnified as they pass from mouth to mouth.

We come now to the other class of shamanistic performance, divination by lifting. In this the shaman's familiar, instead of entering his body and taking possession of him, is supposed to exert its power extraneously by forcing the shade of some dead man or woman to enter the *kila* and manifest itself and give answers by its weight.[1] The *kila* may be either the head or the foot of a patient, his clothes, or the clothes of the shaman himself. The frequency with which Higilak employed the method on her own initiative and for her own satisfaction, together with her indifference to the presence or absence of spectators, all go to show that she herself firmly believed in its credibility and was totally unconscious of any deception. She was quite certain that the *kila* became heavy or light through the active co-operation of the shade, and imagined herself to be more sensitive to its changes than other people. I do not mean that she would have expressed herself in this abstract manner, but that quite plainly she ascribed the uncertainty that others would often feel about the relative weight of the bundle to their not being shamans like herself. It is practically certain that she was deceiving herself unconsciously, and her audience was deceived both with and by her through their assumption of "spiritual" causes. For even a casual observer could hardly have failed to notice that her hand worked differently for the answers "yes" and "no." Apparently she first formulated the answer in her own mind, and the thought unconsciously stimulated a kind of reflex action in the muscles of her hand, so that the *kila* really did seem heavy when the answer was "yes," and light when it was "no."

In concluding this sketch of shamanism I may remark that nothing that I actually saw with my own eyes appeared to suggest the operation of any spiritual or mental forces with which we ourselves are not perfectly familiar. Hysteria, self-hypnosis, and delusion caused by suggestion are well-known to every psychologist and medical practitioner, and everything that I witnessed could be explained on one or other of these grounds. The natives have many tales of far more wonderful phenomena, phenomena which, if true, would be as mysterious and inexplicable as the much-discussed walking over red-hot stones that is practised by a certain Fijian tribe. But of these marvels I myself saw nothing, and until we have the evidence of some more critical eye-witness than the Eskimo himself, it is safest perhaps to attribute them to the over-wrought imaginations of a people whose knowledge of the workings of our universe is far more limited even than our own; a people who have no conception of our "natural laws", but in their place have substituted a theory of spiritual causation in which there is no boundary between the possible and the impossible.

---

[1]Sometimes the natives appeared to regard this shade as the offended power responsible for their misfortunes, in which case they tried to intimidate it or to propitiate it with fair words; sometimes as some other shade that was trying to obstruct their enquiries, or else was friendly towards them and prepared to help them with its superior knowledge. In one instance it was not a shade at all, but the familiar spirits that I was believed to control.

CHAPTER XVII

AMUSEMENTS[1]

It might have been expected that in a land where nature runs to extremes, where at one season of the year every hour of the day is flooded with radiant sunlight, at another only a brief interval of twilight breaks the constant gloom, the natives would have evolved an unusually large number of games and pastimes to relieve in the one case the monotony of the everlasting quest for food outdoors, in the other the tedium of their half-sedentary existence within. But in summer the strenuousness of their migratory life allows them little time for any amenities that do not contribute directly to the general welfare; moreover hunting and fishing amid new and ever-changing scenes gives them a variety of experiences that renders more artificial distractions needless. Children, of course, on whom the cares of life weigh little, will play at every season of the year, running races, or rolling in the snow, or splashing in the water on the margins of the lakes and rivers; but even they in summer are forced to seek their pleasures in the constant round of duties rather than in any organized games, partly through lack of playmates, and partly through the ceaseless activity that characterizes Eskimo life at this season of the year. It is in winter that the need for recreation arises. Some games are limited to this season, being forbidden at all other times; cat's cradles is one of them, and the hoop and pole another. Other pastimes, such as wrestling, may be indulged in at any season, but in actual fact they are seldom practised except in winter.

We may conveniently divide the pastimes of the Copper Eskimos into three classes, children's games, games that require special implements or toys, and athletics. One of the commonest of the children's games is "hide and seek." Half of the children form a ring, keeping their eyes fixed on the ground, while the other half run away and hide. The seekers occasionally intone a kind of chant *e - e - e - e - e*, before breaking off and beginning their search; more usually they merely await the signal from those in hiding.[2] The latter are sought out one by one and captured, when they in their turn become the seekers

Similar to our "tag" are the games of "wolf" and "raven". One child is made the hunter; the others run off, flapping their arms and croaking like ravens or leaping and howling like wolves. Whoever is caught first then becomes the hunter. Adults as well as children sometimes play this game, especially at halts during a migration, when exercise is needed to keep up the circulation of the blood.

In another game a number of children, all facing in the same direction, cling together within a circle of rope. A child in front turns around and faces the rest, and as they try to grab him he backs away against the rope. Thus the whole party is dragged forward until finally one or more of the children trip over and fall to the ground.

Little children have a guessing game that resembles "hidden ball." The seeker has to guess which of a number of players has hidden some object under his coat. A modification of this game is often played by two children only. Sitting opposite, one closes his eyes while the other takes a sliver of wood or any convenient object and hides it, usually on the shoulder or at the side of his

---

[1]For comparisons with other Eskimo areas see the memoir by Stuart Culin, Bureau of American Ethnology, Vol. 24. I have added one or two references to later works.

[2]Cf. Meddelelser om Grønland, Vol. XXX, p. 317. At Barrow, Alaska, the seekers have a proper refrain.

companion. The child then opens his eyes and glances round to see where it lies. If he fails to find it immediately, his rival will point it out with a whoop of delight, then close his eyes in his turn.

Often they have silence competitions. A child says *ika*, and everyone keeps perfectly quiet. The first to break the silence is greeted with roars of laughter and loses the game.[1] Then there are competitions in drinking seal broth, the last one to drain his cup being ridiculed and called by the name of some decrepit old person.

Fɪɢ. 62. Children playing "tag", Dolphin and Union strait

The children naturally have many pastimes that imitate the actions of their elders. Girls make dolls out of scraps of skin, and clothe them like real men and women. Their mothers encourage them, for it is in this way that they learn to sew and to cut out patterns. Both boys and girls play at building snow houses. In summer, with only pebbles to work with, they simply lay out the ground plans, but in winter they borrow their parents' snow-knives and make complete houses on a miniature scale. They trace too figures of men and animals in the snow, and carve them out of single blocks; for example, two small boys one day set up a snow-rabbit on top of a hill; one ran and stabbed it through the heart with his knife, while the other completed its demolition by slicing off its head. Sometimes they make toy sleds of ice, like the real ones that are used by their parents in emergencies. One of their games in which the adults sometimes join imitates the killing and cutting up of a bearded seal. A child lies flat on the ground while the others gather around him and pull him about as though they were hewing him to pieces. In Victoria island the children spent an idle summer's day partly in splashing about in a neighbouring lake, partly in setting up rows of stones and turf, *inyukhuit*, as for a caribou drive, and digging shallow pits, *tallut*, from which they launched their shafts at imaginary deer.

---

[1]At Barrow, Alaska, when a child says *mak* or *tam* all the rest must keep silence. The first to break it loses the game; if a boy he will marry an old woman, if a girl an old man.

Of the games that require special toys or implements one of the commonest is "hoop and pole," played by the children in winter. The hoop, *titkat* or *titkattak*, is made of willow and has a diameter usually of some fifteen inches, while the 'pole' is merely a stick two or three feet long. Sometimes they bowl their hoops at random along the ground and throw their sticks through them, sometimes they fling the hoops into the air and try to catch them on their sticks as they fall.[1]

Fig. 63. Children making houses of pebbles, Colville hills

Two other toys, the bull-roarer, *imilguptak*, and the buzz, *nilitak*, are also confined to children. The buzz I know from description only, for I never saw one in their possession. Juggling was another game I never observed, though it is popular among the Eskimos both east and west of them. Cat's cradles, on the other hand, is just as favourite a pastime here as it is elsewhere.[2] Both children and adults play a game called fishing, *ekaluktok*.   A number of small bones from the flippers of a seal are placed in the toe of a shoe and a noose of sinew set vertically in the heel. The opening is then closed with the left hand and the bones are shaken down to the heel, when the noose is drawn tight and taken out. An expert player will always snare one bone in the noose, and usually several.

Cup and ball is another favourite pastime with natives of all ages. The Copper Eskimos use, as a rule, only the bone from the upper arm of the bearded seal.[3] Holes are pierced in both ends of it and in the side of the larger end. The peg is a short pointed stick of bone. The seal-bone is swung counter-clockwise one half revolution, and impaled on the peg in any hole, while the player counts, "thumb, first finger, second finger, third finger, little finger," first for the right hand, then for the left. If successful in all ten the player swings the sealbone one full revolution and catches it on the second, when the game is finished.

[1]See Stefansson, Anthrop. Papers, A.M.N.H., Vol. XIV, pt. I, p. 391.

[2]A special monograph on Eskimo Cat's Cradles is in course of preparation.

[3]Stefansson, Anthrop. Papers, A.M.N.H., Vol. XIV, pt. I, p. 125, has an illustration of a type that I have never seen in Coronation gulf.

A Bathurst inlet woman who had associated with some Hudson bay (Pallik) natives said that they played the game in a slightly different manner. The seal-bone was swung a half-circle while the player counted consecutively the following rigmarole:

" I sleep, I wake, I rise, I light the lamp, I put on my coat, I put on my boots, I put on my mitts, my knife I take, I open the door, I go outside, my long knife I take, I look around, I look round again, I gaze, I spy (a caribou), I go towards it, I reach it, I shoot, I shoot again, I shoot again."

From the first " I shoot" the seal-bone is swung one complete circle and caught during the second. At the last word " I shoot again," when the caribou is supposed to be killed, the player says " I am dead" and the game is finished. If he misses at any stage he hands the toy to his rival, and whoever is " dead" first wins the game.

Bathurst inlet natives who visited our station in the early spring of 1916 were responsible for the introduction of a new game, *nugluak*, into that region. The natives had learned it from the Eskimos of Backs river, so that it has evidently spread north from Hudson bay.[1] About a dozen men and women were playing it in May beside our station. A short flat bone plate about two inches long was made fast by cords of sinew to the ridge pole of the tent above and to a large stone on the floor below, so that it was suspended taut some two feet above the ground. A small hole had been drilled in the middle of the plate, and the natives, sitting all round in a ring, tried to push darts through it, the darts being shafts of wood from two to four feet long pointed with horn. They were all spearing at once, and their darts rattled together and pushed each other away; the plate too quivered and shook, so that sometimes a minute would elapse before one of them penetrated the hole. As one player grew tired and withdrew another took his place. Half their days for nearly a week were spent in this idle occupation. It was the only game, as far as I know, in which the natives gambled. They would stake knives and cartridges and powder and almost anything else they had, and the same knife would pass through several hands in the course of a single day.

We come now to the more athletic games and pastimes, practiced on stormy winter days in the dance-house, or, in some cases, during sled migrations. Often a stick would be pushed into the side of a sled so that it projected horizontally about three feet above the ground, and one after another the men and women would jump up and kick it with the toes of both feet simultaneously. Novices often fall on their backs in this game, a castatrophe that invariably provokes much laughter.

Skipping is a pastime enjoyed by both sexes, mainly of course by the young, although I have seen adult men skipping during a migration when the train had stopped to rest; in such cases it serves the double purpose of amusing them and of keeping them warm. The Eskimos skip rather differently from us. The rope, which is usually a dog-trace, is swung by two players under the feet of the skipper, then back in the opposite direction. It is thus made to circle backwards and forwards, now in one direction, now in the other, while the skipper hops alternately on each foot. Occasionally he may try to circle round, but usually the rope catches in his feet after the first or second turn. The rope being of raw hide, and very hard, the natives often tie a strip of polar bear skin round the middle to keep it from bruising the ankles.

Wrestling is practiced by the men only as a rule, though children often push and shove each other about in an attempt to imitate their elders. The game usually takes place in the dance-house, especially after a successful seal-hunt, when the people are rejoicing over their good fortune, or in stormy weather,

---

[1] See quotation in Culin, p. 472 *et seq.* Mr. Stefansson mentions a game with the same name at Baillie island (Anthrop. Papers, A.M.N.H., Vol. XIV, pt. I, p. 348.)

when the hunters are confined to their huts. Thus one stormy day in the winter of 1915, after the natives had been dancing for some time in the dance-house, Uloksak suggested a wrestling match. Some one called out "Hold a séance", and immediately everyone began to talk about the ill-luck they had been experiencing owing to the constant storms. Uloksak, however, laid aside the drum he had just been using, and began the tournament by throwing his arms around one of the men and dragging him into the ring. Tripping with the feet is not allowed in these contests; each man grasps his opponent around the neck with one arm, and around the waist with the other, and tries by sheer strength to throw him off his feet. A short man is therefore at a great disadvantage, although he may be quite as strong and active as his opponent.

In the dance-house too the natives often practice some simple acrobatic feats. A stout line of bearded seal-skin is passed through two holes in the roof and clamped with two strong wooden poles.[1] Hanging by his hands the native circles round till his toes are almost touching the rope; then he swings violently back in a half-circle and comes to an upright position, his body balanced against the rope with the weight resting on the hands. From this position he swings round again in a half-circle, throws his legs violently out and swings back again. The exercise is continued until the performer becomes tired or fails to maintain his balance. Very few of the natives, however, could accomplish the feat at all. The women never attempted it, though they sometimes joined in a simpler exercise in which two small loops were made in the rope about a foot apart. Hanging by these the performer circled round and placed a foot in each loop, then released his hands, and hung at full length downwards with his head almost touching the floor. From this position he had to draw himself up again, grasp the loop with his hands, release his feet and drop to the floor.

Foot-ball, or hand-ball, for the ball is both kicked along the ground and thrown from hand to hand, is played occasionally by the natives of Bathurst inlet, who learned it, Ilatsiak said, from the Netsilik Eskimos. The ball, *ekitak*, is made of hairless deer-skin like the membrane of the drum, but no information was obtained on how the game itself is played.

Singing and dancing are the main distractions of the Eskimos. Short stories are sometimes narrated, chiefly in the dance-houses during the winter, but the Copper Eskimos have not the same passion for them as the natives farther west. The only musical instrument they possess is the tambourine or drum, *kilaun*. Children, and even adults at times, frequently produce a scale of notes by flipping their finger-nails in succession against their upper incisors, beginning with the little finger. There can of course be no fixed intervals in their scale, but different notes are made by the different fingers, through modifications probably of the cavity of the mouth, though the movement is difficult to detect.

The drum is merely a circular wooden hoop with a membrane of deerskin stretched over it. One that the Coppermine river natives were using in the winter of 1914-15 was made of poplar obtained near Great Bear lake. The flat lath had been curved round to a rough oval, and the overlapping ends riveted with iron nails. The rim was 7 cm. wide and 2 cm. thick, and the two inside diameters were 85.5 cm. and 77 cm. The handle was a short stout piece of poplar 16 cm. long without any ornamentation; it was notched at one end to fit the rim, to which it was lashed with strands of plaited sinew. The membrane was simply a scraped caribou skin lashed around the rim with cod-line. A new membrane was fitted on during my visit. Three men held the skin taut over the frame while a fourth drew tight the lashings. The edge of the membrane where it protruded below the lashing was wound round a stick, and levered down so that the parchment was stretched still tighter. One

[1]Cf. Amundsen, Vol. II, pp. 17-18.

or two small holes in the skin were left unpatched, as the drum when tested proved to be sufficiently resonant. The Eskimos never tune their drums to any particular note, but if they show signs of slackness and loss of resonance they rub a little water over the surface. The drum-stick is an ordinary heavy baton, perfectly plain; the one used by the Coppermine natives was 33 cm. long. The Eskimos often cover it with seal-skin where it strikes the rim; for the musician, who holds the drum above his head, strikes not the parchment, but the wooden rim on its under side, first on one side of the handle, then on the other.

(Photo by G. H. Wilkins.)

FIG. 64. Angivranna, a Coppermine river native, beating a drum

All the songs of these Eskimos, except incantations and a few children's rhymes, are dancing songs. They are divided into two classes: the *aton* and the *pisik*. A *pisik* is sung when the dancer himself wields the drum, an *aton* when the drum is either dispensed with altogether or is beaten by some one in the ring, the audience sustaining the song while the dancer executes a kind of jig in the centre; the distinction, however, is not always preserved. Both kinds of dancing, together with the ceremonial circling of "dancing-associates" around each other, took place at Bernard harbour when the Eskimos of Bathurst inlet met those of Dolphin and Union strait.

Many of their songs have what may be called standard tunes, to which the native will often improvise words of his own instead of the regular words. Thus the day after we reached their settlement the Coppermine river Eskimos had a song about us, which was simply a new set of words adapted to an old tune. Ikpakhuak was so amused over an adventure of mine with a wolf that before I had finished my story he had improvised a song about it; wherever he was at a loss for any word he simply filled up the gap with the meaningless syllables *ai ye yanga.*

The most usual dance is the *pisik*, and the natives always commence with this. The dancer, whether a man or a woman (for the Copper Eskimos make no difference in this respect), begins with a few beats of the drum as though testing it, then holds it up in both hands and waves it up and down, or else taps the middle of the membrane lightly on the under side. Then he starts his song, balancing himself alternately on either foot. The audience join in when they recognize the words, and as soon as the song is going with a good swing the man begins his dance proper, beating his drum, swaying his body and circling round the ring to the accompaniment of the music. Often he lowers his drum towards the end of the refrain, raps it in the middle a few times and starts the next verse lest his audience may have forgotten the sequence. The time of the music is always very irregular. If the tune runs too high up the scale at any place the men drop an octave for a few notes. The dancer will call on his audience to sing louder if the chorus is not maintained with full vigour, and will himself raise his voice to its highest pitch. Not infrequently though, if the song is a new one, his audience will tell him to change it and he has to begin over again. It is very amusing sometimes to see the wife vigorously leading the singing when her husband is dancing, so that he will be spurred on to put forth his best efforts. A father will often do this for his favourite child, or he will shout words of encouragement and advice. Wild whoops of joy from the dancer always greet support from the ring.[1]

The Eskimos wear their finest clothes in the dance-house, clothes with coloured bands and tasselled fringes. They are often hung with trophies, such as the teeth or claws of a polar bear, or the knuckle-bones of the seal.[2] The white skin of the weasel, worn either on a parti-coloured dancing cap surmounted by a loon's bill or on the back of the coat, is a particularly favourite ornament. Relatives, especially wives, frequently borrow these ornaments when it comes to their turn to dance. Ikpakhuak wore a beautifully striped cap at a dance one evening; half an hour later his niece was wearing it; then soon afterwards his nephew. Fashion ordains the wearing of gloves while dancing, and whenever possible, even in the spring and summer, the feet should be shod with the winter shoes of white seal-skin, especially the kind called *tuatuatsiak*, which are crimped all round the bottom and have a black triangular insertion over the toes. Hence one occasionally sees a curious medley of costumes in the spring; some of the natives will be wearing their finest winter clothes, while others who have cached their property on the sea-shore are forced to appear in their oldest garments, with their feet tucked into long water-boots.

When the Puivlik and Kanghiryuak natives met at Lake Tahiryuak in the beginning of June, 1915, the occasion was celebrated by every variety of dancing known to these Eskimos. A dance-house was erected in a deep snow-drift at the foot of a bank. Only the walls were built of snow, the roof being formed of deerskins and the cloth covering of my sled, as the heat of the sun at this time of the year would have melted a dome of snow. On the first day only one Kanghiryuak family had arrived, Kunana and his wife Allikammik, with their little baby and a young man named Imerak. Ikpakhuak was the most influential man in our party, so it was only natural that his wife Higilak should lead off in the dancing. Despite her portly figure she danced very well, and gave a good exhibition of the ordinary *pisik* in which she beat the drum herself. She called out her visitor Allikammik to run around her, first in one direction, then in the

---

[1] A special memoir on Copper Eskimo music will be published later in this series, based on a large collection of phonographic records now stored in the Victoria Memorial Museum of the Department of Mines, at Ottawa.

[2] A Prince Albert sound native wore at a dance a complete set of polar bear's claws suspended in pairs around his coat like a belt.

other, thus making her a "dancing-associate." Allikammik then retired to the ring again, and the two women ratified their friendship by shaking their noses within an inch of each other.

During all this time the singing had continued uninterruptedly, though Higilak had lowered her drum and stopped beating. She now resumed her dance, and as soon as it was ended handed the drum to Allikammik and executed an impromptu jig on her own account, accompanied by wild whoops that testified to her joy at the meeting. It was now Allikammik's turn. She was very angular in figure, and danced awkwardly, with many jerks and spasms. She laboured, too, under the difficulty of dancing without a full chorus, for the song she started was known only to her husband (and perhaps also to Imerak, but he did not attempt to sing). Ikpakhuak and Higilak gallantly attempted to pick up the tune out of courtesy, but all the rest stood around in silence. Allikammik returned Higilak's compliment by calling her out to run around her, as she had done before. Afterwards some of the Puivlik natives privately ridiculed her dancing, and made rather a laughing-stock of her, but this was partly due to Higilak, who was somewhat jealous of the attentions that Allikammik paid to Ikpakhuak.

Ikpakhuak then took the drum and entered the ring. He was a celebrated dancer, and with lively but graceful movements sprang round and round the ring, leaping on alternate feet, and whirling the great drum to and fro while the low canvas roof puffed up and down with its wind. He struck the drum on the far side of the handle, then, as he swung it back, brought it to a stop on the stick with very little noise; other natives who were less expert made the return swing resound almost as much as the full stroke itself. At the beginning of his dance he called Allikammik out to run around him, then a little later both her and her husband Kunana: the latter, according to custom, took the inside course, the place of honour, allowing his wife to drop back into the ring while he ran back in the opposite direction. He succeeded Ikpakhuak with the drum, for it is the prerogative of two "dancing-associates" to follow one another. Nearly everyone in the company knew his song, so the chorus swelled with some volume; but he was not nearly so skilful a dancer as Ikpakhuak, and moved about very little. During his dance he called out Ikpakhuak and Higilak to run around him, the latter, like Allikammik, running on the outside and leaving her husband to return alone.

The ceremonial portion of the program was now ended, for the visitors had received their formal welcome. It would have been very unnatural, however, to stop a dance in which everyone was finding so much enjoyment, so Okalluk took the drum and entered the ring. His voice was very hoarse and raucous, and he moved about very little, but he compensated for this by flourishing the drum with great vigour and banging it till we were all nearly deafened. Higilak left the dance-house at this stage to attend to her cooking in the camp above.

Kesullik followed Okalluk, and, after him, Kanneyuk; the former was called out by Avranna. He forgot the words of his song in the very middle and broke down for a moment, but recovered again amid a good deal of laughter. The drum, which had been made by Ikpakhuak, was obviously too big and heavy for him, and he handled it rather awkwardly, keeping his feet widely apart and jerking his body spasmodically. Kanneyuk, though a mere child, was much more skilful, and even though she had to lower the drum from time to time on account of its weight, her dancing never stopped for a moment and she continued to beat it just the same.

Avranna took the drum when she had finished, but his dance had hardly started when a sled was sighted and everyone rushed out to welcome the new-comers. It was too late in the day to begin another formal dance, so this was postponed until the morrow. Some of the Puivlik natives, however, went back to the dance-house and amused themselves drumming and singing. A few of them slept there that night, as the skins of their tents had been used on its roof. Kunana, before retiring to his tent, sewed two fur strings on the right shoulder of Higilak's coat in token of their new-formed friendship.

The following morning the natives donned their finest clothing in preparation for the dance in honour of the new-comers, Nilgak and his wife Utuaiyok. Pissuak was an old friend of Nilgak, his dancing-associate in fact, so he naturally opened the welcome. Puivlik and Kanghiryuak natives followed each other in almost regular sequence; Pissuak (Puivlik), Utuaiyok (Kanghiryuak), Avranna (P), Imerak (K), Milukkattak (P), Higilak (P), Kunana (K), Ipkakhuak (P), Allikammik (K), Avranna (P), Utuaiyok (K), Pissuak (P), Nilgak (K) and Kullak (P). When Pissuak danced he called out his friend's wife, Utuaiyok, to run around him, she called out both Pissuak and Avranna, then Avranna called her out in return, Imerak summoned Milukkattak, and she reciprocated immediately afterwards, while Kunana called out, first Higilak, then Ikpakhuak, then Higilak again, and Ikpakhuak had to respond by calling out Kunana's wife Allikammik, and afterwards Kunana himself. Avranna in his second dance called out Utuaiyok, she called out both him and Pissuak, then Pissuak again alone, Pissuak called out both her and her husband together, and then Nilgak called out Pissuak.

Fig. 65. Copper Eskimos holding a dance in the dance-house, from a drawing by the Mackenzie river Eskimo Palaiyak

All the dances on the preceding day had been of the *pisik* type, the dancer, that is, had also beaten the drum. But on this occasion several of the *aton* type were given. Higilak began the change. On entering the ring she rapped the drum a few times to get her song well started, then handed the instrument to Allikammik and the stick to Kunana, and executed a wild kind of jig, waving her arms in the air and swinging around on both feet, only roughly in time with the music. Sometimes she would call on the spectators to sing louder, and swell the chorus herself with her voice; at other times she would utter whoops and shouts of joy, interspersed with remarks to the singers, remarks such as, "Aren't we glad the Kanghiryuarmiut have come." Ikpakhuak, who danced in a similar manner, executed all kinds of fancy evolutions, proving his complete mastery of the art of dancing as far as the Eskimos practise it. He began with a *pisik*, then handed the drum and stick to Allikammik, and gave one *aton* without the drum, then a second with Avranna beating it for him. His second *aton* therefore coincided exactly with the men's dance among the Mackenzie river and northern Alaskan Eskimos. Pissuak and Allikammik both gave *aton* dances, preceded by a *pisik*. The latter was carrying her baby on her back when she began, but finding it too heavy, she handed it over to her husband. The Kanghiryuak natives gave a return dance on the following day, and others were held as long as the two groups remained together; they were less formal than those described, but otherwise differed in no essential respect.[1]

[1]Cf. Stefansson, My Life with the Eskimo, p. 186.

CHAPTER XVIII

PSYCHOLOGY AND MORALITY

There are two standpoints from which we may treat of the psychology of any given people. In the first place we may select a dozen or twenty individuals, regard them as typical of the whole group, and subject them to elaborate experiments that will test their emotional susceptibilities and intellectual powers. We should then try to differentiate between their inherent and their acquired qualities, that is to say, between the qualities that are inherited from one generation to another and those that are superimposed on these either by deliberate training or by the influence of the environment. Generalizing from the data thus obtained, we may arrive at certain conclusions regarding the psychology of the people as a whole and the characteristics that mark them off from other peoples. But a study of this nature, so full of traps and pitfalls even to the trained psychologist, is quite beyond the reach of an ordinary layman. Moreover, as far as the Copper Eskimos are concerned, no one has ever undertaken the necessary experiments.

The second standpoint that we may take, if less scientific in the technical sense of that term, is at least equally valuable. The method adopted is the method of the legislator and the trader, the traveller and the missionary. Regarding the people as a single group, studying their culture and watching their behaviour under the varying circumstances of life, we single out those traits which seem to mark the majority of its individual members and make them characteristic of the people as a whole, without troubling to enquire whether these traits are innate or acquired, the outcome of hereditary factors or the result of education and environment. An analysis of this kind, being more or less empirical, can only be approximately accurate, and when applied to individual cases will be found to fall very wide of the truth. Nevertheless it is largely on such an analysis, conscious or unconscious, that foreigners must always base their judgments and their relations, whether it be, for example, a legislature framing laws for its alien subjects or a Hudson's Bay Company factor trading with Indians or Eskimos. Even though it lacks therefore the precision and exactitude of more scientific enquiries, it has its practical value. It is the object of the present chapter to supply such an analysis, and so to round off the conception I have tried to convey of the life and culture of the Copper Eskimos.

Let us consider first how the limitations of their environment and their ignorance of the great world outside of them react on the minds of these Eskimos. Naturally, we find it reflected in the circumscribed range of their ideas, noticeable more particularly in their topics of conversation. The men are thinking and talking always of their hunting, their fishing, and their sealing. When the hunter returns to camp, every little incident of the day, how he saw a caribou from the top of a ridge, the character of the country, his careful stalking, how he crawled on hands and knees, what the deer was doing, his shooting, the action of the wounded animal, how he skinned it, the thickness of its back-fat and the excellence of its fur, how he packed it home and the other tracks that he came upon, all these are repeated over and over again, down to the minutest detail, to everyone who enters the house. The other hunters describe their adventures, and the women interrupt now and then with a question or an exclamation, or retail the most recent item of gossip around the settlement. The same questions are asked, the same requests made again and again, and so the conversation continues. Even less than with us does it rise to the height of abstract reflection, or to a contemplation of the nature and purpose of the things by which mankind is surrounded. The very religion of the Copper Eskimos, so far from stimulating their intellectual growth, has helped to stunt it, although that religion was itself their own creation, or at least so moulded by them as to fit in with every detail of their daily life. For it has led them to ascribe every mysterious or simply unusual phenomenon to a supernatural agency, an explanation that immediately dampens every impulse to anything in the nature of a scientific enquiry. Incredible and even contradictory assertions (or so they seem to us) are accepted without question, for there is no boundary between the possible and the impossible when spiritual forces are free to intervene at any moment. It is not strange therefore that the Copper Eskimo should be a true Epicurean, holding that life is a short and uncertain thing at the best, and that the wise man will grasp at what pleasures he can in his course without stopping to ponder over those things that do not directly affect his immediate welfare.

It is natural, too, that the natives should believe implicitly in clairvoyance or second sight. More interesting is their peculiar belief in the projection of the human will. I stayed one night with two families who were camped at the mouth of a creek near Cape Lambert in order to spear the migrating salmon. Hardly any salmon at that time had made their appearance, so just as I was leaving, one of the natives asked me to "will" that the fish should enter the creek. That very evening a large shoal of salmon did enter the weir and were speared. The native came to thank me a few days later; he said, "You bade the fish come up, so they came, and we have killed large numbers of them." With a similar idea an old man in Coronation gulf begged Dr. Anderson to cherish good thoughts of him and his family so that they would come to no harm. On another occasion, when the mosquitoes were plaguing us very badly, Kanneyuk circled her finger round her eye and cried "Wind, wind." She seemed to think that if you told the weather to clear or a wind to spring up or anything at all to happen your appeal would very probably take effect. To tease her I summoned the mosquitoes to come, and she earnestly protested against my action. During a storm the natives often cry out, "Be fine, it is very unpleasant when the weather is bad, be fine;" or again, "We can't seal when the weather is stormy, be fine!" Several times I have heard Higilak appeal thus to the weather when her husband was away hunting. It was not the spirit world that the relatives had in mind when they made these appeals, for once when I added, "Hearken and obey," they all burst out laughing; rather they seemed to hold that the very expression of one's thought, the mere utterance of a wish, in some dim and obscure manner worked for its fulfilment.[1]

The intellectual inertia of the natives is apparent in their counting. A woman wanted to tell me that I had six cartridges. She held up three fingers and said "three," *pingahut*, then again held them up and said "three." I tried to make her count consecutively. She began on her fingers "one, two," then for the third finger said "one" again and, on being corrected, "three." For the fourth finger she was quite at a loss, but another native volunteered "four." Beyond this neither of them had any numerals, though there are words for both "five" and "six." Very few of the natives, however, know the word for six, and in ordinary conversation any number above three is "many."[2]

It is significant in this respect that not a single native was encountered who had the slighest conception of a map, with the sole exception of Uloksak. Even he had only a vague comprehension. He understood that certain lines represented the coast and others the rivers, and he seemed to be able to picture a bay as a curve, but he totally failed to comprehend the purpose of a map, and so could not reproduce on paper his own topographic knowledge.[3] Yet the

---

[1]Cf. Stefansson, My Life with the Eskimo, p. 295.
[2]Cf. Stefansson, Anthrop. Papers, A.M.N.H., Vol. XIV, pt. I, p. 343.
[3]A native of Minto inlet, however, drew an accurate sketch of the west coast of Victoria island for one of McClure's people (Armstrong, p. 338 *et seq.*), and Dr. Anderson saw a Tree river Eskimo draw a tolerable outline of the coast near Bathurst inlet, so that there are evidently a few natives who have vague notions of topography.

natives understood pictures without any difficulty, and could draw figures of human beings, especially their clothing, with some approach to accuracy. There drawings of animals, however, and even of the implements that they used every day of their lives, were extremely poor. Probably the making and clothing of dolls, and the cutting out of skins for their own clothes, when the whole pattern is present to the mind beforehand, had accustomed them to think abstractly of the shape and details of the human figure. On the other hand they seldom or never make toys in the shape of animals as other Eskimos do, and so less often conceive of the separate details of the animal body and combine them abstractly into one proportionate whole.

Fig. 66. Okalluk and Tusayok, the former making a cooking-pot from a tin can, the latter making arrow-heads from an antler

Another sign of intellectual inertia is their inability to pursue a logical train of thought. For example, a native will never tell a story straightforwardly from beginning to end. He starts in the middle, returns on himself to explain some allusion, and wanders backwards and forwards in this manner until he has completed all he has to tell. He is easily diverted into another channel or another subject. Direct questions, unless they are simple requests for an enlargement on some remark he has just made, almost invariably confuse him, and he becomes incoherent or silent. This explains to some extent the amazing variations in the accounts that different natives give of the same event or story where the words are not stereotyped into fixed formulæ.

It cannot be said, however, that the Copper Eskimos are altogether lacking in mental alertness. Their daily conversation proves otherwise, their constant use of irony, for example, an irony that consists in saying exactly the opposite of what is meant. Thus when a native remarks to another *aiyuittutin,* "You don't know how to do it," he nearly always means "You are clever, aren't you?" and when Avranna had outstripped the rest of us in his pursuit of two polar bears his wife proudly remarked, "Avranna is slow, isn't he? A regular old woman." Mental alertness is shown again in the quickness with which they adapt themselves to the customs and ways of the white man. They are extremely clever, too, in imitating the peculiarities and mannerisms of one another. My Puivlik companions were always mimicking the peculiar voice inflection of the Prince

Albert sound natives whom we had met. Nothing gives a native more pleasure, for instance, than to single out a rival's or an enemy's peculiarities and to hold them up to ridicule. Higilak was thus constantly ridiculing not only the Prince Albert sound woman Allikammik, but also Ikpakhuak's first wife, until the latter foisted her company on Ikpakhuak again and her presence made her rather too bitter a topic to joke about.

Like all other Eskimos these people display a considerable skill in the treatment of skins, the whittling and carving of wood, and, since iron and brass were introduced, the working of metal. Their talent for imitation has stood them in good stead in these matters now that the whites have introduced new tools and new materials. Iron is beaten into shape just as their copper was, but they are learning also to temper it with fire. Many of them can take their rifles to pieces and put them together again. Ikpakhuak had a bullet stuck in the barrel of his ·30-30 Winchester. He fixed it horizontally in the wall of his snow-hut, and lashed a friend's rifle to it, muzzle to muzzle. Then with the second rifle he fired a blank cartridge into his own, with the natural result that he burst the chamber. Nothing daunted, he tried to weld it together again by hammering on the crack with a stone, and was much chagrined when he found that a method he had employed so successfully with copper failed altogether with hard steel. The women and girls quickly pick up the principle of the sewing machine; after one or two lessons Kanneyuk could run up a snow-shirt or a pair of trousers in about an hour without the slightest assistance. The natives had no idea of twisting the strands of a rope together, or of splicing, up to the time we left their country, but probably before ten years are over there will hardly be a native who is not expert at both these accomplishments. Fox-trapping on an extensive scale is another new departure in their lives, yet they have already adopted all the tricks and devices known to the old trappers in the west.

All these changes indicate the possession of great imitative powers, but little or no originality. The children seemed to be more keen intellectually than their elders, a feature that is common, I fancy, to most, if not all races, whether civilized or uncivilized. They would always grasp what I was trying to say more quickly than the older people, and generally picked up our ways more readily. It is interesting to notice that the inability of the whites to understand their language was frequently ascribed to defective hearing, and the remark or request would be repeated in a louder tone, the natives often forgetting or failing to realize apparently that their language was not intelligible to foreigners. There were great individual differences in intelligence, however, just as there were in manners. Some of the natives were very dull and stupid, and one or two seemed almost half-witted. The majority seemed fairly intelligent in all matters with which they were familiar, and soon adapted themselves to new conditions that did not differ radically from the old. A very few displayed marked intelligence and shrewdness. This was especially noticeable in the case of the two shamans, Ilatsiak and Uloksak, but whereas the former employed his superior intelligence in promoting the welfare of his fellow tribesmen, Uloksak used his for purely selfish ends; the one man therefore was honoured and esteemed for his wisdom and public spirit, the other disliked and feared because of his unscrupulousness and his cunning.

The Copper Eskimos are rather open in their natures as a people, but certain individuals displayed considerable cunning. Uloksak was perhaps the most conspicuous example, as the following episode will illustrate. There was a simple-minded old man named Kingodlik who bought a rifle from us in the winter of 1915-16. He kept it inside his hut against the snow wall at the back of his sleeping platform, but at Uloksak's suggestion removed it to the parapet that ran round the outside of the house, where it lay wrapped in an old deerskin coat securely lashed with a stout sealskin thong. One day it disappeared from the parapet. Some one suggested that the dogs must have dragged it away, and, after chewing up the line and the coat, left the rifle buried somewhere beneath the snow; but no traces of torn skin were visible anywhere, nor were there any tracks of the dogs' feet on the parapet. There was every reason therefore to suspect that some one had stolen it, and the evidence pointed to Uloksak, for not only had he suggested that the rifle be kept outside the hut, but he had been heard to remark several times that it was absurd for an old man like Kingodlik to possess a rifle when he did not know how to use it. Moreover, no one else in the settlement was likely to have the audacity to steal anything so valuable as a rifle. The other natives, however, even if they knew, were afraid to say anything, so Kingodlik appealed to me—he thought "my compass could tell me where the rifle lay." It so happened that just at this time Uloksak had been engaged to tell me some folk-lore, on the agreement that if he proved satisfactory I would give him a ·30-30 Winchester rifle in exchange for his .44. That evening, as we sat alone in my tent with only my interpreter Patsy present, I said to him, "When everyone has gone to bed you take Kingodlik's rifle and put it on my sled." Uloksak raised his eyebrows, assenting, then a moment afterwards, recollecting himself, he said "Oh, but I don't know where it is. Probably the dogs have dragged it away and it is buried somewhere under the snow." I insisted, however, that a great shaman like himself should be able to find it, and said that until it was recovered I would neither trade with the natives nor exchange his rifle. Nothing happened for two days. On the third morning a crowd of Eskimos poured into my tent and woke me up—the rifle was found. Uloksak, they said, had taken his own rifle that morning to shoot a raven that had been hovering round the camp for several days (ravens are never molested as a rule by these Eskimos). Two other natives followed him, and one of them noticed something dark on the surface of the snow. Thinking it was merely a piece of drift-wood he would have turned back, but Uloksak ran forward and picked it up—it was the rifle. Of course the explanation was that the dogs had dragged it there when they tore up the coat!

The Copper Eskimo, as a rule, displays very little independence in either thought or action. He follows the multitude, agrees to whatever is said, and reflects the emotions of those around him. Whenever we laughed the Eskimos laughed, and when we smiled they smiled. If a man, overwhelmed by grief, gave vent to his feelings and wept aloud, the natives around him nearly always wept also. Any individualist like Uloksak, therefore, is fairly certain to become a man of note and influence. The easy merging of one man's will in another's makes for the "tolerance" of Eskimo society, wherein each person may do what he wishes without any interference from the rest. It partly accounts, too, for the ease with which these natives are dominated by Europeans, their pliant natures yielding readily to the aggressiveness of the outsider. Generally speaking they have little strength of character. Even Uloksak, bold as he was, became humble and obsequious when he was confronted with a charge of stealing ammunition and his rifle was held in bond until he should either clear himself or restore the stolen articles. Nanneroak, a native of a rather similar type, carried off a case of pemmican from our station. A sled party pursued him, recovered some of the pemmican, and compelled him to pay two boxes of cartridges for the quantity that he had consumed. The loss of the ammunition was a serious blow, but neither Nanneroak nor his kinsmen had the courage to resist, though they outnumbered the sled party four times over. All this would seem to point to an undeveloped personality. Correspondingly, the gregarious instinct is very strongly marked. It is displayed, for example, in the dances that are held all through the winter, and in the use of the dance-house as a kind of club. It was probably this instinct, rather than any consideration of increased comfort, that led to the adoption of double and triple houses.

To the imperfect development of personality we may perhaps ascribe the deficiency of the natives in a proper sense of responsibility. For instance, a man will be running ahead of the sled, making the trail for the dogs to follow. A seal-hole attracts his attention, his curiosity gets the better of him, and he turns aside to examine it; or it may be that a deer-track crosses his trail, and he will follow it for a hundred yards or so, even when there is absolutely no prospect of securing the animal. The result is that the dogs become entangled in each other's traces and a fight ensues, in which one or more may be injured. Again the inability of the natives to pursue a logical train of thought finds its counterpart in the lack of consistency in their purposes. A native will decide to spend the summer on Victoria island; but a day or two later he takes a sudden whim and joins a party bound for the Coppermine river.[1] Thus they change their purposes from day to day, and, generally speaking, a plan deferred is a plan lost.

The conduct of even the older people is often marked by a naïve childishness and simplicity. Ikpakhuak, usually so dignified, would scuffle with Higilak and playfully give her a slap, while Avranna and Milukkattak, sitting opposite, would make faces at one another or mock each other's words, then embrace with shouts of laughter. Their emotions as a rule lie very close to the surface; they have little of the stoicism so characteristic of the American Indian. Weeping fits are not uncommon; some one mentions a relative who has recently died and begins to weep, whereupon the whole audience weeps in sympathy, not excluding the men. Twice during migrations I saw Kesullik lean against his sled and weep, for no apparent reason; the fit would pass over in a few minutes and he would chatter again as usual. Some of the natives are more prone to tears than others. Itokanna paid a visit to an elder sister in another settlement. The sister buried her face in her hands and wept for joy, but Itokanna sat calmly beside her without a trace of emotion on her face; she was more stolid, however, than the average native. Uloksak induced one of our western Eskimos to clip his hair. His second wife was very much opposed to the operation, and sat on the floor till it ended with the tears streaming down her face. It required much coaxing on the part of her husband to restore her good humour, and induce her to seal a peace by pressing noses.

The majority of the natives are extremely curious, although a few of them keep this feeling fairly under control. They like to pick up and examine everything, to turn a thing over and see what is inside. This was often very annoying to us, although occasionally it led to rather amusing results: Nik, for example, Aksiatak's wife, tasted some cayenne pepper one day, and another native who liked to help himself to our sugar took a mouthful of salt that was left out for him. Some of the older men, however, were models of courtesy and good-breeding, as far as these qualities were understood by the natives. They never imposed their company on us, for example, whenever it was obvious that we wanted to remain alone, and when they did visit us they bore themselves with dignity and respect. In their own houses, too, they always received us as honoured guests, and did their utmost to make us comfortable. The younger men, on the other hand, partly through inexperience of life's vicissitudes, partly through the contamination of foreign influence, were more forward and assuming. Just as among Europeans, however, there were very many different types. Some were very timid and alarmed by anything they could not understand, such as the phonograph or the magnetic needle, others were bold and inquisitive, or sly and cunning, and a few, a very few, frank and straightforward. The majority were cheerful and light-hearted, inclined to be talkative and, in some cases, even garrulous. Their gay and care-free natures make suicide an extremely rare occurrence; in fact I do not remember hearing of more than one case, and that was due not to any morbid weariness of life, but to terror of the revenge that might be exacted for a crime that the man had committed. Some of them are very quick-tempered, and the majority of the murders that occur are committed

---

[1]Cf. Stefansson, My Life with the Eskimo, p. 270.

in a momentary heat of passion provoked by some scornful or sarcastic remark. If a native makes a serious mistake without being greatly to blame—for example, if he unwittingly startles a herd of caribou—he will talk about it for days afterwards in a tone of disappointment or regret. On the other hand if he is blamed for some action—as when I scolded Avranna for using a tiny pair of scissors on a heavy sealskin, with the inevitable result that the scissors broke immediately —he is liable to become very sullen and brood over it for a long time. His anger may pass off after a night's sleep, but sometimes it leads to a violent outburst, when the man will probably pack up his things and move off to another place.

(Photo by J. J. O'Neill)

Fig. 67.   An Eskimo woman and her dog, both carrying packs, Port Epworth

Children show the same individual variation. One will be bold and merry, another bashful and shy, a third forward and presuming, and a fourth an abominable meddler. Two or three children were what we should call "prudes," while one little girl, Tupik, whom I noted as particularly charming (she was about 8 years old in 1916), is declared by the missionaries to have no taint of original weakness or sin, nor to know what wrong is. In many little ways they display the same sensitiveness as European children. Thus Higilak's daughter Kanneyuk slipped on a stone one day and gashed her knee rather badly. Some one noticed her crying and asked her what was the matter, but she angrily brushed the tears from her eyes and moved away, ashamed that anyone should have seen her weeping over a petty injury.

Nearly all the natives have a keen sense of humour. Aksiatak and Anauyak were unable to find the entrance to our house when first it was built. They peered through the window and saw Kaminggok inside, who told them to climb on to the roof and come down the stove-pipe. A little while afterwards the same native was grinning into a mirror and ejaculating, "Who is this? What is his name? Isn't he handsome?" and other remarks of a similar nature that kept his companions in a perpetual state of laughter. A cold snap overtook us once on Victoria island when some of our party had no proper shelters. Higilak, sitting comfortably inside her tent, told me to call out, "Good luck to you people who have no tents." An awkward dancer is sure to be the butt of the other natives, for, like all Eskimos, these people are excellent mimics.[1]   Children especially

---

[1]Cf. Richardson, p. 211.

are fond of mimicking their elders, even their own parents. Practical jokes, while seldom indulged in, are usually taken with great good-humour. A native who had been sampling some of our foods was given a little strong horse-radish. The tears came into his eyes and he choked, but he swallowed it gamely nevertheless and grinned over it afterwards. On the other hand there is a good deal of back-biting and scandal-mongering, especially among the women, who will sit and talk scandal for hours. Mikinrok and Higilak were gossiping about Kullak one day, and on the following day Higilak and Kullak were talking scandal of Mikinrok. The men, who live a more active life out of doors, are naturally less given to such practices.

To the Copper Eskimo goodness means social goodness, that and no more. Whatever directly affects the welfare of the community as a whole is morally good or bad, while whatever relates to the individual alone, or affects the community so remotely that its influence is barely perceptible to their short-sighted view, is neither good nor bad. The foremost virtues therefore are peacefulness and good-nature, courage and energy, patience and endurance, honesty, hospitality, charity towards both the old and the young, loyal co-operation with one's kin and providence in all questions relating to the food-supply. Fair-dealing (apart from the relations with one's kin) and truthfulness have only a secondary place, while sexual purity is hardly considered as coming within the scope of morals at all.

Their peacefulness has been recorded by earlier observers. Thus Collinson remarks, "They have left us with the impression that they are a kind-hearted well-disposed people . . . . They at first with us carried their knives with the blade up their sleeves and the haft in the hand, in readiness for immediate use; but notwithstanding the dread of our firearms may have kept them quiet, I am inclined to think they are an inoffensive race."[1] The lack of any organization for war and their avoidance of the Indians (so much in contrast to the Mackenzie river Eskimos) would alone suffice to prove their peacefulness. A people that lives by the chase and glories in hand-to-hand combats with such adversaries as the polar and the brown bear can hardly be lacking in physical courage. But the Copper Eskimo is the reverse of foolhardy; courage with him is nearly always subordinated to prudence. Except in his hunting, when the tradition of a long line of ancestors makes boldness a merit, a native will never accept a risk unless the odds are greatly in his favour. He will never fight an enemy on equal terms, but will wait until he can overwhelm him with superior numbers or strike him behind his back.

A hunting life under Arctic conditions necessarily calls for great energy, patience and endurance. The Copper Eskimos think nothing of spending twenty-four hours on a hunt, tramping continually over stony hills without a morsel of food, and with only a few short halts to rest their limbs and look around them. In spring I have seen them spend whole days fruitlessly digging one hole after another through the thick ice of the lakes and jigging their lines without ever getting a bite. In winter they sit for hours over their seal-holes even in howling blizzards with the temperature 30° and more below zero Fahrenheit. The patience instilled in them by hunting becomes engrained in their very natures and permeates all their social life, so that tolerance and forbearance are two of the most marked features in Eskimo society. Combined with the lack of a proper sense of responsibility it leads only too often to a passive looking-on when an active interference is more called for. Thus the natives will quietly stand by and witness a robbery or a murder without ever raising a finger. It is no concern of theirs, they will say, so why should they interfere?

Earlier visitors to the country have extolled also their honesty. Rae notices that they had a great respect for caches of any kind. "On the 30th we reached

---

[1]Collinson, p. 286.

our cache of the 16th, and found it, as well as two others, perfectly safe, not-withstanding that one, or perhaps all of them, had been seen by the Esquimaux."[1] Osborn remarked of the Minto inlet natives that "They seemed very simple and honest; and when presented with anything, they appeared incapable of supposing that anyone would give them an article without expecting an equiv-alent." [2] Even as late as 1912 Douglas from the region of Great Bear lake could say, "Everything was all right at the little shack; there were signs that the Eskimos had made a large camp close to it since we had been there, but nothing had been disturbed. Even an axe, an article of inestimable value to them, was just where it had been left.[3] Mr. Stefansson never heard of any thefts nor learned the native word for "stealing." [4] Thefts do sometimes occur nevertheless. Milukkattak was careful to cache a fork that I had given her when we went to look for the Prince Albert sound natives for fear that the latter might steal it; and Higilak accused Mikinrok of stealing some of her sinew. The absolute lack of privacy in their lives, however, makes concealment very difficult, and partly for this reason, and partly because the average native is naturally inclined to be honest and upright, theft is comparatively rare among themselves. Their morality being based on purely social sanctions that hardly operate outside the community, the same restraint is not always observed towards strangers, as we found to our cost. Not only did they steal many articles from our station, but they even robbed one of our caches along the coast, a far more serious offense in the Arctic.

Much kindness and unselfishness is displayed within each little community. During my sojourn on Victoria island I had to diet myself for a time on a little dog-pemmican, in order to recruit my strength after a rather serious illness. According to native etiquette I should have shared my pemmican with the Eskimos of the party, who were indeed very partial to it; but almost invariably they declined it even when they were themselves short of food. One evening not only did they refuse any pemmican, but they even pressed some of their own food on me, although they knew there was nothing left for the morning. I needed it all, they said, and as for them, they could get along very well without it. Under ordinary conditions the aged and infirm are never abandoned, as Hanbury says.[5] Haviron, who died in the spring of 1915, received a regular dole of food from all his kinsmen throughout the winter, though he was confined to his hut during the whole period and could do nothing to help himself. Whenever the Eskimos migrated to another sealing-ground he was carried on one of the sleds, usually, but not always, his son's. In Victoria island we once left Tusayok's old wife all alone for several days with her tent and clothing and a stock of drying meat, because she was unable to maintain the constant travelling. She had an ample supply of food, and was perfectly happy and content, for she knew that her husband and son would rejoin her as soon as they were able. In times of extreme hardship, when the whole community is faced with starvation, I have no doubt that the Copper Eskimos would abandon the old and infirm without much hesitation, but it has apparently never been a regular custom with them, as it was among other Eskimos.

Improvidence is a charge that has sometimes been levelled against the Eskimos, but it is certainly not true of those who inhabit the regions around Coronation gulf. With them it is the duty of every family to preserve carefully for consumption in the early winter all extra supplies of food that are obtained between the spring and the fall. The successful hunter who has the largest reserve on hand in November and December meets with the highest esteem. During my seven months with the Puivlik natives on Victoria island not a single article

[1]Journ. Royal Geogr. Soc., Vol. 22, 1852, p. 80.
[2]Osborn, p. 190.
[3]Douglas, p. 226.
[4]Stefansson, Anthrop. Papers, A.M.N.H., Vol. XIV, pt. I, p. 131 *et seq.*
[5]Hanbury, p. 156.

of food was wasted, or a single serviceable skin thrown away, except during a few days at the end of August, when several deer carcasses were partially wasted. Even of these we took the skins, the sinew, the fat and some of the meat; the rest was left for the foxes and birds. The natives needed the skins for clothing, but they had more meat on hand than they could use, and we could not remain on the spot and consume it because the winter was drawing near. Our base was a hundred miles away, too far for us to pack the meat, while the quantity we were leaving behind was too small to be worth returning for at some later date. They did cache some of the carcasses on the slender chance of other natives finding them the following summer and using the putrid meat for dog-food. The Copper Eskimos may be accused of short-sightedness in some cases, but hardly of improvidence. Caribou are plentiful in their country at the present time, and they know of no reason why they should not always continue so. Consequently, especially in the region between Bathurst inlet and the Coppermine river, they often killed large numbers of deer for the sake of their skins and left the meat for the birds and animals; but wastefulness of this kind is common to all peoples.

Truthfulness is a virtue that varies greatly everywhere with different individuals. Among the Copper Eskimos there were a few natives whose word could be relied upon absolutely on every occasion, others who generally told the truth, but were apt to be influenced by circumstances, and some who would lie deliberately for little or no reason. Ilatsiak, voicing a common opinion, said that the thoughts go round and round in the heart, then the words come up from the body and issue through the mouth. If a man speaks the truth their course is straight, but when he lies they twist and curve in their passage upwards and issue from one corner of his mouth. It is no disgrace to be detected in a lie for no harm is done to the community; *ekkoivaktutin,* "You're a liar," is a common everyday expression of which no one takes very much notice; the culprit usually retorts in kind, or else merely laughs, considering it rather a joke that he should be found out. Their sense of shame, in fact, is not very highly developed; the majority of the natives merely look foolish, for instance, if caught in the act of stealing, and repent their clumsiness, not their wrong-doing.

The Copper Eskimos have not escaped that weakness of every people, cultured or uncultured, viz., a certain insularity and narrow-mindedness that exhibits itself in the constant laudation of themselves and their own ways and the depreciation of other communities. It is a kind of personal vanity enlarged to embrace the group or tribe, and personal vanity is common even among Eskimos. Uloksak sent us a special invitation to attend at the dance-house when he was going to dance, and the women delighted to appear at our station dressed in all the finery they could muster. There are fashions in clothing as imperative as any fashions among us, and here as everywhere you cannot have fine birds without fine feathers. A man (or woman) of fashion and influence should possess, besides two suits of everyday working clothes, one for summer and one for winter, a thick set of heavy winter clothing for travelling and visiting, and a lighter set of short-haired summer skins ornamented with coloured bands and insertions, fringes and appendages of various kinds, to wear in the dance-house on ceremonial occasions. On its social side the same vanity appears in the frequency with which they extol their own virtues and decry those of their neighbours. Dolphin and Union strait natives would often say to us, "We are good people, we never steal. It is the Coppermine river people who steal." Higilak tried hard to persuade me that the Noahognik and Prince Albert sound natives swarmed with vermin, but her people, the Puivlik Eskimos, were absolutely free. Nevertheless the very simplicity and naïveté of their vanity rendered it more amusing than obnoxious.

The social morality of the Copper Eskimos takes no account of personal cleanliness. I have already mentioned their uncleanliness in the matter of food. Normally the natives never wash, nor have they any equivalent for soap. In the winter, indeed, they have no means of washing, for their blubber lamps melt no more water than is required for drinking purposes. They sometimes rub oil on their faces in spring, but rather for its soothing effect on their sunburnt skins than for any other reason. The children enjoy bathing, however, during the two short months that bathing is possible in this climate, and they seemed to like washing with soap and water at our station. They clean the nits from each other's head and eat them, and swallow the mucus from the nose. Yet these same people were horrified to see a white man swallow phlegm, and it must be admitted that they are far less infested with vermin than the Indians or the Eskimos of the Mackenzie river and of North Alaska. Moreover, however they may treat their bodies, they are very careful to keep their clothing scrupulously clean and free from all stains and grease spots, with the exception of course of their ordinary working garments.

Fig. 68. The coming of the missionary. Rev. H. Girling among the Eskimos of Dolphin and Union strait

Every tribe of Eskimos has been notorious for the levity of its sexual morality, and the Copper Eskimos are no exception. The entire lack of privacy in their lives leads to little children of seven and eight years of age knowing more of the mysteries of sex than many an adult among Europeans. Bluntness and plain-speaking in such matters might indicate a trait of manners rather than of morals, were it not that some of the men and a few of the old women exceed the limits of free speech and find a pleasure in bandying coarse and obscene remarks. After the strenuous outdoor summer life the confinement of winter, with its long hours of darkness and its excitation of the emotions through dances and religious séances, creates an almost morbid sexual activity. The interchange of wives, while it is not restricted to winter, is far commoner at that period. Avranna and Uloksak pooled their wives one winter's night—Avranna's one wife and Uloksak's three. All four women, with the two men and a little baby, crowded naked into a single sleeping bag. Towards morning they separated, Avranna with two of Uloksak's wives removing to another sleeping bag, while Uloksak remained with the other two women and the baby.

Whatever the causes may be sexual immorality is certainly very rife amongst them, and as certainly disregarded as a matter of no importance. Even the children are doubtfully pure. A married man deliberately mishandled a little girl in the presence of other people, and his action met with no condemnation. The relatives would doubtless interfere if the children were subjected to any annoyance, but as long as no trouble arises no one takes any notice. I never knew of any girl being a mother before she married, for the simple reason that girls always marry about puberty, and never remain single for any length of time afterwards, at least not as long as they retain their youth. On the other hand I never observed any instance of that hospitality so notorious among other Eskimos, wherein a man lends his wife to his guest. It may occur nevertheless, and an honoured guest who made such a request would certainly be gratified; but travelling natives are almost invariably accompanied by their own wives, and cement their friendships, if they so wish, by the regular method of exchanging wives rather than by borrowing. Of course, in the end, there is very little difference as far as the results are concerned.

Another trait in the character of the Copper Eskimo is a rather thoughtless cruelty. I can better explain my meaning perhaps by the apparently paradoxical statement that while they have much sympathy they have very little real pity. They grieve at the death or misfortune of their relatives, but they calmly look on and allow a helpless babe to be murdered without the slightest compunction. It could not be expected perhaps of a race of hunters that they should feel any pity for their victims; hence we are not surprised that a native should allow a wounded deer to lie in agony for hours when by a little extra trouble he could put an immediate end to its misery. One of Higilak's dogs bore a litter of six pups, only two of which could we possibly carry along with us. It gave Higilak great pleasure to crush the heads of the other four with a stone; "Will you never die?" she cried, as their little bodies lay quivering on the ground. She called Kanneyuk and myself to watch the slaughter, but to Kanneyuk's credit be it said that she fled from the sight with tears in her eyes.

Notwithstanding such cruelty towards blind and helpless pups, the dogs that are reared by the natives are treated with great kindness in most cases.[1] They have the status of servant children, as it were, and are named, like real children, after the dead relatives of their owners. I heard a man tell a woman one day to tie up his "grandfather," meaning a dog that had the same name as his grandfather.[2] Whenever her dog was nosing about the house Higilak would cry in a high-pitched, ironically-seductive tone *arnennoak,* "girl," and the dog would slink out of doors again. A dog began to howl one night outside our tent, and she cried *tikitlutin tikitugalluak* "And yet you have reached the end of your day's journey." Of the two pups that she kept in the summer one was given to Kanneyuk, and both mother and daughter carried them in the hoods of their coats, or in a bag on their backs, until the animals were strong enough to walk. Ayallik's old wife during one winter migration carried a little pup snug and warm in her boot-leg. In winter dogs with pups are sheltered in the house at the back of the sleeping platform, or in a cosy nook especially constructed for them in the wall; their bed is strewn with willow-twigs, over

---

[1]Mr. Stefansson's picture of their life (Anthrop. Papers, A.M.N.H., Vol. XIV, pt. I, p. 241), is nevertheless a little too rosy. Cf. Parry, Vol. IV, p. 28 *et seq.*

[2]Children are never called by the terms of relationship that would be applicable to the persons after whom they are named. Avranna, for example, never called his child "father," though it was named after his father. This is an important point of difference between the Copper and the western Eskimos, reflecting the difference in their conceptions of the after-life.

which is usually laid a seal-skin. The other dogs sleep in the passage, and as soon as their masters have dined they are called in one after another to drink a ladle of broth or eat a little seal-meat and blubber; for the strips of lamp blubber from which most of the oil has been consumed are always reserved for the dogs, who receive in addition, during seasons of plenty, some of the meat and the intestines, besides unlimited quantities of blubber still attached to the skin. As each dog finishes its portion the woman drives it back into the passage again with a raucous sound as though she were clearing her throat, and the command is supplemented with a sharp blow from the snow duster if it dares to delay a single moment. Some dogs are fonder than others of prowling inside the house among the feet of the visitors, and their owners will shout at them, "You dog, you are always inside, will you never go out?"[1] It is not often that the Eskimos strike their dogs, apart from an occasional blow to drive them out of the house; but whenever they do strike they strike hard. Inveterate fighters and trouble-breeders naturally receive the most punishment, and I have seen dogs almost mutilated with a stick. The more usual method, however, of cooling the passions of a troublesome dog is to tie a string round its neck and push one of its fore-feet through the loop so that the animal hobbles along on three legs. In summer, when there is no danger of the limb becoming frozen, a dog may be left in this condition for two or three days. Dogs always fare worse in summer, for they are kept constantly tied up by their harnesses (except when travelling) to prevent them from stealing the meat with which the camp is littered; and they are muzzled as well when there are caribou in the vicinity. Instead of the satisfying seal-meat and blubber they receive only fish-bones, and fish- and caribou-broth, with the entrails and a little of the lean meat of the caribou when food is plentiful. Then they have to work harder at this season; instead of hauling a sled ten miles every fortnight or three weeks they pack an equal distance nearly every day with loads of from twenty to forty and even fifty pounds on their backs. The sleekest and best-nourished dogs of winter become lean and scrawny, with their ribs almost cutting through their skins. Yet their hardships must be attributed to the conditions under which they live, not to the cruelty of their owners. The Eskimo knows that his own comfort, if not his very existence, depends on his dogs, and the better he uses them, the more faithful will be their service. Instances of cruelty do occasionally occur, but the majority of the natives are kind and indulgent masters to their dogs, and reciprocate the affection that their dogs obviously feel for them.

In concluding this sketch of the life of the Copper Eskimos a few remarks are necessary about the influence of the handful of white men with whom they came into contact prior to our expedition. The earliest explorers, such as Collinson and Rae, lingered too short a time, and had too little intercourse with them to produce any considerable effect upon their lives. A quantity of iron was introduced into the country and a feeling of friendliness generated towards the white man, but beyond this they had little real influence. Hardly more was effected by Hanbury's rapid journey along the coast in 1902, or by the brief sojourns of Captains Klengenberg and Mogg in Victoria island between 1905 and 1907, or even by the visit of Mr. Stefansson in 1910 and of Mr. Stefansson and Dr. Anderson in 1911. The first important changes came in when Messrs. Hornby and Melville established themselves on Great Bear lake in 1908 and Captain J. Bernard reached Coronation gulf with his schooner in 1910. Extensive trading was carried on with the natives, who then for the first time came into possession of the high-powered rifles that bid fair to revolutionize their lives. Fox-trapping, too, became profitable now that they had a

---

[1]The Copper Eskimos in speaking to their dogs use either the 2nd person imperative or the 3rd. Thus they may say either "*kimmik takanna annili*" Dog down there, let it go out," or simply "*kimmik takanna itereaglutin*," Dog down there, go out." Cf. Stefansson, Anthrop. Papers, A.M.N.H., Vol. XIV, pt. I, p. 267.

market for their skins, and even those natives who never fell in with the white men began to give some attention to it. The Eskimos were particularly struck by the fact that many articles of inestimable value to themselves, such as tin cans, scrap iron and steel needles, were very little prized by the white men, who set more store on fox-skins and other objects of little use to the natives themselves and therefore of small value in their eyes. The white men again were inferior in hunting, except for the advantage their rifles gave them, and less hardy and enduring. They were ignorant, too, of the art of harpooning seals and of building snow huts, so that they could not move from their houses in

FIG. 69. The influx from the west. Christian Jorgenson Klengenberg (a Dane), his wife (an Eskimo woman from Wainwright inlet, N. Alaska), and their family, all of whom migrated into Coronation gulf in 1916

winter without their tents. Further they often bought meat from the natives, or employed them to hunt for them, and the women to sew their clothes. The journey of the two French missionaries to the mouth of the Coppermine river in 1913 must have opened the eyes of the Eskimos to the difficulties under which the majority of white men labour when they try to cope with Arctic conditions of life and travel. For many different reasons, therefore, the natives conceived a certain amount of contempt for white men, a contempt that was only qualified by a desire to gain some of their most valued possessions, their knives and axes and particularly their rifles and their ammunition. The receipt of indiscriminate presents, however small their value to the donors, undermined the dignity and independence of the natives, especially those of the Coppermine river basin who came more directly under this influence. They quickly dropped the custom of offering an equivalent for everything they received, and learned to beg and clamour for everything they saw without the slighest hesitation or shame. There were still men of grave dignity and self-respect amongst them, especially at the east end of Coronation gulf, where the people had been rather more isolated. There we found them more honest, more hospitable, and more courteous than the inhabitants of the west end of the gulf and of Dolphin and Union strait, where many of the younger men and women were shameless beggars and meddling thieves, who would slyly turn out every bag on one's sled and examine or carry off its contents. For them the unprotected stranger was fair booty, and only the fear of being cut off from all supplies of rifles and ammunition and other articles on which they were learning to depend prevented them from robbing us more extensively than they did. Even among themselves petty stealing became more frequent, and detection more difficult. This degradation in manners and morals was not of course universal. Some of the natives themselves deplored it, and used what little influence they had to check their neighbours and bring about more honourable relations. Two or three of the worst offenders against us received salutary punishments, and the arrest in 1916 of the two murderers of the Roman Catholic missionaries acquainted the natives for the first time with the agents of civilized law. In that year an Anglican mission under the energetic and capable leadership of the Rev. H. Girling took over our station at Bernard harbour, the Hudson's Bay Company established a trading post and several white trappers and traders planted themselves at various points along the coast. In 1917 a second patrol of the Royal North West Mounted Police visited Coronation gulf and a post of the Police was later established at Tree river, and the solitary traveller may now wander with impunity everywhere provided that he exercises a reasonable amount of tact and prudence.

Rapid changes are taking place in the culture of the natives, and implements of iron and steel, rifles, fish-nets, open boats, European textiles and sewing-machines, European foods, cheap musical instruments and the development of trapping at the expense of hunting and sealing will work a complete transformation within the space of a very few years. Already the new culture elements and the new teachings that are filtering in from the west have profoundly modified their social and religious ideas, and before the present generation passes away the primitiveness of the Copper Eskimo will have ceased to exist. How many will remain by that time, and whether they will be able to take any part in the development of this region depends largely on the manner in which we fulfill our trust. For in throwing open their country to outside invasion we have incurred a heavy responsibility towards the natives. We may increase the security of life among them by checking infanticide and murder, we may protect them from unscrupulous exploitation and from the ravages of intoxicating liquors, but all this will be of little avail unless we immediately take measures to secure them against the introduction of our diseases. Smallpox carried off 2,000 of the Greenland Eskimos in 1734 and 1735, and in the same century it destroyed many of the Labrador natives as well. Thirty years ago it was estimated that the Eskimo population of the Mackenzie river delta numbered 2,000; by 1913 it was reduced to barely 500, the majority of the natives having been swept away by measles. The epidemic of influenza in 1918 exacted a terrible toll among the Eskimos of northern Alaska, several settlements being practically wiped out. The Copper Eskimos have no diseases of their own, or at least none were known up to 1916; but white men and western Eskimos are flocking into their country, and in a few more years perhaps they too will fall victims to some of the scourges of our civilization. It may be impossible to prevent this calamity entirely, but at least we could do something to check it, by instituting a kind of quarantine such as the Danes have done for Greenland. At the present time the only practicable route into the Copper Eskimo country is by way of the Mackenzie river, and if no one were allowed to go eastward without a certificate from a medical officer it might be possible to save these natives from the worst of our diseases and a more or less speedy extinction.

APPENDIX.

As the MSS. of this report was going to press Dr. R. M. Anderson, the leader of the southern party of the Canadian Arctic Expedition, received a letter from the pioneer trader, Captain Jos. F. Bernard, who, as I have mentioned in Chapter II, spent three years among the Copper Eskimos prior to the arrival of our expedition. Captain Bernard returned to Coronation gulf in 1916, passed one winter at the Kugaryuak river, 18 miles east of the Coppermine, two at Taylor island, off the south-east corner of Victoria island, and his last winter, 1919-20, at the Kugaryuak river again. His letter, which was written from the Kugaryuak river in February, 1920, gives a résumé of his experiences and observations during the preceding three and a half years, and contains, among other information, some valuable notes on the inhabitants of Dease strait and Queen Maud's sea, the least known of all Eskimo tribes. Through the kindness of Dr. Anderson I am able to publish these passages in their entirety, making only those few changes, mainly corrections in the spelling, necessitated by Captain Bernard's imperfect command of English, his native language being French. While in Ottawa during the winter of 1920-21, Captain Bernard went over and explained the notes more fully. The Eskimo names are given exactly as he wrote them, but are followed by my own interpretations in square brackets.

". . . . I wintered (1916-17) at Kagoryuk [Kugaryuak River], but I found conditions much changed from 1911. In the migration of caribou there were not half the number as in 1910-1911, and none stayed in the vicinity during the winter as they did then. I also find a great change with the natives, · for the best in a few cases but for the worse in others. It is as is general at the first step of civilization.

". . . . We left winter quarters on the 22nd of July. We could have left it sooner but I don't think we could then have gone far, for on the 23rd there was a good deal of ice in the gulf yet. After stopping at the Coppermine river and at Dead Man's island[1] we got to Cape Krusenstern on the 25th, but the strait was full of ice. It was impossible to get through, so we went into the little harbour just east of the cape, after taking on board a man whom I had left at the cape last fall to trade and trap. On the first of August, not finding the ice conditions changed in the strait and apparently no ice to the eastward, we decided to go east. We had clear sailing up to Lind island at the entrance to Victoria strait; here we met considerable and very heavy ice. We sailed into the bay inside of Taylor island on the 16th of August, 1917. The reason for my going in here was to see if we might meet with those natives whom Mr. Stefansson calls the Ecollouctoumeut [Ekaluktomiut] and supposed to be very numerous. As soon as we were in this bay the ice closed in on the entry and never left or opened until the first of September, 1919. For two years it held us prisoners in this deserted land, deserted indeed, for no native abides nearer than Cambridge bay except for an accidental bear hunt in the latter part of March some years; but they never stop long, as the game is scarce and they fear starvation.

"The first year we were here it was an extremely cold winter and the summer following much the same, few places on the land that the snow entirely disappeared during the summer, and on the first of September from three to four feet of ice still remained in the lakes and bay, so you may form an opinion on the cold summer we had. We had a little game during the whole year, not

---

[1]Inyuernerit, in the Duke of York's archipelago.

plentiful, but we managed fairly well. But the second winter was a tough one. Most all our provisions were gone and we had no fuel left, nor was there any chance of getting any seal.

"Victoria strait was practically open until the middle of January, and when it did close up the ice was so rough that it was practically impossible to get across to the nearest natives, whom we supposed were on the ice of Simpson strait. Our nearest neighbours to the west were the Kilelarmut, who were at Cambridge bay until early fall, but moved to the western end of Dease strait in December; so as it stood we could not get any help from the natives.

"In December, I, with a young native whom I had engaged in the summer, went over to the westward looking for game or the natives, cutting across the land from a bay near Cape Adelaide, striking due west up to the southern arm of Albert Edward bay, then across to the sea, and as we hadn't seen anything of game I desired to go to the natives. The weather was extremely cold and stormy. After nine days we found the natives in Wellington bay. They were very friendly. They had but little meat or fish and no oil. Most of the houses were in darkness and they could not, it seems, get any seal, and they were fearing starvation and were moving west to the natives of Bathurst inlet, so we had to turn back without obtaining but little help, a little dried fish and a few frozen fish. After nine days of the worst kind of weather and travelling I have seen we got home, having left two dogs on the trail and the rest of them so fagged out they couldn't stand up. So we had to put through the winter as best we could, using (naphtha) distillate mixed with moss and ashes for fuel in February. We made three unsuccessful attempts to cross Victoria strait, finally in April I succeeded in getting across and found the natives near the mouth of Sherman inlet. They too had not fared too good during the dark days. Two families were reported to have starved to death in Simpson strait.

"It seems as if the same conditions prevailed on the mainland side as around Taylor island, Victoria land. The cause of it, as I believe, was that on the 8th of October a thaw (after a heavy snowfall) brought over the land a sheet of ice two inches thick in places. It seemed to have driven the game inland. Through the spring and summer all game was scarce.

"It was the first of September, 1919, before we could get out of this bay; even then it was only after a hard bucking with ice, but once we got around De Haven point we had open sea to the westward. Considering the season too far advanced to make around Point Barrow [in Alaska] we decided to winter in Coronation gulf. . . . We went into winter quarters Kogaryuk [Kugaryuak]. If I found conditions changed in 1916 there is also as much change in 1919, that is in game. There were not fifty head of caribou landed within a radius of twenty miles, and it seems, from what I can find out from the natives, that they have been scarce all along the coast. . . .

"Although there are few islands marked on the chart in Queen Maud's sea I believe they are as numerous as they are in Coronation gulf. They are of a much different formation, mostly all low and rocky and gravel bars formed by ice pressure; some are of considerable size. Lying south of Lind island there is practically a chain of them from the land seen by Rae to the mouth of Sherman inlet. Amundsen when he sailed through there laid a couple of them on his chart. . . . .

"I note quite a distinct difference comparing the people of Adelaide peninsula, the King William land and the Great Fish river with those of Victoria island and Coronation gulf, both in stature, life habits, and dialect. They average heavier and taller. Their clothing too is much different from the gulf people. The Natchelengmut [Netsilingmiut] or King William land people are by far the most numerous of the three tribes. In winter time they are on the ice in Simpson strait and to the east of King William land, and the most of them spend the summer on Boothia Felix peninsula. Some of them journey as far south as Committee gulf (bay) where they barter with the Ivelinmiut [Aiviling-miut]. The Eleneremeut are the smallest of these three tribes and are perhaps the most local tribe of natives I have ever known. Adelaide peninsula in summer and the portion of Queen Maud's sea up to the Royal Geographical Society's islands and Lind island in winter, this is about the limit of their hunting ground, although some individuals have been as far south as Committee gulf (bay).

"The third tribe, the Olcokishalugmiut [Ukkusiksaligmiut] are the people who live at the mouth of Great Fish river whose other name is not Arkelanik [Akilinnik or Thelon] but the Olcohisluk [Ukkusiksalik.][1] The Arkelanik [Akilinnik] seems to be a branch of the Great Fish river[2] leading to the eastward or towards Chesterfield inlet, here where the Bathurst inlet and the Coronation gulf people used to go and meet the Chesterfield people to barter—hence its name. Those Olcohishicamiut [Ukkusiksaligmiut] are probably the most miserable people in the winter time I have ever seen or heard of. They have no seal or oil for their lamps nor fuel for fire. All of their grub is composed mostly of fish in winter, caribou and ox [musk-ox] in summer. There seems to be a close relation between the three tribes and they seldom come in contact with western people, but very often with eastern people. It seems by all accounts that they are on the decline, and to add to their misery syphilis is among them; some cases are far advanced. The Victoria island people are all clean and healthy, even more so than the gulf people.

"The Ecolotock [Ekaluktok] does not empty into Albert Edward bay as stated by Mr. Stefansson, but empties into Wellington bay, Dease strait. It is a river of considerable size apparently, from its mouth and from native report. Its head rises near the headwaters of a river which flows into Prince Albert sound and is the common highway for the natives of Prince Albert sound to communicate with the Kilelarmut.

"There are two rivers in Albert Edward bay, neither one of much importance. The Oherackquak [Oyaragyuak] (so named from the rocky country it flows through). It runs in a westerly direction and leads near the Ekelolocktuock [Ekaluktok]. The other river's name is the Ekitegoggeyock [Ikittigagyuak] flowing in a northerly direction in a chain of lakes of the same name (so named from the large number of Sabine's gulls that breed along their banks). It is a favourite hunting place for the Kililermiut, particularly in the fall, on account of the large number of lake trout they get in those lakes. These fish are the largest and best eating fish I have ever known in the Arctic. The boundary of these lakes, which lies in about 70 [degrees] north, seems to be about the farthest north those natives hunt on the eastern coast of Victoria island.

ARCHÆOLOGY.

"I want to tell you that we did quite a little work in archæology at Krusen-stern. We located the site of three villages, apparently of different age. Two of them were on the gravel bar immediately west of the cape, two or three hundred yards from the beach. The site of the third was on the highest part of the divide where the trail crosses the neck of land inside of the cape. At this latter one we did no excavation. Mr. A. H. Anderson, the man that I brought with me, had stopped at Krusenstern to trap and trade, and did a considerable amount of excavation on the site of the two lower villages, where he succeeded

---

[1]Strictly speaking, Ukkusiksalik seems to be only the delta of the river, with the adjoining region, the river itself being called Saningaiyok.

[2]The Akilinnik or Thelon is not a branch, however, of Backs or the Great Fish river, though the sources of the two rivers are not far apart.

in obtaining an extensive and interesting collection. The floors of these houses were three to four feet below the level of the surroundings. Many men might have tramped over them without suspecting it. In fact it was only after a very careful examination of the surface that we were able to locate the site of the house. I also located the site of two houses on Dead Man island [Inyuernerit, Duke of York archipelago]. They were very old.

"I have also the knowledge of the site of the large village on the Mackenzie river, Victoria island. Mr. Anderson in the summer of 1919 located two houses on one of the Jameson islands. We also saw some excavation on three houses done twenty or thirty miles east of Tree river close to Hepburn island."

It would seem from Captain Bernard's account that there is only one tribe of Eskimos inhabiting southeast Victoria island, a tribe that he calls Kililarmut, or, in one instance, Kililermiut. This may possibly be a mis-rendering of the word Kiglinirmiut, a term that is often applied to all the inhabitants of Victoria island by the Bathurst inlet Eskimos, and by the Netsilingmiut and Ugyulingmiut to natives coming from the direction of Coronation gulf[1]. The Eskimos whom Lieutenant Hansen met near Taylor island called themselves, as he understood, Kilnermiun, which is another rendering of the same word.

On the other hand both Mr. Stefansson and myself heard of the Ekaluktomiut, a tribe that seals in winter on the ice of Dease strait, and in summer hunts inland on Victoria island and communicates with the Kanghiryuak natives from Prince Albert sound. Moreover, an Anglican missionary, the Rev. E. Hester, visited a village of the Ekaluktomiut in Dease strait in the winter of 1918. Now the Ekaluktok river flows, not into Albert Edward bay, as Mr. Stefansson supposed, but into Wellington bay. There can be little doubt therefore of there being two groups in Dease strait, though in winter they sometimes, perhaps usually, fuse into one. The first group is the Ekaluktomiut, who gather in spring and fall at the head of Wellington bay, and hunt in summer around the head-waters of the Ekaluktok river, in which neighbourhood they meet the Eskimos who have come inland from Prince Albert sound. The other group, the Kililarmiut (or Kiglinirmiut?), gathers in spring and fall at Cambridge bay, where they were encountered both by Captain Bernard and by his predecessor nearly seventy years before, Captain Collinson. The hunting grounds of this second group lie between Cambridge bay and Albert Edward bay (probably there is an easy sled route between the two places), and extends no farther north than about 70° N. latitude. In winter the two groups would unite in the vicinity of the Finlayson islands[2] or in Wellington bay, and work westward in the direction of Coronation gulf to meet the Bathurst inlet people. The united band would then be called indifferently either Ekaluktomiut or Kililarmiut (Kiglinirmiut). Late in the winter a party sometimes travels eastward towards Lind and Taylor islands to hunt the polar bears, but as a rule this part of the coast is little frequented. Rae, it will be remembered, found no indications of Eskimos having recently visited the several points he touched at between Cambridge bay and Pelly point.[3]

The inhospitable character of the region of Queen Maud's sea, and the discovery that the Ekaluktok river flows, not into Albert Edward bay, but into Wellington bay, throws a new light on Mr. Stefansson's trade route from Prince Albert sound to the Akilinnik river. We know that the Kanghiryuak natives go inland from Prince Albert sound about the beginning of June, and that the Ekaluktok natives must also be taking to the land at the same time. The Kanghiryuak natives whom I met in 1915 said that the two groups meet in the interior of the island near the head of a river, which must either be the Kagloryuak or some similar river flowing into Prince Albert sound, or else the

---

[1] Schwatka, Science, Vol. IV, 1884, p. 543.
[2] Collinson, p. 284.
[3] Journ. Royal Geogr. Soc, Vol. 22, 1852, p. 89.

Ekaluktok river flowing southeast. This meeting can hardly take place, therefore, before the middle of June. Now at this season, in a normal year, the snow is fast leaving the ground, the rivers are breaking out, and the lakes are becoming surrounded with a margin of water. Travelling by sled, especially with an Eskimo sled shod with frozen mud, grows more and more difficult every day. It is very improbable then that the Kanghiryuak natives travel any farther by sled until the fall. Even if they did push down to the coast, as Mr. Stefansson supposed[1], and reach the mouth of the Ekaluktok river in Wellington bay, they would find the natives either already inland, or else caching their stocks of blubber on the shore before going into the interior of the island to fish and hunt, not, under ordinary circumstances at least, preparing to cross the strait to the mainland. We must assume therefore that the Kanghiryuarmiut cache their sleds in the interior (as the Puivlirmiut did in the summer of 1915), spend the summer hunting and fishing in the neighbourhood, recover their sleds in the fall, and, travelling down to Wellington bay, become merged for the winter with the Ekaluktomiut on Dease strait. Theoretically, of course, they might cross over to the mainland as soon as the sea was frozen solidly over (in November), and either make their way west to Bathurst inlet, or east to the Ellice river or to Ogden bay; then during the dark days of winter they might push on south to the Akilinnik and return to the coast in the spring. Such a course might appeal to the European explorer, equipped with a light steel-shod sled and a high-powered hunting rifle, and anxious to make the journey as quickly as possible. But to the Eskimo time is of no value; his hunting weapon is the bow and arrow, and his cumbersome sled with its heavy mud shoeing is little adapted to inland travel over the soft snow of early winter. Moreover, owing to the scarcity of game and fuel along the Arctic coast at this season of the year, after the caribou have migrated south (very few seals are obtainable before the new year), the Copper Eskimo is compelled to lay in a stock of provisions to last him over Christmas at least, while for fuel he utilizes the blubber that he has cached on the coast the previous spring. Hence a long journey at this season of the year, when the daylight does not last more than five hours, with a sled loaded down with provisions and blubber, is not practicable. The Bathurst inlet natives who travel to the Akilinnik in the fall of the year and return to the coast in the spring take their sleds and stocks of blubber with them inland the previous spring, and have their journey half completed before the summer overtakes them. It is not unlikely indeed that they reach the Akilinnik, or one of its tributaries in the neighbourhood of Aberdeen lake, before Christmas, perhaps even before the dark days set in, when travelling, with its concomitant fishing and hunting, becomes more difficult.

We must suppose, therefore, that the migrating Kanghiryuarmiut remain with the Ekaluktomiut during the early winter. They could lay in a store of dried and frozen meat and fish during the summer and fall, but for blubber they would have to rely on the supplies that were cached by the Ekaluktomiut during the spring. This factor alone would be sufficient to limit the number of migrating natives to two or three families. Towards spring, when the Ekaluktomiut visit their western neighbours, the usual reshuffling of groups would occur, and some Kanghiryuak and Ekaluktok natives might join the Bathurst inlet people and travel southward. Again they would cache their sleds inland when the snow melted, and either pack across to the Akilinnik in the summer, returning with the first snows, or else make the journey by sled in the early winter and return the following spring. They could then rejoin the Ekaluktomiut before the latter abandoned their sealing on the ice, travel with them up the Ekaluktok river in the late spring, and join their countrymen from Prince Albert sound in the interior of Victoria island about the middle or end of June, exactly two years after they had left them.

[1]G.S.C., Museum Bulletin, No. 6, 1914, p. 6.

It will be noticed that I have stressed the route by way of Bathurst inlet. The accounts of the Bathurst inlet natives themselves, and the information obtained by Captain Bernard, indicate that the Eskimos of southeast Victoria island maintain closer contact with their neighbours to the west than with any of the tribes to the east of them. This is indeed what we should expect from their geographical position, and from the greater resources and population of the region west of Kent peninsula. Kent peninsula itself, as far as we know, was uninhabited until the last year or two, the Asiagmiut who visited the Bathurst inlet people travelling behind it by way of Melville sound.

Captain Bernard does not mention the Asiagmiut in his letter, probably because he never fell in with any members of the tribe, who seem to range between Kent peninsula and Ogden bay. Whether they are to be included among the Copper Eskimos, or considered as an intermediate link between them and the eastern Eskimos, must remain for the present uncertain; the geographical position of the tribe favours the latter course. Captain Bernard confirms the reports of earlier explorers as to the location and range of the Netsilingmiut and Ukkusiksaligmiut, but the third tribe of which he speaks, the Eleneremiut, is new to us. It seems to coincide with Schwatka's Ugyulingmiut, who inhabited Adelaide peninsula in the middle of last century, but were gradually merging with the Netsilingmiut.[1] Probably the Eleneremiut are a surviving remnant who clung to their old hunting-grounds around Sherman inlet and Simpson strait. With regard to the Ukkusiksaligmiut it is strange that they have never learned the art of sealing from their neighbours. I imagine that instead of seal oil they use caribou tallow in their lamps during the winter, like the natives on the upper reaches of Backs river, the Saningaiyomiut, who are probably only a branch of the Ukkusiksaligmiut with a little admixture from Hudson bay tribes.

Captain Bernard has made some very important archæological discoveries which enable us to extend the limit of wood and sod houses to the eastern end of Coronation gulf. The number of ruins that he found would indicate a considerable population, while their great antiquity is shown by the depth at which the floors were submerged below the ground, even after discounting the thickness of the sod roofs that doubtless caved in on top of them. These ruins must certainly be older than some at least of those that dot the coast between Cape Lyon and Cape Krusenstern, and while the latter may still indicate transitory settlements by parties travelling along the coast, as I have suggested in Chapter IV, the former undoubtedly mark the earlier, perhaps the earliest inhabitants of the region of Coronation gulf, and predate, I suspect, the influx of the Copper Eskimo tribes into this area. The evidence cannot be given here, but there are certain facts that seem to indicate that the Copper Eskimos were an inland people until a few centuries ago, and that their culture has changed considerably since their immigration to their present home.

Note.—Captain Bernard reached Ottawa on December 22, 1920. He stated that the Copper Eskimo country had undergone a profound change during the last few years. Four Hudson's Bay Company trading posts had been established, one at Bernard harbour, one at the mouth of the Coppermine river, a third at the mouth of Tree river and a fourth at Kent peninsula. The Eskimos were leaving their winter sealing grounds about two months earlier than usual, and devoting their attention to the trapping of foxes. In the winter of 1919 all the inhabitants of southeast Victoria island migrated to Kent peninsula, where a large supply of blubber fuel had been accumulated by the trader in order that the natives might be able to give all their time to trapping. Hardly a bow remained in the country, nearly every man possessing a rifle. Caribou

---

[1]Boas, Central Eskimo, p. 456 *et seq.*

meat had therefore become the predominant article of food, and the destruction of the caribou was proceeding so rapidly that within ten years, be believed, hardly one would be left in the vicinity of Coronation gulf. The old copper culture had given place to one of iron—even the copper ice-pick had disappeared —and the old style of dress was being abandoned in favour of western models. Infanticide had become exceedingly rare, partly through police and missionary influence, partly, Captain Bernard thought, because the Eskimos were shamed out of the practice by the Indians. He seemed to notice an increase, therefore, in the number of little children. On the other hand tuberculosis had already made its appearance among the Copper Eskimos. Clearly, for better or for worse, the new era has dawned, and only the future can decide whether the natives will survive or go under.

BIBLIOGRAPHY

Amundsen, R.   The North West Passage. 2 vols., London, 1908.
Anderson, Dr. R. M.   Appendix, pp. 456-527, to Stefansson, V. My Life with the Eskimo, New York, 1913.
————Eskimo Food—How It Tastes to a White Man. Ottawa Naturalist, October, 1918, pp. 59-65.
————Recent Explorations on the Canadian Arctic Coast. The Geographical Review, New York, Vol. IV, No. 4, October, 1917, pp. 241-266 (The Copper Eskimos, pp. 261-263).
Armstrong, Alexander. A Personal Narrative of the Discovery of the North-West Passage. London, 1857.
Back, Capt. G.   Narrative of the Arctic Land Expedition to the Mouth of the Great Fish River, London, 1836.
Boas, Dr. F.   The Central Eskimo. Sixth Annual Report of the Bureau of Ethnology, Washington, 1888.
————The Eskimo of Baffin Land and Hudson Bay. Bulletin of the American Museum of Natural History, vol. XV, 1907.
Collinson, Capt. R.   Journal of H.M.S. Enterprise. London, 1889.
Crantz, D.   A History of Greenland. 2 vols., London, 1767.
Culin, Stewart.   Games of the North American Indians. Twenty-fourth Annual Report of the Bureau of American Ethnology, Washington, 1907.
Dease and Simpson.   Arctic Discovery on the North Shore of America. Journal of the Royal Geographical Society, London, vol. 9, 1839.
————Progress of Arctic Discovery on the North Shore of America. Journal of the Royal Geographical Society, London, vol. 10, 1840.
Douglas, G. M.   Lands Forlorn. The Knickerbocker Press, New York and London, 1914.
Egede, Hans.   A Description of Greenland, London, 1818.
Franklin, Sir John.   Narrative of a Journey to the Shores of the Polar Sea. London, 1823.
————Narrative of a Second Expedition to the Shores of the Polar Sea. London, 1828.
Gilberton, A. N.   Some Ethical Phases of Eskimo Culture. Journal of Religious Psychology, vol. VI, No. 4, October, 1913, and vol. VII, No. 1, January, 1914.
Hall, C. F.   Arctic Researches and Life Among the Esquimaux. New York, 1865.
Hanbury, D. T.   Sport and Travel in the Northland of Canada. London, 1904.
Hearne, Samuel.   Journey from Hudson Bay to the Northern Ocean. Edited by J. B. Tyrrell, Champlain Society, Toronto, 1911.
Jenness, D.   The Copper Eskimo. The Geographical Review, New York, Vol. IV, 1917, pp. 81-91.
————The Eskimos of Northern Alaska: A Study in the Effect of Civilization. *Ibid.*, Vol. V, 1918, pp. 89-101.
————The Cultural Transformation of the Copper Eskimo. *Ibid.*, Vol. XI, 1921, pp. 541-550.
————The 'Blond' Eskimos, American Anthropologist, Vol. 23, No. 3, July–September, 1921.
Kroeber, Dr. A. L.   The Eskimos of Smith Sound. American Museum of Natural History, vol. XII, 1899.
Leffingwell, E. de K.   The Canning River Region, Northern Alaska, U.S. Geol. Survey, Professional Paper 109. Washington, 1919.
MacMillan, D. B.   Four years in the White North, New York and London, 1918.
Markham, C. R.   Papers on the Greenland Eskimos. Arctic Papers for the Expedition of 1875. London, 1875.
Mauss, M.   Essai sur les variations saisonnières des sociétés eskimos. Essai de morphologie sociale. L'Année Sociologique, 9me année, 1904–1905.
McClintock, Capt.   The Discovery of the Fate of Sir John Franklin. London, 1859.
Murdoch, John.   The Point Barrow Eskimo. Ninth Annual Report of the Bureau of Ethnology, Washington, 1887-'88.
————On some Popular Errors in Regard to the Eskimos. American Naturalist, January, 1887.
Nelson, E. W.   The Eskimo about Bering Strait. Eighteenth Annual Report of the Bureau of American Ethnology, Pt. 1, Washington, 1896-1897.
Osborn, Sherard.   The Discovery of the North-West Passage. London, 1857.
Parry, W.   Three Voyages for the Discovery of a North-West Passage. 4 vols., London, 1835.
Peary, Robt. E.   The Secrets of Polar Travel. The Century Co., New York, 1917.
Rae, Dr. John.   Journey from Great Bear Lake to Wollaston Land, and Explorations Along the South and East Coast of Victoria Land. Journal of the Royal Geographical Society, vol. 22, 1852.
Rasmussen, Knud.   The People of the Polar North. Ed. by G. Herring. London, 1908.
Reports regarding the Great Bear Lake Patrol, Royal North West Mounted Police, 1916. Ottawa, 1917.
Report of the Bathurst Inlet Patrol, Royal North West Mounted Police, 1917-1918. Ottawa, 1919.

Richardson, Sir J. Arctic Searching Expedition. 2 vols., London, 1851.
Rink, Dr. H. Tales and Traditions of the Eskimos. Ed. by Dr. R. Brown, Edinburgh and London,1857.
————Eskimo Tribes. Meddelelser om Grønland, vol. XI, supplement, Copenhagen, 1891.
Russell, F. Explorations in the Far North. Univ. of Iowa, 1898.
Simpson, T. Narrative of the Discoveries on the North Coast of America. London, 1843.
Stefansson, V. My Life with the Eskimo. New York. The Macmillan Company, 1913.
————The Stefansson-Anderson Arctic Expedition. Anthropological Papers of the American Museum of Natural History, vol. XIV., pt. 1, New York, 1914.
————Prehistoric and Present Commerce Among the Arctic Coast Eskimos. Geological Survey of Canada, Museum Bulletin, No. 6, Ottawa, 1914.
Thalbitzer, W. A Phonetical Study of the Eskimo Language. Meddelelser om Grønland, vol. XXXI, Copenhagen, 1904.
————The Ammassalik Eskimo. Meddelelser om Grønland, vol. XXXIX,Copenhagen, 1914.

Bibliography

... ...

PLATE II

A. A hut built in the autumn while the snow was still shallow. The travellers have therefore unloaded
one of their sleds and are using it to convey snow-blocks. The builder's head is just
visible inside the structure. Southwest Victoria Island, 1915

(Photo by J. J. O'Neill)

B. The man on the right has been cutting snow-blocks outside and passing them in to his companion.
The latter is closing the roof; his hand can be seen holding a snow-block in place.
On the left his wife is shovelling soft snow around the edge.
Bernard Harbour, 1915

PLATE III

A. Two snow huts, their entrances and windows facing south. Sticks and sealing harpoons are planted in the walls, and the two sleds are raised on snow-blocks, partly to keep them from being buried in a snow-storm and partly to protect their rawhide lashings from the dogs

B. A view of the whole settlement, showing the dance-house on the right. In the foreground are the tracks of the sleds

PLATE IV

(Photo by G. H. Wilkins)

A. An old woman drinking caribou broth from a ladle of musk-ox horn. Moore Islands, 1915

B. Two Prince Albert sound natives, Kunana and Nilgak, eating boiled caribou meat. A Puivlik woman in the back-ground. Lake Tahiryuak, Victoria Island, June, 1915

C. Outdoor cooking with *Dryas integrifolia* for fuel. The camp is littered with caribou meat drying in the sun. Bernard harbour, 1916

A—A Tree River native adjusting his wife's pack. Tree River, 1915   (Photo by J. J. O'Neill)

B—Coppermine River Eskimos packing overland to Great Bear Lake, June, 1916   (Photo by K. G. Chipman)

C—Sleeping under a wind-break, Colville Hills, S.W. Victoria Island, May, 1915

(Photo by G. H. Wilkins)
A—An alignment of stones, *inyukhuit*, for a caribou drive. Cape Krusenstern, 1915.

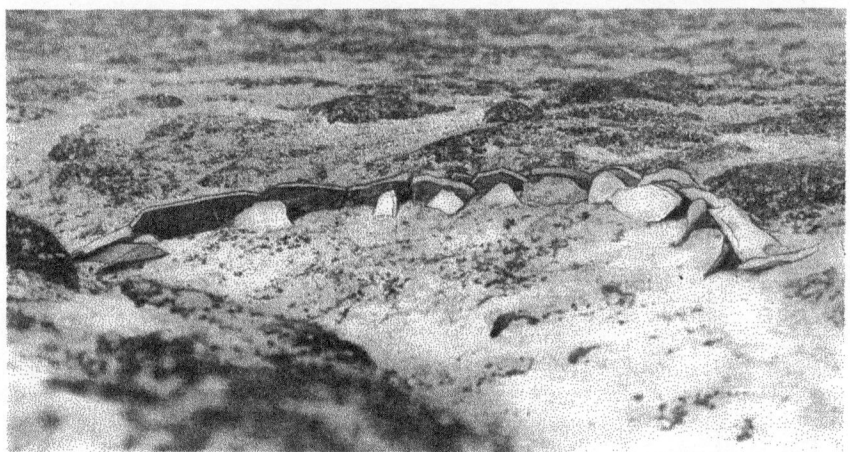

(Photo by G. H. Wilkins)
B—A pit, *tallu*, where a hunter has concealed himself from approaching caribou. Bernard Harbour, 1915.

C—Two stones, *nakkatain*, pointing to a good fishing site on a lake behind Cape Lambert. July 1915.

A—General view, showing the weir. The man at the mouth of the creek is keeping guard over the entrance to prevent any fish from escaping

B—The men are plying their spears; the women, clustering around the small stone caverns in which the fish try to hide, are catching them in their hands and stringing them on rawhide lines

C—Returning to camp with the salmon

PLATE VIII

(Photo by G. H. Wilkins)

A—A shy little Coronation gulf boy. Bernard Harbour, 1915.

B—On the left, Kaulluak, the widow who married the Alaskan Eskimo, Natkusiak; on the right, Tupik, the maiden to whom he first paid his addresses. Although of marriageable age, Tupik still wears the costume of a young girl. Moore Islands, 1915

(Photo by J. R. Cox)

C—Uloksak and his three wives. The one on the left is Hakungak, whom he took from her first husband, Kikpak. Bernard Harbour, 1916.

A—Front view—Kila on the left, Kanneyuk on the right

(Photos by G. H. Wilkins, Bernard Harbour, 1916)

B—View from behind

INDEX

A

G

Gambling, 221.
Game animals, 15; disputes concerning ownership of, 90.
Games, chap. xvii; children's, 115, 138, 218–220.
Gathering-places of Eskimo groups, 15, 16, 19, 25, 33, 35, 37–39, 110, 246.
Geology, general character of, 14, 17–18, 21, 22, 25, 26.
Giants, belief in, 180.
Girling, Rev. H., 8, 9; on Dolphin and Union strait Eskimos, 36; on Kiglinirmiut, 39; on creation
     of new Eskimo groups, 39; on Ekaluktomiut, 40; on Kanghiryuarmiut, 41; on Coppermine
     river route, 19; on marriage of cousins, 84; on marriage by capture, 160; on respect for
     mothers, 170; on hunter's scars, 114; establishment of mission by, 242.
Graves, 175–176; stone cairns used as, 29, 50, 174; avoidance of, 174, 177.
Great Bear Lake, visits of Eskimos to, 19, 20, 47, 124.
Groups, instability of, 32, 36; classification of, 33–42; creation of new, 39; homogeneity of, 42;
     intercourse of, 24, 25, chap. iv; assembling of, 125; rearrangements of, 116; disbandment
     of, 122.
Gulls, eating of, 105; trapping of, 133; towels from skins of, 105, 106.
Gymnastics, 222.

H

Hanbury, explorations of, 30–31; on Eskimo groups, 39; on the country of Asiak, 23, 40; on the
     route to Akilinnik river, 48; on snow-huts in spring, 77.
Hanerak, 23, 34.
Haneragmiut, extinction of, 34, 140; intercourse with other groups of, 24, 36, 50.
Hansen, Lieutenant, encounter with Eskimos of, 40, 246.
Health of Eskimos, 42–43, 245, 249.
Hearne, Samuel, journey of, 28; on salmon fishing, 123.
Heather, for fuel, 14 *et passim;* for curing snow-blindness, 171.
Hepburn island as gathering-place of Pingangnaktomiut, 38, 39, 110; old houses near, 246.
Holm, on size of Eskimo family, 163.
Honesty of Copper Eskimos, 30, 235–236.
Hornby, J., at Great Bear lake, 31.
Houses, *see* Dwellings.
Hudson bay, journeys to Coronation gulf from, 30, 31; contact with Copper Eskimos of natives
     of, 48, 49; peace sign in, 55; stone houses in, 58; snow houses in, 77.
Hudson Bay Company, establishment of posts of, 31, 242, 248.
Hunting, chap. xi; part of sexes in, 88; weapons used in, 145; distances travelled while, 124;
     taboos on, 185.

I

Ice, thickness in lakes of, 153; water from sea, 107; fishing through holes in, 153–154.
Igloryuallik as gathering-place of Eskimos, 39, 110.
Implements, for sealing, 113; for hunting, 145; for fishing, 153; broken on grave, 174, 176;
     introduction of new, 242.
Incantations, 187; to weather, 187; to Kannakapfaluk, 188.
Independence of Eskimos economically, 89.
Indians, trade of Eskimos with, 19–20, 37, 47; conflicts of Eskimos and, 28, 47; hunting method
     of, 146; dancing of, 208; Eskimos afraid of, 124.
Indicators for seals, 113.
Infanticide, 91; frequency of, 166; decrease of, 249.
Infirm, care of, 86, 95, 236.
Inhabitants, earlier, 56, 58, 248.
Inheritance, 92.
Inland Eskimos, *see* Backs river Eskimos.
Inman river, ruins near, 56.
Intercourse of Copper Eskimos, with western Eskimos, 28–29, 44–47; with inland Eskimos,
     48–49; with eastern Eskimos, 49–50; with each other, 24–25, 32, 34, 36, 40, chap. iv, 116,
     120.
Intonation of voice, variation in, 42.

J

Jamieson islands, natives at, 8, 13, 38; old houses on, 246.
Johansen, Mr. F., description of country by, 26; meets Eskimos in Wilbank bay, 38.

K

L

M

W

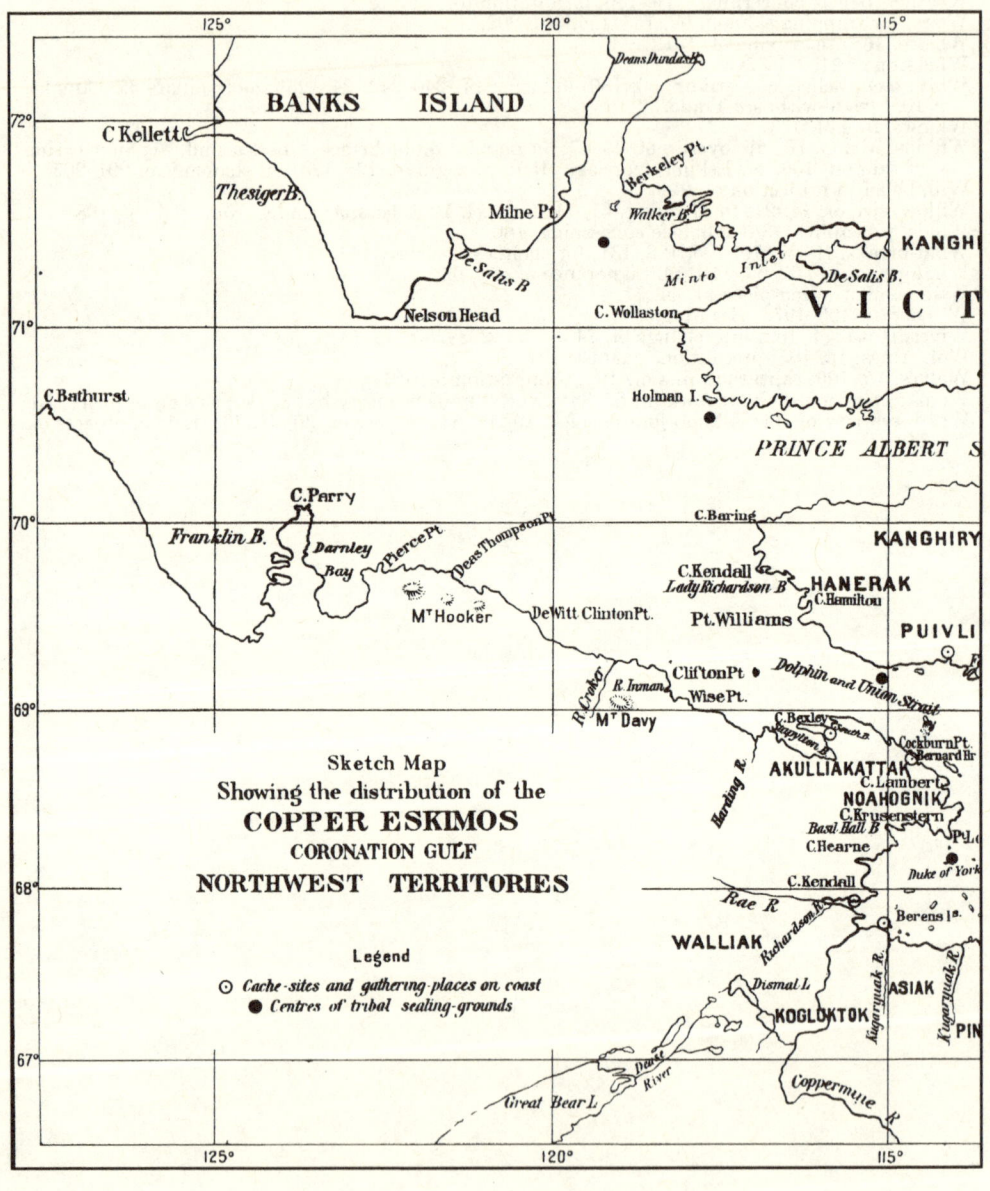

Sketch Map
Showing the distribution of the
COPPER ESKIMOS
CORONATION GULF
NORTHWEST TERRITORIES

Legend
⊙ Cache-sites and gathering-places on coast
● Centres of tribal sealing-grounds